# HITLER'S WAR AGAINST THE PARTISANS DURING THE KURSK OFFENSIVE

# HITLER'S WAR AGAINST THE PARTISANS DURING THE KURSK OFFENSIVE

THE THIRD REICH'S LAST OFFENSIVE ON THE EASTERN FRONT, SPRING TO AUTUMN 1943

DR ANTONIO J. MUÑOZ

FRONTLINE
BOOKS

# HITLER'S WAR AGAINST THE PARTISANS DURING THE KURSK OFFENSIVE

The Third Reich's Last Offensive on the Eastern Front, Spring to Autumn 1943

First published in Great Britain in 2025
by Frontline Books
An imprint of
Pen & Sword Books Ltd
Yorkshire - Philadelphia



ISBN 978 1 03612 865 4


A CIP catalogue record for this book is available from the British Library



Typeset by Lapiz Digital
Printed and bound in the UK by CPI Group (UK) Ltd,
Croydon, CR0 4YY.

Printed on paper from a sustainable source by
CPI Group (UK) Ltd, Croydon, CR0 4YY

Pen & Sword Books Limited incorporates the imprints of Archaeology, Atlas, Aviation, Battleground, Digital, Discovery, Family History, Fiction, History, Local, Local History, Maritime, Military, Military Classics, Politics, Select, Transport, True Crime, Air World, Claymore Press, Frontline Publishing, Leo Cooper, Remember When, Seaforth Publishing, The Praetorian Press, Wharncliffe Books, Wharncliffe Local History, Wharncliffe Transport, Wharncliffe True Crime and White Owl.

For a complete list of Pen & Sword titles please contact
PEN & SWORD BOOKS LTD
47 Church Street, Barnsley, South Yorkshire, S70 2AS, England
E-mail: enquiries@pen-and-sword.co.uk
Website: www.pen-and-sword.co.uk
or
PEN & SWORD BOOKS
1950 Lawrence Rd, Havertown, PA 19083, USA
E-mail: uspen-and-sword@casematepublishers.com

*This book is dedicated to my parents,*
*Olga Muñoz and Antonio Muñoz*
*R.I.P.*

# CONTENTS

# LIST OF PLATES

15. A Russian child has been discovered in the woods by SS troops during an anti-partisan operation. The forests of the USSR offered protection for not only the partisan forces but citizens seeking to hide from the Germans. Jews in particular would hide in the vast forests, swamps and marshes of the USSR, as a way of surviving the war. It is unlikely that this child lasted the war. (*Bundesarchiv*)
16. A German patrol in search of the enemy. (*Bundesarchiv*)

# LIST OF FIGURES, MAPS AND TABLES

**Figures and Maps**

## Tables

# AUTHOR'S NOTE

A regime, of whatever kind, collapses only under the weight of defeat.
Benito Mussolini

## History is cyclical

John Gray was one of only a few academics in the world who anticipated, and warned of, the coming economic collapse of 2008. He claims that economic boom periods in the market can be deceptive, given that history is cyclical. The key word we should take note of is 'cyclical', meaning that history is never progressive but recurring. In simple terms, history repeats itself. With regard to history repeating itself, I have observed numerous parallels between Adolf Hitler and Vladimir Putin, proving Dr Gray's analysis of repeating cycles. Back in the 1930s and 1940s it was expansionist dictatorships that threatened the world. Although Benito Mussolini and the Empire of Japan were a threat to peace, it was Adolf Hitler and Nazism who were the greater dangers. Today Xi Jinping is pushing Communist China into a more aggressive stance with regard to the South China Sea and the issue of Taiwan.

Yet, it is Vladimir Putin of the Russian Federation who is now the larger danger to world peace. During the past ten years, our world has seen the rise of autocrats all over the planet. Many nations are now run by authoritarian regimes. Examples that immediately come to mind are Kim Jong-un of North Korea, Bashar al-Assad of Syria, Viktor Orbán of Hungary, Recep Tayyip Erdoğan of Turkey, Daniel Ortega of Nicaragua, Nicolas Maduro of Venezuela, Miguel Diaz-Canel of Cuba, Aleksander Lukashenko of Belarus, Ramzan Kadirov of Chechnya, and of course, Vladimir Putin of the Russian Federation. The list of autocrats is much longer. In fact, in the past 17 years, there has been a decline in democracy around the world. Only twenty-five nations have seen improvements in human rights and advances in liberal reforms, while a whopping sixty nations have slipped into authoritarianism.[1]

That is more than double the number of nations who have come closer to democracy. If our twentieth-century history is our guidepost, and if this trend continues, then the twenty-first century will likely see more conflicts brought on by men calling themselves General Secretary, Chairman, Supreme Leader, or even 'President for Life'. In particular, Vladimir Putin has been active in exporting his despotism beyond the borders of the Russian Federation. That is what sets him apart from other despots. While most authoritarian leaders today are content with oppressing their own people, Vladimir Putin has begun 'exporting' his dictatorship to other nations. Of course, I'm referring to the current invasion of Ukraine. The parallels between Hitler and Putin, as we shall see, are there for anyone to observe if they care to notice.

Waiting in the wings, much like Benito Mussolini did from 1939–40, Xi Jinping of China is looking to see if Putin gets away with carving up Ukraine. Like Putin, Xi Jinping has an eye on conquering land outside of the current borders of mainland China. In addition to building artificial islands in the South China Sea, then claiming 'territorial waters' around them, the Chinese communist government in Beijing has always claimed that Taiwan is a 'breakaway' province that rightfully belongs to mainland China. Taiwan was established on the island of Formosa after General Chiang Kai-shek and the Nationalist forces lost the Chinese civil war in 1949. If Putin succeeds in taking Ukraine, the Chinese communist leader may feel emboldened to make a similar attempt to grab Taiwan by force, sooner rather than later.

## The long Russian authoritarian winter

In 1960 Gerald Reitlinger published a groundbreaking study titled *The House built on Sand: The Conflicts of German Policy in Russia, 1941-1945.* Dr Reitlinger explained how the German attempt at empire building in the East failed, given the absurd and counterproductive Nazi policies towards the very people in that they wished to rule. This work was released around the height of the Cold War. It was timely then because it showed, among other things, that many of the people who inhabited the Soviet Union had been and continued to be unhappy with the communist system. The establishment of the 'Iron Curtain', as Winston Churchill described it in 1946, imprisoned not only those peoples living within the borders of the USSR, but all of Eastern Europe as well. The population in these areas chafed at the lack of freedom and inaccessibility to even basic consumer goods that were needed for everyday life. The Soviet system stifled individuality and only offered repression, deprivations and harshness to its citizens.

Vladimir Lenin's Bolshevik state was not that dissimilar to the Tsar's rule when it came to repression. In fact, Lenin's government proved to be harsher than the Tsars had ever been. Joseph Stalin's rule (1924–53) was even more severe. Current estimates by Russian scholars as to the number of people who perished as a result of Stalin's regime stand at around twenty million. The only one to beat that record is Adolf Hitler. The communist state that followed under Nikita Khrushchev (beginning in 1953) and Leonid Brezhnev (in 1964) was, in many ways, not as repressive as the Stalinist period, but the system had not altered substantially enough for the population of the Soviet Union to enjoy the benefits that come from living in a free society. In that communist 'utopia', individuals could not question or criticise the state. Doing so was to risk ostracism, alienation or even imprisonment. People also lived in virtual fear that someone would inform on them if they were overheard complaining about the state or said the 'wrong thing'.

Free travel was not permitted and individuals could not enjoy the benefits that come from economic independence, except for high party officials who received rewards that the common Soviet citizen could only dream of. In essence, the autocracy of the Tsars and dictatorship of the Leninist and Stalinist period gave way to the oligarchy of the old guard in the Central Committee of the Communist Party. Throughout the communist period, citizens of the USSR would spend hours standing in bread lines or lines at the local department store, hoping to be able to purchase provisions or scarce consumer goods. This was because most of the nation's GDP was going to the production of military hardware.

## Why did Russia end up as a kleptocracy?

When Brezhnev died in 1982, another old-timer from the Central Committee, Yuri Andropov, was elected General Secretary of the Communist Party. Andropov died in 1984 after serving less than two years, at which point another old-timer, Konstantine Chernenko, was elected. Chernenko lasted an even shorter time than Andropov, dying in 1985, not even a year after assuming office. Members of the Central Committee thereupon chose a candidate who was significantly younger than most of the old guard who had served up until then. The hope was that this new General Secretary would not have to be replaced in a couple of years. This turned out to be Mikhail Gorbachev. Gorbachev was born in 1931 of a Russian father and Ukrainian mother. Employing what he called *Glasnost* (openness) and *Perestroika* (restructuring), Gorbachev set about trying to reorganise the Soviet economic and political system. The job seemed insurmountable, but Gorbachev began to make slow progress.

However, the changes that he was implementing seemed so progressive and democratic that in 1991 the hardliners in the Communist Party attempted a coup against Gorbachev. The coup ultimately failed. That failure led directly to the collapse of the USSR and the formation of the Russian Federation under Boris Yeltsin. The establishment of the Russian Federation in 1991 seemed to bring hope that perhaps the long Russian 'authoritarian winter' might break, and democracy could finally take hold. Unfortunately, two things occurred which quickly halted that swing towards democracy. First, instead of trying to support the newly created democratic institutions in Russia, the United States declared victory in the Cold War and went about establishing itself as the sole superpower in the world. Secondly, the appointment of Vladimir Putin as president of the Russian Federation in 1999 eventually relegated Russia's newly born democracy to a slow death.

Putin, a KGB hardliner and a true believer in the Soviet communist system, worked slowly at first, crippling and undermining the newly created democratic institutions in Russia. In this he took the old Benito Mussolini adage: 'if you pluck a chicken one feather at a time, no one will notice'. So, following this method, Putin usurped the democratic checks and balances in the country and slowly created the kleptocracy that exists in Russia today. Putin was not alone in this. He had help from people who felt as he did. The Weimar Republic was also undermined by officials who resented democracy and longed for a return to the rule of the Kaiser. Still others wished a new authoritarian leader to emerge. These men worked against the republic from within, subverting the government. The parallels here between the failed Weimar Republic and the failed attempt to bring true democracy to Russia are obvious.

## Where was the United States?

Following the collapse of the USSR, the United States involved itself in several conflicts, some of which were not of its making, like Saddam Hussein's invasion of Kuwait in 1991, and the 2001 attack on America by Al Qaeda. But in 2003 the United States elected to invade Iraq. This was a war of choice that ultimately proved to be costly and debilitating to the US in terms of lives lost, the huge financial expense of the conflict, and the loss of political capital around the world. George Bush Jr. opted for a pre-emptive policy that said the United States would act if it saw a threat in the making. This unnecessary conflict also helped to destabilise the delicate political balance in the Middle East. While it was true that Al Qaeda was responsible for attacking the United States on 11 September 2001, its presence was in Afghanistan, not Iraq. In order to justify the invasion of Iraq, the US government accused Saddam Hussein of having weapons of mass destruction. Saddam was also blamed for conspiring with Al Qaeda, even though those in the US government knew very well that he was a secular tyrant, who would not have allowed a fundamentalist theocratic movement like Al Qaeda into his country.

By 2003 Saddam Hussein was no longer a threat to the United States or even to his Arab or Persian neighbours. After his defeat in 1991, he had been content to remain within the borders of Iraq and butcher his own people. However, the neo-conservatives under the George Bush Jr. administration saw an opportunity for regime change, under the guise of the pre-emptive policy and of fighting Al Qaeda. They felt this change could occur at the point of a gun, and that ousting Saddam would alter the political landscape of the Middle East in favour of the United States. The political situation of the Middle East did change after the invasion of Iraq. But this is not the change for which the neo-conservatives had hoped. The nation that in the end benefitted most from Saddam Hussein's fall, was the Islamic Republic of Iran. Today Iraq has close relations and partners with Iran, while the United States has lukewarm relations with Iraq. At great cost in human life and financial expense, the United States has inadvertently aided a sworn enemy (Iran).

Hubris, it seemed, had taken the United States to a place where it was completely invested in what would become the longest conflict that America had ever fought. Initially in Afghanistan, only small American forces were employed, backed up by local warlords whose allegiance was not guaranteed. The United States had used few forces at the start of the Afghan war because it was saving the bulk of the troops for the invasion of Iraq. As a result, the one chance to capture Osama bin Laden early, at Tora Bora, was lost because one of America's Afghan 'allies' was bought off and turned a blind eye while Bin Laden and his cohorts slipped away. Mistakes were also made in Iraq once the country was occupied.

The first mistake was placing a minority Shiite leader to head the new Iraqi government. After a lifetime of being abused by the Sunni majority, the Shiites were dying for payback. Nouri al-Maliki began to favour the Shiites, while the Sunnis were marginalised. Another mistake was the US government's decision to disband the entire Iraqi Army, using the Coalition Provisional Authority. The Iraqi Army employed hundreds of thousands of Sunnis. The consequences of demobilising so many Sunni men would prove to be detrimental. These decisions, and others, led directly to further alienation and resentment by the Sunni population. Many former Iraqi soldiers, now out of work, and seeing their country led by a Shiite leader bent on weakening the power of the Sunni majority, were easily radicalised. These ex-Iraqi Army soldiers became ready recruits for a new terrorist organisation: ISIS. Slowly but steadily, attacks against US troops in Iraq began to increase.

## The demise of the fledgling Russian democracy

While the United States was distracted with its Iraqi adventure, Russia was struggling to establish its democratic institutions. The period from 1991–9, I would venture to say, was very similar to the period of the Weimar Republic from 1921–33. A nation that was only accustomed to one form of authoritarianism or another (Germany in 1921 and Russia in 1991) was asked to accept democratic institutions and to embrace them willingly. As stated earlier, like the Weimar Republic, there were people in the new Russian government who opposed democracy. The principal opponent in Russia's bid for liberalism was Vladimir Putin. When he was appointed President of the Russian Federation (after Boris Yeltsin retired), he was in a perfect position to attack that nascent Russian democracy from within. Just like Putin was given the position of President of the Russian Federation in 1999, Hitler was given the position of Chancellor of Germany in 1933, and just like Putin, he began to undermine the Weimar Republic until he obtained the dictatorship that he wanted. Again, the parallels between both men are obvious.

Putin was a child of the communist system and was wholly indoctrinated in the principles that had kept the USSR together. Using patience and the dirty tricks of his former KGB trade, he employed bribery, coercion, blackmail, and even worked with the Russian and Chechen mafia to eliminate or intimidate politicians, industrialists, and reporters, forcing them to bend to his will. Those who refused to be subverted were killed. Those critics whom Putin could not reach because they were living outside of the Russian Federation were eventually killed as well. It became quite common for Russian dissidents to be poisoned with Polonium-210 by Federal Security Service of the Russian Federation (FSB) agents, many of whom were former KGB members. For example, Russian dissident Alexander Litvinenko was poisoned in 2006. In 2015, another dissident, Boris Nemtsov, was assassinated while taking a walk near the Kremlin. Those who are in the know claim that it was the Chechen mafia that killed Nemtsov. The person who benefited most from Nemtsov's murder was Vladimir Putin. While living in the United Kingdom, Sergei Skripal and his daughter were poisoned using Novichok in 2018. In 2020 Alexei Navalny, a brave critic of Putin, was poisoned. He survived, only to be charged with false corruption charges that sent him to jail for 13 years. Navalny died on 16 February 2024. He was only 47 years old. Many warned Navalny not to return to Russia, for fear of what would happen. Nevertheless, this brave critic of Putin refused to be cowed. Like so many before him, he paid the ultimate price for defending democracy in Russia. Since the start of the Second Chechen War (in 2000) and today, over 200 politicians and reporters from television and print media have been assassinated in Russia, a number that parallels the number of moderate and left-leaning German politicians and newspaper editors who were killed by right-wing assassins during the period of the Weimar Republic. Slowly, Putin has destroyed or usurped the new democratic institutions in Russia, including a free press. Adolf Hitler did the same thing.

The Russian parliament has become simply a rubber stamp for Putin's wishes and desires in much the same way that members of the Reichstag became a rubber stamp for Hitler. Newspaper and TV reporters in Russia must toe the line and only present to the Russian people the version of history and events that Putin wants to show them. This is yet another parallel with Hitler's Third Reich. Once he was certain that his position as President of the Russian Federation was secure for another 20 years, Putin lamented openly that the collapse of the Soviet Union was the greatest calamity to befall the world in the twentieth century. We hear today, as the Russian invasion of Ukraine continues to wreak destruction, pain, misery, and death, that the majority of Russians support Putin's war and his version of events. The ludicrous and spurious accusation by Putin that he is eliminating Nazis from the Ukrainian government is simply an excuse for aggression.

Unfortunately, he is believed by the majority of Russians. It's not merely the *babushkas* who believe him, but middle-aged people and even young adults. This is because Vladimir Putin has turned what were independent and impartial Russian news outlets into the political mouthpiece of his regime. Those who are not fooled do not dare to speak openly. The situation has not been helped by the fact that the majority of the Russian people have not experienced true democracy and its advantages for any serious amount of time. Not knowing any better, perhaps some Russians actually prefer the harshness and repression of a police state, simply because it is familiar to them. Professor Jeffrey Herff, an expert on the history of the Weimar Republic, remarked in 1986 that the Weimar Republic 'was a republic without republicans'. This was echoed by Sebastian Ulrich in a work that was published in 2009.[2]

Both claimed that the German people at the time were only accustomed to authoritarian rule, and therefore were less inclined to support a democratic government when it was offered to them, especially when there were anti-democratic agents working from within to undermine that very democracy. This is the same scenario that Russia has experienced since 1999. It is also another reason why democracy was not firmly embedded in Russian society. Granted, there were some in Russia who tried to defend the newly-created independent institutions, like a free press. Many who did so were targeted and paid the ultimate price. Putin and his cronies made sure of that, and that democracy would not flower in Russia. Taking all of this into account, we can say that the parallels between the history of the Weimar Republic and the Russian Federation are undeniable.

## A forgotten lesson from the past

While the United States was spending much human capital and economic effort being the sole superpower of the world, fighting both a war of consequence and a war of choice, what it should have been doing was supporting Russia's young democracy by all means. Frankly, America dropped the ball. The United States forgot its own history. Back in 1918, when the First World War ended, President Woodrow Wilson wished to aid the newly-established democracies of Europe that had been created from the ashes of four former empires. He wanted to do this by sending both money and experts to those new democratic nations in Europe. Two things put a stop to this. First, Wilson had a stroke towards the end of his second term which incapacitated him for about a year. Second, the US Congress refused to allocate any funds towards supporting the new democracies of Europe. Instead, the United States became isolationist and ignored Europe altogether.

Within 20 years (by 1938), the only true democracy left in central Europe was Czechoslovakia.[3] In that same year, Adolf Hitler's threats yielded appeasement from the West yet again.[4] At Munich, he was able to acquire the Sudetenland, a stretch of frontier border between Germany and Czechoslovakia that contained a sizeable *volksdeutsch* (ethnic German) population. The Sudetenland also happened to contain the principal mountain defences for Czechoslovakia. At Munich, Édouard Daladier of France and Neville Chamberlain of the United Kingdom didn't even bother inviting the Czechs to the negotiating table. Benito Mussolini, who really had nothing to do with the problem, showed up at the meeting uninvited, but was given a seat, while the Czechs, whose future was being decided, were left out.

When the Germans acquired the Sudetenland, they effectively stripped the country of its defensive fortifications along the Czech-German border. Months later, in March 1939, Hitler's armies quietly marched in and took over what was left of the Czechoslovakian nation. Hitler's troops entered Prague during a heavy snowstorm, which ironically intimated the dark period ahead for the Czech people. Had the United States supported the new democracies of Europe after the First World War, things might have had a different outcome. In 1991, instead of declaring victory in the Cold War, the United States should have assured that victory over the USSR by supporting democracy in Russia by any and all means possible.

## Edmund Burke was right

We can speculate that things might have been different if in 1991 the United States had concentrated on making sure that democracy would take a firm hold in Russia. Today the nation of Ukraine, and indeed all peaceful nations of the world, are suffering from Russian aggression, directly or indirectly, either at the point of a gun, or through rising food and fuel prices, all because for years many nations turned a blind eye to Russia's bullying. Ukrainians are dying by the thousands and people around the world are starving because the war is affecting grain shipments. The world had to suffer the Second World War because Adolf Hitler was appeased from 1934 until 1938, as he became stronger and more dangerous. Vladimir Putin has been emboldened by the apathy and lethargy of the West. Europe in particular has had a large dependence on Russian oil and natural gas. This has led the nations of Europe to ignore Russia's growing belligerence in exchange for a steady energy supply. The Russian Army, long known for its brutality and heartlessness, devastated Grozny, the capital of Chechnya, in 1994. The Russian Army did horrible things in Georgia, when Russian backed separatists in the South Ossetian *Oblast* declared their independence from Georgia in 2008 and sought Russian 'protection'.[5]

The heinous tactic of targeting civilians, as seen in Ukraine, was perfected by the Russian Army during the Syrian civil war in 2016. Entire cities in Syria were levelled by Russian artillery and air strikes. In particular, hospitals and schools were targeted as a way of demoralising their opponents. In the twisted logic of tyrants, killing the children of your enemy limits the rise of future soldiers who will oppose you. Even chemical weapons were used against the Syrian civilian population. Although President Obama warned Bashar al-Assad of Syria that employing chemical weapons was a line he should not cross, Assad, who benefitted from the protection of the Russian Army, employed those chemical weapons to horrific effect.

The United States and others condemned this barbaric act, but in the end, nothing was done by any Western leader, just as nothing had been done when the Russians committed war crimes in Chechnya and in Georgia. Employing terror and targeting the civilian population has become part of the *modus operandi* of the Russian Army. That sounds awfully familiar if we think back on the Nazi period with its politicised army, which committed untold war crimes. During the Second World War the Third Reich kidnapped tens of thousands of Nordic-looking children from all across Europe. They did so in order to raise them as Nazis. Today, Putin's regime has admitted to stealing as many as 700,000 Ukrainian children, under the guise of protecting them from the war. The woman in charge of coordinating this massive effort is Maria Lvova-Belova, one of Putin's stooges. Stories are now filtering out of Russia that indicate Putin has ordered the indoctrination of these Ukrainian children in order to raise them as Russians. Again, the parallels between what the Nazis did and what Putin is doing are there for anyone to see.

## Empty promises

In 1991, when the Soviet Union collapsed, both the newly created Russian Federation and the United States made a promise to Ukraine that if it would give up its nuclear arsenal (there were nuclear missiles stationed in Ukraine), the United States and the Russian Federation would guarantee and protect the territorial integrity of Ukraine's borders. In February 2014 Vladimir Putin ordered the invasion and occupation of the Crimea and its annexation from Ukraine for the Russian Federation. This was followed up on 6 April 2014, when Russian-backed separatists began a war against the Ukrainian government in the Donbas region of eastern Ukraine. The attempt aimed to wrest control of this eastern Ukrainian province, rich in minerals and industrial capacity, from Ukraine and unite it with Russia. Russia supplied these separatist rebels with an abundance of military equipment and continue to do so today. It appears then, that Ukraine might have done better had it kept its nuclear arsenal as a deterrent to any would-be invader, rather than depending on the empty promises of both the United States and the Russian Federation to guarantee its borders.

As with all other acts of Russian aggression, the United States and Europe's leading powers employed words of condemnation in 2014, but not much else. This is exactly what happened between 1934 and 1938. Was it a surprise to the United States and the European nations that, after years of turning a blind eye to what Putin was doing, he felt emboldened enough to invade another sovereign nation? In order to find an excuse to swallow up the rest of Ukraine, Putin has made the baseless accusation that the country is being run by Nazis.

This is truly a classic case of psychological projection, given that Ukraine's president, Volodymyr Zelensky, happens to be Jewish, and the only person behaving like a Nazi happens to be named Putin. Just as the Western leaders had appeased Hitler for years, culminating in the signing of the infamous Munich Agreement, so has the West appeased Putin by allowing him to run roughshod over his neighbours for years.

With the formal invasion of Ukraine on 24 February 2022, the birds of appeasement and economic pragmatism have come home to roost, and only too late has the West realised that Putin needs to be confronted. Only when Adolf Hitler's forces marched into what was left of Czechoslovakia in March 1939, ending that nation's liberty, did the British Prime Minister, Neville Chamberlain, and France's Prime Minister, Édouard Daladier, finally realise that Hitler, like all schoolyard bullies, needed to be opposed. The months between September 1938 and March 1939 have gone down in history as a testament to what happens when democracies fail to confront tyranny. We must now also add February 2014 to this shameful list. Confronting Hitler much earlier might have avoided war, or at least reduced the terrible cost in lives that the Second World War brought. By the same token, opposing Vladimir Putin earlier might have also prevented further Russian aggression. If he were alive today to witness the tragic events unfolding in Ukraine, Edmund Burke, the Irish-born British statesman, would have repeated his famous warning: 'All tyranny needs to gain a foothold, is for people of good conscience to remain silent'. Again, the parallels between the Nazi period and now are uncanny.

## The same old dream of empire building

Today we are faced with a Hitler-want-to-be in the guise of the Russian President. Putin's goal is no less than the re-establishment of a Russian empire like the one that existed during the time of the USSR. Realising that he can't live forever, and contemplating how Russians will remember him, Putin is attempting to re-establish the territorial boundaries of what used to be the USSR as his legacy. Like all other tyrants before him, he will ultimately fail, but not before tens of thousands, or even hundreds of thousands of innocent people lose their lives. The only thing that will defeat Vladimir Putin is the will and military support of the West, coupled with the resistance of the brave Ukrainian people. Unfortunately, Western support for Ukraine is faltering. This is especially true with regard to the United States, given that the election of 2024 will most likely decide if the US will continue to fight aggression by supporting Ukraine, or allow Ukrainian democracy to fall.

At home in Russia, there are stirrings of dissent, but Putin's police state is now firmly entrenched. In 2017 he created the *Natsional'naya gvardiya* (National Guard), known as the Special Police Force. This organisation is a police formation of some 340,000 soldiers, whose members are only answerable and loyal to Putin himself. This paramilitary organisation sounds very similar in make-up and allegiance, to Hitler's SA Storm Troopers, or even the SS. Now, the only way that Putin will fall from power is if military affairs take a further bad turn for Russia. Putin knows that his future as leader of the Russian Federation depends on victory in Ukraine, no matter what that victory might cost. If Putin is thwarted in taking Ukraine, he will lose power and most likely, his life. Therefore, he will continue to act ruthlessly and show no mercy. His past track record suggests he will be willing to sacrifice everything, including the lives of the Russian people, to obtain that victory. Recently, some politicians in the West have been pushing the Ukrainian government to make peace with Russia. What these 'armchair generals' don't realise is that allowing Vladimir Putin to keep what land he has stolen from Ukraine will only encourage him to continue his aggression at a later date. The temporary peace will also give him time to reequip and retrain the Russian Army. The Ukrainians understand that they cannot compromise or try to reason with a man like Putin. To Putin, compromise is a sign of weakness. The only thing he understands is brute force. In this, he is accompanied by a legion of Russian tyrants who came before him, going all the way back to Ivan the Terrible. Putin is merely the latest Russian tyrant.

Behind the lines, the Ukrainian partisan movement has begun to take a toll on the Russian invader. The war, it seems, will last longer than Putin expected. Hopefully, Putin's attempt at empire-building will fail. In the meantime, those politicians, generals, and rich oligarchs around Putin, who support his kleptocracy, are waiting to see if the Russian *Führer* suffers more military reversals, or if the West abandons Ukraine. If history is a harbinger, then this war of aggression will decide not only Ukraine's future, but Putin's ultimate place in history. Just as the Nazis failed at building an empire in the East, Putin too, it is hoped, will fail in his attempt to create an empire along the lines of his beloved USSR. Dr. John Gray's observation that history is cyclical has to be considered, given the many parallels between the Nazi period and now. If Putin suffers more military reversals on the battlefield, like Hitler discovered, he may find himself inside a house of cards that is about to collapse on him. Benito Mussolini's famous quote, 'a regime, of whatever kind, collapses only under the weight of defeat' will then have been proven true.

# INTRODUCTION

## A different kind of war

Why was it that Nazi Germany was unable to create an eastern empire, that many historians agree could have supplied land and resources that would have kept the Third Reich alive for a thousand years? The answer lies in the nature of the Nazi system itself. During the Second World War Nazi policy regarding the combating of partisans, especially in Eastern Europe, including the USSR, involved the tactic of *kollektive gewaltmassnahmen.*[1] This policy punished all for the acts of a few. For example, an attack by guerrilla forces against German units or interests made the local population near that attack as responsible as the guerrillas themselves. This and other German policies dealing with civilian and military matters would eventually work to undermine German rule in the East. The idea behind *kollektive gewaltmassnahmen* was the German belief that, fearing reprisals, the local population in an occupied region behind German lines would inform on the partisans before the guerrillas had a chance to launch any attacks against German interests. In addition, several orders created shortly before the start of the Russian campaign, collectively referred to by historians as the *Verbrecherbefehle*, were meant to give an air of 'legality' to such policies as *kollektive gewaltmassnahmen* that were criminal and illegal in wartime. These official announcements would quickly become standard policy in the East. They would also end up costing the lives of many civilians.

With the invasion of the Soviet Union on 22 June 1941, various Nazi ideologies were used that would come together in a deadly cocktail which would shape the German struggle in the East. Anti-Polish and anti-Jewish sentiments were already causing the deaths of thousands in German-occupied Poland. The idea that the Jewish, Romani and Eastern European people were inferior to Germans, and natural enemies of Germany, made it easier for the Nazis to prosecute the Russian campaign in a more barbaric manner. In effect, dehumanising these people made it easier for Germans to kill them. It's an established fact that anti-Semitism was the principal factor in the Nazis' eventual decision to attempt to murder the entire Jewish population of Europe. Christopher Browning states that the society in which Germans lived at the time was imbued with a steady dose of anti-Semitic propaganda, which denigrated and marginalised the Jews to the point where they began to be seen as less than human and, by extension, 'life unworthy of life' (*Lebensunwertes Leben*):

> As *Leutnant* Drucker said with extraordinary understatement, 'Under the influence of the times, my attitude to the Jews was marked by a certain aversion'. The denigration of Jews and the proclamation of Germanic racial superiority was so constant, so pervasive, so relentless, that it must have shaped the general attitudes of masses of people in Germany, including the average reserve policemen.[2]

Just as importantly, however, Christian Streit has described very persuasively how anti-communism was 'a factor of crucial importance' in the process of creating an extermination policy during the period prior to and during the Russian campaign.[3] A perfect example of this is the infamous 'Commissar Order', which gave all German troops, irrespective of branch of service or rank, the ability to execute any and all Red Army commissars either right after capture, or immediately after interrogation. While the Nazis had behaved and continued to behave harshly towards the Polish nation, their cruelty in this instance did not compare to that which they planned to inflict during their campaign in the Soviet Union.[4] That is not to say that Poland would be spared the full brunt of the Nazis' wrath. On the contrary, as soon as the German invasion of the Soviet Union began, Poland would feel the full weight of this *vernichtungskrieg*. Repression begets cruelty, and the Germans would increase their campaign of terror against the Polish nation as the war in the East progressed. In effect, these criminal orders allowed the *Ostheer* to operate under a completely different set of rules than those that had been employed when the *Wehrmacht* conquered Western Europe.[5] In this new form of warfare, simply being a Jew became synonymous with being a partisan. As such, all Jews were subject to execution on sight.

In addition, the Russian military and civilian population would have no legal protection from killings of any kind. Since the USSR had never signed the Geneva Convention on the treatment of captured enemy prisoners, the Nazis considered they had *carte blanche* in treating all captured enemy combatants and civilians in whichever way they wished. This included the use of immediate executions if it was deemed necessary by the local German commander, meaning that the lowest-ranked German soldier (even a lowly corporal) had the right to execute captured prisoners if he deemed it necessary. Nazi ideology, coupled with what was virtually a mandate to kill, fused together in the Russian campaign to create the *Weltanschauungskrieg* (ideological struggle) against what the Nazis referred to as the 'Judeo-Bolshevist' threat. Given such wide latitude, the struggle in the East would be unprecedented in terms of its intensity, ferocity, and brutality. With the Nazi belief that the Jewish race was a polluting factor in German life and *lebensunwertes leben,* this idea was now further expanded upon to suit the circumstances of the war in the East. This was accomplished by (as stated earlier) making the killing of Jews synonymous with fighting the partisans. Adolf Hitler even said that the war in the East was an opportunity to kill all those they felt opposed them.

The belief that *Jeder Jude ist ein Guerrillakampfer* (every Jew is a guerrilla fighter) was hammered home by officers not only within the SS and *Ordnungspolizei,* but the entire *Wehrmacht.* As if to reaffirm this view, Wilhelm Keitel issued the following order, dated 16 December 1942, regarding the combating of partisans. The command seemed to reiterate the criminal orders completely – almost a year and a half after the German invasion. A portion of it reads:

> The troops therefore have the right and the duty to use, in this fight, any means, even against women and children, provided they are conducive to success. Scruples, of any sort whatsoever, are a crime against the German people and against the front-line soldier who bears the consequences of attacks by bands and who cannot understand why any should be shown to them or their associates. These principles must serve as a basis for operations against bands in the East. No German participating in action against bands or their associates is to be held responsible for acts of violence either from a disciplinary or a judicial point of view. Commanders of troops engaged in action against the bands are obliged to see to it that all officers of units under their command be immediately and thoroughly notified of this order, that their legal advisers be immediately acquainted therewith and that no judgments be passed which are in contradiction thereto.[6]

This policy made it easy for regular German Army troops to (1) work side by side with SS units fighting the partisans and assisting the SS *Einsatzgruppen* in eliminating the Jewish population, and (2) commit crimes against the Jewish and non-Jewish population under the guise of combating the guerrillas. Romani were added to the category of *lebensunwertes leben,* so they too would be targeted wherever they were encountered. In many instances these murders were carried out independent of the SS mobile killing units, the *Einsatzgruppen*. Even rear-area army garrison commands have been shown to have cooperated with the SS and to have undertaken operations against Jews and Romani on their own initiative. The above order, issued by Keitel, stipulated that no soldier was to be punished for any acts which he committed while under the pretext of fighting the guerrillas and keeping order behind the lines. In addition, women and children were specifically mentioned as not being an exception to this rule.

What Keitel meant is clear enough: the killing of women and children in the East would be permitted. Notice also that all of this served, as he put it, as 'a basis for operations in the East', meaning that the war and the tactics which the *Ostheer* was employing in the Soviet Union were unique to this particular front. Was this the case because the Germans saw the Eastern Europeans as subhuman and less worthy of life? Was it because Josef Stalin did not subscribe to the Geneva Convention? Was it anti-communist hatred? Was it the brutalisation which occurred on the Eastern Front, as Omer Bartov and others have argued, which contributed to the barbarisation of the German soldier? Was it anti-Semitism? Was it hatred of the *Zigeuner*? The answer (sadly) is all of the above. All of these representative biases and bigotries were inflamed by Nazi propaganda and indoctrination. The Germans brought these biases to the East, and when coupled together with criminal military orders, permitting brutality and mass murder, engendered in the *Ostheer* a feeling that immoral conduct would be condoned. A major role in combating the partisans in the USSR was played not only by SS and police forces, but by the *Ostheer*. This included ancillary and volunteer auxiliary units of the German Army. In addition, Keitel's order also reinforced the German Armed Forces High Command directive against communist insurrection in occupied territories, issued on 16 September 1941, and also the infamous 'Reichenau Order' of 10 October 1941, on the conduct of troops in the eastern territories, which partly read as follows:

> The most important objective of this campaign against the Jewish-Bolshevik system is the complete destruction of its sources of power and the extermination of the Asiatic influence in European Civilization . . . Therefore, the soldier must have full understanding for the necessity of a severe but just revenge on subhuman Jewry. The Army has to aim at another purpose, i.e., the annihilation of revolts in hinterland which, as experience proves, have always been caused by the Jews . . . This is the only way to fulfil our historic task to liberate the German people once forever from the Asiatic-Jewish danger.[7]

In 2004, Ben Shepperd published a work detailing the war guilt of principally two such German units: two security divisions as they operated in central Russia from 1941–3.[8] Although his work covered only two security divisions, the author argued that their behaviour proved how National Socialist indoctrination, combined with the brutality of the war in the East, created the conditions that allowed for widespread murders under the guise of combating the Soviet partisans. Shepperd's approach was to build his case from the bottom up, by illustrating a consistent pattern of action within the battalions and regiments of these security divisions. His study was important because it reinforced existing research on the criminal excesses of the *Wehrmacht* in the East.

The book, however, would have been aided further if Shepperd had been able to cite other cases in similar German rear-area and front-line commands, to support the theory that this type of behaviour in the *Ostheer* was widespread and commonplace throughout the entire width and scope of the Eastern Front. By citing examples of atrocities committed by these units, Shepperd showed how, in the region of central Russia and Belarus, the degenerative brutality that National Socialism caused, when combined with the constant and vicious combat of the war in the East, worked to harden the German soldier and accustomed him to murder, even illegal killings.[9] This work will argue that similar criminal behaviours were perpetrated by German rear-area security forces throughout the East, including Poland, and what comprised the USSR at the time.

My research has affirmed what Dr Shepperd and other academics refer to as the brutalisation theory. But this is just one piece of the puzzle if we are to understand Nazi *Ost* policy. In this work, I have covered a wider area, citing numerous examples from the occupation of Poland, the Baltic States, Belarus, Ukraine, and European Russia. The conclusions provide verifiable evidence of this widespread practice of criminal conduct which even seeped into the Nazi civilian administration in the East. Like Shepperd and other researchers, I have worked from the bottom up by going through reels of captured German records detailing the history of these rear-area forces which operated in the East from 1939 until 1944. Cases also abound of front-line troops behaving criminally during anti-guerrilla sweeps. All of what happened in the East was in keeping with a strategy prepared before the invasion. *Generalplan Ost* was a Nazi plan developed as a blueprint for the genocide and democide that would take place in the East as a precursor to German colonisation. This plan required the Germans to be brutal and ruthless in the East. Employing the typical

German penchant for fulfilling obligations, the *Ostheer* carried out this order to devastating effect.

### The debate over German Army criminality in the East

Gerald Reitlinger was one of the earliest historians, if not the first, to have brought up the subject of possible participation of the German military in the heinous murders of the Jewish population of the USSR. Prior to this early work, the only substantive reference to this German Army and Holocaust connection were the High Command trials that occurred within the context of the Nuremberg War Crimes Trials of 1946–8. Reitlinger pointed to this in his ground-breaking 1956 study, *The SS: Alibi of a Nation.*[10] He began there, and others followed after him, with further proof that it wasn't just the Jewish people who were targeted, but the civilian population as a whole, and the *Ostheer* was knee-deep in it all.

With this work, Reitlinger established a foundation upon which others would follow and contribute, in much the same way that the base of a house is built, and other workers later add the walls and roof. The crux of his argument was that by blaming all of the evils committed by the Nazi regime on the SS, the German Army and therefore the nation as a whole, could be exculpated from any guilt. Reitlinger followed that classic work four years later, in 1960, with *The House Built on Sand: The Conflicts of German Policy in Russia, 1939-1945.*[11] In it, he detailed how the Nazi leaders and their German Army counterparts had prepared for a different kind of war in the Soviet Union. The criminal orders made the campaign different, in that these orders were a virtual licence to kill. In this he was repeating points already made by Alexander Dallin in *German Rule in Russia, 1941-1945: A Study of Occupation Policies*, in which Dallin described the 'Commissar Order' among other documents linking the German Army to the Holocaust and the illegal killings of the general population.[12]

Reitlinger pointed to documents written to senior German Army commanders by the Nazi leadership – collectively referred to by historians as the 'criminal orders', which provided the *Ostheer* with its 'mandate' to allow for the killing of the local population, especially the Jewish population. These orders document how German military courts would not apply to Russian civilians, how the SS and police units were to work outside military commands, and also included the infamous Commissar Order and the Barbarossa Jurisdiction Order, to name a few. The Jurisdiction Order in effect gave a virtual *carte blanche* to any German soldier fighting in the East, to shoot or kill anyone that was considered as being either 'agitators', 'partisans', 'partisan helpers', 'saboteurs', 'political commissars', or 'Jews', without fear of prosecution by any German court or tribunal. As stated earlier, the terms 'partisan' and 'Jew' were made synonymous, since treatment of both groups would be the same: execution. While many former German Army officers point to the fact that no order originated from the *Wehrmacht* which specified that the Jewish population was to be targeted for premeditated murder, historian Yitzhak Arad was correct when he stated that because Jews were included in the list of those persons who could be shot on sight, the effect was the same as if the *Wehrmacht* itself had written the order for the murder of the Jewish population.[13]

The criminal orders, therefore, directly link the Holocaust in the USSR to the German Army. Reitlinger related how shortly after the start of the Russian campaign, a meeting was held on 16 July 1941, in Angerburg. In attendance were Göring, Keitel, Rosenberg, Lammers, Bormann, and Adolf Hitler. The *Führer*, Reitlinger explained, 'declared that Stalin had ordered partisan warfare behind the German front'. Hitler also commented that this partisan war gave them the ability to eliminate everyone who opposed them.[14] This of course not only included the Jews, but anyone considered by the Nazis as an enemy. As a result, on 22 July 1941, a new expanded order was put forth by Hitler and added to the Barbarossa Jurisdiction Order, which stated implicitly that where SS and other security forces were not available, the German Army itself was to take all measures necessary, even draconian steps, to control the rear areas and those who populated them. They were also to eliminate the partisan threat or 'other dangers' that placed the German armed forces or the war effort at risk. This, Reitlinger wrote, 'became the German soldier's charter for anti-partisan warfare'.[15]

In spite of these early and impressive starts, the study of this German Army connection to the Holocaust and other illegal murders in the East did not really begin to be considered fully until the mid-1980s. It was then that Professor Omer Bartov published his now-classic work, *The Eastern Front, 1941-45, German Troops and the Barbarisation of Warfare*. In it, he proposed that the rigours of the Eastern Front, that is, the very nature of the warfare being fought between the Soviet Union and Nazi Germany, as well as preexisting Nazi ideology, quickly accustomed the typical German soldier to brutalisation, which made it easier for him to kill Jewish and non-Jewish civilians, captured soldiers, and partisans with little thought to the legality or morality of his actions. Indeed, as stated decades before by Reitlinger and Dallin, the 'criminal orders' gave the members of the German Army, from officers down to even the lowly *landser*,[16] the feeling that any action taken under the pretext of these orders would protect them from punishment by any German Army military tribunal.[17]

Bartov's incisive work was followed up three years later, in 1989, by a study titled *The German Army and Nazi Policies in Occupied Russia* by Professor Theo J. Schulte. Professor Schulte proposed that not only had the German Army been complicit in the Holocaust, but that it was part of a Nazi aim which sought 'the total destruction of another society as a fundamental prerequisite for the refashioning of German society'.[18] Here, Schulte was echoing the thoughts of historian Michael Geyer, who argued that the war of ideologies, the *Weltanschauungskrieg*, was not just fought with mere words, but was practised in the East with physical vigour.[19] Two years later in 1991, Yitzhak Arad reappraised the various criminal orders and expounded and developed on their implications as part of the Yad Vashem Yearbook Series. This important article added 'cement' to the arguments that authors like Bartov and Schulte were developing. Even when discussing the non-military leadership that ruled the German Eastern empire, we see the same ideology and action. Why did it take several decades from the publication of Reitlinger and Dallin's works for them to be followed by further research on the criminality of the *Wehrmacht* in the East? This is an important question.

It is beyond the scope of this work to go into the personal, social, or political reasons why the topic remained relatively dormant for so many years, but in 2007, Professors Ronald Smelser and Edward Davies published a study which proposed several reasons for this apparent 20-year hiatus.[20] Although this study was fraught with numerous assumptions, the authors did conclude correctly that the Cold War may have played a role in sanitising the German Army from its complicity in the horrors perpetrated in the East. This was done in order to use the full capacity of a revitalised West German state to help block Soviet aggression and intentions during the Cold War.[21] Throughout this period, Smelser and Davies argue, an entire myth about the valour and chivalry of the *Wehrmacht* was created by numerous American and European writers. In addition, at the end of the Second World War various powers were scrambling to grab as many Nazi scientists as they could get their hands on. The Americans and Russians were the biggest hoarders of German scientific knowledge. Professor Werner von Braun, the Nazi scientist who worked at Peenemünde perfecting the V-1 and V-2 missiles, and who later helped the United States reach the moon, immediately comes to mind. The Cold War was also a time when former Nazis, some involved in the Holocaust, were sought by

Western intelligence agencies because of their supposed knowledge of the Soviet Union and its people.

An important study as to understanding how it came to pass that 80 million Germans fell sway to Hitler and the Nazis and aided in the destruction of European Jewry came when Christopher R. Browning published his definitive study, *Ordinary Men: Reserve Police Battalion 101 and the Final Solution in Poland*. A few years later, in 1995, German author Paul Kohl published a little-circulated work called *Der Krieg der Deutschen Wehrmacht und der Polizei 1941-1944* ('The War of the German Armed Forces and Police 1941-1944'). In it, he argued that indeed, the German Army had followed the *Führerprinzip* (Leader Principle) of the *Weltanschauungskrieg* to its inevitable conclusion.[22]

Following the work by Kohl, Walter Manoschek edited a book in 1996 titled *Die Wehrmacht im Rassenkrieg: Der Vernichtungskrieg Hinter der Front* ('The [German] Armed Forces in the Race War: The War of Annihilation Behind the Front'). The numerous contributors to this work, who included such notables as Raul Hilberg, Manfred Messerschmidt, Wolfram Wette, Christian Streit, Hans Safrian, Hannes Heer, Bertrand Perz, Ela Hornung and Reinhold Gärtner, referenced incidences that occurred in the Soviet Union, but went a step further by describing the political and propaganda preparations and conditioning Germans were subjected to by the Nazi state before they even set foot on Soviet soil. The editor of this significant work, Walter Manoschek, also managed to document a comparable occurrence of German Army atrocities in Serbia, thus further cementing the truth of unlawful activities prevalent in the Nazi-era German Army.[23] Willi Dreßen had also recorded *Wehrmacht* atrocities in Serbia and Russia in an article published in the 1993 edition of the Yad Vashem Yearbook Series.[24] The numerous eyewitness reports in his book cemented those accounts with apparent indelible ink. That same year Hannes Heer and Klaus Naumann edited and published an extremely important study, *Vernichtungskrieg: Verbrechen der Wehrmacht 1941 bis 1944* ('War of Annihilation: Crimes of the [German] Armed Forces 1941 to 1944') that propelled the topic of German Army complicity in atrocities to a whole new level by attacking the question from the top and bottom – that is, by presenting not only documentary evidence of guilt, but showing in a very lucid and straightforward manner how the very nature of the Nazi regime worked to create the conditions leading to complicity from all corners of the *Wehrmacht* and civilian apparatus.[25] The book turned out to be so popular and important that in 2000 it was translated into the English language in annotated form.[26] *Vernichtungskrieg: Verbrechen der Wehrmacht 1941 bis 1944* proved very successful in the US, but interest was especially high in Germany, where there was a growing awareness of what had been a taboo subject until 1990: German Army complicity in atrocities and sanctioned murder. An exhibit was eventually created. That exhibit toured Germany for many years in the 1990s and was considered extremely controversial.[27]

German military veteran groups protested that this exhibition was negatively painting too broad a stroke on the *Wehrmacht*. A huge, oversized volume was produced in 2002: *Verbrechen der Wehrmacht: Dimensionen des Vernichtungskrieges 1941-1944* ('Crimes of the Armed Forces: Dimensions of the War of Extermination'). Its 764 pages are chock-full of documents, photographs, reports from diaries, interviews, eyewitness accounts, and other documentary evidence about the crimes of the German Army during the Nazi period. The sheer size and scope of this volume attests to the extent of the German Army's participation in these crimes, for surely if today the institute that produced it, the *Hamburger Institut für Sozialforschung* (Hamburg Institute for Social Research) could have amassed such a work, what other crimes were committed during the Second World War that for lack of evidence we shall never know about? That same year Wolfram Wette, who, until then, had been a contributing writer to this topic, published his first single and full study on the subject,[28] translated into the English language as *The Wehrmacht: History, Myth, Reality*. In it, Wette studied not only the top generals and middle-management officers but read reports and testimonials from the lowly privates as well. In his closing analysis, he stated:

> In recent years we have gained greater insight into the experience of the 'average Joe' in uniform meaning the many millions of enlisted men and non-commissioned officers who participated in the exterminationist campaign on the Eastern Front. Many of them followed the generals' ideological guidelines reluctantly, while others supported the campaign on the basis of their own convictions. Recent research has revealed a considerable amount of agreement with and support for the regime's goals at the bottom of the military hierarchy. Very few summoned the courage to resist this war – to the extent that it was possible at all. While the *Wehrmacht* was officially dissolved after the capitulation of May 8, 1945, that did not put an end to its history. Some believe that only after that date did the *Wehrmacht* achieve its ultimate victory, namely, in its struggle to preserve its image as an army with 'clean hands' in the eyes of the public both at home and abroad. The myth of the *Wehrmacht* lived on. The policy of apology evident in the memoirs of former generals – in concert with like-minded people in West Germany – worked successfully for decades.[29]

Wette reached the conclusion that, perhaps by 2002 – the year when his work was published and several years after the *Hamburger Institut* exhibit – Germany was now ready to admit that the legend of the *Wehrmacht*'s 'clean hands' could finally be consigned to the past.[30] However, old habits are hard to break. During the mid-1990s, an American political scientist would reopen the old wounds caused by German war guilt that perhaps the travelling exhibit on *Wehrmacht* crimes had merely opened slightly. So heated and controversial was this author's assertion to be that the national media both in the United States and in Europe picked up on it and carried the story for months. That author's name was Daniel J. Goldhagen, and the debate about the German Army's war guilt was about to expand to the German nation's guilt as a whole. By the early 1990s, the question over the extent of German Army complicity in *ha Shoah* almost certainly helped to partly inspire Goldhagen's work, *Hitler's Willing Executioners: Ordinary Germans and the Holocaust*.[31]

Goldhagen's book sold over 80,000 copies in its first print run – catching the attention not only of academics but the general public. American and European media covered the story about the controversy that the book produced. It also stirred up a hornets' nest of arguments among academics for and against the theory which Goldhagen proposed. In the book he argued that the majority of Germans were willing participants in the Holocaust because of their predisposed negative conditioning towards Jewry. Accusations and counter-arguments appeared from every corner of academia. Julius H. Schoeps edited the first work which appeared in Germany to counter Goldhagen's argument: *Ein Volk von Mordern? Die Dokumentation zur Goldhagen-Kontroverse um die Rolle der Deutschen im Holocaust*.[32] Not all of the recriminations against Goldhagen's book came from Germany. Domestic scholars like Fritz Stern, a German-Jewish refugee who, at the time Goldhagen's work was released, was teaching at Columbia University, had some tough criticism to dish out as well. Stern's counter-argument seemed as persuasive, as did the strength of his words:

> Goldhagen singles out those murderers who were 'ordinary Germans' and who, he insists were motivated solely by their 'cognitive model' of the Jew. He then moves from specific and harrowing examples to a grotesque extrapolation: having examined the acts of some hundreds or perhaps even thousands of people, he insists that almost all Germans were moved by the same hatred, approved the killing, and would have acted in like fashion if chance had so decreed. As he writes, '. . . the

> institutions treated here . . . should permit the motivations of the perpetrators in those particular institutions to be uncovered, and also allow for generalizing both to the perpetrators as a group and to the second target group of this study, the German people'. The leap from individual cases to the German people at large is unpersuasive, but necessary for his indictment of his 'second target group'.[33]

That was but a taste of the argument that all Germans were willing participants in the Holocaust, based on several hundred or several thousand Germans who willingly took part in the Holocaust. Dr Stern was pointing out the fact that you cannot assume that 80 million Germans were willing participants, based on thousands who did have a leading role in the Holocaust. This argument was reinforced when further research about the complicity of German Army units in the Holocaust began to be studied in greater detail (which began in the mid-1980s). It only affirms the continued importance of researching this topic even today. The implication of Goldhagen's work is clear: all Germans bear responsibility for the deaths of six million Jews. Thus, Goldhagen stirred many passions which have very real personal, social, and political implications. Geoffrey P. Megargee, whose work *War of Annihilation: Combat and Genocide on the Eastern Front, 1941* is perhaps one of the better studies to be released, and referred to what Goldhagen was claiming. In it, Megargee merges some of the theories expounded by Goldhagen, arguing that Germans in general were predisposed to the kind of annihilation war waged in Russia. Most academics, however, have only proven the guilt of the *Wehrmacht* during the war. In his conclusions, Megargee states, according to his premise, the crux of German Army guilt:

> In order to ensure their victory, the generals also helped lay the plans for Hitler's vision of an exterminationist war. Later they would claim that the SS was solely responsible for the crimes in the East, but in fact the military's role was crucial. At the most basic level, the crimes could never have taken place if the *Wehrmacht* had not conquered the ground, but the generals' culpability extends well beyond that fact. They encouraged their soldiers in an attitude that placed little or no value on the life of Soviet civilians, in fact, they ordered their men to use the harshest conceivable means to establish German dominance. They planned for the deliberate starvation of millions of people and for forced labour by millions more. They laid the groundwork for the fatal neglect of Soviet prisoners of war, whose care was their responsibility by international law. And they played a key role in planning for the elimination of the Communist leadership and intelligentsia, including

> those in uniform, as well as anyone who resisted German rule. That last goal provided the perfect cover for the SS *Einsatzgruppen* and other killing units to murder anyone whom they saw as a threat, including hundreds of thousands of Jewish men, women, and children. Since most of the military's leaders believed that Jews were fundamentally hostile and dangerous, they were able to persuade themselves, with little apparent difficulty, that killing all the Jews was necessary to secure the conquered territories.[34]

The only drawback to Megargee's book is that he only used published works and as a result, could only come to conclusions from observations and assessments of other authors. However, he laid out exactly what the *Wehrmacht* generals did which stained their escutcheon of honour forever. Another important work regarding German attitudes and decisions made in the East was published a year earlier, in 2005. It was titled *Abgehort: Deutsche Generale in britischer Kriegsgefangenschaft 1942-1945* ('Monitored: German Generals in British War Captivity 1942–1945'). This work, edited by Sönke Neitzel, is a massive compilation of secret conversations taped by British intelligence of German officers held in British POW camps from 1942–5. The book was thought important enough to be translated into English in 2008. The importance of this study is that in many of these secret conversations, German officers talked openly of the annihilation war in the East. Not knowing that they were being recorded, they showed emotions ranging from arrogant joy to total indifference. One such example from the book describes a conversation secretly recorded in a POW camp by the British on 6 May 1945, between *Generalleutnant* Karlimilian Siry, the former commander of the German *347. Infanterie Division*, and *Generalstabsintendant* Pauer of the *Oberkommando des Heeres* (OKH).[35] Pauer just listened while Siry expounded on how he would have handled the massive POW problem which the *Ostheer* had to deal with during the Russian campaign:

> Siry: One mustn't admit it openly, but we were far too soft. All these horrors have landed us in the soup now. But if we'd carried them through to the hilt, made the people disappear completely – no one would say a thing. These half measures are always wrong. In the East I suggested once to the *Korps* [command] – thousands of POW were coming back, without anyone guarding them, because there were no people there to do it. It went quite well in France, because the Frenchman is so degenerate that if you said to him: 'You will report to the POW collecting point in the rear' the stupid idiot really did go along there. But in Russia there was a space of 50–80 km, that is to say a 2 to 3 days' march, between the

> armoured spearheads and the following close formations. No Russians went to the rear, they lagged behind and then took to the woods left and right, where they could live all right. So, I said: 'That's no good, we must simply cut off one of their legs, or break a leg, or the right forearm, so that they won't be able to fight in the next four weeks and so that we can round them up'. There was an outcry when I said one must simply smash their legs with a club. At the time, of course, I didn't really condone it either, but now I think it's quite right. We've seen that we cannot conduct a war because we're not hard enough, not barbaric enough. The Russians are that all right.[36]

This outlook did not just arise out of the blue. The Nazis had nine years (1933–41) to imbue the German nation with a hatred of Jewry and the Slavic people in the East. This hatred was nurtured, fed, and finally legalised by a series of orders that, when combined with anti-Semitic and anti-communist ideology, worked to create conditions that caused criminality on a grand scale. However, we must admit that there existed in the German nation (and indeed, in most European countries) a base level of antipathy by the Gentile community towards the Jewish people. Religious anti-Semitism had existed in Europe for hundreds of years. What made the Nazi period different was that racial anti-Semitism was now added, in much the same way that one adds more kindling to a fire. The Nazis were able to exponentially increase that basic anti-Semitic sentiment to the point of madness. There is no doubt now that the German Army bears a good portion of the guilt for the horrors that occurred in the East. The outcome of the debate as to the degree of that war guilt on the part of the *Wehrmacht* is still incomplete. This work will hopefully add additional brick and mortar to the studies mentioned in this introduction, but more precisely, it provides additional documentation to Dr. Timothy Snyder's *magnum opus, Bloodlands: Europe Between Hitler and Stalin,*[37] and Mark Mazower's equally important study, *Hitler's Empire: How the Nazis Ruled Europe.*[38] The documentation herein affirms a cruel and extremely genocidal comportment on the part of the Germans, that was particular to these regions of Eastern Europe. This comportment was led by an ideology of exclusion and genocide. It was also the very reason why ultimately Germany was not able to establish an eastern empire as envisaged in *Mein Kampf.*

## *Fall Blau*

In the spring of 1942, the *Ostheer* was attempting to regain its footing after four months of a Soviet winter counteroffensive that not only pushed the German Army in Russia back with serious casualties, but forced it to employ a large number of rear-area and security forces as front-line units for lack of sufficient conventional forces. The Red Army winter offensive which began on 5 December 1941 also had repercussions behind the German lines, where the nascent Soviet partisan movement was attempting to grow and gain a foothold. By the spring of 1942 those early partisan units were ready to expand. The Germans, aware of the military situation both on the front lines and in the rear of their armies, also prepared to counter the growing partisan threat. As the German military planned to continue the Russian campaign into the summer of 1942, new security forces were gathered together and sent to the Soviet Union, and a new headquarters, specifically organised to fight the guerrilla menace, was established. In 1942 the *Ostheer,* acting on Adolf Hitler's orders, launched *Fall Blau* (Case Blue), the 1942 summer offensive which was aimed at capturing the Caucasus Mountains and the Russian oil fields that lay there. As the German southern armies began to advance further into southern Russia, the German anti-partisan effort behind the lines or *Heeresgruppe Süd* grew. The *Wehrmacht* eventually reached the Don River bend, where the city of Stalingrad (today's Volgograd) was located, one part of the southern army group veered towards Stalingrad, while the bulk of the German forces moved south, into the Caucasus Mountains.

Meanwhile, during the spring and summer of 1942 a strong guerrilla presence coalesced in Belorussia, central and northern Russia. This was a force composed of former Red Army soldiers, Communist Party functionaries, Komsomol members, university students and ordinary citizens that took up arms and were now threatening the very lifeblood of the German *Ostheer*. The war in the East in 1942 was as spectacular as it had been in 1941. This time however, the focus of the German assault would be southern Russia. The *Ostheer* could no longer launch a full-scale attack all along the entire width and breath of the Russian Front. It was incapable of doing what it had done in the summer and autumn of 1941. In the spring of 1942 Adolf Hitler was faced with a momentous decision. Should the German Army strike towards Leningrad, and link up with the Finnish Army? Should it take Moscow, and thus capture the political and all-important communications hub of the Soviet Union? Should Sevastopol be conquered so that the Crimea could finally be taken? Or should the Germans strike towards the Caucasus Mountains and the vast oil fields that lay there? This decision would have far-reaching consequences for the outcome of the war in the East.

In the end, the *Führer* attempted to capture three of the four objectives, but in incremental steps. He would first capture Sevastopol with the *11. Armee* and clear the Crimea of Russian forces. Then he shifted half of the *11. Armee* to the Leningrad sector while the other half remained to be employed in the German drive on the Caucasus Mountains. This is where the plan began to go wrong. By dividing *11. Armee*, the forces that were sent to the Leningrad sector proved insufficient for the task of capturing that city. The German summer offensive in the region of *Heeresgruppe Süd* envisioned numerous envelopment operations, where Red Army forces would be encircled by the panzer divisions, only to be finished off by the advancing infantry. Instead, the Soviets opted for an orderly withdrawal east, thus avoiding large encirclements and husbanding their forces by trading space for time. Time in which to reinforce the South and evaluate the enemy's intentions. Time in which to plan a counterstroke that would deal the Axis invader a fatal wound. By August 1942 it was clear that Hitler was once again dividing his forces because he wanted more than one objective. While the German *6. Armee* was tasked with capturing the city named after the communist leader, eventually more and more German forces were sent into the bloody fight. Before October 1942 a good part of *4. Panzerarmee* was also drawn to Stalingrad, while 3rd Romanian Army, the German *17. Armee, 1. Panzerarmee,* and parts of 4th Panzer Army headed for Ploesti and Tiflis in the Caucasus Mountains.

The *6. Armee* and the adjacent Axis armies would have been sufficient a force to act as a mobile left flank screen for the Axis advance on the Caucasus Mountains. There was no need to capture Stalingrad. With the employment of the entire *4. Panzerarmee,* Grozny and Tiflis could have been taken. The *Wehrmacht* would have been set for the rest of the war as far as petrol was concerned, while the Red Army would begin to suffer inadequate supplies. That, however, was not to be. Hitler wanted to boast that he had taken the city named after his opponent, so he ordered *6. Armee* to capture Stalingrad. That decision cost the Germans the defeat of their 1942 summer campaign, the loss of almost five entire armies (*6. Armee* and half of *4. Panzerarmee,* and three crushed Axis armies). Their defeat at Stalingrad and their withdrawal from the Caucasus also brought the realisation that after 1942, Germany could not defeat the Soviet Union. The defeat of Operation Zitadelle, conducted seven months later (July 1943), guaranteed that Germany would lose the war in the East. All of this occurred because Adolf Hitler attempted to gain too many objectives in 1942 with insufficient forces. The consequences of his military decisions, like deciding to capture Stalingrad, turned the war against the Germans. Behind the lines, the war also began to change in favour of the defender. The year 1941 saw the nascent partisan army sprouting small branches from a small bud. The year 1942 saw its growth to proportions that required more and more German security forces behind the front lines. By 1943, the war behind the lines was similar in intensity and size as the war on the front lines. The year 1943 is also the year that saw the greatest number of anti-partisan drives. It is the year that the Germans began to surrender large tracks of land behind the lines to the partisans. It is the year when more and more people, soldiers and civilian alike, died as a result of this partisan and anti-partisan struggle. 1943 is where we pick up the story of this, the greatest guerrilla war in the history of the world.

Chapter 1

# REINFORCEMENTS AND REORGANISATION IN THE EAST, 1942–1943

The battle is fought and decided by the quartermasters, long before the shooting begins.

Field Marshal Erwin Rommel

## German losses mount

As the autumn of 1941 turned into the winter of 1942, the principal areas where the *Heer* was fighting (and taking losses) were in North Africa and in the Soviet Union. On 26 December 1941, Rommel's *Afrika Korps* was finally able to halt the British 8th Army. Almost a month later, on 21 January 1942, the Desert Fox launched an unbridled counter-attack that caught the British by complete surprise. In the face of this German *Blitzkrieg*, the 8th Army withdrew in disorder and was forced to give up most of the newly-won territories in Cyrenaica (eastern Libya). United Kingdom and Commonwealth forces were finally able to regroup along a front between Bir Hakim and Gazala, just west of the important port town of Tobruk. Soon after, as both forces lay exhausted, the *Afrika Korps* and 8th Army rested and received fresh reinforcements, in anticipation of further hostilities. In the meantime, the German campaigns from October 1941 to December 1942 caused heavy casualties. In total during this period, German losses stood at 455,635 killed, 386,316 wounded, and 58,049 missing. This totalled some 900,000 casualties. Of this figure, roughly 120,000 were losses taken in North Africa from February 1941 to December 1942 (killed, wounded, missing, or taken prisoner).

Clearly, the Russian Front continued to cause the German Army the heaviest casualties.

As the German armies reeled back on account of the violent Red Army winter offensive of 1941–2, the *Ostheer* was scrambling for reinforcements with which to replenish the exhausted and depleted divisions along the Eastern Front. Given that (by sheer necessity) many of the German rear-area security forces were already fighting on the front lines, the situation behind the lines began to worsen. Some Soviet partisan units were able to support the Red Army attacks or disrupt the flow of German reinforcements arriving at the front. Guerrilla bands that had been on the verge of being destroyed in the autumn of 1941 were given a respite due to the Germans having to shift anti-partisan forces to the front lines. *Reichsführer*-SS Heinrich Himmler was personally tasked by Hitler to reinforce those security forces in the USSR in order to regain control of the rear areas. The German Army in the East was complaining about the interruption of troops and war materiel caused by the growing partisan menace. The *Oberkommando der Wehrmacht* (OKW) was pointing an accusing finger at the SS and police, even though the Army was just as responsible for securing the rear areas. Himmler promised the *Führer* additional SS and police forces for the Eastern Front. For their part, the *Wehrmacht* made the conscious decision to transfer field training divisions from Germany to the rear of the Russian Front in order to help garrison the countryside.

## SS and *Polizei* reinforcements

Police reinforcements for the Russian Front in 1942 proved to be quite substantial. Between January and July 1942 no fewer than twenty-one police battalions appeared in the territories of the Baltic States and Soviet Union (Russia, Belarus, and Ukraine). The largest numbers of battalions were sent to northern Russia. There, the *Ordnungspolizei* (Order Police) dispatched twelve battalions. These were *Polizei Bataillonen 2, 10, 42, 56, 61, 74, 84, 102, 121, 305, 306,* and *310. Polizei Bataillon 121* arrived in January 1942, while *Polizei Bataillon 2* arrived in July. *Polizei Bataillon 84* was the last police unit to reach *Heeresgruppe Nord.* It arrived there in October 1942. However, heavy losses in the *4. SS-Polizei Division* forced the unit to absorb *Polizei Bataillon 84.*[1] German forces operating in Ukraine and southern Russia only received one police battalion, and that proved to be *Polizei Bataillon 305,* which was transferred in mid-1942 from northern Russia as the newly redesignated *I. Bataillon* of *Polizeiregiment 15.* Central Russia and Belarus received a total of nine police battalions, eight from the Reich and one (*Reserve Polizei Bataillon 11*) transferred from northern Russia. The first police battalion to be sent to the front lines in 1942 was *Polizei Bataillon 313,* which arrived from Belarus in January 1942.[2] The last battalion to arrive was *Polizei Bataillon 134* which reached Belarus in late May or early June 1942. The police battalions included *Polizei Bataillonen 6, 11, 13, 22, 51, 91, 111, 134,* and *313.* The bulk of these police forces were used to create the new police regiments that were being established, although in many cases these new police regiments were split up amongst the rear-area security divisions. Some of these new police regiments were also distributed to the local SS and *Ordnungspolizei* commands. Interestingly, the distribution of these police reinforcements paralleled the threat of the Soviet guerrilla movement which in the spring of 1942 was strongest in northern, central and White Russia. It seems then, that the Soviet partisan movement was effectively drawing in more and more German forces. By the spring of 1942 it was apparently clear to the German command that the number of rear-area security forces that had initially been employed had been wholly inadequate for the tasks assigned.

Finally, *Gendarmerie Bataillon 1 (motorisiert),* newly organised in Poland on 24 June 1942, was sent to Belarus in July 1942 under Himmler's personal orders.[3] The SS also allocated more units for employment in central Russia and Belarus.[4] In January 1942 an SS penal formation, *Sonderkommando Dirlewanger,* made its appearance on Russian soil and began to wage war indiscriminately against both the partisans and the Belarusian civilian population.[5] This battalion was led by Oskar Dirlewanger, a convicted child molester who had supposedly obtained a PhD.[6] Some of the most horrific accounts of the war would emerge from the history of this unit. In February 1942 an SS *Feldrekrutendepot* (SS Field Recruit Depot) was established in Bobruisk under SS *Standartenführer und Oberst der Schutzpolizei* Rudolf Pannier (1897–1978). These three recruit battalions would contain a large proportion of ethnic Germans from all over Eastern Europe and the USSR. Its three *Waffen-SS* recruit training battalions would be employed again and again, beginning in June 1942, in numerous anti-guerrilla operations throughout White Russia.[7] At times SS units were detached from front-line fighting and employed in anti-partisan operations. A case in point was *1. SS Infanterie Brigade* (*mot.*) which was used in the Osipovichi region of Belarus in February and March 1942 and later south of Slonim in September and October 1942.[8] This brigade did not return to front-line fighting until January 1943.[9]

## Special *Heer* troops

During the spring and summer of 1942, the German Army formed special *Jäger Bataillonen* (Hunter Battalions), which were geared specifically to track down and eliminate Russian partisan units. They were formed from volunteers and specialised soldiers who had particular knowledge, such as language skills, forestry experience, etc. which was thought would aid in hunting down the guerrillas. In addition, several 'penal' battalions, created from dishonoured officers, NCOs and men who were disciplinary cases or were disgraced in some way, were sent to Russia. In the case of *Heeresgruppe Mitte* only one battalion, *Infanterie Bataillon z.b.V. 550 (bewährungs)*[10] was sent to serve under the *3. Panzerarmee* and was stationed in Vitebsk from 1942–4.[11] This unit ended up fighting in the front but was also employed behind the lines against the partisans. The following *Jäger Bataillonen* were formed and stationed in the region of *Heeresgruppe Mitte*. They were used extensively in fighting the guerrillas:

Table 1. Jäger Battalions on the Russian Front

| Unit | Location | Comments |
|---|---|---|
| *Jäger Bataillon 1* | Nevel (1942), Vitebsk (1943) | Lost in the winter of 1943–4. |
| *Jäger Bataillon 2* | Cholm (1942), Vitebsk (1943) | To *1. Skibrigade* in 1943. |
| *Jäger Bataillon 3* | Smolensk (1942), Velikiyeye Luki (1943) | Sent to Finland in 1944. |
| *Jäger Bataillon 4* | Smolensk (1942–3) | To *1. Skibrigade* in 1943. |
| *Jäger Bataillon 7* | Vitebsk (1942) | Absorbed into *Jäger Bataillon 13.* |
| *Jäger Bataillon 9* | Orel and Gomel (1942–3) | To *1. Skibrigade* in 1943. |
| *Jäger Bataillon 10* | Bryansk (1942), Orel (1943) | Disbanded Dec 1943. Its remnant personnel given to *Divisionsgruppe 137.* |
| *Jäger Bataillon 11* | Bryansk (1942), Orel (1943), Gomel (1943) | To *1. Skibrigade* in 1943. |
| *Jäger Bataillon 13* | Rzhev and Orel (1943), Gomel (1943) | Disbanded Dec 1943. Its remnant personnel given to *292. Infanterie Division.* |
| *Jäger Bataillon 14* | Orel and Bobruisk (1943) | Disbanded Dec 1943. Its remnant personnel given to *253. Infanterie Division.* |

*Jäger Bataillon 14* was actually formed in the autumn of 1943 but disbanded soon after, in December 1943. Most of these *Jäger* battalions were withdrawn to help create *Skijäger Brigade 1* (1st Ski Brigade), which was created in the autumn of 1943.[12] Finally, a two-battalion Air Force infantry regiment, *Luftwaffe Infanterie Regiment Moskau* (Air Force Field Infantry Regiment 'Moscow'), complete with 1,300 men, was stationed in Vitebsk.[13] A replacement battalion of 300 men was also located there.

## Reserve and training divisions

In September 1942 three *Feldausbildungsdivisionen* (field training divisions) were sent to the USSR. They were placed behind the front lines as part of the occupation force. The theory behind this order was that the German infantry recruits would gain much valuable experience fighting the partisans, while at the same time acclimatising themselves to the Soviet Union and helping to garrison the German rear areas. In this way the *390. Feldausbildungs Division* and the *391. Feldausbildungs Division* were sent to central Russia and Belarus in October 1942. In the *Ostland* region, the *141. Reserve Division* was similarly brought in and placed behind the lines. The *141. Reserve Division* was spread out over the triangle bordering Kaunas–Vilnius–Daugavpils. It was operating in this area by the second week of September 1942. The *151. Reserve Division* also arrived and was initially located between Lida and Baranovichi. It had begun operations in October 1942. A list of the major reserve and replacement divisions brought into Belarus and the surrounding areas from September to October included the following formations:

***390. Feldausbildungsdivision***
CO: *Generalmajor* Walter Hartmann.
Ia: *Hauptmann* Hartmut Sprotte.
IIa: *Major* Herbert Gaertner.[14]
Location: Bobruisk–Mogilev, September–October 1942, then Vitebsk.[15]
*Feldausbildungs Infanterie Regiment 635* (three battalions).
*Feldausbildungs Infanterie Regiment 636* (three battalions).
*Feldausbildungs Infanterie Regiment 637* (three battalions).[16]

***391. Feldausbildungsdivision***
CO: *Generalmajor* Albrecht Baron Digeon von Monteton.
Ia: *Hauptmann* Friedrich Allmer.
IIa: *Major* Walter Meissner.[17]
Location: area of Polotsk, Vitebsk, and Orsha September–October, then Mogilev beginning November 1942.[18]
*Feldausbildungs Infanterie Regiment 718* (three battalions).

*Feldausbildungs Infanterie Regiment 719* (three battalions).
*Feldausbildungs Infanterie Regiment 720* (three battalions).[19]

***143. Reservedivision***
CO: *Generalleutnant* Paul Stoewer.
Ia: *Hauptmann* Otto Rusche.
Location: Sarny–Pinsk–Kobrin–Brest–Kovel (Pripet Marshes region).[20]
*Reserve Grenadier Regiment 68*: Brest-Litovsk (169th, 188th, and 512th Battalions).
*Reserve Grenadier Regiment 76*: Luzk (230th, 323rd, 386th, and 479th Battalions).
*Reserve Grenadier Regiment 208*: Kovel (122nd, 337th, and 397th Battalions).
*Reserve Artillerie Abteilung 257*: Beresina–Kartuska.
*Reserve Pionier Bataillon 68*: Plozk.

***151. Reservedivision***
CO: *Generalleutnant* Wolf Schede.
Ia: *Hauptmann* Heinrich Walter.
Location: Lida–Baranovichi from September–October 1942, then in and around Vilnius.[21]
*Reserve Grenadier Regiment 21*: Daugavpils (24th, 176th, and 301st Battalions).
*Reserve Grenadier Regiment 217*: Molodechno (2nd, 3rd, and 311th Battalions).[22]
*Reserve Artillerie Abteilung 1*: Pabrade.[23]

***141. Reservedivision***
CO: *Generalleutnant* Heinz Hellmich.
IIa: Major Theodor Postels.
Location: Kaunas–Vilnius–Daugavpils, September–October 1942, then Stolpce beginning in November.
*Reserve Grenadier Regiment 1*: Stolpce (1st, 43rd, and 45th Battalions).
*Reserve Grenadier Regiment 61*: Baranovichi (23rd, 44th, and 389th Battalions).
*Reserve Grenadier Regiment 206*: Minsk (22nd, 162nd, and 312th Battalions).
*Reserve Artillerie Abteilung 11*: Baranovichi.
*Reserve Pionier Bataillon 1*: Stolpce.

In addition to the above-listed reserve and training forces, a static division was created in Bialystok on 24 September 1942. The unit was designated as 'Division Nr. 461' from the following units:

***Division Nr. 461***
CO: *Oberst* Gottfried von Erdmannsdorff.

IIa: *Hauptmann* Erwin Walz: Bialystok.
*Grenadier Ersatz und Ausbildung Regiment 11*: Bialystok (151st, 346th, and 400th Battalions).
*Grenadier Ersatz und Ausbildung Regiment 491*: Modlin (356th, 492nd, 493rd, and 494th Battalions).
*Grenadier Ersatz Regiment 521*: Allenstein (2nd, 23rd, 162nd, 311th, and 389th Battalions).

## The Slovak Security Division

In July 1942 the Slovak Security Division was transferred to Mozyr, basically to cover the Pinsk–Gomel railway line. Thus, on the southern fringes of Belarus, the unit could be counted on to perform some limited garrisoning duty. The division performed poorly against the local partisan forces during 1942. However, after the Stalingrad debacle, its morale sank. Desertions occurred although the worst thing to happen was that beginning in the spring of 1943, the division agreed to a *modus vivendi* with the Kovpak and Saburov partisan brigades. The Germans soon realised the ineffectiveness of the unit and withdrew it to Minsk in early August 1943, where it was ordered to reorganise into a regular infantry division. The unit was eventually disbanded on 3 November 1943, due to low morale and a high desertion rate.[24]

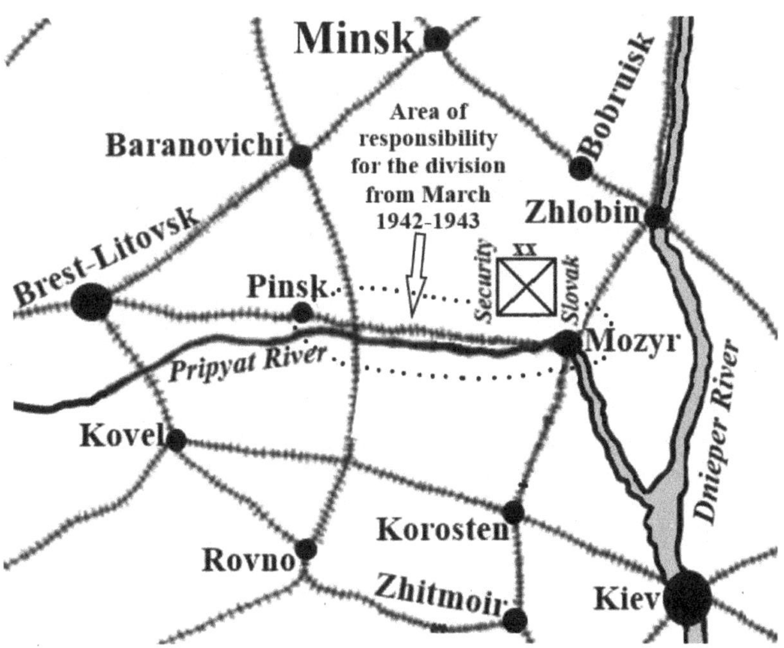


Figure 1. Area of operations of the Slovak Security Division, 1942–3.

***Slowakische Sicherungs Division***[25]
CO: *Oberst* Gustav Malar – located in Mozyr.
*Sicherungs Regiment 101* (two battalions).
*Sicherungs Regiment 102* (two battalions).
*Artillerie Regiment 31* (two artillery battalions).
*Panzerjäger Abteilung* (three anti-tank companies).
*Reiter Abteilung* (two cavalry squadrons).
*Nachrichten Abteilung* (two companies).
*Pionier Kompanie* (engineer company).
*Divisionseinheiten* (smaller divisional units).[26]

Figure 2. Location of the Slovak Security Division, April–August 1943. The demoralised division was moved just north of Minsk, where it was to reorganise as a regular infantry division, but continued desertions eventually forced the Germans to transfer what was left of the unit to Ravenna, Italy in November 1943, and use it as a construction brigade.

## *Wehrmacht Befehlshaber Heeresgebiet Mitte*

To these German army and Slovak forces, we must add those units under the *Wehrmacht Befehlshaber Heeresgebiet Mitte 102*.[27] Between

April and July 1942 a large portion of these forces were brought together in a battlegroup under its commander (*Generalleutnant* Karl von Schenckendorff)[28] as *Gruppe von Schenckendorff* and employed against the partisans.[29] In 1943 the reserve forces available to the Commander of Rear Area Forces *Heeresgruppe Mitte* were increased when *Kavallerie Regiment Mitte* (formed in April 1943) was added. In addition, a battalion of French armoured vehicles was also attached.[30] One additional division, which made its appearance in the spring of 1942 in the area of *Heeresgruppe Mitte*, was *Divisionsstab z.b.V. 442* (Division Staff for Special Employment 442). In May 1943 this unit was located between Yelnya and Spas-Demensk.[31] This formation only brought with it two regiments and was commanded by *Generalleutnant* Karl Bornemann. The regiments contained regional defence as well as guard battalions. The divisional 'Ia' was *Major* Dr. Horst Mueller, while the 'IIa' was *Hauptmann* Georg Heiland.[32] These reinforcements, although sizable, were very necessary. The guerrilla movement was only growing in size and by the spring of 1942 was better organised. The Red Army made every effort to supply the partisans. The following tables shows the forces available to the *Wehrmacht Befehlshaber Heeresgebiet Mitte 102* (German Army Rear Area Commander in 1942):

Table 2. Forces Available Under the Army Group Centre Rear Area Command 102

| Date | HQ Staff | Units Available for Employment |
|---|---|---|
| 2 Jan '42 | *Wehrmacht Befehlshaber Heeresgebiet Mitte 102* | *707 Infanterie Division:* temporarily under to the command of the *Militär Befehlshaber Ostland,*[33] two-thirds of *339. Infanterie Division,*[34] part of *221. Sicherungs Division, 286. Sicherungs Division, 403. Sicherungs Division,* 202 and 203. *Sicherungs Brigade.* Reserve forces: *Radfahr Sicherungs Regiment 2, Kosaken Abteilung 102, Graukopf Brigade,* and the *Druzhina SS Verbände.* |
| 6 Feb '42 | *Wehrmacht Befehlshaber Heeresgebiet Mitte 102* | *286. Sicherungs Division,* part of *403. Sicherungs Division, (verstärktes) Französisches Infanterie Regiment 638, 707. Infanterie Division,* attached to *Militär Befehlshaber Ostland. 201. Sicherungs Brigade* plus the HQ of *203. Sicherungs Brigade.* Reserve force: *Radfahr Sicherungs Regiment 2; Kosaken Abteilung 102, Graukopf Brigade,* and the *Druzhina SS Verbände.* |

| Date | HQ Staff | Units Available for Employment |
|---|---|---|
| 10 Mar '42 | *Wehrmacht Befehlshaber Heeresgebiet Mitte 102* | Bulk of *286. Sicherungs Division,* part of *403. Sicherungs Division, 707. Infanterie Division,* attached to the *Militär Befehlshaber Ostland* command. *201. Sicherungs Brigade* plus the HQ of *203. Sicherungs Brigade.* Reserve force: *Radfahr Sicherungs Regiment 2; Kosaken Abteilung 102, Graukopf Brigade,* and the *Druzhina SS-Verbände.* |
| 5 Apr '42 | *Gruppe von Schenckendorff* | Staff plus parts of *10.* and *11. Panzer Division.* Reserve; bulk of *286. Sicherungs Division,* part of *403. Sicherungs Division, 707. Infanterie Division,* attached to the *Militär Befehlshaber Ostland* command. *201. Sicherungs Brigade* plus the HQ of *203. Sicherungs Brigade.* Reserve force: *Radfahr Sicherungs Regiment 2, Kosaken Abteilung 102, Graukopf Brigade,* and the *Druzhina SS-Verbände.* |
| 11 May '42 | *Gruppe von Schenckendorff* | Staff plus parts of *10.* and *11. Panzer Division.* Reserve; bulk of *286. Sicherungs Division,* part of *403. Sicherungs Division, 707. Infanterie Division,* attached to the *Militär Befehlshaber Ostland* command. *201. Sicherungs Brigade* plus the HQ of *203. Sicherungs Brigade.* Bulk of the *221. Sicherungs Division.* Reserve force: *Radfahr Sicherungs Regiment 2; Kosaken Abteilung 102, Graukopf Brigade,* and the *Druzhina SS-Verbände.* |
| 8 Jun '42 | *Gruppe von Schenckendorff* | Bulk of *286. Sicherungs Division,* part of *403. Sicherungs Division, 201. Sicherungs Division* and *203. Sicherungs Division.*[35] Bulk of *221. Sicherungs Division, SS-Kavallerie Brigade, (verstärktes) Französisches Infanterie Regiment 638.* Reserve force: *Radfahr Sicherungs Regiment 2, Kosaken Abteilung 102, Graukopf Brigade,* and the *Druzhina SS-Verbände.* |

| Date | HQ Staff | Units Available for Employment |
|---|---|---|
| 4 Jul '42 | *Gruppe von Schenckendorff* | *286. Sicherungs Division,* part of *201. Sicherungs Division* and *203. Sicherungs Division, (verstärktes) Französisches Infanterie Regiment 638.* Reserve force: *Radfahr Sicherungs Regiment 2, Kosaken Abteilung 102, Graukopf Brigade,* and the *Druzhina SS-Verbände.* |
| 5 Aug '42 | *Wehrmacht Befehlshaber Heeresgebiet Mitte 102* | *286. Sicherungs Division,* staff and part of *201. Sicherungs Division* and *203. Sicherungs Division.*[36] Reserve force: *Radfahr Sicherungs Regiment 2, Kosaken Abteilung 102, Graukopf Brigade,* and the *Druzhina SS Verbände.* |
| 7 Sep '42 | *Wehrmacht Befehlshaber Heeresgebiet Mitte 102* | *286. Sicherungs Division,* part of *201. Sicherungs Division* and *203. Sicherungs Division,* staff and parts of *221. Sicherungs Division.* Bulk of *201. Sicherungs Division* and *203. Sicherungs Division, Graukopf Brigade,* and the *Druzhina SS-Verbände.* |
| Oct '42 | *Wehrmacht Befehlshaber Heeresgebiet Mitte 102* | *286. Sicherungs Division, 201. Sicherungs Division* and *203. Sicherungs Division.* Reserve force: *Radfahr Sicherungs Regiment 2; Kosaken Abteilung 102, Graukopf Brigade,* and the *Druzhina SS-Verbände.* |
| Nov '42 | *Wehrmacht Befehlshaber Heeresgebiet Mitte 102* | *286. Sicherungs Division,* part of *221. Sicherungs Division* and *201. Sicherungs Division, 203. Sicherungs Division.* Reserve force: *Radfahr Sicherungs Regiment 2, Kosaken Abteilung 102* and *Graukopf Brigade.* |
| Dec '42 | *Wehrmacht Befehlshaber Heeresgebiet Mitte 102* | *286. Sicherungs Division,* part of *221. Sicherungs Division* and *201. Sicherungs Division, 203. Sicherungs Division.* Reserve force: *Radfahr Sicherungs Regiment 2, Kosaken Abteilung 102*[37] and *Graukopf Brigade.*[38] |

These additional German and native auxiliary forces were indeed needed. The Red Army was making a point of trying to supply its partisan forces whenever possible. In 1943 there were few Soviet offensives that were coordinated with partisan units. That changed dramatically beginning in 1944. Between July 1942 and September 1943, the following arms and supplies were dropped by air in Belarus:[39]

Table 3. Supplies Dropped by Air, July 1942–September 1943

| | |
|---|---|
| Rifles and submachine guns | 7,685 |
| Anti-tank weapons | 266 |
| Grenades | 45,000 |
| Explosives (kg) | 950 |
| Rounds | 6,500,000 |
| Uniforms | 17,000 |
| Food (tons) | 145,000 |

The guerrilla war began in earnest in the spring of 1942. A series of small- and large-scale anti-partisan operations were now undertaken in the region of central and White Russia which was hoped would stem the increasing numbers of guerrilla units and threatened areas. Yet, in spite of these anti-guerrilla drives, the Belarusian partisans had enough success to claim the destruction of 500 bridges and about 1,000 enemy vehicles between June and November 1942.[40] In the beginning of 1942, the German armies in the East were reeling back from the Soviet winter counter-attack. This offensive continued into the spring of 1942 and in many places along the German front, actually managed to break through and advance deep into German-occupied territories. These breakthroughs allowed the Soviet partisan units to link up with the advance elements of the Red Army and join them in their attacks. One such example was the region bordering Spas Demensk–Yelnya–Dorogobush–Vyazma. Between 24 May and 3 June 1942, the Germans launched an operation to eliminate a combined

Red Army-partisan force (Operation Hannover). By February–March, however, a measure of stability had been brought to some regions of the German front lines and in some instances, the foremost units of the Red Army now found themselves cut off and surrounded. In these cases, the local partisan formations in each particular area supported these trapped units for mutual defence. In February 1942 the distribution of German police battalions was as follows:

Table 4. Location of Police Battalions in February 1942

| Location | No. of Battalions | Men |
|---|---|---|
| USSR | | 12,070 |
| In the security divisions, USSR | 9 | |
| With the security police, USSR | 1 | |
| With *Organisation Todt*, USSR | 1 | |
| *Reichskommissariat Ostland*, USSR | 3 | 3,439 |
| *Generalgouvernment*, Poland | 9 | 10,997 |

It was this situation along the immediate rear of the German front that necessitated a series of anti-partisan operations in which regular front-line units of the *Heer* (Army), as well as rear area army and SS security forces would be employed. The primary security divisions behind the rear areas of *Heeresgruppe Mitte* in February 1942 stood at four. The initial drive would be codenamed 'Bamberg'. This drive would set the standard for brutality that would be seen throughout the German occupation of the USSR. As stated previously, *Division z.b.V. 442* had arrived in central Russia in April 1943. It contained *Landesschützen Bataillonen 452, 453, 454* and *455*, two companies of *Wachbataillon 522*, and two companies each of *Panzerjäger Bataillon 8* and *Panzerjäger Bataillon 211*. The division remained in the region of *Heeresgruppe Mitte* until 22 August 1944, when it was disbanded after heavy fighting during the Soviet 1944 summer offensive. The various rear-area divisions were located in the following regions:[41]

Table 5. German Rear-Area Divisions, February 1942

| Rear-Area Division | Commander | Region |
|---|---|---|
| *221. Sicherungs Division* | *Generalleutnant* Pflugbeil | Gomel-Mogiliev |
| *286. Sicherungs Division* | *Generalleutnant* Müller | Orsha-Borisov |
| *339. Infanterie Division (bod.)* | *Generalleutnant* Pflugradt | Bobruisk-Slutsk |
| *403. Sicherungs Division* | *Generalleutnant* von Ditfurth | Vitebsk-Velikiye Luki |
| *442. Landesschützen Division* | *Generalleutnant* K. Bornemann | Jelnya-Spas Demensk |

Some of these commanders would be replaced. For example, *Generalmajor* Richert assumed command of *286. Sicherungs Division* on 5 June 1942. *Generalleutnant* Pflugbeil (*221. Sicherungs Division*) was replaced by *Generalmajor* Karl Freiherr von Lersner from 18 June 1942.[42] Ditfurth was replaced on 15 May 1942, by *Generalleutnant* Russwurm, who assumed command of *403. Sicherungs Division*.

## Hungarian forces

The Hungarian contribution to the invasion of the USSR proved substantial. While the initial batch of Hungarian units were employed at the front, by the beginning of 1943 it was clear to the Germans that Hungary's troops were not up to the task of confronting the Red Army. As a result, the German strategy evolved into giving Hungarian forces a greater role in rear-area operations, like patrolling railway lines and other occupation duties, such as launching anti-partisan drives. Many of the initial units brought in to protect the rear areas were brigades before they were redesignated as 'divisions'. Five of these light brigades were brought in by the Hungarians to help with the occupation. The 105th Hungarian Light Brigade was formed between 30 October and 5 November 1941. It arrived in Berdichev that same month, but it took another three weeks until the division's sub-units had reached their deployment locations. The 105th was one of five brigades, and had arrived in Ukraine in early 1942 to help secure the rear areas. These Hungarian brigades were numbered 102, 105, 108, 121, and 124.[43] The brigade (later redesignated division) had an area of 26,000 square kilometers to control! This was a vast area for one brigade to cover. In March 1942 that was expanded to 46,000 square kilometers! Of this figure, 16,000 square kilometers were practically uncontrollable swamps and forests that was the home of around 10,000 partisans.

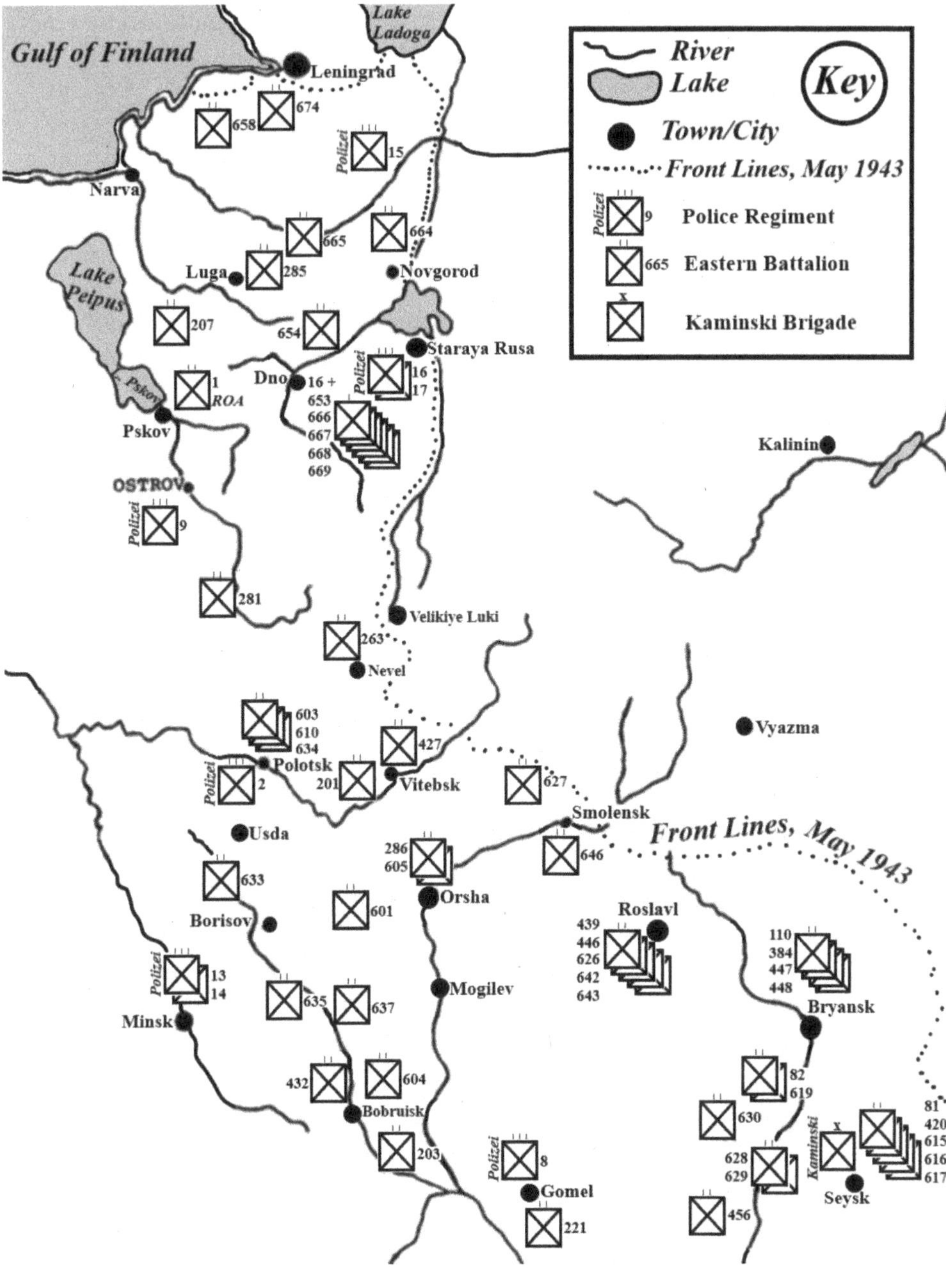


Figure 3. German police and locally-raised units in the region of Army Group North and Central Russia, autumn 1942–spring 1943.

The first contact with partisans by the 105th Light Brigade occurred on 7 December 1941, based on a report from *Feldkommandantur 197*,[44] which said that a punishment detachment was formed and sent in an omnibus to Komarovka, Nosowka and Crimea. However, no losses were suffered. The first partisan attack in the division's war diary is recorded on 1 January 1942, when a Honvéd soldier from the division was killed.[45] The 102nd, 105th, and 108th Light Brigades (later 'divisions'), were sent to operate in central Russia, in the Bryansk region. In May 1943 the Hungarian VIII Army Corps was once again activated and brought in to cover western Ukraine, while the Hungarian VII Army Corps was activated in June 1943 and brought in to cover the area behind *Heeresgruppe Mitte*. Their order of battle was as follows:

Commanding General of all Hungarian Rear Area Troops
Headquarters: Kiev
17 Feb 43 – 15 May 43 Gusztáv Vitéz Jány
15 May 43 – 7 Apr 44 Géza Vitéz Lakatos

VIII Hungarian Army Corps[46] – *Heeresgruppe Mitte*
Headquarters: Chernigov
Commanding General:
18 May 43 – 6 Jun 43 Szilárd Vitéz Bakay
16 Jun 43 – 30 Apr 44 Vitéz Lászlo

1st Hungarian Light Division – *Korück 580, 2. Armee*
Headquarters: Krolovetz
Seredina Buda–Konotop (Bryansk–Kiev railway)

2nd Hungarian Light Division[47] – *Befehlshaber rückwärtiges Heeresgebiet 102*
Headquarters: Gomel
Gomel and Gomel–Chernigov (Kiev–Vilna railway)

5th Hungarian Light Division[48] – *Befehlshaber rückwärtiges Heeresgebiet 102*
Headquarters: Neshin
Konotop–Kiev (Bryansk–Kiev railway)

Figure 4. By December 1943 a sizable number of Hungarian divisions were operating as security troops behind the front lines, along the border between the *Gebietskommissariat Weissruthenien* and *Reichskommissariat Ukraine.*

8th Hungarian Light Division[49] – *Befehlshaber rückwärtiges Heeresgebiet 102*
Headquarters: Starodub
Konotop–Gomel (Bryansk–Kiev railway)

201st Hungarian Light Division – *Befehlshaber rückwärtiges Heeresgebiet 102*
Headquarters: Rogatchev
Rogatchev–Gomel (Kiev–Vilna railway)

VII Hungarian Army Corps – *Wehrmacht Befehlshaber Ukraine*[50]
Headquarters: Korosten
Commanding General:
Jun 1943 Ödon Vitéz Sziklay

18th Hungarian Light Division – *Wehrmacht Befehlshaber Ukraine*
Headquarters: Narodychi
Kiev–Korosten (Kiev–Warsaw railway)

21st Hungarian Light Division – *Wehrmacht Befehlshaber Ukraine*
Headquarters: Shepetovka
Rovno–Bereditchey (Vennitsa–Leningrad railway)

24th Hungarian Light Division – *Wehrmacht Befehlshaber Ukraine*
Headquarters: Proskurov
Vennitsa–Proskurov (Odessa–Warsaw railway)

25th Hungarian Light Division – *Wehrmacht Befehlshaber Ukraine*
Headquarters: Ovrutch
Korosten–Mosyr (Vennitsa–Leningrad railway)

## Reorganisation of the lower commands under the *Korück* system

The employment of additional troops to combat the growing partisan menace not only entailed increasing the strength of the occupation forces, but it also involved organising them in the most efficient manner in order to make full use of them. To this end some of the *Feldkommandanturen* and *Ortskommandanturen* were shuffled around, depending on need. Additional commands were also sent to the *Ostfront*. Some lower *Kommandeur des Rückwartige Heeresgebiete* (*Korück* – Commander of the Army Rear Area) headquarters remained where they had been placed in 1941, but others were shifted. The following table lists the lower *Korück* commands for Belarus and the Bialystok District:

Table 6. German Army *Kommandantur* in Belarus and the Bialystok District.

| Command | City | Period Served |
|---|---|---|
| *Oberfeldkommandantur 392* | Minsk | 1942–4 |
| *Oberfeldkommandantur 399* | Bobruisk, Polotsk | Bobruisk (1942–4), Polotsk (1943) |
| *Oberfeldkommandantur 400* | Baranovichi | 1943–Apr 1944 |
| *Oberfeldkommandantur 579* | Brest Litovsk[51] | 1941 |
| *Feldkommandantur 812* | Molodechno | 1942–3 |
| *Feldkommandantur 813*[52] | Mogilev | 1942–3 |

| Command | City | Period Served |
|---|---|---|
| *Feldkommandantur 812* | Minsk | Minsk (1941–2), Slutsk (1943) |
| *Feldkommandantur 551* | Lida | 1 Mar 1943–1944 |
| *Feldkommandantur 749* | Polotsk, Lepel | Polotsk (1941–2), Lepel (1943) |
| *Feldkommandantur 181* | Lepel | Lepel (1943), Velikiyeye-Luki (1944) |
| *Feldkommandantur 754* | Pinsk, Polotsk, Yanov | Pinsk, Polotsk (1943), Yanov (1944) |
| *Feldkommandantur 191* | Mogilev | 1941–2[53] |
| *Feldkommandantur 199*[54] | Kobryn[55] | 1943–4 |
| *Feldkommandantur 820* | Beriza | 1944 |
| *Feldkommandantur 549* | Bielski[56] | 1941 |
| *Feldkommandantur 550* | Stari-Dorogi | 1942–3 |
| *Feldkommandantur 581* | Bobruisk, Shlobin | Bobruisk (1941–Apr 1942), Shlobin (1943–4) |
| *Feldkommandantur 244*[57] | Vitebsk, Borisov, Vitebsk | Vitebsk (1941), Borisov (1942–3), Vitebsk (1944) |
| *Feldkommandantur 516* | Borisov | 1944 |
| *Feldkommandantur 815* | Vitebsk, Polotsk, Gorodok | Vitebsk (1941), Polotsk (July 1942–Jan 1943), Gorodok (1943–4) |
| *Feldkommandantur 619* | Lachva, Mosyr[58] | 1943 |
| *Feldkommandantur 197* | Neskin | April 1942, 1944 |
| *Feldkommandantur 683* | Orsha | 1941–3 |
| *Feldkommandantur 194* | Pinsk, Polotsk | 1944 |
| *Feldkommandantur 660* | Vileika / Glebokie, Postavy | Vileika (8 Feb 1942–1943), Glebokie (1943), Postavy (1944) |
| *Feldkommandantur 528* | Rogachev | 10 May 1941–2 |
| *Feldkommandantur 250* | Slonim | Nov 1943–1944 |
| *Ortskommandantur 282* | Vitebsk | 1942 |
| *Ortskommandantur 427* | Vielke | 1941 |
| *Ortskommandantur 593* | Vetrino | 1944 |

| Command | City | Period Served |
|---|---|---|
| *Ortskommandantur 848* | Chasniki | 1944 |
| *Ortskommandantur 525* | Starobin | 1943 |
| *Ortskommandantur 508* | Svislotch | 1943 |
| *Ortskommandantur 309* | Slutsk | 1942 |
| *Ortskommandantur 343* | Slutsk | 1943–4 |
| *Ortskommandantur 360* | Slavkovitschi | 1944 |
| *Ortskommandantur 552* | Shuravitschi | 1944 |
| *Ortskommandantur 737* | Shlobin (Zhlobin) | 1943 |
| *Ortskommandantur 846* | Senno | 1942 |
| *Ortskommandantur 858* | Sapolje | 12 Jun 1942–1944 |
| *Ortskommandantur 363* | Rogachev | 1943 |
| *Ortskommandantur 930* | Polotsk | 1944 |
| *Ortskommandantur 335* | Polotsk | 1943 |
| *Ortskommandantur 431*[59] | Podvoloczyska | 1941–2 |
| *Ortskommandantur 292* | Schventschionys, Pinsk | Schventschionys (1941), Pinsk (1943) |
| *Ortskommandantur 760* | Pinsk[60] | 1942–4 |
| *Ortskommandantur 311* | Pasherevizy | 1944 |
| *Ortskommandantur 737* | Paritschi | 1942–4 |
| *Ortskommandantur 842* | Orsha | 1942–3 |
| *Ortskommandantur 844* | Niesviez | 1943–4 |
| *Ortskommandantur 619* | Mosyr[61] | 1944 |
| *Ortskommandantur 843* | Mogilev | 1942–3 |
| *Ortskommandantur 292* | Mogilev | 1941 |
| *Ortskommandantur 850* | Grodno[62] | 1941 |
| *Ortskommandantur 906* | Minsk, Orsha, Sherven | Minsk (autumn of 1941), Orsha (1942–3) Sherven (1943) |
| *Ortskommandantur 650* | Minsk | 1943 |
| *Ortskommandantur 352* | Minsk | 1942 |
| *Ortskommandantur 411* | Minsk | 1941 |
| *Ortskommandantur 436* | Minsk | 1941 |

| Command | City | Period Served |
|---|---|---|
| *Ortskommandantur 864* | Metvedy | 1941 |
| *Ortskommandantur 340* | Marina-Gorka | 1943 |
| *Ortskommandantur 845* | Luniniec | 1942–Feb 1944 |
| *Ortskommandantur 355* | Lida | 1942–3 |
| *Ortskommandantur 851* | Lepel | 1941–3, then Logoisk (1943) |
| *Ortskommandantur 278* | Krupka | 1943 |
| *Ortskommandantur 532* | Krugloye | 1941 |
| *Ortskommandantur 685* | Kostyukovitschi | 1943–4 |
| *Ortskommandantur 353* | Korma, Chechersk | Korma (1941), Chechersk (1941–3) |
| *Ortskommandantur 889* | Koydanov | 1943 |
| *Ortskommandantur 452* | Kobrin | 1942 |
| *Ortskommandantur 935* | Iasionovo | 1944 |
| *Ortskommandantur 352* | Hansevicze | 1942 |
| *Ortskommandantur 763* | Gorodok | 1942 |
| *Ortskommandantur 827* | Gomel | 1942–3 |
| *Ortskommandantur 339* | Glebokie | 1942, 1944 |
| *Ortskommandantur 256* | Postavy, Glebokie | Postavy (1941), Glebokie (1943–4) |
| *Ortskommandantur 262* | Rossono, Schumilino, Drisa, Beschenkovichi | Rossono (1941), Schumilino (1941) Beschenkovichi (1943), Drisa (1943) |
| *Ortskommandantur 532* | Cholopenichi | 1944 |
| *Ortskommandantur 194* | Bychov | 1941–2 |
| *Ortskommandantur 327* | Brest-Litovsk[63] | 1941 |
| *Ortskommandantur 899* | Brest-Litovsk[64] | 1942, 1944 |
| *Ortskommandantur 335* | Braslav | 1944 |
| *Ortskommandantur Borisov*[65] | Borisov | 1941, 1943 |
| *Ortskommandantur 841* | Boguschevskoye | 1941–2 |
| *Ortskommandantur 273* | Bobruisk | 1943 |

| Command | City | Period Served |
|---|---|---|
| *Ortskommandantur 264* | Baranovichi | Jul 1941–Sep 1944 |
| *Ortskommandantur 826*[66] | Baranovichi | 1941–2 |
| *Ortskommandantur 425* | Beresina-Kartuska | Kobrin (1942–4), Beresina (1944) |
| *Ortskommandantur 344* | Beresina | 1943–4 |
| *Ortskommandantur 79* | Beschenkovichi | 13 Oct 1941 – 31 Mar 1942 |
| *Ortskommandantur 929* | Beriza, Zabinka | Beresina (1943), Zabinka (1944) |

Chapter 2

# OPERATIONS IN THE BALTIC STATES AND THE POLISH-RUSSIAN-LATVIAN BORDER REGION, 1943

## The establishment of *Kampfgruppe Knecht*

Kampfgruppe Knecht was an SS and police anti-guerrilla force that was organised for emergency action along the Latvian-Russian border in November 1941, and again from mid-February to early April 1943. In early February 1943 it was reconstituted and placed under the same commander: *Oberst der Schutzpolizei* Karl Knecht.[1] This battlegroup was raised in conjunction with *Kampfgruppe Schröder* and was to perform operations against the growing partisan menace on the Latvian-Russian frontier.[2] *Gruppe Schröder* (as it was more commonly referred to) was led by *SS-Brigadeführer und Generalmajor der Polizei* Walther Schröder.[3] Both battlegroups were under the control of Friedrich Jeckeln's anti-partisan headquarters, and would, when necessary, coordinate drives. However, they were to operate independently of one another. As stated previously, the initial units comprising *Kampfgruppe Knecht* were:[4]

*(lettische) Schutzmannschaft Bataillon 276.*
*(lettische) Schutzmannschaft Bataillon 277.*
*(lettische) Schutzmannschaft Bataillon 278.*
*(lettische) Schutzmannschaft Bataillon 279.*

*Polizei Nachrichten Zug Lewinski.*
*Luftwaffe Flak Zug Hatje.*
*Gendarmerie Zug Nr. 10. (motorisiert).*[5]
*2. Kompanie der Landesschützen Bataillon 232.*[6]
*SS und Polizeiführer Kompanie.*
*(lettische) Schutzmannschaft Bataillon 282.*[7]

Members of the staff of this battlegroup, from 4 February to 2 April 1943, included the following:[8]

*Oberst der Schutzpolizi* Karl Knecht – *Kommandeur.*
*Major der Schutzpolizei* Heinrich Oberwinder – *Ia.*
*Oberleutnant der Schutzpolizei* Karl Wutz – *Adjutant.*
*Oberleutnant der Gendarmerie* Bruno Stark – *Ordnanz Offizier.*
*Leutnant der Schutzpolizei der Reserve* Kurt Arnold – *Ib.*
*Ober Sekretar* Kilian Körber – *Verwaltungs Beamt.*
*Leutnant der Luftwaffe* Albert Hatje (Reserve-Flak-Abteilung 613) – *Flak kampftruppeführer.*
*Revier Leutnant der Schutzpolizei* Lewinski – *Nachrichten Zugführer.*
*Hauptmann der Schutzpolizei* Reinhold Girndt – *Verbindungs Offizier mit (lettische) Schutzmannschaft Bataillon 276.*
*Major der Schutzpolizei* Alfred Kopka – *Verbindungs Offizier mit (lettische) Schutzmannschaft Bataillon 277.*
*Hauptmann der Schutzpolizei* Franz Müller – *Verbindungs Offizier mit (lettische) Schutzmannschaft Bataillon 278.*
*Hauptmann der Schutzpolizei* Egon Nasedy (4 February to 5 March 1943) – *Verbindungs Offizier mit (lettische) Schutzmannschaft Bataillon 279.*
*Hauptmann der Schutzpolizei* Franz Lehner (3 March to 2 April 1943) – *Verbindungs Offizier mit (lettische) Schutzmannschaft Bataillon 279.*
*Hauptmann der Schutzpolizei* Ernst Friese (25 March to 2 April 1943) – *Verbindungs Offizier mit (lettische) Schutzmannschaft Bataillon 282.*
*Hauptmann der Schutzpolizei* Neuberh (20 March to 2 April 1943) – *Verbindungs Offizier mit (estnische) Freiwilligen Polizei Bataillon 50.*[9]
*Hauptmann der Schutzpolizei* Beyer (20 March to 2 April 1943) – *Verbindungs Offizier mit (litauisch) Schutzmannschaft Bataillon 2.*
*Hauptmann der Schutzpolizei* Siehm – *SS und Polizeiführer Kompanie Chef.*
*Oberleutnant der Schutzpolizei* Fritsche – *Zugführer der SS und Polizeiführer Kompanie.*
*Leutnant der Gendarmerie* Nimmergut – *Zugführer der SS und Polizeiführer Kompanie.*
*Oberleutnant* Artel – *2. Kompanie der Landesschützen Bataillon 232* (18–20 February 1943).

The location of these units in February 1943 (when they began their anti-partisan sweep) was as follows:[10]

*SS und Polizeiführer Kompanie* – Pustina.
*2. Kompanie der Landesschützen Bataillon 232* – Pustina.
*(lettische) Schutzmannschaft Bataillon 276* – Pustina.
*(lettische) Schutzmannschaft Bataillon 277* – Pustina, Asune, and Pizani.
*(lettische) Schutzmannschaft Bataillon 278* – Between Asune and Pizani.
*(lettische) Schutzmannschaft Bataillon 279* – In and around the south-west region of Redkevice, Veterovice, and Vorzowa.
*Polizei Nachrichten Zug Lewinski* – Held in reserve in Pustina.
*Luftwaffe Flak Zug Hatje* – Held in reserve in Pustina.
*Gendarmerie Zug (motorisiert) Nr. 10* – Held in reserve in Pustina.

German and Latvian-language sources which record the history of *(lettische) Schutzmannschaft Bataillon 275* concur that the men from this company-sized battalion ended up with the *(lettische) Freiwilligen Polizei Regiment 1.* [11] Indeed, records state that both the *(lettische) Schutzmannschaft Bataillonen 276* and *278* were also absorbed into *(lettische) Freiwilligen Polizei Regiment 1* when it was formed in August 1943. We can see from the order of battle that several additional formations were brought into the battlegroup after the *kampfgruppe* had been established:[12]

*SS und Polizeiführer Kompanie* (beginning 6 March 1943).
*SS und Polizei Kompanie z.b.V.* (beginning 7 March 1943).
*(litauisches) Schutzmannschafts-Bataillon 2* (beginning 20 March 1943).
*(estnische) Freiwilligen Polizei Bataillon 50* (beginning 20 March 1943).
*(lettische) Schutzmannschaft Bataillon 282* (beginning 27 March 1943).

The following table lists the number of losses which the *kampfgruppe* took during the anti-partisan sweep of 15 February to 30 March 1943.

Table 7. Losses taken by *Kampfgruppe Knecht*: 15 February –30 March 1943[13]

| 1943 | Killed | Wounded | Missing |
|---|---|---|---|
| | | | |
| 15 Feb | 2 | 2[14] | |
| 16 Feb | | 1 | |
| 17 Feb | 1 | 1 | |
| 22 Feb | 4 | 16[15] | |
| 25 Feb | | 2 | |
| 27 Feb | | 1 | |
| 2 Mar | | 3 | |
| 3 Mar | | 6[16] | |
| 4 Mar | 1 | 3 | |
| 6 Mar | | 6 | |
| 9 Mar | | 10[17] | |
| 10 Mar | 2 | | |
| 11 Mar | 2 | 2 | |
| 15 Mar | 8 | 2 | 3[18] |
| 16 Mar | | 1 | |
| 18 Mar | | 3 | |
| 19 Mar | | 2 | |
| 22 Mar | 2 | 4 | |
| 30 Mar | 2 | 1 | |
| Total: | 24 | 66 | 3 |

According to the after-action report, between 16 February and 31 March 1943 *Kampfgruppe Knecht* killed 77 guerrillas in battle, took nine partisans prisoner, and executed 875 people in what was listed as 'Special Treatment of Bandits and Bandit Helpers'. In addition, the battlegroup handed over 1,389 people to the *Sicherheitsdienst*.[19] The final tally of friendly troops killed seems to contradict the earlier, written tally of twenty-four killed and sixty-six wounded. It lists only twenty-two killed, plus twenty-four severely wounded and fifty-three lightly wounded. Likely, the Germans did not count the two Latvian *panje*[20] drivers that had been killed on 15 February, but that still does not explain the difference in wounded (sixty-six as opposed to seventy-seven).

## The anti-partisan drive

According to the war diary of the unit, *Kampfgruppe Knecht* set off on 5 February 1943. The *(lettische) Schutzmannschaft Bataillon 276* was directed to go to Pustina and just east of the town, while *(lettische) Schutzmannschaft Bataillon 277* was directed to move on three localities: Pustina, to support its sister battalion, then to Asune and finally, Pisani. Similarly, *(lettische) Schutzmannschaft Bataillon 278* was to aid *(lettische) Schutzmannschaft Bataillon 277* in taking Asune and Pisani. *(lettische) Schutzmannschaft Bataillon 279* was ordered to cover the flank of the other battalions by making a south-westerly sweep, through the area bounded by the localities of Redkevice, Veterrovice, and Worzowa (Vorzova). On 7 February the advance command headquarters, consisting of the lower staff officers and *Gendarmerie Zug 10 (motorisiert)*, marched to the town of Asune. On 8 February *Oberst der Schutzpolizei* Karl Knecht, *Major der Schutzpolizei* Heinrich Oberwinder, and *Oberleutnant der Schutzpolizei* Karl Wutz departed for Daugavpils for a meeting with Friedrich Jeckeln. On 9 February Knecht, Oberwinder, and Wutz had to remain in Daugavpils because of a heavy snowstorm and also on account of engine trouble with the vehicle they were using.[21]

The men left on the morning of the following day. On that day (10 February) the entire staff of the battlegroup was assembled in the town of Dagda. For operational purposes, the command staff of *Kampfgruppe Knecht* would be referred to as 'Runo Command'.[22] Due to another large snowfall, the planned journey to Asune could no longer take place on the same day. In Dagda, details about the procurement of the missing equipment for the operation were discussed. On 11 February the entire command staff marched towards Asune. They arrived there around midday. The school in Asune was chosen to be the location for the headquarters of the battlegroup. On 12 February preparations were made to issue the operational order for attack. However, armament, equipment and even clothing issues in the rifle battalions were inadequate. These problems took almost an entire week to resolve. In order to partly remedy this situation, *Feldkommandantur 818*, whose headquarters was located in Daugavpils, loaned the battlegroup six heavy machine guns for the operation.[23]

February 13th brought a heavy, blowing snowstorm. Since the motor vehicles were immobilised due to the heavy snowfall, *panje* sledges had to be used for all of the battalions and units involved in the operation. On 14 March the strong wind kept the visibility low due to blowing snow. That day preparatory measures were taken for deployment. A day later, on 15 March, the weather got worse. In addition to the blowing snow, frost also developed. That morning a meeting of the group commanders was held at the 'Runo' command post in the school building in Asune. The battlegroup commander announced the day and time of the attack. The group staff then set off towards Vorsova. In Vorsova, the liaison officers with the various *Schutzmannschaft* battalions, were made aware of the date and time of the attack. A day later, on 16 March, the frost ended and a thaw began to settle, although it snowed occasionally throughout the day. The action was detailed in Operational Order No. 1, dated '14 February 1943 Ia No. 22/43 (appendix page 1)'. The battalions and anti-aircraft troops marched to their staging areas. The attack was scheduled for 6:00 a.m. on 16 March, but due to another heavy snowfall which pretty much hid all paths in a blanket of snow, the attack was delayed by 40–60 minutes. The group headquarters went forward with the *4. Kompanie* of the *(lettische) Schutzmannschaft Bataillon 278,* which had been pulled out as group reserve, and released from the forest north of the village of Kaljuti (Kalyuti).

The German command reported taking heavy machine-gun fire from Kalyuti, including the northern edge of the village. Partisans (the Germans referred to them as 'bandits') had apparently taken up position there with a captured German machine gun. After a short firefight, Kalyuti was taken by the battlegroup. The 'bandits' escaped into the forest to the east of. Several 'bandit suspects' were apprehended in Kalyuti, and were handed over to the *Sicherheitsdienst Einsatzkommando* for interrogation. The village was partly burned down. Later in the day, *(lettische) Schutzmannschaft Bataillon 278* still faced enemy resistance in Forvalkova. Three bandits encountered there were shot. *(lettische) Schutzmannschaft Bataillon 278* reached its assigned position at around 4:00 p.m. *(lettische) Schutzmannschaft Bataillon 277* was only able to reach the staging area at 6:15 a.m. on the following day due to heavy snow. The battalion thereupon attacked. The village of Paproha was captured at 7:15 a.m. At 8:30 a.m. a successful firefight occurred with the bandits west of the village of Sekolova. There ten partisans and ten people suspected of being 'bandit suspects' were shot dead. At 9:20 a.m. a brief firefight ensued with partisans north of the village of Anisskovo. After the skirmish, the battlegroup discovered three dead bodies left behind. This was unusual given that the standard operating practice for the guerrillas was to carry their dead when they withdrew. This was so the German command could never be sure how many partisans had been killed.

South of Vasnova, two men wearing Soviet insignia were killed in battle. The daily objective for *(lettische) Schutzmannschaft Bataillon 276* was reached at 11 a.m. and the attack proceeded on time. Two more 'bandits' were shot dead in area surrounding the village of Rosica. *(lettische) Schutzmannschaft Bataillon 279* began its attack 40 minutes late. The bunkers of the former Stalin line located in the attack area were found to be unoccupied. These were mainly earthen bunkers that were not reinforced with concrete or cement. During the fighting on 16 February, a total of fifteen 'bandits' were killed in battle. The *Sicherheitsdienst* reported separately to the Runo Command, about executions of 'bandit suspects' that SD men had taken part in during the day. During the attack, no radio communication could be established with the battalions on the field and vice versa, as radio communication was not operational during the advance. This circumstance had an unfortunate effect. The registration of livestock, agricultural goods and equipment caused great difficulties due to the lack of agricultural managers to account for them. On the night of 16/17 February, 'bandits' shelled the houses in the village of Muschina, where men of *(lettische) Schutzmannschaft Bataillon 277* were quartered. The mortar fire came from the forest north-east of Mushina. In addition to mortars, the partisans moved several machine guns to the edge of the village and began to spray the houses with fire. Likewise, the village of Rakschni came under indirect mortar fire from the forest area east of Ssaryanka. One company each from *(lettische) Schutzmannschaft Bataillonen 277* and *278* were assigned to reconnoitre in the direction of Kolbovschina, Barsuki, and Medvedevo, to see if they could locate more guerrillas. Partisans of an unknown strength were identified in all three localities. The reconnaissance patrols received machine-gun and submachine-gun fire from the western direction of Kolbovschina and Barsuki. The patrols returned fire and withdrew to report the incident.

A thaw now began to set I after the previous days' frost. One man from *(lettische) Schutzmannschaft Bataillon 278* was shot in the head by a sniper. Action against the aforementioned 'bandit nests' was to be planned as soon as further reconnaissance would become available. On the night of 17/18 February, two rounds of artillery fire were fired at Schamuzina (Šamucina) from the area around the village of

Kolbovdschina (Kolbovdščina). On 18 February, one platoon of the *2. Kompanie* of *(lettische) Schutzmannschaft Bataillon 277* conducted a reconnaissance operation near Seljanki, about 4km east of Kaljuti (Kalyuti). A 'bandit post' was discovered 1km south of the town. The guerrillas immediately withdrew under fire. According to statements from local residents, there was a large number of bandits stationed in the village of Kolbovchina, who were well armed with machine guns. One statement from a resident in the village said that on 15 February, the 'bandits' had received around twenty sleds of ammunition. One platoon of the *4. Kompanie* of *(lettische) Schutzmannschaft Bataillon 277* advanced to Sharnosseki (Šarnoseki), Sharvonochki (Šarvonočki), Helmniki and Seljanki. Except for three residents who were arrested, the towns mentioned were deserted. All of these localities were burned down.

On 19 February the weather was expected to be overcast with frost. A '*Säuberungs und Räumungsaktion*' ('cleansing and evacuation operation') was launched, as directed by operational order of 18 February, Ia No. 31/43 (appendix, page 6). On 19 February, shock troop operations were carried out in the forest 2km north-east of Mushina. The following units were deployed for this operation: *1. Kompanie* of *Landesschützen Battalion 232* and *1. Kompanie* of the *(lettische) Schutzmannschaft Bataillon 277*. Since there was somewhere between 70–80cm of snow (approximately 27–31in) in the forest, the operation was very lengthy and strenuous. About 150m (164 yards) from the northern edge of the forest, *1. Kompanie* of *Landesschützen Battalion 232* began to receive fire from two machine guns and several submachine guns. After a short firefight, the northern edge of the forest was reached. After reaching the northern edge, *1. Kompanie* of *Landesschützen Battalion 232* began to receive sustained machine-gun fire from the direction of Kolbovdschina and mortar fire from the direction of Seljanki. The company returned fire with three light machine guns. On the company's return march, a member of *(lettische) Schutzmannschaft Bataillon 273* was found wounded. This man had been reported killed two days earlier. He had been lying wounded in the field for two whole days. In addition to his wound, he was suffering from frostbite.

The towns of Bandzeli, Kriwosseltsevo (Krivoselttsevo), Schilowo (Žilevo), Pleusski (Pleusskis), Dubniki (Dubņiki) and Trischewa (Triževa) were burned down by the *Sicherheitsdienst*. 'Bandits' were not found in the aforementioned towns. Some 204 people, 16 horses, 62 cows and 95 other livestock were also seized from these localities. The *(lettische) Schutzmannschaft Bataillon 278* combed several areas of the forest north and south of Waznowa (Vaznova). During the sweep, two people were discovered in the forest. Although they carried no weapons, they were arrested and handed over to the *Sicherheitsdienst*. Also found in the sweep of the forest were two unusable anti-tank guns and sixty rounds of German artillery ammunition. The ammunition was destroyed by a *Wehrmacht* sergeant.

20 February Weather: Overcast. Assault troops moved from a line near Ssaryanka and east of the locality, as per the order of 19 February, 'Ia No. 30/43 (appendix page 7)', as well as an 'evacuation and cleansing' operational order of 19 February 'Ia No. 37/43 (appendix page 8)'. *Schutzmannschaft Bataillon 278* combed the forest east of Kalyuti and Anisskovo. During the sweep, eighteen people were encountered who were then handed over to the *Sicherheitspolizei*. The SS and police company and one company from *(lettische) Schutzmannschaft Bataillon 277*, which were subordinate to the group on 20 February, cleaned out the forest area near Saarjanka (Sārjanka), between Poporotnovo and Ssokolovo. The forest area was free of guerrillas. *Schutzmannschaft Bataillon 276* cleared the area between Rosica, Lipovka, Tirschewa, Dubniki, and Pessky. No partisans were discovered there. The battalion then roamed the forest area in a north-westerly direction from Koslovo, Buli, Saborovzi, and Borki. A group numbering thirty-five people was identified. This group also included women and children. After a short firefight, fourteen 'bandits' were shot dead. Among those shot was a woman wearing men's clothing. One man was wearing parts of a Russian uniform.

The start of Sunday, 21 February, was frosty but it remained cloudless throughout the day. Preparations for the next day's operation got underway. The area in question was the region bordering Kolbovdzchina (Kolbovdžina), Barsuki, Medvedevo, and Vesnino (Vesņino). For this meeting, all liaison officers, battalion commanders as well as *Leutnant* Hatje, the commander of the anti-aircraft platoon, gathered with the battlegroup commander, *Oberst der Schutzpolizei* Knecht. On his orders, the village of Lipova was burned because it was known to be a base for partisan operations. On Monday, 22 February, further operations were planned east of the Ssaryanka village perimeter, as per 'Order No. 2 of 21 February, 1943 – Ia No. 43/43 (appendix page 11)'. A thaw had set it that day, making everything wet and slippery.

On 22 February a thaw in the weather set in. Further operations east of the Sarjanka area proceeded as per 'Order No. 2 of 21 February 1943 – Ia No. 43/43 (appendix page 11)'. At 8:00 a.m. the attack began from the north and west. The 'bandit towns' of Kolbovdzchina (Kolbovdčina),

Barsuki and Medvedevo (Medvedevs), Kolbovdzchina (Kolbovdčina) and Barsuki were taken by *(lettische) Schutzmannschaft-Bataillon 278* and *(lettische) Schutzmannschaft-Bataillon 279* without resistance. The Hatje anti-aircraft platoon supported the batallion's mission.

At around 9:00 a.m. the town of Medvedevo was attacked. *(lettische) Schutzmannschaft Bataillon 278* received heavy machine-gun fire from the town. About 50 'bandits' retreated to the small forest south of Medvedevo, while about 80–100 'bandits' continued to resist in town. When the attack stalled, the battlegroup commander immediately deployed a company from *(lettische) Schutzmannschaft Bataillon 276* on the right flank.[24] After about 15 minutes, a second company from *(lettische) Schutzmannschaft Bataillon 276* was also deployed on the right flank. The 'bandits' then fled to the east, protected by the village. At around 10:00 a.m. Medvedevo was taken. Parts of *(lettische) Schutzmannschaft Bataillon 278* immediately continued the attack on to Vesnino, which was taken without any significant resistance. The town of Medvedevo was heavily fortified. On the west and south edges, two large earthen bunkers were found, as well as numerous well-camouflaged riflemen's nests with trenches. When the attack on Medvedevo began, three shots were fired at short intervals from a flare gun.

During an attempt to recover the body of a non-commissioned officer from *(lettische) Schutzmannschaft Bataillon 273,* who had died a few days earlier, a mine was triggered. The 'bandits' had tied the body to a mine. One man was seriously injured. Another mine was triggered while our troops were passing the edge of the forest in the western part of Kolbovdschina (Kolbovdščina). One officer was seriously injured in that incident. A company from *(lettische) Schutzmannschaft Bataillon 277,* was made subordinate to *(lettische) Schutzmannschaft Bataillon 278*. That attached company received active fire as it approached the woodlands about 1km north-west of Ssakeli. After the end of the firefight, the company observed that about 50 sleds were fleeing the scene, followed by about 100 'bandits' on foot. These guerrillas left the village of Ssakeli and moved in the direction of Buchanovo. Given the great distance, it was not possible to prevent the 'bandits' from escaping. The operation was over at 12:00 noon. All captured towns were burned down. The loss of air operations, the lack of communications equipment and the inadequate training of the battalion had a negative impact. Four men were killed in the operation, four were seriously wounded and twelve were lightly wounded. Bandit losses could not be determined.

In the cemetery of Medvedevo a grave was found that bore the following inscription in Russian script: 'Fallen on 21 January 1943 in the fight against the German occupiers'. A thaw set in on 23 February. Based on the orders of the Runo Command, the battalion's radio stations were withdrawn. Otherwise, there were no incidents on this day. On 24 February the thaw in the weather continued. Preparations were made and reconnaissance was performed for the operation schedule on 25–26 February east of Saarjanka (Sārjanka), in a north-easterly direction to Velikoye-Sselo, as per Operational Order No. 3 of 23 February, Ia No. 47/43. The thaw continued on 25 February, but this day the weather was also windy. Our forces attacked up to the Kochnowitschi–Zaicevo–Strelki (Kočnoviči–Zaicevo–Strelki) road junction immediately east of the area Velikoye–Sselo, as per Operational Order No. 4 of 24 February 1943, Ia No. 54/43 (appendix page 16). The area combed was 'gang-free'.

According to local residents, most of the bandits fled before the attack began. The *(lettische) Schutzmannschaft Bataillon 276* received heavy machine-gun and rifle fire from the Budzhanovo and Barkova area, about 1km north-east of Medvedev. Barkova was taken at 8:00 a.m. The 'bandits', who stubbornly resisted, fled from the threatening encirclement of the town, in a north-easterly direction towards Szashorkovoskoye (Szashorkovoskoje). They fled around 10 o'clock, not giving much resistance as they withdrew. During the approach to Dobreniki, *(lettische) Schutzmannschaft Bataillon 276* received fire. Although heavy fire was taken, it was immediately suppressed after the anti-aircraft platoon was deployed. Dobreniki was taken around 11:00 a.m. When Dedino was attacked, there was a surprise attack on the flank. When an all-out attack was attempted, 'bandits' withdrew in a north-easterly direction. Two bandits were shot by members of *(lettische) Schutzmannschaft Bataillon 279*, during the capture of Wischnarowo (Višnarovo). Numerous traces of blood on the scene suggested that the 'bandits' had additional losses. *(lettische) Schutzmannschaft Bataillon 276* suffered one soldier seriously wounded and one lightly wounded. The daily goal for the first day was achieved by all battalions. Thirty-six 'bandit suspects' were executed by the *Sicherheitsdienst*. Bushanovo, Sukhorukovskye, Brobiniki, Rubani, and Salino were all burned down.

February 26th began as an overcast day, then turned partly sunny. On the second day of the attack, no 'bandits' were found in the occupied areas. The villages of Shlyki, Sherebzovo, Satloishchina, Demidovo, Dubrovy, Osetki, Popeļuševo, Kurashi, and Chervony, plus six isolated farmsteads were captured without any significant resistance. The headquarters staff as well as *Gendarmerie Zug 10 (motorisiert)* and *Luftwaffe Flakkampf Zug Hatje* were fired upon with grenades in the Shlyki area. This day the *Sicherheitsdienst* executed 204 'bandit helpers'. The above-mentioned villages were all burned to the ground. The daily goals were achieved by the battalions. On 27 February at around 8:00 a.m., the 3. *Kompanie* of *(lettische) Schutzmannschaft Bataillon 276,* which was on the march from Velikoye-Sselo to Budy, was fired upon from the east by 'bandits' numbering about 200 men. The 'bandits' occupied Height 192.4, about 4km north-east of Velikoye-Sselo and the village of Tserkovno (Cerkovno). To support the 3. *Kompanie,* two companies from *(lettische) Schutzmannschaft Bataillon 279,* one company from *(lettische) Schutzmannschaft Bataillon 277,* and the *Flakkampftroop Hatje* were deployed. After a fierce firefight, the 'bandits' were repulsed. They fled eastwards, taking their wounded with them. A 'bandit' was caught and handed over to the *Sicherheitsdienst.* The villages of Cerkovno and Gorodilovich (Gorodilovičs) were then burned down. During the interrogation of a prisoner, it was established that the 'gang' that had attacked were people who came from the area about 50km north-west of Cerkovno. An English carbine, an anti-tank rifle, a Russian rifle and a hand grenade were captured. The *(lettische) Schutzmannschaft Bataillon 279* had one slightly wounded man. The 'bandits' left three of their dead in the field. In Cerkovno, traces of blood were found in some houses, apparently from wounded or dead 'bandits'.

On 28 February the weather was overcast with continued thaw. 'Cleansing operation' in the area west of the Sebesh-Strelki road, as per Operational Orders Nr. 5 of 27 February, Ia Nr. 55/43, and Nr. 6, Ia Nr. 56/43 (appendix pages 20–22). During the search of the houses, *(lettische) Schutzmannschaft Bataillon 278* found an album with records containing Stalin's speech to the Eighth Special Assembly of the Soviet Socialist Republics on 28 November 1936, and was handed over to the *Sicherheitsdienst.* The *(lettische) Schutzmannschaft Bataillon 276* roamed the western border area of Lake Osveja, and the towns of Asvieja and Abraozvo, as well as the eastern border region of the highway running through Sebesh, Budy and Strelki. In Daglevo, two remaining houses were burned down. In Galkovdschina two men were arrested and handed over to the *Sicherheitsdienst.* Battalion 278 cleared the towns of Scriptschina and Belany. 122 people were handed over to the SD. The *(lettische) Schutzmannschaft Bataillon 278* carried out the ordered clearing operation south of the Osveya-Velikoye-Sselo road. The area was 'gang-free'. The village of Kal'kovshchina was burned down. Around forty-five 'bandit helpers' were executed by the *Sicherheitsdienst.*

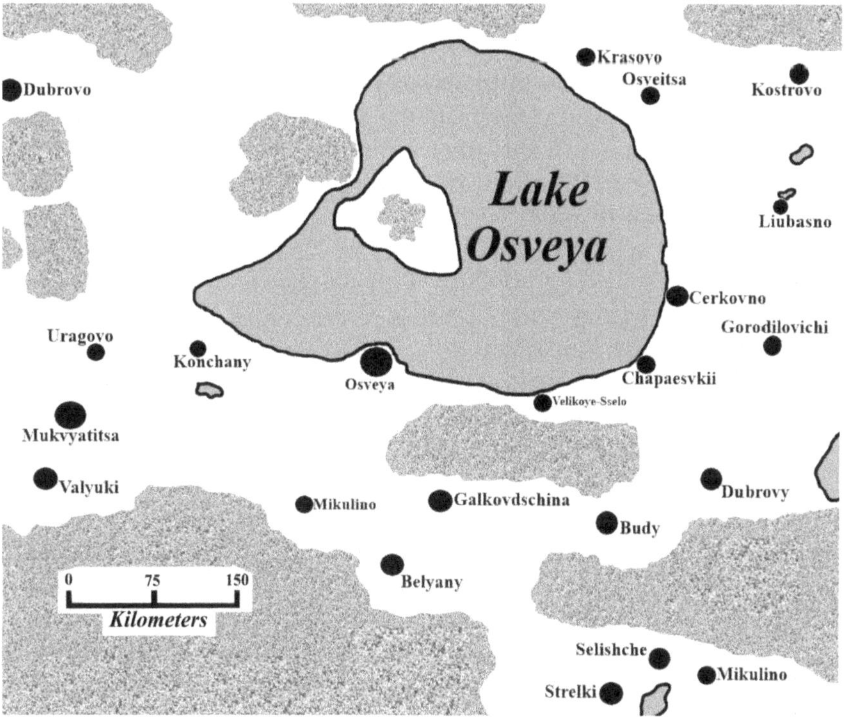


Figure 5. General view of the villages and towns in the area of Lake Osveya.

March 1st: The weather was cloudy, with continued thaw. Reorganisation of the group sections were performed as per Operational Order No. 7 of 1 March 1943, Ia No. 57/43 (appendix page 23) and establishment of a patrol service as per Operational Order No. 8 of 1 March 1943, Ia No. 58/43 (appendix, page 24), and reinforcement of the field guards at Velikoye-Sselo, as per Operational Order No. 9 of 1 March 1943 (appendix, page 25). On 2 March a snowstorm hit the region. Velikoye-Sselo was attacked several times throughout the day by enemy mortar fire and heavy machine guns. Two men from *(lettische) Schutzmannschaft Bataillon 279* and one man from *(lettische) Schutzmannschaft Bataillon 277* were killed. Zerkovono and height 192.4 were occupied by the enemy. At around 3:00 p.m., a horses was killed by machine-gun and rifle fire on the Sebesh-Strelki road, in the direction of height 179.4. Two battalions: *(lettische) Schutzmannschaft Bataillonen 277* and *279* responded to the firing. They quickly set up a defence, in battalion strength, at Velikoye-Sselo.

The *(lettische) Schutzmannschaft Bataillonen 278* had been in action since early in the morning. In the morning, about 1km east of Selishche, it received machine-gun and mortar fire. *(lettische) Schutzmannschaft Bataillonen 278* discovered that Yaroshi was occupied by 'bandits'. Reconnaissance forces sent to investigate were attacked with artillery, machine-gun and mortar fire from the Yaroshi area. According to local residents, five bandits were killed and five were wounded in the battle in Medvedevo on 22 February. The wounded 'bandits' were said to have been transported through Velikoye-Sselo to the hospital in Milovidy. At around 10 a.m., the field guard of *(lettische) Schutzmannschaft Bataillonen 278* observed 'bandits' with sleighs about 1km south of the Velikoye-Sselo road junction, who were driving towards height 161. A platoon with two heavy machine guns and a mortar were immediately deployed, before the 'bandits' retreated towards Demidovo, taking with them the dead or wounded.

On 2 March the weather brought a snowstorm with wet snow. Advances were planned against the villages located east of the starting line, as per Operational Order No. 10 of 2 March 1943, Ia Nr. 62/43 (appendix page 26), and an attack on Gorodilovichi was planned based on Operational Order No. 11 of 2 March 1943, Ia Nr. 63/43 (appendix page 27). The *(lettische) Schutzmannschaft Bataillon 279* attacked Gorodilovichi on the right flank at 7:30 a.m. and took possession around 11 a.m. Enemy resistance mainly from the forest east and north-east of the town of Gorodilovichi, as well as from the villages of Nish-Lybass. An aircraft dropped bombs on height 192.4 which was heavily occupied by the enemy. After the air raid, *Flakkampftrupp Hatje*'s anti-aircraft platoon shelled height 192.4 as well. In Gorodilovichi, seven 'bandit helpers' were shot. The attack by *(lettische) Schutzmannschaft Bataillon 279* was carried further north of Nish and Bubasny. The battalion took both villages. One 'bandit' was killed. The 'bandits' fled north-east into the woods on sleighs. From the battalion command post, the retreat of around 150 'bandits' and 30 sleighs were observed. They were moving in the direction of Gory to the north-east and east. Strong 'bandit' forces in the forest south-east of Gorodilovichi were also identified. The headquarters of the battlegroup received mortar fire. From what was observed, 'bandits' suffered casualties when fire was returned. The *(lettische) Schutzmannschaft Bataillon 278* reported that 'bandits' fired incendiary ammunition at Kisseli in the morning hours. A house was burned down as a result. Furthermore, the *(lettische) Schutzmannschaft Bataillon 276* was peppered with rifle and machine-gun fire from the Selichi heights throughout the day and until nightfall. As a result of that continued fire, two houses were set ablaze by incendiary ammunition. Strelki was hit around 10 a.m. with twelve rounds of artillery (calibre 75cm). In addition, around fifteen to twenty rounds of mortar fire also landed on the town. In order to relieve Strelki from direct fire from the heights near Selichi, an advance was made on Selichi at 3 p.m. and the 'bandits' were driven away. The height in front of Selichi was occupied by a strong field guard. Two men from *(lettische) Schutzmannschaft Bataillon 279* were seriously wounded and four were lightly wounded. No enemy losses could be determined.

On 3 March 1943 the thaw continued, but occasionally throughout the day, snow blew hard. The attack on Velikiyeye-Pole, Plyushchik, Nishcha and Dubrovo now proceeded. This assault was based on Operational Order No. 22 of 3 March 1943, Ia Nr. 66/43 (appendix page 31). The *1. Kompanie der (lettische) Schutzmannschaft Bataillon 279,* which arrived on 4 March at 11 a.m., was made subordinate to *(lettische) Schutzmannschaft Bataillon 277.* Velikiyeye-Pole, Plyushchik, Nishcha and Dubrovo were all reached on that day. The localities were searched and found to be free of 'bands'. The localities that had already partially burned down were now completely destroyed. The battalion received heavy machine-gun, grenade and anti-tank fire from the forest and south-east of these villages. The air force that was deployed did not attack the target in the forest opposite the battalion, even though the target area was marked by burning houses. Bombs were instead dropped on another target. According to information, during the air raid on Seletsevo on 3 March, bandits left the village with fourteen sleighs. They left in the direction of the eastern edge of Lake Svonets.[25] After the air raid was over, the 'bandits' returned with 60 sleighs and positioned two heavy machine guns to the north-east of Seletsevo. Another air strike on Seletsevo was therefore requested.

On 4 March 1943, *(lettische) Schutzmannschaft Bataillon 276* cleared Mikulino on the eastward edge of the forest and the heights north of Mikulino. These areas had been heavily manned by the 'bandits' who employed machine guns and mortars. The battalion had not made any further advance because the towns east of the base had already been burned down by *Kampfgruppe Marder.* During the fighting, a 'bandit' sniper (up on a tree) was shot, and a horse with a sleigh was destroyed by mortar fire. Further enemy losses were certain to occur. One man from *(lettische) Schutzmannschaft Bataillon 277* was killed, one man from *(lettische) Schutzmannschaft Bataillon 276* was slightly wounded, and two men from *(lettische) Schutzmannschaft Bataillon 279* were also slightly wounded.]

On 5 March the weather was windy but the thaw continued. The *(lettische) Schutzmannschaft Bataillon 278* reported that at 12:25 p.m. when an airplane approached, about forty bandits fled on seven sleighs into the forest north-east of Yaroshi. On the second approach, another twenty-two 'bandits' fired a white flare as they fled. The battalion also reported that at 10:15 a.m. thirty-one bandits came from the forest north-east of Selevo and carried out fortifications work in groups of four to seven men on the western and southern edges of the village. There was a lot of 'bandit' traffic between Yaroshi and Selevo. A reconnaissance patrol in the direction of Dubrovy-Demidovo, consisting of one platoon, was involved in a firefight near Demidovo after they were fired upon with mortars from the corner of the forest about 600m north-east of Kurashi. The mortar fire was silenced. On the return march, the column was attacked with machine guns and mortar fire from a height north-west of Selevo and from the town itself. At around midnight, about fifteen bandits attempted to attack a field station about 1km north of Budy. During this attack, the 'bandits' employed submachine-guns and rifles. After fire was returned, the 'bandits' continued to retreat. After daybreak, traces of blood were discovered. German bullet casings were also found where the 'bandits' had been.

On 6 March the thaw in the weather continued. Attacks were ordered in and around *Beloye See*[26] as per Operational Order No. 13 of 5 March 1943, Ia Nr. 67/43 (appendix page 32). The area between Osveya Lake and Beloye Lake was cleared of 'bandits' and 'bandit helpers' on 6 March 1943. The *(lettische) Schutzmannschaft Bataillon 279* encountered enemy resistance on the west side of Zerkovo, as well as from the forested region east of Kostrova. Immediately after starting the attack from the forest east of Gorodilovichi, *(lettische) Schutzmannschaft Bataillon 277* received automatic weapons and mortar fire. As the battalion continued north, the fire grew stronger. The battalion was attacked using artillery and anti-tank guns. The *2. Kompanie* of *(lettische) Schutzmannschaft Bataillon 277*, which was advancing on the right wing, was prevented from proceeding for a long time by sustained heavy fire. It was only through the deployment of the *1. Kompanie* that the *2. Kompanie* managed to break away despite the heavy enemy fire. In the process, four men from *2. Kompanie* were wounded. During the entire attack to the northern edge of Lyubasno, the battalion constantly received strong flank fire from the forest to the east. The 'bandits' employed mortar, anti-tank and automatic weapons fire. Although the battalion lacked heavy weapons, they stood their ground and were able to continue the ordered attack in a northerly direction. The first attack target were the villages of Oddbor'ye, Kostrova and Kaplyar. These were reached at 10 a.m. The bandits withdrew to the large forest area north of Lake Beloye. The localities were judged 'bandit free' and burned down. Shortly before Oddbor'ye, forty 'bandit suspects' were apprehended in a small forest and handed over to the *Sicherheitsdienst*. The second attack objective was reached around 1 p.m. Ignalino, Osveytsa, and Krasovo were burned down. About twenty-five 'bandit suspects' were handed over to the *Sicherheitsdienst*. Enemy losses were unknown, but traces of blood were found on various occasions. One 'bandit' was captured. *(lettische) Schutzmannschaft Bataillon 279* had one soldier seriously injured in a mine explosion, while another man broke his leg due to a fall on the ice. The *(lettische) Schutzmannschaft Bataillon 277* had four wounded. A *panje* driver was killed. A horse was also killed and another was injured. In the early hours of 6 March 1943, a road patrol from *(lettische) Schutzmannschaft Bataillon 278* recovered two mines about 200m north from the bridge just north of Strelki.

On 7 March *Gendarmerie Zug Nr. 10 (motorisiert)* was assigned to *SS und Polizei Kampfgruppe Isserstedt* (commander: *Major der Schutzpolizei* Otto Wilhelm Heinrich Isserstedt).[27] The *SS und Polizei Kompanie z.b.V.* and the *1. Kompanie* of the *(litauische) Schutzmannschaft Bataillon 2* reported to the *kampfgruppe* on 7 March. Otherwise, no incidents occurred on this day. On 8 March the *1. Kompanie* of *(lettische) Schutzmannschaft Bataillon 276* received strong infantry and machine-gun fire from the forest area about 1km east and south-east when moving from the western heights of Gorodilovichi. The fire of the 'bandits' was silenced. The 'bandits' retreated into the forests. At around 5.30 a.m. our group came across a freshly laid mine on the Sebesh–Strelki road, near Strelki. The first mine was placed behind the makeshift bridge which had been built by *(lettische) Schutzmannschaft Bataillon 278*. The mine was about 2km north of Strelki on the left side of the roadway. When run over by an ammunition sled, the mine exploded and damaged the sled and ammunition. The second mine was found behind the same bridge on the right lane. This mine was not touched and was later removed by *Kampfgruppe Isserstedt*. According to findings, both mines must have been laid after *(lettische) Schutzmannschaft Bataillon 276*, which had passed the road shortly before, had moved on. The mines were placed into the lanes and were covered with snow.

In order to burn down and 'cleanse' the towns of Ostrov, Petino and Sukoli, the *Sicherheitsdienst* was given two platoons of heavy machine guns. The *(lettische) Schutzmannschaft Bataillon 279* provided the weapons and soldiers. March 9th was overcast, with the spring thaw continuing. An attack to the east of the village of Svolnatal' was organised, as per Operational Order No. 14 of 7 March (appendix page 34). The *(lettische) Schutzmannschaft Bataillonen 278* and *279* attacked the towns of Osveya and Lissno. They deployed on the south-eastern edge of Lake Osveya. With the exception of the town of Melnitsa, the daily objectives ordered were achieved. Because of darkness, Melnitsa was not taken by *(lettische) Schutzmannschaft Bataillonen 278* until dawn on 10 March 1943. *(lettische) Schutzmannschaft Bataillonen 277* and *279* followed the assault battalion as reserves. Enemy resistance was encountered, employing automatic weapons fire from the forest east of Gorodilovichi, Velikoye Sselo and Pole. Further enemy fire was received from the edges of the forest on the road from Velikoye Sselo to Lissno. A suspicious person was apprehended and turned over to the *Sicherheitsdienst* for interrogation. The battalion's advance was effectively supported by our artillery half-battery, which fired on the forest area on both sides of the road. At the fork in the road east of Sagradyasnaya, a *Sicherheitsdienst Kommando* ran into two mines. Three men were seriously wounded and two were slightly wounded. No enemy losses were recorded. The 'gangs' withdrew into the woods in a fighting withdrawal. The towns of Kobylnitsv, Sayel'nitsa and Maleshkovo were burned down. A 'bandit' was arrested. In addition, forty-seven 'bandit helpers' were handed over to the *Sicherheitsdienst*. The *(lettische) Schutzmannschaft Bataillon 276* had one seriously and three lightly wounded.

An attack by *(lettische) Schutzmannschaft Bataillon*en *276–279* to the south of Kobylnitsv, Sayel'nitsa and Maleshkovo was ordered. As a result of effective air raids, most of the 'bandits' withdrew further east. There was no apparent plan of defence of the 'gang camps' located in the attack region. The sweep by *Schutzmannschaft Bataillonen 276–279* encountered and overcame weak enemy resistance. The 'gangs' continued with their previous tactics of stalling and evading. The battalions encountered numerous tree barriers in various places which the 'bandits' had set up. The German forces surprised about forty 'bandits' at Makuty who were fleeing to the east. In the process, a 'bandit' was shot dead. The villages of Isubritsa, Ardavskaya and Makuty were burned down. Ardavskaya had already been partially destroyed by air raids.

A 'bandit cemetery' with fresh graves was discovered near Dobroplessi. A telephone cable line which had been established between Velikiyeye-Sselo and Lissno was cut several times by 'bandits' along the Velikiyeye-Sselo–Lissno road. Both *(lettische) Schutzmannschaft Bataillonen 277* and *279* achieved the required daily goals. After taking possession of Makuty, *(lettische) Schutzmannschaft Bataillon 278* halted their advance after darkness fell, apparently due to the exhaustion of the men. The daily assigned target was not reached by *(lettische) Schutzmannschaft Bataillon 276*. It bivouacked east of Yaroshi. During the day, a 'bandit leader' was shot dead in battle. Six 'bandit' camps and 'bandit helper' camps were destroyed. One hundred and sixteen suspicious persons thought to be 'bandit helpers' were handed over to the *Sicherheitsdienst*. A soldier in *(lettische) Schutzmannschaft Bataillon 278* died due to his own carelessness. The battalion captured a gun mount, ten rounds of 75mm artillery ammunition, one German field kitchen, two radio sets, one German carbine, one pistol, and two full Russian machine-gun magazines. A soldier from *(lettische) Schutzmannschaft Bataillon 279* was killed. The *SS und Polizei Kompanie*, which marched at the head of the group headquarters and was the group reserve during the attack on 10 March, encountered 12–15 'bandits' about 1km to the north. This group immediately fled into the deep forest area to the east. The majority of the *SS und Polizei Kompanie* immediately opened fire with submachine guns and rifles. The 'bandits' escaped despite the immediate arrest attempt.

On 10 March, after reaching the daily objective, *(lettische) Schutzmannschaft Bataillon 279* occupied the enemy bases in the Svolna Valley and set up a hedgehog-like defence. The day of 11 March began sunny and ended with a night frost. The other battalion, *(lettische) Schutzmannschaft Bataillon 276*, which bivouacked in the forest on the night of 10/11 March, continued the approach in the early hours of 11 March and reached the day's goal as ordered. Due to swampy terrain, as well as numerous tree barriers and metres of snow, the advance of *(lettische) Schutzmannschaft Bataillon 278* was slowed. On 10 March it lost its bearings and did not reach its daily goal. According to orders, *(lettische) Schutzmannschaft Bataillon 278* continued the interrupted advance at daybreak on 11 March, reaching the daily objective ordered for 10 March without coming into contact with the enemy. Otherwise, no incidents were reported from 10–11 March. Like the day before, 12 March started sunny and ended with a night frost. According to Operational Order No. 16 of 11 March 1943, Ia No. 71/43 (appendix page 41), a 'cleansing' operation took place in the forest area west of the village of Svolna.

The 3. *Kompanie* of the *(lettische) Schutzmannschaft Bataillon 277* was fired upon in Milovidy by 'bandits' from the woods east of the town. This firefight left one man slightly wounded and three *panje* horses slightly injured.

The company responded immediately with return fire. Thereupon, the 'bandits' retreated east across the Svolna River. An armed 'bandit' was shot while trying to escape near Gnil'zy. In the afternoon hours of 12 March, Milovidy was again attacked with machine-gun fire from the forest to the east. The fire was stopped by friendly fire. On 12 March *(lettische) Schutzmannschaft Bataillon 277* continued the 'cleansing' operation in the area that had been taken over on 11 March 1943. Numerous enemy machine-gun and rifle fire, especially in the Makuty area, were silenced. In Makuty, a newly built bakery and a blacksmith shop were found and destroyed. A *bataillonkommando* from *(lettische) Schutzmannschaft Bataillon 277*, which accompanied a slightly wounded man to Chernoki, was fired upon by 'bandits' about 1.5km south-west of Dobroplesy, and west of the Svolna. One man from the escort squad was slightly wounded. A horse was also killed. As a response for these incidences, orders were passed for the battalion to clear the entire area.

The weather on 13 March was sunny but ended with frost at night. Men from *(lettische) Schutzmannschaft Bataillon 277,* who occupied village of Melovidy, were machine-gunned in the morning hours from the forest to the east of the town. Fire was returned which silenced the enemy fire. The 'cleansing' of the area continued on 11 March and any forest camps found were destroyed. A forest camp was found by *(lettische) Schutzmannschaft Bataillon 278* in the Zagrosnaya area at altitude 168.9. The camp was destroyed. In Kobylnitsa, two howitzers and one anti-tank gun were found, as well as a number of artillery shells. The guns were rendered unusable and the ammunition was destroyed. Apparently, there was an artillery workshop in the town of Kobylnitsa. The men from *(lettische) Schutzmannschaft Bataillon 277* continued the cleanup operation in Svolna. At around 10:30 a.m. the *2. Kompanie* of *(lettische) Schutzmannschaft Bataillon 277* accepted a 'bandit defector'. During his interrogation he stated that there was a 'bandit' camp of some sixty men in the forest, about 2km south-east of Dobroplessy and Lonnizabakhe.

At 3:30 p.m. a company from *(lettische) Schutzmannschaft Bataillon 277* deployed with a *Sicherheitsdienst Kommando.* The forest area was extensively attacked. A large number of the 'bandits' fled. In the firefight, six 'bandits' were shot dead. A female 'bandit' was captured. The weather on 14 March started out sunny but ended with frost as nightfall began. The SS *und Polizei Kompanie* was deployed on 14 March to assist in cleaning up the area between Lissno and Lake Beloees. Several forest camps were discovered and burned down or destroyed. The villages of Belaya, Mylenki and Dubnoye to the north of Lake Beloees, which were found deserted, were completely burned down. Seventy bodies were discovered by *(lettische) Schutzmannschaft Bataillon 279* during a combing operation west of Stradnoye. According to prisoner statements, those seventy killed were probably refugees who were shot at by aircraft or machine-gunned by 'bandits' from the forest east of Dobroplessy. Two companies of *(lettische)*

*Schutzmannschaft Bataillon 277* were attacked by the 'bandits' before fleeing. Enemy losses could not be ascertained. A man from *(lettische) Schutzmannschaft Bataillon 277* was slightly wounded.

The weather on 15 March, like the day before, started sunny but ended with a night of frost. After the town of Milovidy had already been shelled several times from the east, in the early hours of 15 March a company belonging to *(lettische) Schutzmannschaft Bataillon 277,* together with an *Sicherheitsdienst Kommando* deployed against three accommodation and storage bunkers that were supposed to be occupied by Latvian 'bandits' east of Svolna, and south of the Lonnitsa River. As the two companies approached the bunker positions, it received heavy machine-gun and machine-pistol fire. The 'bandits' had also deployed snipers in trees. According to the company commander, the bunker position could not be taken with the forces deployed. Ten 'bandits' were killed by machine-gun fire from the two companies. Eventually the enemy broke and ran, but not before two men in the Latvian company were wounded. In the midday hours of 15 March Milovidy was again fired upon by 'bandits', with a non-commissioned officer from *(lettische) Schutzmannschaft Bataillon 276* fatally wounded by a bullet that pierced the wall of a home. An eighteen-strong sled column from *(lettische) Schutzmannschaft Bataillon 279*, travelling on the Lissno-Osveya road in the morning of 15 March, was ambushed near Saye'nitsa by about fifty 'bandits'. Five soldiers and a *panje* driver, as well as five *panje* horses, were killed in the attack. One wounded man arrived in Osveya and one wounded man in Lissno. Two soldiers and two *panje* drivers were also reported missing after the engagement. *Oberleutnant der Schutzpolizei* Turks, who was appointed by the group commander as a mine expert in Lissno, began his work teaching the units how to locate and defuse mines. Turks destroyed artillery ammunition that was found in a nearby forest.

The weather on 16 March was the same as the day before. In the aftermath of the attack on the sleigh column belonging to *(lettische) Schutzmannschaft Bataillon 279* on 15 March, the following individual units were reported: the sleigh column was subjected to enemy fire that lasted around 20 minutes. The barrage of enemy weapons fire was returned by the escort team. Another man who was seriously wounded in the battle dragged himself a short distance towards Velikoye-Sselo. When he was exhausted and could crawl no further, he shot himself in order to avoid falling into the hands of the 'bandits'. His death increased the number of casualties to six. A missing soldier subsequently arrived at the command post in Velikoye-Sselo. Three sleighs with all of their cargo were captured by the 'bandits'. The fallen soldiers were stripped of their clothes which were stolen by the 'bandits'. The *(lettische) Schutzmannschaft Bataillon 278,* which was used to comb the forest area north of Lake Beloye, made no contact with the enemy. To destroy the bunker positions south of Lonnitsa, about 1km east of point 121.4, one company from *(lettische) Schutzmannschaft Bataillon 277* and three companies of *(lettische) Schutzmannschaft Bataillon 276* used. The bunker positions were attacked extensively from the north and south. The bunkers, which were located in a well-camouflaged valley basin, consisted of six large residential bunkers with a capacity of forty men each. All the bunkers, which were built deep into a slope and had special access trenches, were burned out by the troops. Planes from *1. Staffel der Luftwaffe Fliegergruppe 7* were deployed to provide support against the bunker positions, but they could not target the bunkers given that they were well camouflaged. Five 'bandits' were shot dead in the battle, including a lieutenant in a Russian uniform. According to his papers, he was a demolitions platoon leader. Judging by the traces of blood, the 'bandits' must have suffered significant losses. The *(lettische) Schutzmannschaft Bataillon 277* suffered one soldier slightly wounded.

The weather on 17 March was the same as the day before. Based on Operation Runo's orders, a platoon-strong patrol was deployed indefinitely to cover the Lissno-Osveya road. Patrols were sent out by *(lettische) Schutzmannschaft Bataillon 278* in the early morning hours of 17 March, which came across a gang about 4km west of Lissno. The strength of the band could not be determined. A 'bandit leader' was shot dead by the patrol. He carried on him a Russian identity card with inscriptions and a personal diary. Both items were handed over to the *Sicherheitsdienst.* The *SS und Polizei Kompanie* and the *1. Kompanie* of *(lettische) Schutzmannschaft Bataillon 278* were deployed on 17 March in order to comb the forest area between Lissno and Lake Beloye. No contact with the enemy was reported. Combat training was ordered for the remaining battalions. During the day, the Melovidy base was repeatedly attacked by 'bandits' with mortars and automatic weapons. One man was slightly wounded. The *3. Kompanie* of *(lettische) Schutzmannschaft Bataillon 277* returned fire and shot at some 'bandits' emerging from the forest in southern Melovidy. Two non-commissioned officers were slightly wounded in this firefight. 'Bandits' thereupon retreated into the forest. Losses among the 'bandits' could not be determined. On the night of 16/17 March, *(lettische) Schutzmannschaft Bataillon 278* took up ambush positions in the forest on the Lissno-Selikoye Selo road, as well as north and west of Lake Beloye. A man who stumbled into the ambush was shot while trying to escape.

18 March: sunny with frost in the evening. In the midday hours, a group crossing Lake Beloye from the forest area north-east of Lissno, was shot at by rifle fire. Two companies of *(lettische) Schutzmannschaft Bataillon 278* were immediately dispatched for reconnaissance and a combing out of the area. Due to the repeated shelling of Melovidy during the course of 18 March, two men were killed from *(lettische) Schutzmannschaft Bataillon 276.* Two companies from this battalion were used to comb the forest strip between Avlasovka and Milovidy, along the eastern bank of the Svolna River. Only light contact with the enemy was encountered. The gang that was encountered quickly withdrew. In the forest area east of Milovidy, wooden shacks that served as shelter for the 'bandits' were burned down. The combing operation continued to Borlevo. The rest of Borlevo was likewise burned down. In addition, underground bunkers fitted with embrasures were destroyed. Two additional companies of *(lettische) Schutzmannschaft Bataillon 276* were used to comb the forest area east of Milovidy. A company from *(lettische) Schutzmannschaft Bataillon 277* was deployed south of Milovidy to combat any gangs there. Two companies of *(lettische) Schutzmannschaft Bataillon 278* combed the forest area north-east of Lissno. A platoon from *(lettische) Schutzmannschaft Bataillon 278,* which was sent to the forest area east of Lake Lissno for reconnaissance, observed that a train from the Isubriza area was shot at by three 'bandits'. The platoon returned fire and one 'bandit' was killed. The other two 'bandits' escaped towards Takuny. The rest of the town of Isubriza was burned down. The *(lettische) Schutzmannschaft Bataillon 279* was used for subsequent combing operations of the Ladigovo-Ardavskaya area. *Oberleutnant der Schutzpolizei* Turks was able to defuse and remove two anti-tank mines and one anti-personnel mine which were found. Furthermore, unexploded bombs in Lissno, Melnitsy and Kobylnitsa were rendered harmless. On 18 March a man was shot while trying to escape. Three soldiers from *(lettische) Schutzmannschaft Bataillon 277* were slightly wounded. On 19 March there was sunshine throughout the day, but after frost in the evening. In the morning hours of 19 March there was a brief clash between 'bandit' scouts and the advanced posts of *(lettische) Schutzmannschaft Bataillon 276*. The 'bandits' withdrew in a north-easterly direction. Losses for *(lettische) Schutzmannschaft Bataillon 276* included two men slightly wounded. No enemy losses could be determined. As far as the battalion was concerned, it was not used for security purposes given that at the time, combat training was being conducted.

On 20 March the forest area in the region of Makuty was once again combed out by a company from *(lettische) Schutzmannschaft Bataillon 279*. A 'bandit' camp was found and disrupted. No further contact was made with the enemy that day. In the early hours of 20 March, a mortar attack took place on Melnitsy. The return fire was carried out by *(lettische) Schutzmannschaft Bataillon 279*, which responded with heavy machine-gun fire which eventually silenced the mortar fire. A company from *(lettische) Schutzmannschaft Bataillon 278* was dispatched from Lissno to assist. Those battalion forces not deployed, continued combat training.

On 21 March the day was sunny but ended with night frost. Regrouping and deployment was done in accordance with Operational Order No. 17 of 20 March 1943, Ia No. 76/43 (appendix page 48). Because of the 'bandits' were aware of their location, *(lettische) Schutzmannschaft Bataillon 276* and one company from *(lettische) Schutzmannschaft Bataillon 277* were ordered to take up new lodgings. Milovidy was once again burned down and the bridge over the Svolna River was destroyed. Otherwise, no other incidents occurred. For the remaining battalions, combat training was carried out.

Like the previous days, the weather on 22 March was sunny all day, but the night brought on a frost. The detachments from the battalion employed against the enemy was carried out without any particular hindrance. The villages of Gnil'tsy, Dobroplesy, Chernoki, Reuty, Lissno, and Saluchye were burned down after the troops abandoned them. Furthermore, the Svolna River Bridge near Lissno was destroyed. Strong explosions occurred repeatedly when houses are burned down, implying that munitions had been hidden in the homes. After moving to Denisenki, *(lettische) Schutzmannschaft Bataillon 277* received machine-pistol and mortar fire from the forest north of the town. The enemy fire was immediately returned. The battalion then combed the forest, but no enemy losses could be determined. The *4. Kompanie* of *(lettische) Schutzmannschaft Bataillon 277* led the search. A platoon from the *1. Kompanie* of *(litauisch) Schutzmannschaft Bataillon 2*, that was escorting a German Army telephone construction unit, walked over a mine in the morning hours, about 2km from the Velikoye Selo road junction. One man was killed, two lightly wounded and two seriously wounded. The weather on 23 March was the same as in the previous days. The battalion performed a 'cleansing' operation of the area east of the Latvian border, between Lake Osveya and Lake Lissno, to the south of the Rozenov–Sebesh railway line.

23 March: sunny with frost in the evening. According to Operational Order No. 18 of March 20, Ia No. 77/43 (appendix page 50). The battalion and other units have achieved the ordered daily objective. The *(lettische) Schutzmannschaft Bataillon 279* encountered light enemy resistance along the Beresviza River. Eight fleeing 'bandits' were shot dead, but there was no further contact with the enemy. The village of Lipnyagi and eleven forest camps were burned down. Combing the forests was difficult and time-consuming due to deep snow, dense undergrowth and stumpy terrain. There were newly-dug 'bandit' trenches dug nearby village of Bondari. The daily goals for today were achieved.

24 March: Sunny during the day, with frost at night. The battalions launched the attack at the ordered time. No contact with the enemy occurred. On the Osveya–Sebesh road, three destroyed bridges were repaired by the assigned *Technische Nothilfe* bridge construction team. The daily territorial goal for all units was achieved.

25 March: The battalions launched the attack as ordered and achieved the daily territorial objectives. No contact with the enemy was made.

26 March: continued Sunny weather during the day with frost at night. No incidents were reported. The SS *und Polizei Kompanie z.b.V.* and *Gendarmerie Zug Nr. 10 (motorisiert)* was attached to *II. Bataillon* / SS *Polizei Regiment 9.*

27 March: No incidents were reported. *(lettische) Schutzmannschaft Bataillon 282* was placed under the control of the *kampfgruppe*.[28]

28 March: A new staging area was chosen according to Operational Order No. 19 of 26 March 1943, Ia 28/43 (appendix page 56). The chosen area was reached by the battalions. No contact with the enemy occurred.

On 29 March the weather was overcast and cloudy. Cleansing operation in the area bounded by the Latvian border in the west, the Rosenov–Sebesh road in the south, the Issa River line to Kopina and then the Kopina–Mosuli road in the east, with the northern region bordering the Ustinova–Koslovo–Yasvintsy areas. This procedure was planned according to Operational Order No. 20 of 26 March 1943, Ia No. 83/43 (appendix page 59). The battalion launched the attack at the time that was ordered. However, no contact with the enemy was made. The town of Lubievo, which was known as a 'bandit base', was burned down. According to statements by the residents, there were still around fifty 'bandits' in Blonty on 29 March who had then moved north. The daily territorial goals were achieved despite the most difficult terrain conditions.

On the night of 29/30 March 1943, 'bandits' tried several times to get through the security posts, employing machine-pistol fire. The enemy fire was silenced by the sentries of *(lettische) Schutzmannschaft Bataillon 279*. One Latvian medical non-commissioned officer was seriously wounded by machine-gun fire from the Armenian Battalion (*Wehrmacht*), which was deployed to cordon off the right group border, when *(lettische) Schutzmannschaft Bataillon 279* was deployed in Zerovka. The battalion's combat strip north of Lyukhova was partially occupied by the *Wehrmacht*. Likewise, the towns of Lyukhova and Glinishchi were also occupied. In the area in front of Lyukhova, the men of *(lettische) Schutzmannschaft Bataillon 279* were fired upon, despite sending up numerous recognition flares and shouting in German. *Wehrmacht* guards continued to fire on the men of the battalion, so that further combing operations were no longer possible. The *3. Kompanie* of *(lettische) Schutzmannschaft Bataillon 279* had two deaths on account of this friendly-fire incident. The liaison officer reported the incident to the *Wehrmacht* general controlling the army cordon. During the further combing out operations, the combat strip in question was also occupied by *(lettische) Schutzmannschaft Bataillon 279* even though it received sustained heavy mortar fire. The mortar fire was suppressed by the Armenian cordon forces.[29]

31 March: rain all day. SS *und Polizei Kampfgruppe Knecht* returned to Latvia and was billeted in the towns of Jaski, Lineja, Jarkuti, Plaudise, Kalvi and Dolseji. 1 April: sunny and windy at times. The battalions were assigned to new bases on the Latvian border.

2 April 1943: occasional sunshine interspersed with rain. Processing of the battlegroup staff. A 'liquidation commando' of the group remained in Ludsen (Ludsens) until 6 April 1943.

This anti-partisan operation which lasted about a month is a perfect example of the tactics of warfare and terror, and the coded terminology which the Nazis employed in going after the guerrillas and the Jewish population. Throughout this detailed report, one sees the terms 'bandit(s)', 'bandit helper(s)', 'bandit camp(s)', 'suspicious person(s)', etc. The area of operations encompassed eastern Latvia, as well as the north-eastern tip of Poland that today is part of Belarus, as well as the northern Belarusian-Russian border region. The operation also highlighted the close relationship that existed throughout the war, between the police, SS, *Sicherheitsdienst* and the locally-raised volunteer battalions. The burning of towns and villages and the expropriation of livestock, grain and other foodstuffs, was typical of the wanton destruction and theft that the people living in these occupied areas endured at the hands of the Nazis.

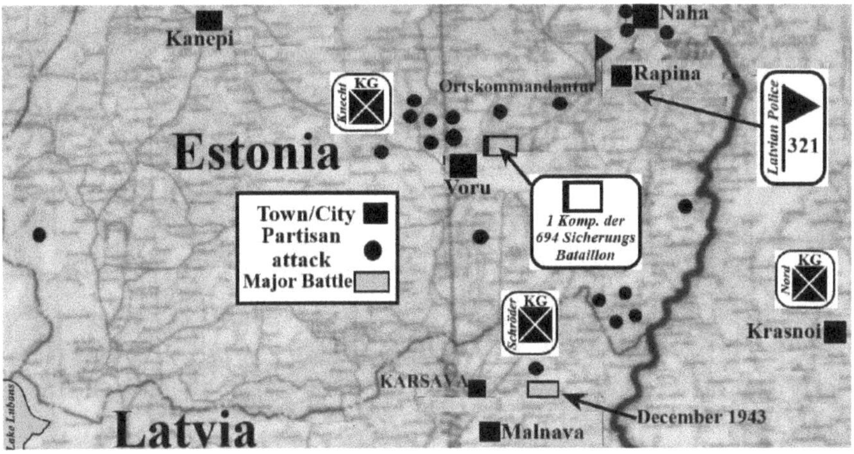


Figure 6. Location of *Kampfgruppe Knecht* in early December 1943. This SS and police battlegroup would continue to operate in the Baltic States as well as the border regions of north-eastern Poland, Belarus and north Russia.

The major partisan attacks for 1943 in the region of Army Group North centered on four regions: the Pskov region, Novgorod region, along the Estonian border, and along the Latvian border region. The forested areas around Ostrov, Dedovichi, and Strugi Krasnye (Pskov Oblast) were targeted. In particular, the railway line. The principal guerrilla unit was the 3rd Leningrad Partisan Brigade, which blew up trains and rail bridges. All of this caused delays in troop and ammunition deliveries. The Wehrmacht was forced to deploy security battalions for defense of that rear-area. In the area of Novgorod (especially in the Võru and Petseri regions), the partisans concentrated their attacks south of Lake Ilmen, around Staraya Russa and Parfino. The targets were small German outposts and supply convoys. In Estonia, the guerrillas concentrated in the southeastern region of the country. The guerrillas targeted communication lines, bridges and collaborators. In Latvia the partisans concentrated on the railway corridor between Daugavpils and Rēzekne. German positions near Nevel and Pskov were also targeted.

Chapter 3

# PARTISAN AND ANTI-PARTISAN ACTIVITY IN THE REGION OF ARMY GROUP NORTH

## The *Wehrmacht Befehlshaber Ostland* command

The *Wehrmacht Befehlshaber Ostland* was in overall charge of all military formations (except for the SS and police) withing the region designated as the *Ostland.* The region of the *Ostland* included the Baltic States, that is, the former independent states of Latvia, Estonia, Lithuania and the Belarusian Soviet Socialist Republic (also referred to as White Russia).[1] The command therefore was the one that allotted army units for operations in that region that mostly comprised the Baltic states of Lithuania, Latvia and Estonia. The German officers who served as the commanding officer were as follows:

*General der Kavallerie* Walter Brämer: 1 June 1943 to 30 April 1944.
*General der Panzertruppen* Franz Werner Kempf: 1 May to 31 August 1944.
*General der Infantry* Anton Grasser:[2] 1–25 September 1944.

## Partisan war in the Baltic States, 1943

Beginning in autumn 1942 the tempo of German anti-partisan drives began to increase. By the spring of 1943 there were more than 350,000 Axis troops actively involved in fighting the guerrillas behind the lines along the entire Eastern Front. These forces not only included German as well as indigenous troops, but Hungarian, Romanian and Slovakian units. The following operations were considered major affairs and took place in the region of *Heeresgruppe Nord* in the winter of 1942–3 and the spring of 1943.

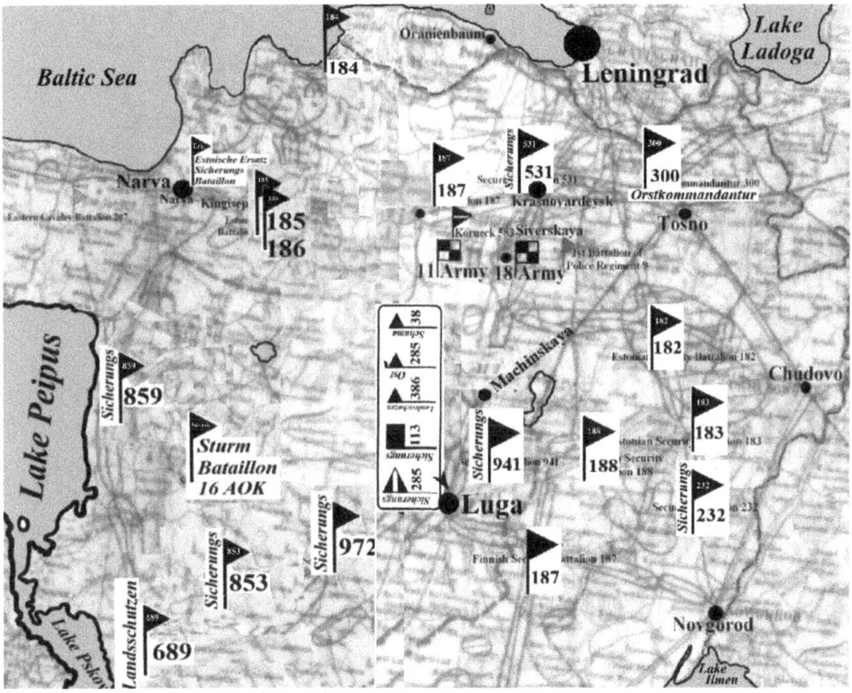


Figure 7. German and Baltic anti-partisan forces in the rear of Army Group North, 1–12 September 1942.

### *Unternehmen Zeithen: 1 February–19 March 1943*

This operation was a local anti-partisan drive that was launched in the region of Demyansk by elements of *123. Infanterie Division.*[3] The operation was to coincide with the evacuation by the Germans of Demyansk. By 1 March 1943, the Russians had taken the town. Forces from the local *Feldkommandantur* were also employed (about two battalions). The result netted thirty-two partisans killed and four were captured. The captured guerrillas were then shot after interrogation. During this month (January 1943), *123. Infanterie Division* was under the control of *II. Armeekorps.*

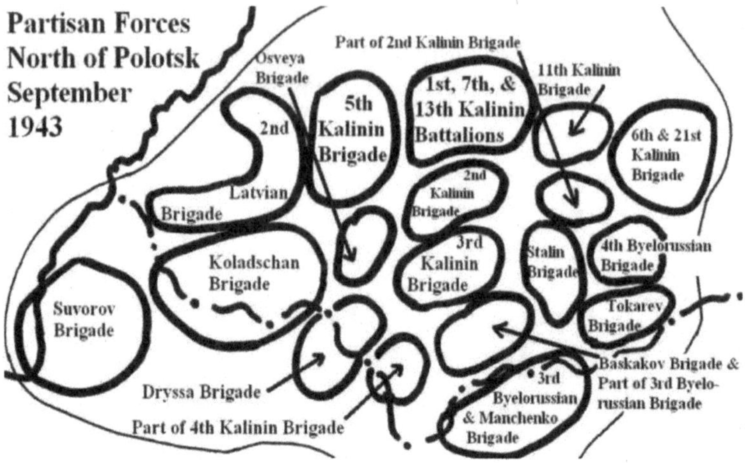


Figure 8. Partisan brigades north of the Polotsk region, September 1943.

### *Unternehmen Günther: 7 February–7 July 1943*

This operation was centred in the Logoisk–Rudnia region including the Rudnya and Manili woods.[4] The region was an area north-east of Minsk including Logoisk and Borisov.[5] There were several units which were employed in this drive. One was *Regiment von der Goltz: Grenadier Regiment 2* of *11. Infanterie Division*.[6] This was an Army regiment led by *Oberst* Freiherr von der Goltz.[7] The *11. Infanterie Division* at this time was located in the Volkov front region by Lake Ladoga and under *XXVI. Armeekorps* of *18. Armee*.[8] Other units which took part in the operation included *SS-Sonder-Bataillon-Dirlewanger*, and *SS-Regiment Griep*, aka *SS-Polizeiregiment 2* under *Oberstleutnant der Schutzpolizei* Hans Griep.[9] Another formation included in this drive was *Polizei-Panzer-Kompanie 1*.[10] The operation was quickly concluded but no reports have been uncovered listing partisan, civilian, or German losses. *Unternehmen Günther* was considered a minor operation that netted negligible results.

### *Unternehmen Heinrich: 25 October–15 November 1943*

On 6 October 1943, the Red Army broke through the German lines in and around Nevel. The partisans who had been operating behind Nevel and north of Polotsk in the Rossono forest region were causing severe supply and reinforcement problems to the German *23. Infanterie-Division* at Nevel and other units trying to hold back the Soviet advance.[11] This area was referred to as the Rossono Partisan Republic because it had been dominated by the guerrillas for so long. On 14 October Adolf Hitler personally instructed *SS-Obergruppenführer* Erich von dem Bach-Zelewski to stage an operation against the Rossono partisans in order to relieve the pressure behind the lines.[12] Von dem Bach complied and launched a two-pronged attack with two division-sized formations stationed in a north-south direction which eventually numbered about 20–21 battalions of police, Latvian volunteers and Army security troops. One source states that 29 battalions were employed:[13]

***SS-Polizei Kampfgruppe von Gottberg***[14]
*SS-Polizeiregiment 2*
*Polizei-Panzer-Kompanie 1*
*SS-Polizeiregiment 13* (minus *II. Bataillon* which remained in Smolensk during the action)[15]
*Polizei-Panzer-Kompanie 4*
*SS-Polizeiregiment 24* (minus *III. Bataillon*)
*Polizei-Panzer-Kompanie 9*
*Polizei-Panzer-Kompanie 12*
***SS-Polizei-Kampfgruppe Jeckeln***[16]
*Sicherungs-Regiment 113*
- *I. Bataillon* (ex-*Sicherungs-Bataillon 853*)
- *II. Bataillon* (ex-*Sicherungs-Bataillon 941*)
- *III. Bataillon* (ex-*Sicherungs-Bataillon 972*)
- *III. Bataillon der SS-Polizeiregiment 9*

*Sicherungs-Regiment 773*
- *Sicherungs-Bataillon 591*
- *Landesschützen-Bataillon 597*
- *Sicherungs-Bataillon 663*
- *(lettische) Schutzmannschaft-Bataillon 319*

*Polizeiregiment 1 Riga (lettische)* [17] (as part of the Latvian SS Brigade)
- *I. Bataillon* (ex-*lettische Schutzmannschaft Bataillon 276*)
- *II. Bataillon* (ex-*lettische Schutzmannschaft Bataillon 277*)
- *III. Bataillon* (ex-*lettische Schutzmannschaft Bataillon 278*)
- *IV. Bataillon* (ex-*lettische Schutzmannschaft Bataillon 312*)

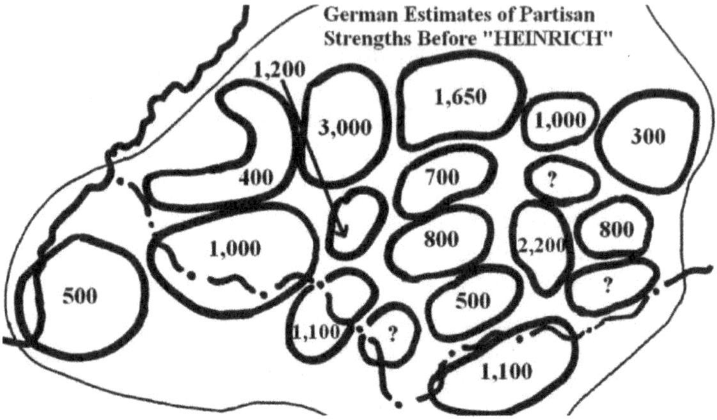


Figure 9. Partisan strengths north of Polotsk, November 1943.

The attack was scheduled for 25 October but did not begin in earnest until 1 November, and was to run until the middle of the month. The newly re-established *Polizei-Panzer-Kompanie 3,* which arrived in the region of *Heeresgruppe Nord* in early November, was attached to *SS-Polizeiregiment 16* but did not join the *Jeckeln* battlegroup until after the conclusion of *Heinrich.*[18] Before the operation was completed German reversals in front of Nevel required that von Gottberg's and Jeckeln's *kampfgruppen* be employed as a screen behind the lines connecting *Heeresgruppe Nord* and *Heeresgruppe Mitte.*[19] A serious breach in the direction of Dvinsk was thus averted by aggressive action on the part of both SS *kampfgruppen.*[20] So great was the loss of these anti-partisan troops that *Heeresgruppe Mitte* advised the OKH that it could no longer mount any anti-partisan operations until these two SS *kampfgruppen*were withdrawn from front-line service.[21] In early December 1943 the military situation in the region of Nevel forced the Germans to commit Jeckeln's anti-partisan force to front-line fighting. His combat group was still in the front lines in March 1944. In this month, it was arrayed midway between Opochka and Polotsk (north to south). As the military situation at the front continued to deteriorate, more and more SS, police, and locally-raised auxiliary units would be thrown into front-line fighting. These forces would prove mostly incapable of standing up to the rigours of combating regular Russian troops. As a result, they would suffer unusually high casualty rates.

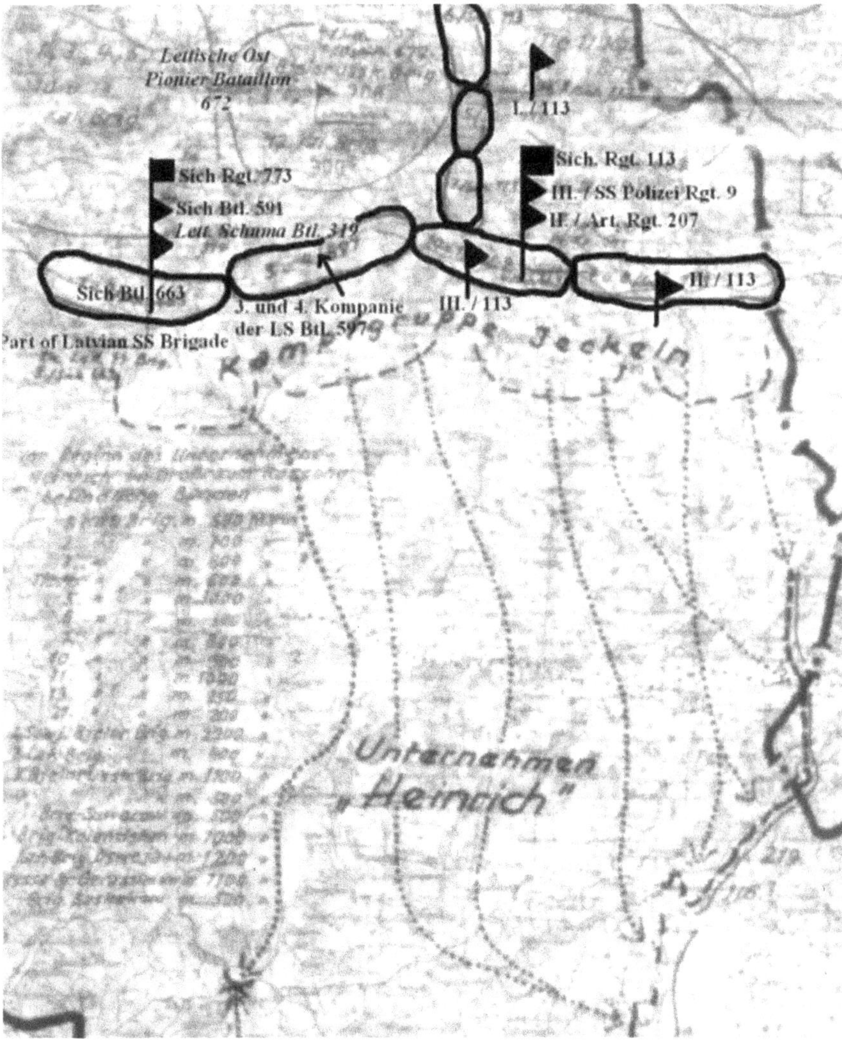


Figure 10. The northern wing of *Unternehmen Heinrich*.

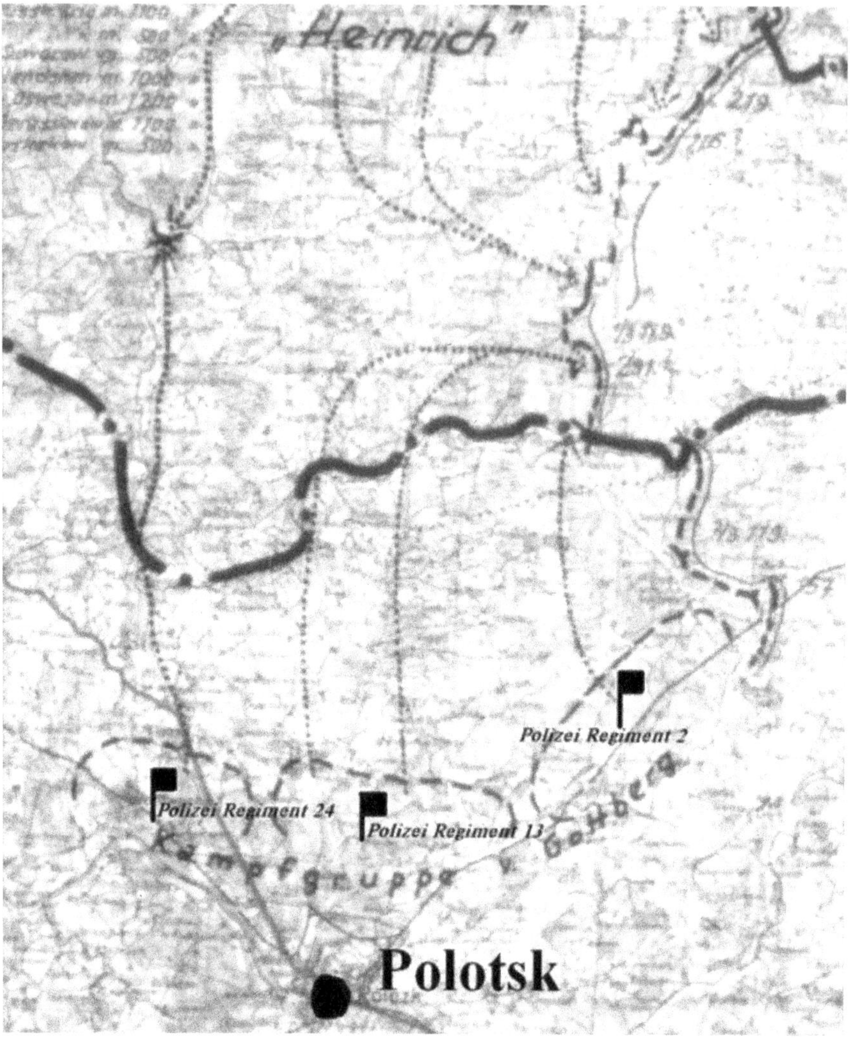


Figure 11. The southern wing of *Unternehmen Heinrich*.

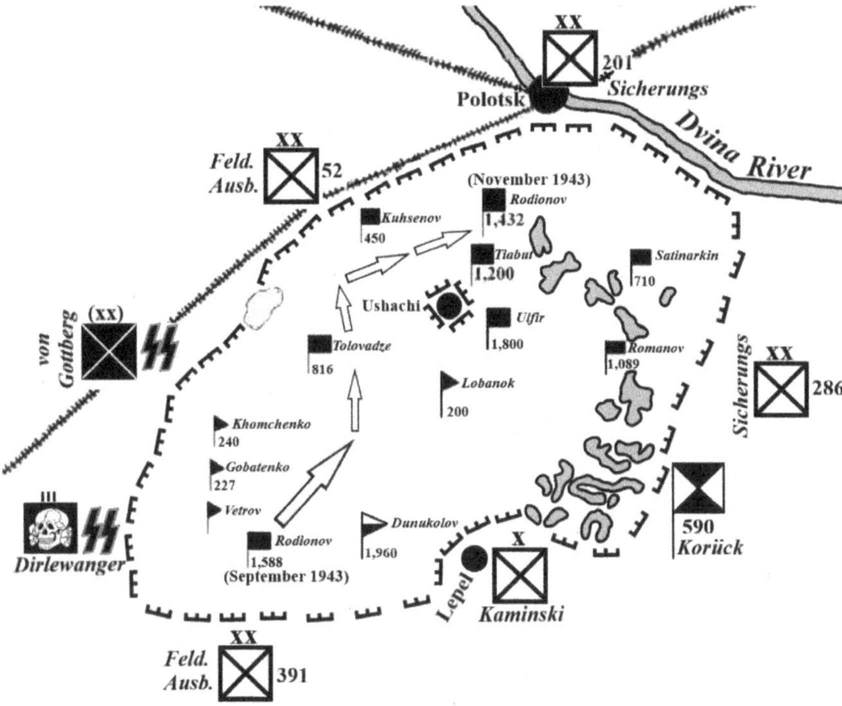


Figure 12. Partisan strengths and location of partisan formations in the region of the Polotsk Lowlands, November 1943.

German front-line forces were indeed short-handed all along the Eastern Front. This was proven by an OKW (Armed Forces High Command) war diary entry dated 7 August 1943. In it, the narrator stated that a request was made to transfer the 18th and 23rd Hungarian Divisions for a planned anti-partisan drive behind the lines in and around Velikiyeye Luki.[22] At this time, the 18th Hungarian Reserve Division was under the *Wehrmacht Befehlshaber Ukraine* while the 24th Hungarian Reserve Division was already a part of *Befehlshaber Heeresgruppe Mitte*.[23] As for the partisans, they had avoided giving battle during the operation and once the SS and police units turned east to face the Red Army, they proceeded to re-establish their authority over the region.

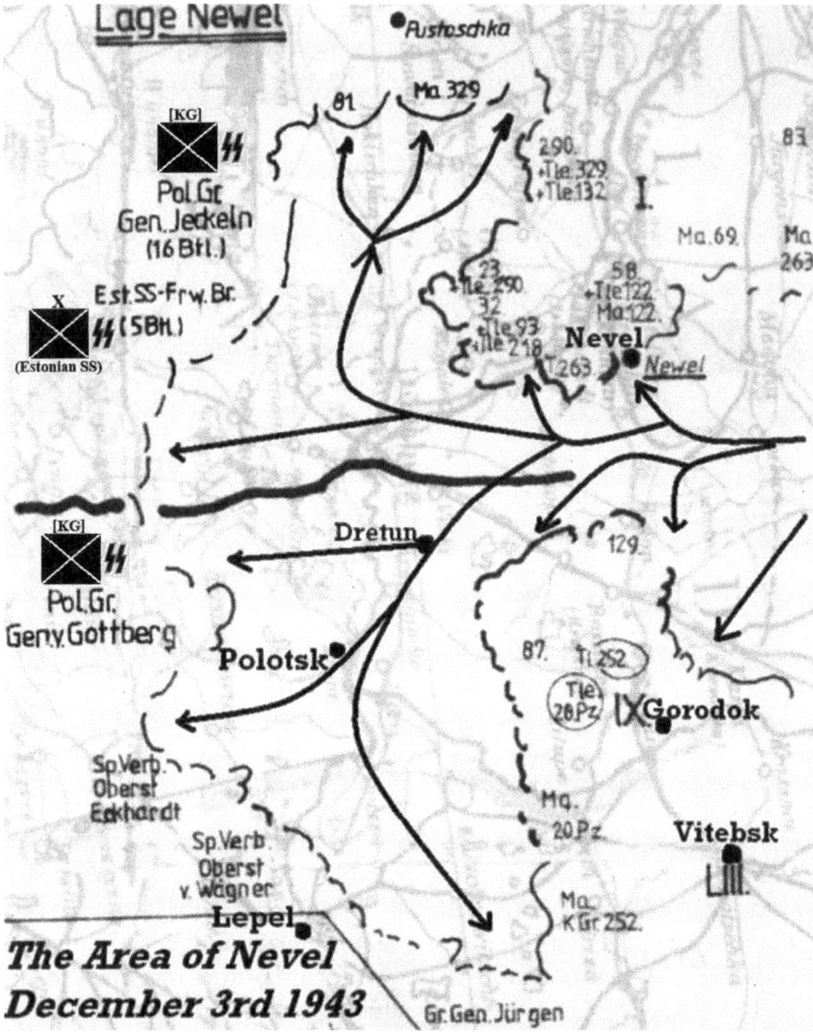


Figure 13. Beginning in November 1943, Russian Army successes at the front required the employment of SS and police forces in the front lines. They were employed in the region bordering Army Group North and Army Group Centre

The Red Army vanguard temporarily advanced into the Polotsk Lowlands before the region was retaken by the Germans and the front was stabilised in January 1944. The northern prong of the Soviet attack that had swung around the Nevel positions included three powerful Soviet armies: 6th Guards Army, 3rd Shock Army and 10th Guards Army.[24] The situation had developed as follows:

On November 26, 1943 the Red Army took Sselitsche and widened the breach between Army Group North and South. The gap was now 20km wide and getting bigger. Both army groups sent combat groups to try and plug the gap. This only managed to slow down the enemy drive. On December 9, 1943 a light frost came down and covered the cold countryside. The Soviets struck four days later. Their attack resumed on that day, this time aiming the brunt of their effort specifically against units of *3. Panzermee.*[25]

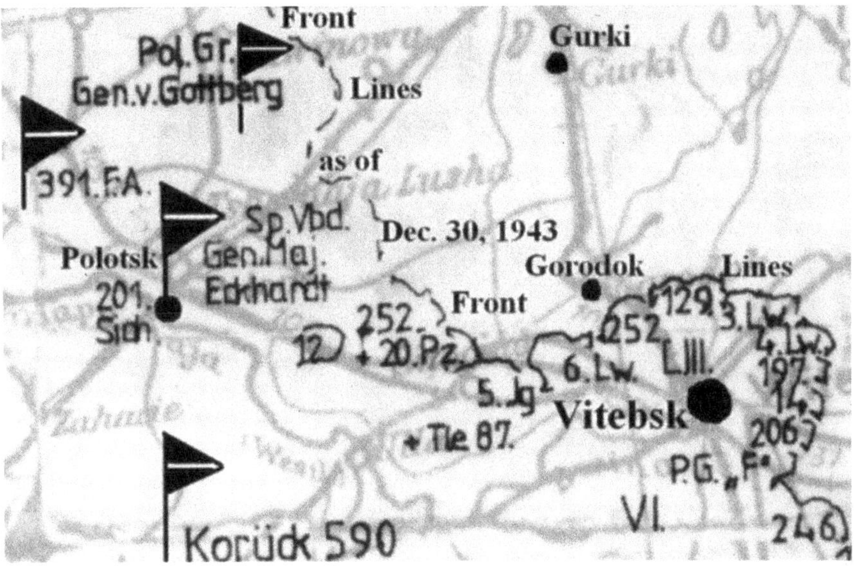


Figure 14. *SS-Kampfgruppe von Gottberg* fighting in the front lines, December 1943.

The employment of emergency police, SS and indigenous volunteer units in the front lines became a permanent necessity by the winter of 1943–4. During those winter months, *SS-Kampfgruppe Jeckeln* was diverted from rear area anti-partisan operations and placed under *10. Armeekorps,* which had recently taken a beating from the Russians. Also attached to *X. Armeekorps* were *(lettische) Polizeiregiment 1* and *(lettische) Polizeiregiment 2* (1st and 2nd Latvian Police Regiment). The importance of *X. Armeekorps* was that it was the lynchpin connecting *Heeresgruppe Nord* with *Heeresgruppe Mitte.* That rear-area forces, only suitable for fighting irregular forces, were deployed on the front lines, shows the level of desperation on the part of the German command, to mitigate the desperate military situation. To these SS/police units, the Germans brought up whatever additional forces which they possessed.

These troops included *SS-Kampfgruppe Jeckeln* and SS *Kampfgruppe von Gottberg*. In December *SS-Kampfgruppe Jeckeln* was reinforced by the arrival of *Polizeiregiment 26*.[26] It was not until the end of December 1943 that the front lines between *Heeresgruppe Nord* and *Heeresgruppe Mitte* were reconnected and the Polotsk region was once again stabilised.

Chapter 4

# THE CENTRAL SECTOR

## Lost opportunities: the Russian National People's Army

As 1943 came into sharp focus and 1942 became a mere shadow in the rear-view mirror of history, the realisation that the war in the East was headed towards disaster, like a runaway freight train, weighed heavily on the minds of many German commanders. Although the first year of the campaign had brought amazing successes, the second year had ended in unmitigated disaster. Behind the lines the news was no better. What had been scattered remnants of the Red Army behind the lines in 1941 had coalesced into a hard-core group of guerrilla formations that by the autumn of 1942 had begun to seriously threaten many regions of the German rear areas on the Eastern Front. Still, the year 1942 had also brought promise that the people of the USSR could still be harnessed and employed to help destroy the communist government in Moscow. On the initiative of several enlightened German officers, several experimental formations had been established in 1942 that, it was hoped, would eventually form the nucleus of a large anti-communist army that would help defeat Stalin and Stalinism. Colonel Rudolf Christoph Freiherr von Gersdorff, an intelligence officer for *Heeresgruppe Mitte*, had been a principal party in the establishment in April 1942 of the so-called *Russkaya natsional'naya narodnaya armiya* (RNNA, Russian National People's Army). The unit was the brainchild of the German Armed Forces intelligence service – the *Abwehr*. It was created around a core of White Russian émigrés that were stationed in the town of Osintorf, about 35km north of Orsha in Belarus. Members included Sergei N. Ivanov, Igor K. Sakharov, Konstantin G. Kromiadi, Count Grigoriy von Lamsdorf, and Count Sergey von der Pahlen. On 1 September 1942, Colonel Vladimir Boyarsky was appointed head of the RNNA.

Starting out with only a company of former Red Army soldiers who had been captured by the German Army and placed in local prisoner of war transit camps, the formation quickly grew to numerous battalions and proved to be quite effective. The majority of its Russian officers, as well as the German liaison officers, principally Colonel Gersdorff, wished to commit the unit as a whole against the Red Army on the front lines. However, 1942 was a time where Adolf Hitler was still adamant about refusing any Russian formation larger than battalion size to take to the field. His prejudice against the Slavic people prevented him from seizing on an opportunity to destroy the communist regime from within by using the very Soviet people to do so. Nevertheless, the battalions of what was now being unofficially referred to as the *Graukopf Brigade* (Grayhead Brigade – named after its Russian commander) proved to be effective in battle. Throughout most of 1942 the battalions proved to be cohesive with excellent morale. The first battalion to be readied and detached from the *Graukopf Brigade* was *Ost Kampf Bataillon Dnieper* which was deployed as an independent unit in April 1942. It was employed behind the Soviet lines during *Unternehmen Hannover* (Operation Hannover) in May–June 1942. The next battalion to be deployed was *Ost Kampf Bataillon Beresina* in June 1942.[1] The third, fourth, and fifth battalions in the brigade were all formed in July 1942. These were *Ost Kampf Bataillon Duna, Ost Kampf Bataillon Pripjet* (Pripet), and *Ost Kampf Bataillon Wolga* (Volga). The brigade reached a strength of some 3,000 men, complete with its own staff and intelligence groups.[2] Equipment included three Russian BA-64 armoured scout cars, one BA-6 heavy armoured car, dozens of mortars, sixty-five Degtyaryov DP 28 light machine guns, twenty-one Maxim heavy machine guns, twelve 45mm anti-tank guns and four Soviet 76mm M 1927 artillery pieces.

Although the brigade seemed promising, Hitler absolutely refused to allow the employment of its battalions together as a brigade. As the volunteers began to realise that the Germans had no intention of creating a post-war Russian state, morale began to wane. The unit began to experience problems beginning in August 1942 when nearly 200 members of the brigade deserted to the partisans.[3] During a discussion over the fate of the formation in December 1942, Field Marshal von Kluge, following Hitler's obvious sentiments, basically stunted the unit's further growth and reliability when he announced that he intended to split up the *Graukopf Brigade* and send its battalions to serve under separate German commands. To Colonel Freiherr von Gersdorff, this decision by von Kluge was narrow-minded and counter-productive. Gersdorff knew that Colonel Vladimir Boyarsky's willingness to support the Germans was based on anti-communist, nationalist ideology. Boyarsky was willing to betray Stalin and communism, but only if the Germans were willing to guarantee a Russian state that was not a puppet of the Germans.

Again, we see the divide that existed within the German camp regarding what to do with the Eastern peoples and Eastern volunteers. With its officers and most of its volunteers demoralised, the *Graukopf Verband* was eventually dissolved and its battalions were renamed and used singly behind the German lines. Desertions soon followed and only increased. Hitler had never wanted to recruit soldiers from the East – considering the recruitment of these *untermenschen* (subhumans as he saw them) as anathema to Nazi ideology. However, even as early as 1941 there existed in the German command those who understood that the way to topple the Soviet regime was from within. Unfortunately for the German war effort, there was no unanimity of thought regarding how to approach the matter of recruitment of Eastern volunteers. In the beginning, the German officers who wished to recruit Eastern volunteers had to do so clandestinely. Only as the war turned against the Germans did practicality take over and ideology was eventually tossed aside. However, by then the opportunity to employ large numbers of Soviet citizens in large-scale formations and actually have willing volunteers to man them had passed. Once the volunteers (including the émigré elements) in the *Graukopf Brigade* realised that the Germans had no intention of allowing a Russian state to exist after a Nazi victory, morale quickly collapsed. The battalions were stripped of the leadership that had hoped for the establishment of an independent Russian state and restructured. In spite of this, desertions mounted and several mutinies within the battalions occurred. Throughout its existence the men wore their Russian Army uniforms. Their flag was the Russian white-blue-red Tsarist tricolour. After the unit was disbanded, the soldiers were given *Wehrmacht* uniforms.

## Lost opportunities: The 1st Russian National SS Brigade

As stated in my previous work on this topic, in 1942 the German *Sicherheitsdienst* (SD, or SS Security Service), had not yet absorbed the *Abwehr*.[4] The SS Security Service was therefore still in direct competition with the *Abwehr* to become Nazi Germany's chief intelligence gathering service. Copying the actions of Admiral Wilhelm Canaris, the SD also moved to create their own experimental Russian unit, for planned operations behind the Soviet lines. This decision was taken purely for competitive reasons, given that Walter Schellenberg, who headed *Amt VI* (Department 6) of the *Reichssicherheitshauptamt* (RSHA) was attempting to outdo his equivalent in the *Abwehr*. The formation was variously named, but most often referred to as the *SS-Druzhina Verbände*. The unit had its early beginnings in February 1942 when a battalion-sized formation was organised near Smolensk but stationed initially in Nevel. In 1942, it would operate between Polotsk, Lepel and Bogomil (also spelled Begomyl). At the time of its creation, the *Abwehr*'s rival *Graukopf Brigade* had a strength of two battalions.

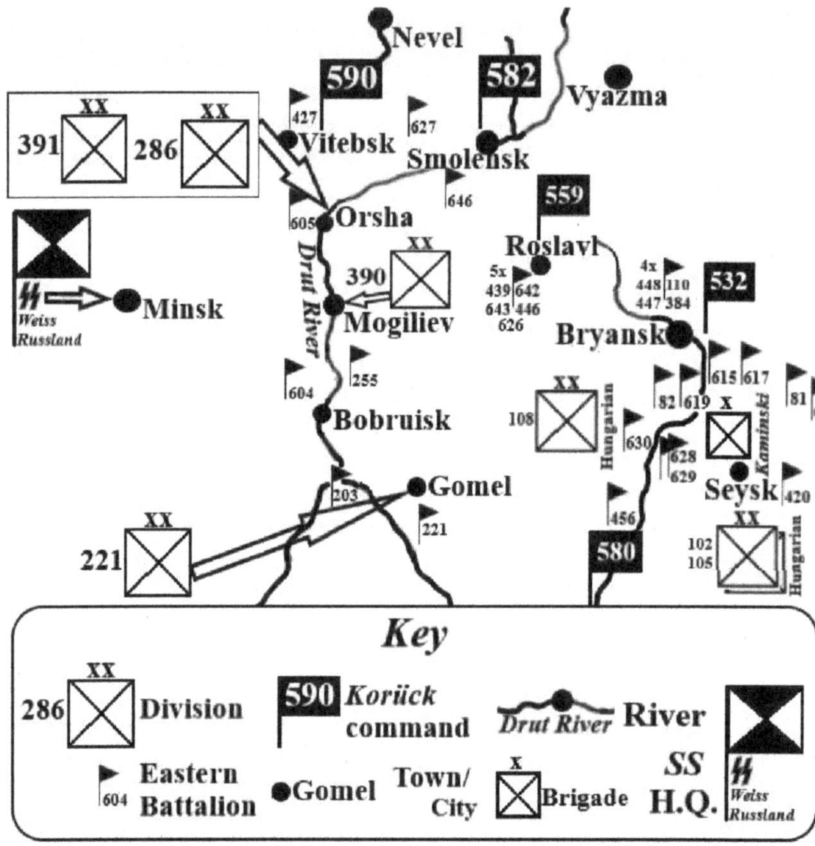


Figure 15. Anti-partisan forces in eastern Belarus and western central Russia, November 1943.

A month later, in March the SS *Druzhina* formation was transferred to Glebokie, where it remained through September 1942. It was there that it was attached to the *Befehlshaber der rückwärtigen Heeresgruppe Mitte*.[5] From Glebokie it launched successful anti-partisan operations. By April of that same year, the unit was up to a strength of four battalions.

In March 1943 its listed TO&E strength was 150 officers, 1,050 men, 60 artillery pieces, 95 machine guns, 18 mortars and 200 submachine guns.[6] By July it had reached a force of 3,000 men. This formation would prove to be the most effective indigenous anti-partisan unit in the German arsenal in Belarus until it would defect to the partisans on 13 August 1943.[7]

## Volunteers nevertheless

In spite of the absurd German policies regarding the Eastern peoples encountered in the Soviet Union, there were men who were still willing to serve on *an deutscher Seite* (on the German side). A roster of volunteer units for the *Ostheer*, dated March 1943, lists a significant number of units:[8]

***Heeresgruppe A***
*Platov Kosaken Regiment*
*Kuban Kosaken Regiment*
*1. und 2. Kosaken Kompanien der 97. Jäger Division*
*Ostbataillon mit 73. Infanterie Division*
*Ostbataillon mit 198. Infanterie Division*
*4. und 5. (georgisch) Kompanien, mit Pionier-Bataillon 71*
*4. Ost Kompanie, mit Pionier-Bataillon 97*
*Ost Bau Kompanie, mit 198. Infanterie Division*
*Ost Bau Kompanie, mit 101. Jäger Division*
*15. Ost Telefonleitung Bau Zug*
*27. Ost Telefonleitung Bau Zug*
*43. Ost Telefonleitung Bau Zug*
*51. Ost Telefonleitung Bau Zug*
*55. Ost Telefonleitung Bau Zug*
*62. Ost Telefonleitung Bau Zug*
*63. Ost Telefonleitung Bau Zug*
*3. Kompanie / 125. Ost Leichte LKW-Säule*

***Heeresgruppe Süd***
*Kommandeur der Osttruppen z.b.V. 720*
*Kosaken Regiment von Jungschultz*
*III. Kosaken Bataillon der 57. Sicherungs Regiment*
*Kosaken Bataillon 213*
*Kosaken Bataillon 403*
*I. und II. Bataillone / 444. Kosaken Regiment*
*I. und II. Bataillone / 454. Kosaken Regiment*
*Don Kosaken Bataillon 557*
*Kuban Kosaken Bataillon 448*
*Kosaken Ausbildungs Bataillon*

*Kosaken Kompanie (motorisiert) der III. Panzerkorps*
*Kosaken-Kompanie 404*
*1. und 2. Kalmücken Schwadron 66*
*553. Kosaken Artillerie Batterie*
*551. Ost Bataillon*
*555. Ost Wach Bataillon*
*45. Ost Kompanie*
*1. und 2. Ost Kompanien / Jäger Regiment 75 (5. Jäger Division)*
*182. Ost Kompanie*
*323. Ost Kompanie*
*340. Ost Kompanie*
*377. Ost Kompanie*
*383. Ost Kompanie*
*387. Ost Kompanie*
*407. Ost Kompanie*
*455. Ost Kompanie*
*552. Ost Kompanie*
*1., 2. und 3. Ost Kompanien / Infanterie Regiment 556 (330. Infanterie Division)*[9]
*4. und 6. Ost Kompanien der Wach Bataillon 122*
*4. bis 10. Ost Kompanien der Wach Bataillon 552*
*4. und 5. Ost Kompanien der Wach Bataillon 571*
*4. bis 10. Ost Kompanien der Wach Bataillon 81*
*4. bis 7. Ost Kompanien der Feldgendarmerie Bataillon 581*
*Ostreiter Bataillon 580*
*9. Östliches Kavallerie Schwadron der Fahrrad Regiment 4*
*168. Ostreiter Schwadron*
*4. Ost Kompanie der Pionier Bataillon 370*
*Ost Munitions Bataillon 550*
*Östliches (ukrainisches) Versorgungs Bataillon 551*
*1.-3. Ostsäule, Versorgungs Bataillon 128 der 23. Panzer Division*

***Heeresgruppe Mitte***
*Kommandeur der Osttruppen z.b.V. 700*
*Kommandeur der Osttruppen z.b.V. 701*
*Kommandeur der Osttruppen z.b.V. 702*
*Kommandeur der Osttruppen z.b.V. 703*
*Kommandeur der Osttruppen z.b.V. 704*
*Kommandeur der Osttruppen z.b.V. 709*
*Kosaken Bataillon 443*
*Kosaken Battalion 600*
*Kosaken Battalion 622*
*Kosaken Battalion 623*
*Kosaken Battalion 624*
*Kosaken Battalion 625*

*Kosaken Battalion 631*
*1. und 2. Kosaken Kompanien der Infanterie Regiment 137*
*638. Kosaken Kompanie*
*Ost Bataillon 82*
*Ost Bataillon 84*
*Ost Bataillon 134*
*Ost Bataillon 229*
*Ost Bataillon 308*
*Ost Bataillon 339*
*Ost Bataillon 406*
*Ost Bataillon 412*
*Ost Bataillon 527*
*Ost Bataillon 439*
*Ost Bataillon 441*
*I. und II. Bataillone der Ost Regiment 447*
*Ost Bataillon 456*
*Ost Bataillon 601*
*Ost Bataillon 602*
*Ost Bataillon 603*
*Ost Bataillon 604*
*Ost Bataillon 605*
*Ost Bataillon 615*
*Ost Bataillon 616*
*Ost Bataillon 617*
*Ost Bataillon 618*
*Ost Bataillon 619*
*Ost Bataillon 620*
*Ost Bataillon 627*
*Ost Bataillon 628*
*Ost Bataillon 629*
*Ost Bataillon 630*
*Ost Bataillon 633*
*Ost Bataillon 634*
*Ost Bataillon 635*
*Ost Bataillon 636*
*Ost Bataillon 637*
*Ost Bataillon 642*
*Ost Bataillon 643*
*10. Ost Kompanie*
*25. Ost Kompanie*
*34. Ost Kompanie*
*1. und 2. Ost Kompanien*
*151. Ost Kompanie*
*178. Ost Kompanie*
*195. Ost Kompanie*

*1. Ost Kompanie der Infanterie Regiment 203*
*Ost Kompanie der Infanterie Regiment 205*
*1. Ost Kompanie der Infanterie Regiment 221*
*253. Ost Kompanie*
*260. Ost Kompanie*
*1. Ost Kompanie der Infanterie Regiment 263*
*1. Ost Kompanie der Infanterie Regiment 367*
*268. Ost Kompanie*
*331. Ost Kompanie*
*409. Ost Kompanie*
*420. Ost Kompanie*
*1. Ost Kompanie der Infanterie Regiment 446*
*453. Ost Kompanie*
*612. Ost Kompanie*
*613. Ost Kompanie*
*626. Ost Kompanie*
*4. Ost Kompanie der Sicherungs Bataillon 555*
*4. Ost Kompanie der Wach Bataillon 551*
*4. und 5. Ost Kompanien der Wach Bataillon 508*
*5. Ost Kompanie der Wach Battalion 722*
*5. Ost Kompanie der Landesschützen Bataillon 587*
*5. Ost Kompanie der Landesschützen Bataillon 675*
*5. Ost Kompanie der Landesschützen Bataillon 826*
*156. Ost Wach Kompanie*
*606. Ost Wach Kompanie*
*1.-3. Ost Kompanien der Wach Bataillon 607*
*608. Ost Wach Kompanie*
*609. Ost Wach Kompanie*
*1. und 3. Ost Kompanien der Wach Bataillon 610*
*611. Ost Kompanie*
*639. Ost Kompanie*
*640. Ost Kompanie*
*644. Ost Kompanie*
*645. Ost Kompanie*
*201. Ostreiter Schwadron*
*2. Ostreiter Schwadron der Wach Bataillon 203*
*2. Ostreiter Schwadron der Wach Bataillon 221*
*1. und 2. Ostreiter Schwadron der Wach Bataillon 447*
*Ost Artillerie Bataillon 621*
*582. Ost Batterie*
*614. Ost Batterie*
*Ost Bau Bataillon 134*
*1. und 2. Ost Signals-Bau Kompanien der Bau Bataillon 515*
*221. Ost Versorgungs Kompanie*
*286. Ost Versorgungs Kompanie*

*4. Ost Kompanie der Versorgungs Bataillon 622*
*4. Ost Kompanie der Versorgungs Bataillon 687*
*4. Ost Kompanie der Versorgungs Bataillon 690*
*4. und 5. Ost Kompanien der Versorgungs Bataillon 604*
*4. Ost Ersatz Bataillon*
*I. und II. Bataillon der Ost Ersatz Regiment Mitte*
*582. Ost Ersatz Kompanie*
*582. Ost Unteroffiziersschule*

**Heeresgruppe Nord**
*Kommandeur der Osttruppen z.b.V. 711*
*Kommandeur der Osttruppen z.b.V. 710*
*655. Kosaken Schwadron*
*Ost Bataillon 653*
*Ost Bataillon 654*
*(estnische) Ost Bataillon 658*
*(estnische) Ost Bataillon 659*
*(estnische) Ost Bataillon 660*
*Ost Bataillon 661*
*Ost Bataillon 662*
*Ost Bataillon 663*
*(finnisch) Ost Bataillon 664*[10]
*Ost Bataillon 665*
*Ost Bataillon 667*
*Ost Bataillon 668*
*Ost Bataillon 669*
*59. Ost Kompanie*
*647. (estnische) Ost Kompanie*
*650. (litauische) Ost Wach Kompanie*
*651. (litauische) Ost Wach Kompanie*
*652.(lettische) Ost Wach Kompanie*
*Ost Reiter Bataillon 207*
*Ost Reiter Bataillon 281*
*Ost Reiter Bataillon 285*
*1. und 2. Ost Artillerie Batterien der Artillerie Abteilung 670 (717. Infanterie Division)*
*Ost Pionier Bataillon 666*
*Ost Versorgungs Bataillon 574*
*671. Ost Signals Kompanie*
*Ost Ersatz Bataillon 16*
*(estnische) Ost Ersatz Bataillon Narva*

**XX. Gebirgsarmeekorps**
*690. Ost Kompanie*

## Other collaborator forces

The recruitment of Belarusian collaborator forces had continued, in spite of the fact that reliability had become an issue by the second half of 1942. Yet, as the following maps reveal, by the end of 1942 and beginning of 1943, there were substantial collaborator units still under German command in Belarusia (White Russia). German rear area units are also depicted. These forces were located as shown by the next three maps:

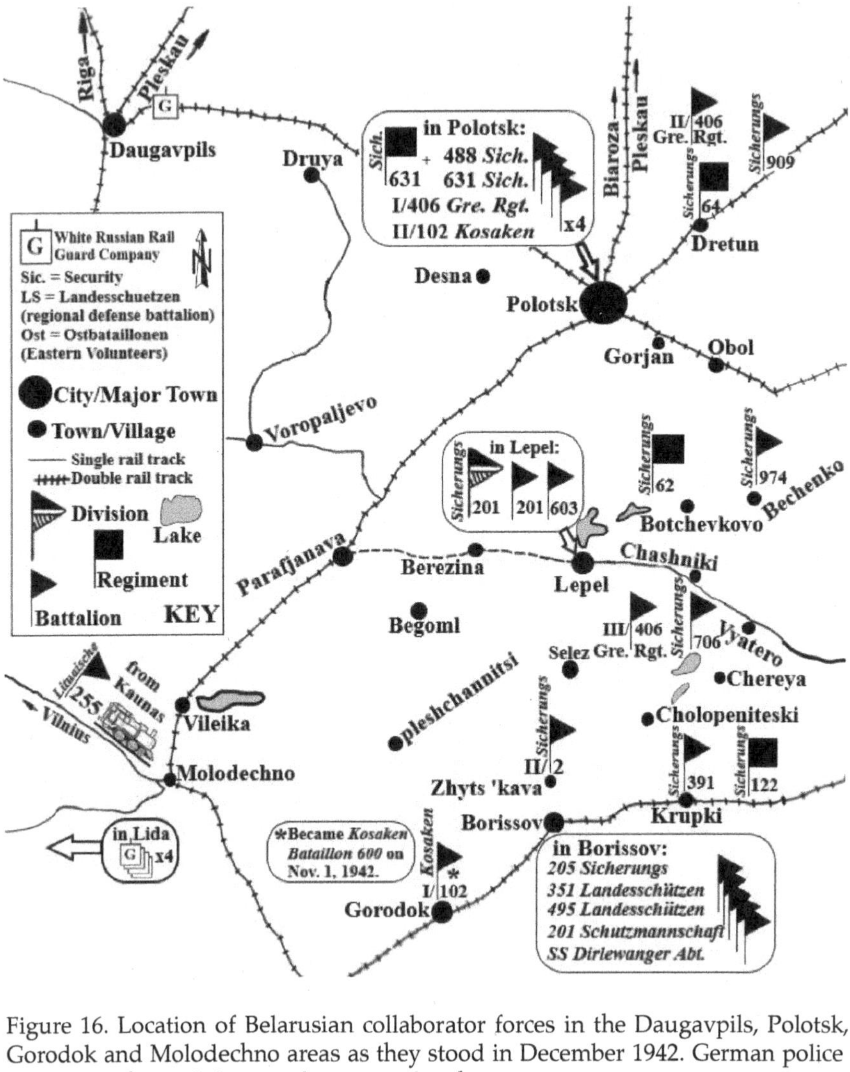


Figure 16. Location of Belarusian collaborator forces in the Daugavpils, Polotsk, Gorodok and Molodechno areas as they stood in December 1942. German police units and other collaborator forces are also shown.

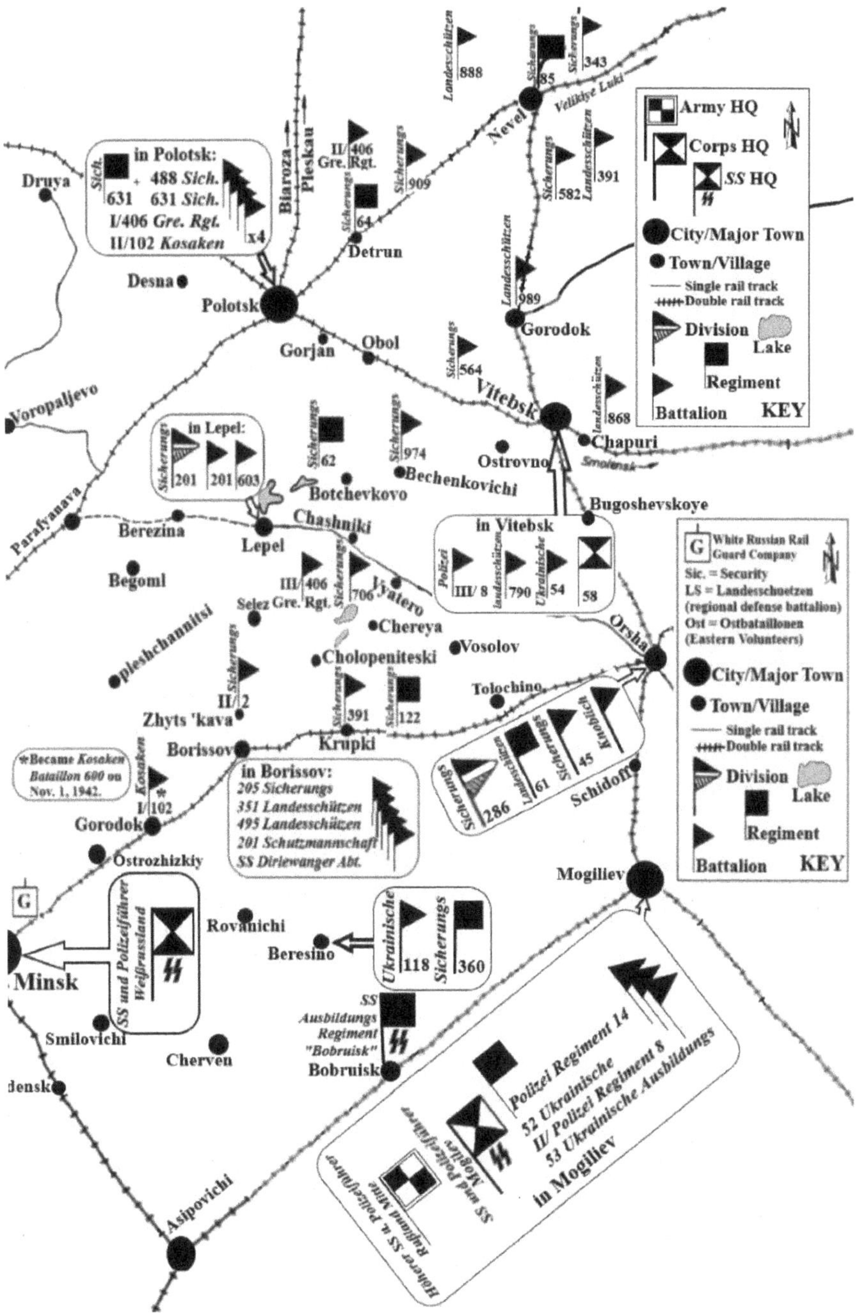


Figure 17. Location of Belarusian collaborator forces in the Polotsk, Nevel, Vitebsk, Orsha, Mogilev and Asipovichi areas as they stood in October 1942. German police units and other collaborator forces are also shown.

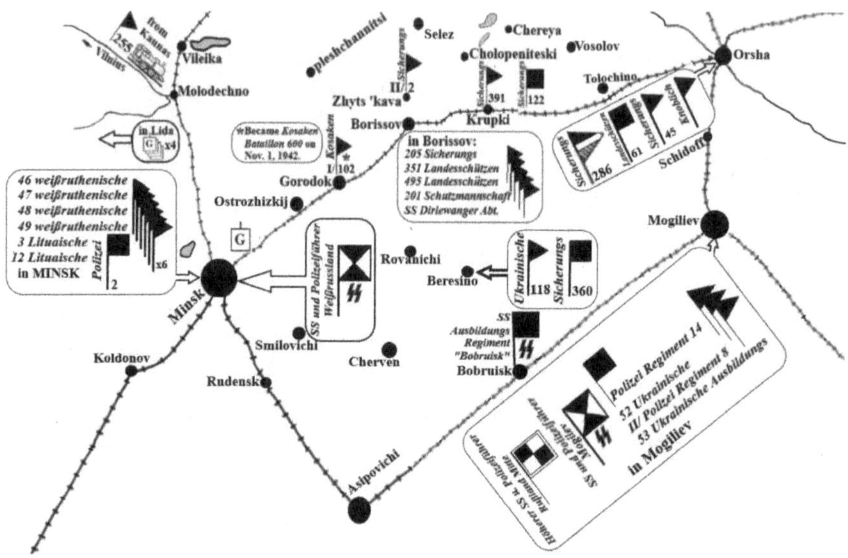


Figure 18. Location of Belarusian collaborator forces in the Orsha, Minsk, Asipovichi and Mogilev areas as they stood in October 1942. German police units and other collaborator forces are also shown.

## Partisan activity between Vitebsk and Orsha, and the Polotsk Lowlands

Since the summer of 1942 the region between Vitebsk and Orsha had become inundated with numerous partisan forces. This did not seem random, but appeared to be a premeditated attempt to influence the front lines nearby. Further south-east from the line Orsha–Vitebsk lay the large Rzhev salient – a pocket of some twenty German divisions who were in a close-enough position to strike towards Moscow if supplies of men and materiel allowed it. The Red Army had been placing pressure on the front lines between Vitebsk and Nevel, hoping to achieve a breakthrough that would force the Germans to give up the salient. This is why large numbers of partisan forces had been gathering in that region since the summer months. Further north, in the region of the Polotsk Lowlands, guerrilla forces would begin concentrating in the winter of 1942–3 and spring of 1943. The situation called for two drives. The first occurred in October 1942 and concentrated on attacking partisan units located between Vitebsk and Orsha. The second operation occurred in the Polotsk Lowlands and took place in June 1943, or eight months later.

By the end of the year 1942 German anti-partisan forces had inflicted substantial losses on the partisans, but that was offset by the fact that recruitment of volunteers for the partisans continued to increase. According to Soviet sources, the Red Army partisan movement had lost somewhere in the neighbourhood of about 20,000 men during 1942. Official Red Army estimates give a total of about 70,000 effective fighters operating behind the lines of the *Ostheer* in the spring of 1942. By the end of the summer of 1942 however, that number had increased to about 125,000 fighters. Also in 1942, the headquarters of the partisan movement, which was located in Moscow, increased its effort to better control and coordinate partisan forces. It ordered the placement of all local guerrilla forces under one regional commander who was in direct communication with the Moscow headquarters and therefore, could better coordinate efforts between the Red Army offensives and partisan activity. The following table lists just a portion of the partisan losses suffered in the region of *Heeresgruppe Sud* and *Heeresgruppe MitteSüd.* To understand these figures and compare them to the estimated 20,000 guerrillas which Moscow claimed were killed, we should consider that the numbers shown on this table most likely also includes innocent civilians who were murdered simply to raise the tally of enemy killed.[11]

Table 8. Partisan Losses by Region and Commands, 1942[12]

| Command | Date | Captured/ Executed | Killed, missing, or wounded |
|---|---|---|---|
| *Geheime Feldpolizei von Wehrmacht Befehlshaber Mitte* | Oct 1942 | 1,001 | ? |
| *Besatzungstruppen von Heeresgruppe B* | Aug 1942 | 862 | 165 |
| *Besatzungstruppen von Heeresgruppe B* | Oct 1942 | 387 | 234 |
| *Geheime Feldpolizei von Heeresgruppe B* | Aug 1942 | 291 | ? |
| *Geheime Feldpolizei von Heeresgruppe B* | Sep 1942 | 693 | ? |
| *Besatzungstruppen von Heeresgruppe Mitte* | Apr 1942 | 6,283 | 381 |
| *Besatzungstruppen von Heeresgruppe Mitte* | May 1942 | 2,248 | 725 |

| Command | Date | Captured / Executed | Killed, missing, or wounded |
|---|---|---|---|
| *Besatzungstruppen von Heeresgruppe Mitte* | Jul 1942 | 2,672 | 876 |
| *Höhere SS und Polizeiführer Nord, Mitte, und Süd* | Sep–Nov 1942 | 24,159 | 997 |
| *Geheime Feldpolizei Heeresgruppe Süd* | Oct–Dec 1941 | 6,550 | ? |
| *Geheime Feldpolizei Heeresgruppe Süd* | May 1942 | 2,729 | ? |
| *Geheime Feldpolizei Heeresgruppe Süd* | Jul 1942 | 5,599 | ? |
| *Wehrmacht Befehlshaber Ukraine* | 20 Jun–20 Jul 1942 | 2,372 | 589 |
| *Korück 580* | Dec 1941–May 1942 | 8,800 | 1,161 |

### *Unternehmen Karlsbad*: 11–23 October 1942

This operation may have concluded on 25 or 26 October. It concentrated on the wooded region between Orsha and Vitebsk. *Feldkommandantur 812* was the highest headquarters command involved in the operation. Other units that took part were *SS-Infanterie Brigade 1 (motorisiert), Polizeiregiment 14, (ukrainische) Schutzmannschaft Bataillon 54* and *(ukrainische) Schutzmannschaft Bataillon 201*. Total partisan losses were 1,676 killed, 58 taken prisoner and 480 who surrendered were shot. As far as which unit took losses, the numbers were the following:

> *Feldkommandantur 812* lost 156 killed, 64 wounded and one missing. It killed 1,003 partisans and later shot an additional 480 after they surrendered.
> *Polizeiregiment 14* suffered 3 wounded and only managed to kill 5 partisans.
> *(ukrainische) Schutzmannschaft Bataillon 201* lost 26 killed, but killed 89 partisans and took 20 prisoners.
> *(ukrainische) Schutzmannschaft Bataillon 54* lost 3 killed and took prisoner 5 partisans.
> *SS-Infanterie Brigade 1 (motorisiert)* lost 4 killed, 1 missing, 3 wounded. The brigade only managed to kill 11 partisans.
> *Kompanie z.b.V. Minsk* lost 3 killed and 1 wounded. The company killed 22 partisans.

The operation cost the lives of 2,156 people but it is difficult to gauge how many of these were actually partisans.

### *Unternehmen Kottbus*: 3–23 June 1943

Very soon, the actions and practices of the Germans during these drives would begin to sap the morale of the men in the *Druzhina* SS unit. One particularly horrendous drive was *Unternehmen Kottbus,* in which 16,662 Germans and native auxiliary troops were used.[13] It was launched against a 'partisan republic' on the eastern border of the General Commissariat White Ruthenia, in the region of Begoml–Lepel–Ushachi. The Germans encountered stiff resistance, and suffered just over 672 casualties with 127 killed.[14] The operation would be the last operation in which the *Druzhina* SS *Brigade* would participate in before its defection. It would also be one of the largest German anti-guerrilla drives of the war in the Soviet Union. SS Lieutenant-General Kurt von Gottberg was placed in charge. The slaughter began after the partisans slipped through the ring of SS, police, and *Schutzmannschaft* (*Schuma*) units that had been arrayed against them. Kurt von Gottberg claimed that his forces had killed 6,042 guerrillas, and that an additional 3,709 'other criminals' had been liquidated, while 599 prisoners were taken to the rear. Of this total number of 9,720 people, only 1,000 rifles and machine guns could be found.[15] In addition von Gottberg stated that 'another two to three thousand civilians were blown up in helping to forcibly clear the partisan minefields'.[16] As horrible as this practice was, it appears to have taken place on a regular basis.

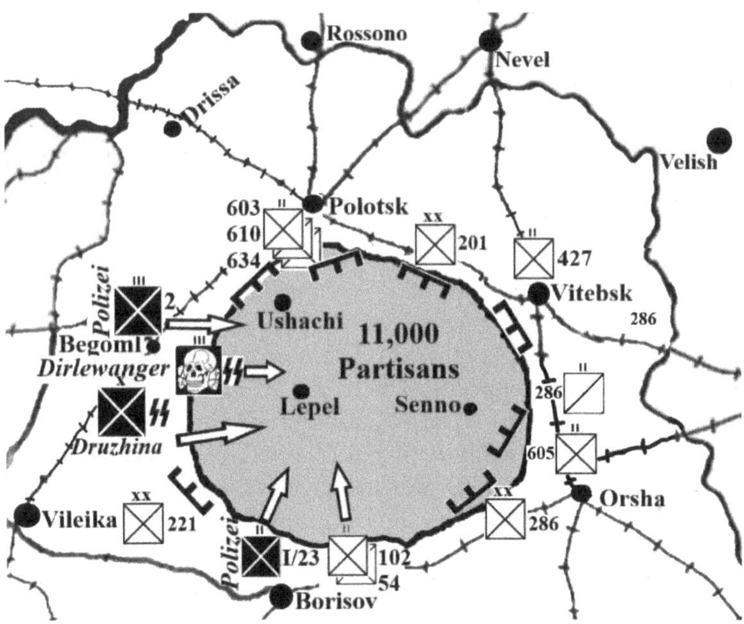


Figure 19. Location of Axis and Russian partisan forces during *Unternehmen Kottbus*, June 1943.

The Germans even had a cynical term for the forcible employment of Russian civilians in front of their troops, in order to detonate mines. They called this the '*1942 Minensuchgerät*' ('1942 Mine Detector'). In both cases, the numbers seem to be about the same, although the latter is slightly higher, to the tune of 850 people. One final source states that altogether 13,000-plus people died during the operation.[17] In any event, the numbers of weapons captured by the Germans was not in proportion to the numbers of people killed. In fact, only 492 rifles were found among the dead, leading one to conclude that a massacre of the local population had taken place. In fact, author John A. Armstrong confirmed as much when he quoted a letter from General Commissar for Belorussia, Wilhelm Kube:

> He [Kube] also argued that if for 4,500 enemy dead only 492 rifles were captured, the implication clearly was that the dead included many peasants who were not necessarily partisans.[18]

Even SS officers on the headquarters staff of Erich von dem Bach-Zelewski's anti-partisan unit complained about the manner in which *Unternehmen Kottbus* had been conducted. *SS-Brigadeführer und Generalmajor der Polizei* Eberhard Herf, who was the head of the *Ordnungspolizei* in Minsk and the Chief of Staff of von dem Bach's headquarters, had this to say:

> Yesterday a Gauleiter . . . broadcast certain secret reports [intended for the *Führer*] showing that some 480 rifles were found on 6,000 dead 'partisans'. Put bluntly, all these men had been shot to swell the figure of enemy losses and highlight our own 'heroic deeds'. I am under no illusions that, this being the system, the winter of 1943–44 will see the beginning of the end in the rear areas and probably at the front as well. The increase in guerrilla warfare is simply and solely due to the way the Russians have been treated.[19]

Given the brutal manner in which the war was being waged, we can only speculate as to what negative effect this all had on Russian volunteer units, but certainly it could not have been positive. This is not to say that Rodionov and his unit were free of acts of cruelty like their German benefactors. For example, in the village of Zembin, Rodionov's men killed three young men and two girls solely because they were wearing Belarusian (nationalist) emblems on their shirts and blouses.[20] In the village of Sloboda, Gil himself played at 'God' by first sentencing some poor peasants to death, but conditionally commuting their death sentence 'if' the peasants could ask for their pardon in good literary language. Apparently, they didn't please Rodionov and they were summarily shot.[21]

We can perceive his callous indifference to the lives of the local peasants as perhaps a premeditated attempt to continue to alienate the population against the Germans, or perhaps an even simpler reason – pure savagery and chaos for its own sake. Whichever is the case, it seems pretty clear that Colonel Rodionov's eventual decision to defect had been made before *Unternehmen Kottbus* even began. If anything, it is possible that his decision might have aided the guerrillas since he might have given them vital information about the coming offensive which would have allowed them to evade destruction. With such cruel and radical practices, the Soviets found it quite easy to employ effective propaganda against the collaborationist forces. Already the actions and practices of the Germans during these drives were sapping the morale of the men in the *Druzhina* SS unit and other indigenous voluntary formations.

A taste of things to come occurred on the night of 24/25 November 1942, when sixty-three men from the *Druzhina* SS battalion stationed at Kolitschenko killed five German SD men of the battalion liaison staff and deserted to the partisans. Yet, in spite of this incident, nothing was done to check the allegiance or morale of the *Druzhina* unit. According to Sven Steenberg, the chief SD officer in the *Druzhina SS Brigade, SS-Sturmbannführer* Appel, was an incompetent. Steenberg states that Appel, a former SA leader, had limited his control over Rodionov and the rest of the officers in the unit to teaching them how to conduct themselves in an officers' club.[22] That left the entire *Druzhina* SS unit under the sole control of Rodionov. Also deserting during the winter of 1942–3 were about fifty members of *Schutzmannschaft Bataillon 115*, who joined the local partisans. In addition, dozens of members of *Schutzmannschaft Bataillon 118* deserted and joined the Ukrainian UPA insurgent army. The UPA was seeking independence for Ukraine from both the Germans and Russians. A German document titled *Verteiler* (dispatch) listed the following partial list of units for *Unternehmen Kottbus*:[23]

*1st Battalion/ Polizei Schutzenregiment 31* – Borisov.
*Schutzmannschaft Bataillon 54* – Borisov.
*Schutzmannschaft Bataillon 51* – Voloshin (Woloczin).
*Schutzmannschaft Bataillon 12* – Poloczeny.[24]
*Schutzmannschaft Bataillon 15* – Lida.
*Schutzmannschaft Bataillon 57* – Baranovichi.

*Schutzmannschaft Bataillon 118* – Novogrudok (397 men).
*Schutzmannschaft Bataillon 102* – Borisov / Stoplce.
*Gendarmerie Zug* (platoon) – Borisov / Stolpce.
*Schutzmannschaft Bataillon 3* – Slonim.
*Schutzmannschaft Bataillon 115* – Slonim (537 men).
*Schutzmannschaft Bataillon 271* – Slutsk.
*SS-Polizeiregiment 2* – Begomyl.
*SS-Druzhina Verbände* – Begomyl (south-west of Lepel) and surrounding area.
*SS-Sonder Bataillon Dirlewanger* – Begomyl and surrounding area.
*Gendarmerie Einsatzkommando 'Kreikeborn'* – Begomyl and surrounding area.
*Gendarmerie Kommando 'Plechtschenicze'* – (north-east of Minsk).

The intent of the operation was the destruction of what was considered a partisan republic in Belorussia – an area that had been under constant guerrilla control. This 'republic' was located on the eastern border of the *Generalbezirk Weissruthenien*.[25] One of the principal units in this 'republic' was the Zhelezniak Partisan Brigade which coincidentally, would feature prominently in the desertion of the *Druzhina* SS unit. This unit was an important component of the Belarusian partisan movement.[26] The Staff of the Partisan Headquarters based in Moscow directly charged the Zhelezniak Partisan Brigade with targeting the 1st Russian National SS Brigade (aka the *Druzhina* SS Brigade) with a concerted campaign of propaganda, aimed at getting its commander, Vladimir Gil, and its men to desert to the Red Army partisans. The concerted propaganda by the Zhelezniak Partisan Brigade, coupled with further German military defeats in the USSR, finally convinced Gil (aka 'Rodionov') to consider defection. It is interesting to note that while negotiations for the *Druzhina* unit to defect were begun in June 1943 – a period when *Unternehmen Kottbus* began, the Zhelezniak Partisan Brigade and other partisan forces were able to evade the tens of thousands of Axis troops trying to trap them. One does not need to stretch the imagination to consider that perhaps Gil may have provided valuable intelligence to the partisans, which allowed them to mostly escape the German trap. The numbers of people killed in the anti-partisan drive vary slightly. Two reliable sources state that 5,000 people were shot for suspicion of collaborating with the partisans after being taken prisoner, while another 4,500 enemy were left dead in the field.[27] By May 1943, large regions of Belarus and to the north were under partisan control.

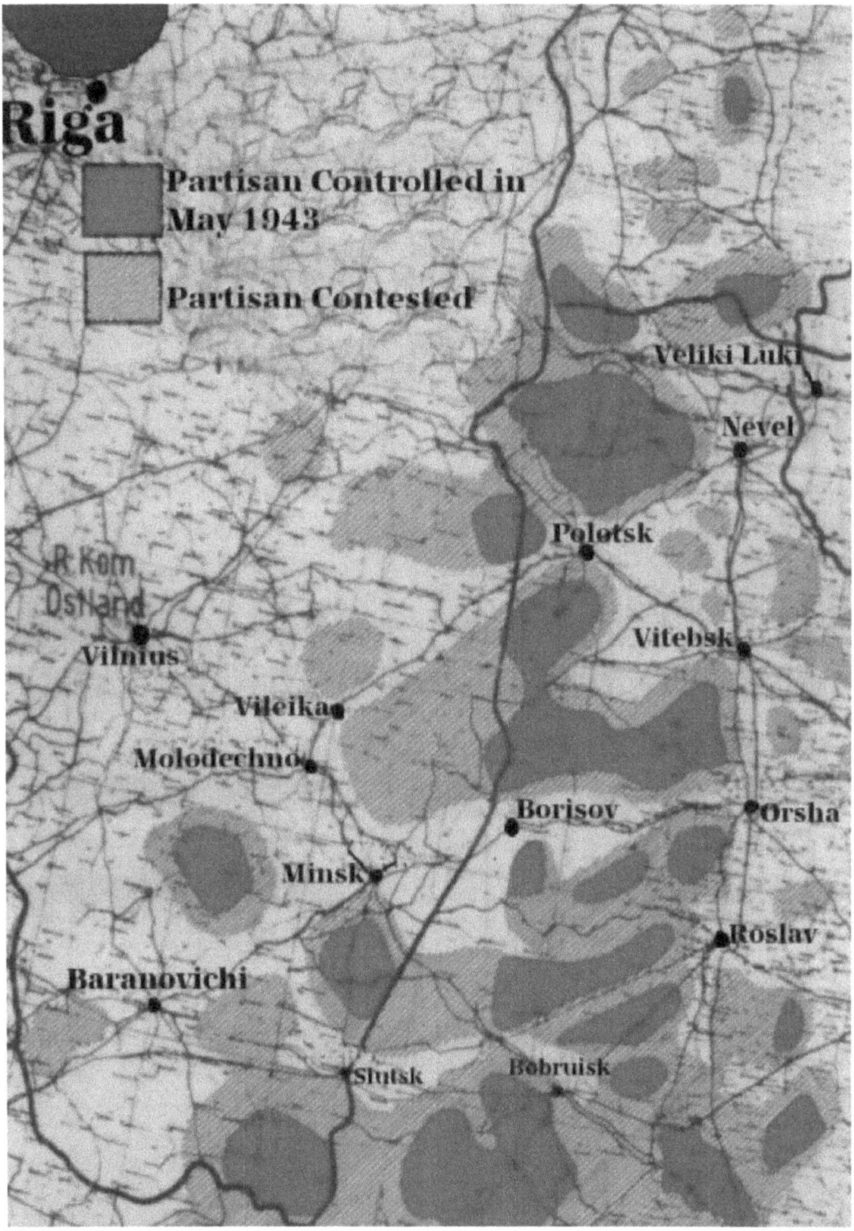


Figure 20. Areas under partisan control and areas that were partisan-contested in May 1943.

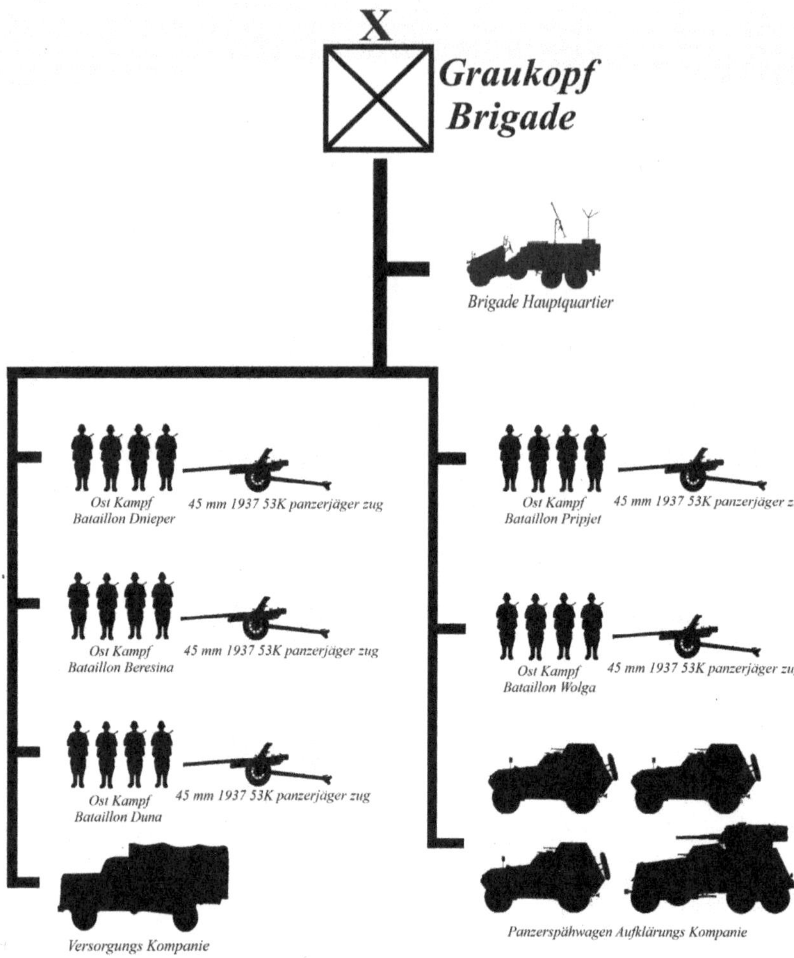


Figure 21. Illustrative schematic of the organisation of the Russian National People's Army (RNNA) at its height in 1942.

Chapter 5

# THE SOVIET PARTISANS IN BELARUS AND RUSSIA, 1943

'The conventional army loses if it does not win. The guerrilla wins if he does not lose.'

Henry Kissinger

It was clear by the autumn of 1942, that the guerrilla movement behind the German lines was picking up steam. The Germans themselves had admitted as much by their reorganisation of rear-area forces and the substantial increase in units assigned to anti-partisan warfare. The Soviet partisan movement had grown dramatically, beginning in the second half of 1942. While some parts of Belarus had no formal partisan unit in June 1942, a year later every district in the country had regular guerrilla forces stationed on a permanent basis. In June 1943 the remaining numbers of units and men stood as follows:[1]

Table 9. Soviet Guerrilla Bands and Strengths in Belarus, 1942–1943

| District | Bands in Jul 1942 | Partisans | Bands in Jun 1943 | Partisans |
|---|---|---|---|---|
| Bialystok | 3–4 | 300 | 3–4 | 800 |
| Brest-Litovsk | 12 | 500 | 25 | 2,645 |
| Pinsk | 9 | 3,000 | 27 | 5,609 |
| Baranovichi | 5 | 2,000–3,000 | 25 | 2,469 |

| District | Bands in Jul 1942 | Partisans | Bands in Jun 1943 | Partisans |
|---|---|---|---|---|
| Minsk | 4 | 400 | 126 | 21,024 |
| Mozyr | 31 | 4,000 | 35 | 4,500 |
| Gomel | 9 | 600 | 41 | 7,974 |
| Mogilev | 11 | 2,000 | 84 | 9,481 |
| Orsha–Vitebsk | 75 | 9,000 | 140 | 19,080 |
| Total | 160 | 20,100 | 507 | 73,582 |

In January 1943 the number of partisans in Belarus had stood at 57,700. As the table above shows, the partisan forces in Belarus numbered around 74,000 men in early June. This was about almost a quadrupling of forces available to the partisan movement in Belarus from June 1942 to June 1943. In late June 1943 that figure rose even higher, to 80,700. In September there were 103,600 partisans behind the German lines in Belarus.[2] In the beginning of 1943, the primary partisan concentrations in the region of *Heeresgruppe Mitte* were located in (1) the wooded areas of Orel and Bryansk, (2) the Pripet Marshes region which roughly divided Belorussia from Ukraine, and (3) the White Russian forests west of Mogilev–Orsha–Vitebsk.[3] The areas of central Russia around Bryansk held an estimated 16,000 partisans in 1943.[4] In addition, the area around Smolensk had an additional 9,000 guerrillas and the area between Konotop and Bryansk, that is, the region of *2. Armee*, had another 3,000–5,000 partisan units. When we add the guerrilla forces in both central and White Russia, we come up with a total of some 76,000–78,000 partisans in the central sector of the Eastern Front. The majority of these guerrilla forces was pretty much under the command of regular Red Army officers with specialised training in partisan warfare and were better armed, equipped and trained than they had been a year ago. For example, three partisan brigades located just north of the city of Bryansk altogether had three 76mm guns, three 45mm anti-tank guns and eighteen heavy mortars plus dozens of submachine guns, some anti-tank rocket launchers and a few heavy machine guns.[5]

The situation was so difficult for the Germans that entire territories of their rear were labelled as partisan regions where their control did not extend. In some places where the Germans held sway, the guerrillas impeded rail and road traffic, attacked isolated garrisons and harassed the rear of the German forces. For example, the 2. *Panzerarmee* reported on 1 April 1943, that guerrilla activity had temporarily impeded its supply operations.[6] Soviet guerrilla operations in 1943 had been geared towards the stopping of German rail and road movement and disruption of strategic supplies and reserves being sent forward to the front lines. This was the primary mission of the Soviet guerrillas in 1943.[7]

## The battle for the rails: summer 1943

Between May 1943 and May 1944, the Soviet guerrillas would lose an estimated 12,700 men out of 27,000 partisans which they had in the region of 3. *Panzerarmee* alone.[8] Yet, during that same time period, less than a thousand men would desert to the Germans from this area. What this showed was that by mid-1943 the average Soviet citizen knew that it was better for him to either remain neutral or stay with the Soviet partisans. German statistics on Russian desertions proved to be an increasingly small figure beginning in mid-1943 onwards. By the time the summer of 1943 arrived, the partisan movement was sizable and strong enough to try and make a large and coordinated strategic effort behind the German lines in order to better influence the outcome of the military campaign in the front lines. This 'push' would be the so-called 'battle of the rails' which would aim at paralyzing German rail transport through central and White Russia. In May between Shlobin and Gomel alone the guerrillas were able to destroy 35 locomotives and 106 rail cars in 69 separate attacks.[9] Also on 1 May a 50-mile stretch of the Roslav–Bryansk rail line was placed under constant pressure by no less than five partisan brigades.[10]

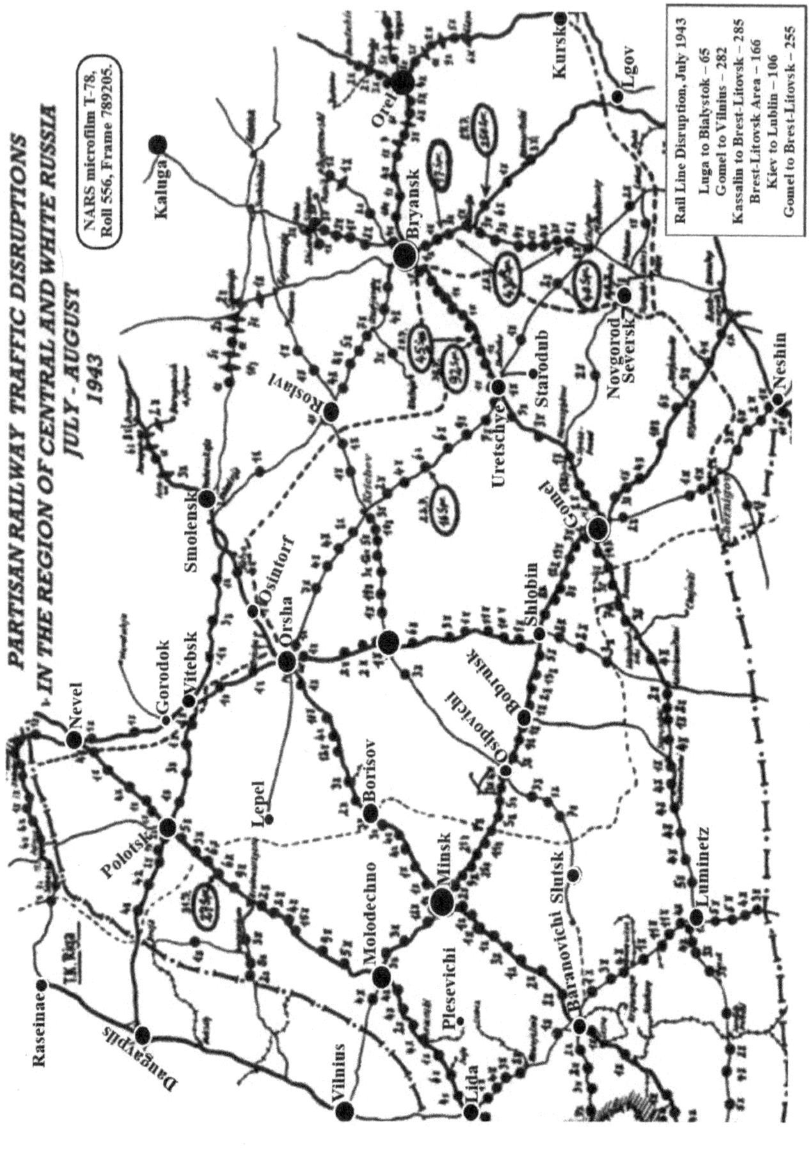


Figure 22. Partisan rail demolitions in Russia and White Russia, July–August 1943.

Beginning in June 1943 the guerrillas stepped up their attacks on the rail lines. The partisans in that month managed to damage or destroy 298 locomotives and 1,222 railway cars. In addition, 44 railway bridges were blown up and the rail lines were interrupted in 746 separate places. All of these incidents took place in the region of central and

White Russia in June alone.[11] But these numbers, although high, would pale in comparison by the numbers or actions against the rails two months later in August. This plan for the disruption of German railway communication was so important that even Joseph Stalin inquired on 13 July 1943, just exactly when the campaign against the German rails could begin.[12]

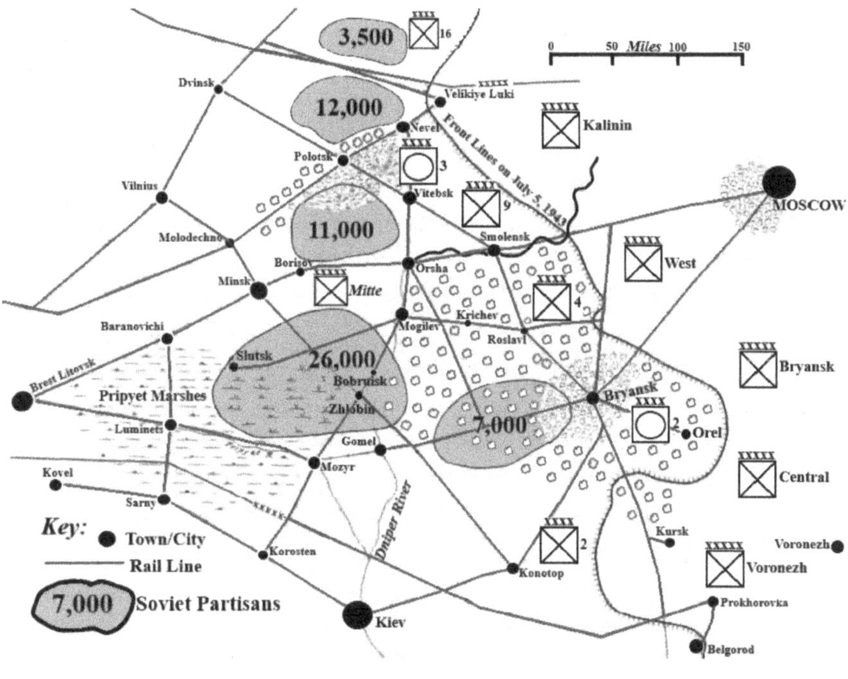


Figure 23. Partisan concentrations in White Russia and Central Russia, July 1943.

The Chief of Staff of the Central Staff of the Partisan Movement, P.K. Ponomarenko, told the Soviet dictator that operations against the rails could begin as early as 25 July 1943. In late July the partisans cut off the main north-south rail line between *Heeresgruppe Mitte* and South at the Bryansk–Konotop rail line for 48 hours. Worse still, two ammunition trains, one fuel train and a trainload of badly-needed Tiger tanks went up in flames at the Osipovichi station on 22 July 1943.[13] In the beginning of August 1943, the Red Army began its counter-offensive in the region of Kursk and Orel which quickly widened in operations north and south, completely engulfing the regions of Army Group Centre and South. In order to support this major offensive, the guerrillas in the region of Belorussia and central Russia launched a coordinated attack against the entire rail system in these two regions. In total, the month of August saw the rail lines in White Russia cut in 40,000 separate places. In the region of *Heeresgruppe Mitte,* the rail system was cut in 8,300 separate places in the Smolensk region while 13,700 separate attacks were conducted in the region of Orel.[14] Orel itself was captured by the Red Army on 5 August 1943.[15] Its fall was surely accelerated due to the above-mentioned guerrilla activities. These guerrilla strikes against the German rail system in central Russia and Belorussia were substantial and significant as shown by an excerpt from the war diary of the Chief of Transportation, *Heeresgruppe Mitte*:

> Despite the employment of special alert units for the protection of the railway lines, partisan activity increased 25% during August 1943 and reached a record 1,392 incidents as compared with 1,114 in July. The daily average amounted to 45 demolitions. In 364 cases the rails were cut simultaneously in more than ten places. Individual demolition points amounted to 20,505 while 4,528 mines could be removed. During the night from 2 to 3 August the partisans began to put into effect a program of large-scale destruction. Numerous demolitions were carried out which caused a serious curtailment of all railway traffic and a considerable loss of railway materiel. Within two nights the six to seven thousand miles of track in the area were cut in 8,422 places, while another 2,478 mines were detected and removed prior to exploding. Several lines could not be put back into operation for a considerable time. Another major handicap in the operation of the railways was the increasing number of sabotage acts, committed chiefly by native workers under partisan orders. In many instances, the so-called eastern volunteer units were employed to protect the railway lines made common cause with the partisans and took German weapons along with them. In one case for instance, an entire Russian security detachment of 600 men went over to the partisans. On 17 August 1943 this force attacked the Krulevshchizna Railway Station. Using machine guns, mortars, and anti-tank guns which they had taken with them at the time of their desertion, the Russians caused considerable damage. German losses in that engagement amounted to 240 dead and 491 wounded. Altogether, partisan activities from 1 to 31 August 1943 resulted in damage to 266 locomotives and 1,373 railway cars; about 160 miles of track were also rendered unserviceable.[16]

The battle for the rails affected the movement of German supplies and reinforcements being sent to the front. For example, *68. Infanterie Division* and *125. Infanterie Division* had been traveling by rail through the region, but were forced to debark at the station in Olekh-Novichi on the Molodechno–Minsk rail line.[17] Some of the component parts of both divisions had to be trucked to the front lines from there while the rest of them had to march on foot. The guerrillas thus delayed the arrival of two entire German infantry divisions to the front lines for at least a week.

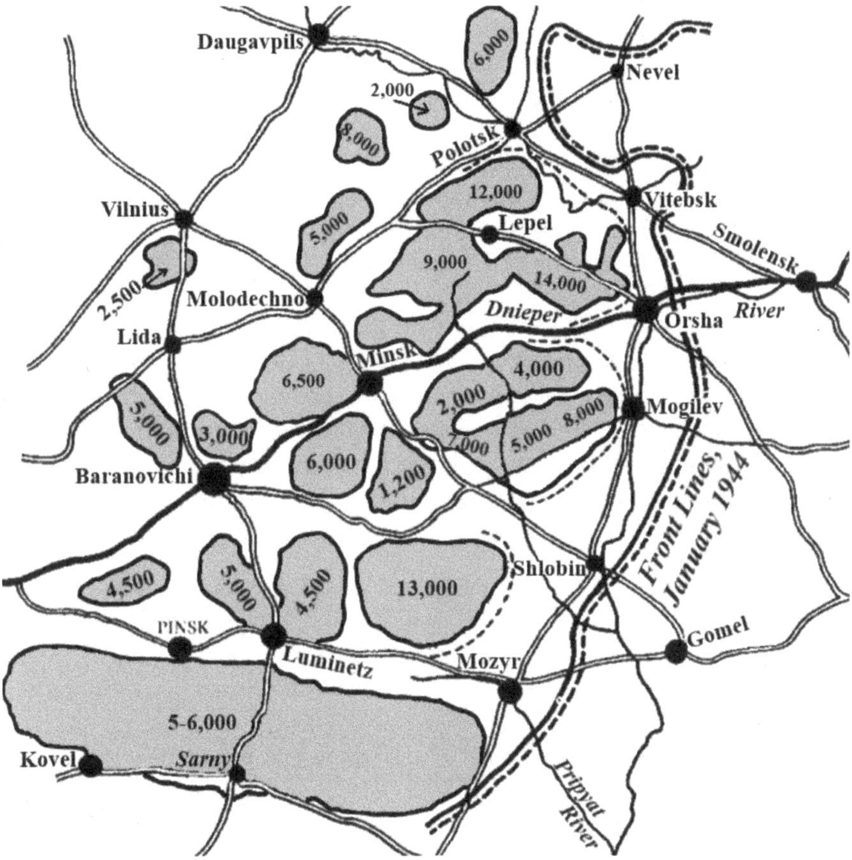


Figure 24. Partisan strengths in Belarusia (White Russia), December 1943–January 1944.

## Increase in partisan strength

Immediately after the failed German offensive around Kursk in the summer of 1943, the German army in Russia was finally placed on the strategic defensive. The debacle of the Battle of Stalingrad had showed that Nazi Germany would not defeat the USSR. The grievous losses taken by the Germans during the Battle of Kursk indicated that Nazi Germany would lose the war in the East. The Kursk defeat was therefore a cue for all Russians who had previously doubted in a

Soviet victory and had remained neutral, to come off the fence and cast their lot with the partisans. In addition, those Russian volunteers on the German side who could set aside their hatred for the Soviet regime began to consider how they could switch sides. A large defection occurred towards the middle of August when the majority of the *Druzhina SS Brigade* defected to the guerrillas on 13 August 1943.[18]

Partisan strengths had been growing throughout the autumn of 1942 and beginning of 1943. The largest concentration was around Lepel, Mogilev and Mozyr. In March 1943 guerrilla strengths had been as follows. In the Baltic States there were under 1,000 partisans; in the region of *Heeresgruppe Nord* there were 4,203 men, while Belorussia had 57,700.[19] The regions of central Russia (Smolensk, Bryansk, Orel) had another 44,000 guerrilla troops, while Ukraine contained 7,039 and the Crimea had about 500 men.[20] By the summer of 1943 the number of Soviet partisans along the entire Eastern Front would number 142,000. As the table below illustrates, by the beginning of the summer of 1942 the Germans had killed some 80,000 partisans behind the lines of *Heeresgruppe Mitte* alone. Still, the partisan movement continued to grow and cause ever-increasing problems for the Germans behind the front lines.

Table 10. Losses sustained behind the lines of Army Group Centre, June 1941–May 1942[21]

| | 22 Jun 1941–1 Mar 1942 | 2 Mar–31 May 1942 | Total |
|---|---|---|---|
| Guerrillas killed | 63,257 | 16,743 | 80,000 |
| Germans killed | 638 | 456 | 1,094 |
| Germans wounded | 1,174 | 668 | 1,862 |
| Germans missing | 181 | 147 | 328 |
| Total German losses | 1,993 | 1,291 | 3,284 |
| Russian collaborators assassinated | 22 Jun 1941–31 May 1942: 500 | | 500[22] |
| | | Grand Total | 87,068 |

As we have seen, these numbers grew dramatically, especially in the region of central Russia and Belarus by the summer of 1943. What is interesting about the growth of the partisan movement and the battle for the rails is that they all occurred during a time when the German rear-area army, SS and police forces were conducting the largest anti-partisan operations of the war. Some of these operations involved two or three entire corps-sized units and numbered 40,000–50,000 men. One would say that perhaps German moves and operations behind the lines in 1943 merely slowed down the growth of the guerrilla movement. In addition, the eventual loss of control in vast swathes of land in the German rear areas was, by the summer of 1943, a forgone conclusion. In fact, by the summer of 1943 large tracts of land were completely controlled by the Soviet partisans and behaved like liberated territories or small partisan 'republics'. German forces could only enter these regions employing large numbers of troops. By the end of 1943, the Soviet partisans were claiming to control approximately 60 per cent of the territory of Belarus. By the autumn of 1943 there were 15,000 guerrillas in the Rossono Rayon north of Polotsk; with another 14,000–18,000 partisans situated along the Ushach River, between Borisov and Lepel. Another 12,000–13,000 partisans were operating in the swamps along the Beresina River, between Lepel and Borisov; while 8,000 men were located near Minsk, 9,000 were operating in and around Senno, and 14,000 guerrillas were launching operations around Vitebsk. By June 1944, the number of guerrillas in Belorussia was somewhere in the neighbourhood of 150,000 men split up into 150 partisan brigades and 49 independent detachments.[23]

Chapter 6

# MAJOR ANTI-PARTISAN OPERATIONS IN 1943

'We lost in the East because we were too soft; we should have behaved more ruthlessly.'

Captured German general, Trent Park, North London

## *Unternehmen Dreieck und Viereck*: 17 September–2 October 1943

This anti-partisan operation was named 'Triangle and Quadrangle'. *Korück 532*, which was responsible for the southernmost rear area of *2. Panzerarmee*, would direct the operation. The region was an area south and south-east of Bryansk, where approximately 4,000 partisans were operating. All villages were to be combed out and the residents were to be deported. The orders specifically said that the area should be made uninhabitable.[1] Two *kampfgruppen* were organised, named *Zebisch* and *Schlegel* (after their respective commanders). Units from *Korück 532*, plus elements of *18. Panzer Brigade* (*2. Panzerarmee*). Elements of *707. Infanterie Division* also took part in the operation. Specifically, *Infanterie Regiment 727*, which at this time was led by *Oberst* Karlimilian Lasalle von Louisenthal. The *Korück 532* command, which was led by *Generalleutnant* Friedrich Bernhardt, could employ the following forces for the operation:

*Sicherungs Bataillon 242*
*Landesschützen Bataillon 238*
*Landesschützen Bataillon 551*
*Landesschützen Bataillon 981*
*Ost Bataillon 615*
*Ost Bataillon 616*

*Ost Bataillon 617*
*Ost Bataillon 618*
*Ost Bataillon 619*
*Ost Bataillon 620*
*Infanterie Ausbildungs Bataillon 500* (not used)

An armoured train was also available for use (*Panzer Zug Nr. 30*). Elements of the Hungarian 102nd and 108th Infantry Division also took part in the operation. Finally, several Russian auxiliary battalions would take part in the drive. The region in question where the operational sweep was to take place was known to be heavily mined, so the Nazi command requested that Jews from several labour battalions be gathered together and formed into mine-clearing groups. These groups would go ahead of the German troops, ostensibly either finding and defusing the mines or getting blown up by them. Specific orders were given that rope be tied around the waist of each Jewish person, in order to prevent their escape. The Germans sarcastically named these Jewish mine-clearing groups, the *Minensuchgerät 1942* ('1942 mine detector').[2] A report from 11 September 1942 clearly defined how the mine clearing would take place during the operation:

> Because throughout the 'Triangle' region enemy mines are to be expected, '*Minensuchgerät 1942*' are to be available in sufficient quantities. Units are to equip themselves with cords to use as leashes with which to control the Jews or bandits.[3]

An after-action report from the *II. Bataillon* of *Infanterie Regiment 727* further affirmed the implementation of this illegal use of prisoners:

> Second Battalion, 727. Infanterie Regiment which was deployed as the leading battalion, broke through the enemy defences, breaking their resistance in a lightning attack, in spite of the fact that the advance proceeded slowly due to the region being heavily mined. Four '1942 mine detectors' were blown up, flying into the air, thus sparing any losses on our side.[4]

The results of the operation were as follows: 973 civilians were apprehended and sent to POW Camp No. 142, where many were coerced into joining a pro-German local self-defence militia, if they wished to be released. Only eighty-six partisans were taken alive. The Germans counted 1,064 dead on the field, out of which three were women who were shot after being captured. The German *Korück* command claimed that 366 guerrillas defected to the Germans during the operation.[5] Axis losses were said to be only forty-five men, most of whom were Hungarian. About 400 sheep, 1,500 cattle, and an unspecified number of pigs were plundered from the area, as well as most of the wheat harvest.[6]

## *Unternehmen Lenz Süd und Nord*: 30 March to 7 April 1943 (*Süd*), 4–13 April 1943 (*Nord*)

The date for the start of this anti-guerrilla drive has been given variously as 1 April 1943,[7] 31 March 1943 and 30 March 1943.[8] The probable date of the beginning of this drive is most likely either 30 or 31 March. The drive aimed at destroying any guerrilla units located in the regions of Borisov, Sloboda, and Smolevichi. *SS-Kampfgruppe Schimana* was assigned to this operation. At this time, it was composed of the following units:

*I. und II. Bataillon / Polizeiregiment 13*
*Polizei Panzer Kompanie 4*
*Polizei Panzer Kompanie 12*
*I. Bataillon / Polizeiregiment 23*
*(ukrainische) Schutzmannschaft Bataillon 57*
*(pol.) Schutzmannschaft Bataillon 202*
*Ein Kompanie (1) der Landesschützen Bataillon Wendland*
*SD Sonderkommando Kompanie*
*SS-Sonder Bataillon Dirlewanger*

This force went up against an estimated 3,000 partisans with 14–16 tanks, 4–8 guns, and 102 machine guns. Because these guerrillas had been spotted wearing German uniforms, it was ordered that a white armband be worn on the left shoulder strap of the tunic in order to better differentiate between the partisans and the SS and police forces. Operation 'Spring South' officially ended on 7 April and a day later, 'Spring North' began with basically the same forces minus *Polizeiregiment 13*, which was withdrawn for another mission.[9] The same regions of Borisov and Smolevichi were combed and the areas of Lahoisk (Logysk) and Sembin (Zembin) were now also added. These two towns were located north of Smolevichi. Sembin lay exactly north-west of Borisov and north-east of Lahoisk. 'Spring North' ended on 13 April 1943.

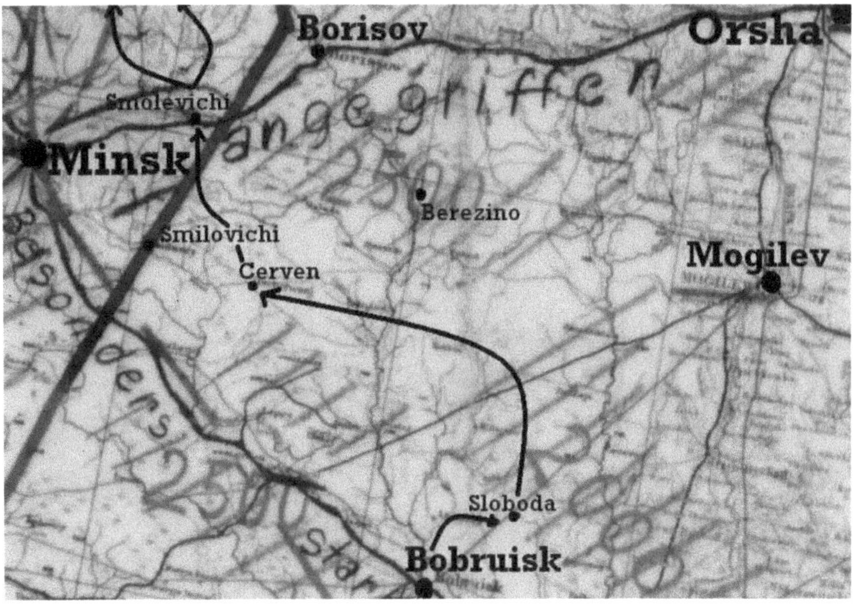


Figure 25. Area of operations for *Unternehmen Lenz I* and *II*.

## *Unternehmen Donnerkeil*: 21 March–2 April 1943

This operation centred on partisan forces located around Mossoyova, and the swampy region between Dretun and Obdol River. This was in the area of operations of *3. Panzerarmee*. Units employed in this drive included forces under *201. Sicherungs Division* and *286. Sicherungs Division*, including numerous indigenous formations such as Cossack and *Ost* battalions. Some units under direct *3. Panzerarmee* control also took part, like *Wolgatatar Infanterie Bataillon 825*. Native units under *201. Sicherungs Division* and employed in the drive included the following:[10]

*Kosaken Bataillon 622*
*Kosaken Bataillon 623*
*Kosaken Bataillon 624*
*Kosaken Bataillon 625*
*Ost Wach Bataillon 508*

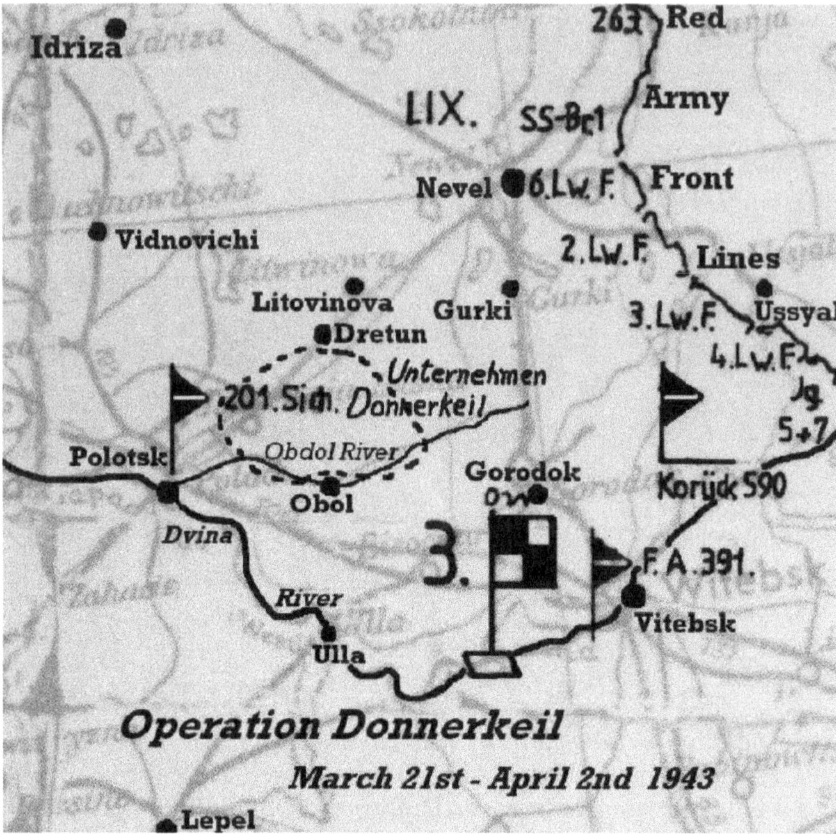


Figure 26. Area of operations for *Unternehmen Donnerkeil.*

This anti-partisan drive lasted a little over a week and was jointly directed by *201.* and *286. Sicherungs Divisionen.* According to researcher Professor Christian Gerlach, the two divisions killed around 6,500 people in the Polotsk and Vitebsk region from August 1942 to February 1943, while losing just 159 dead over the span of three anti-partisan operations (*Schneehase, Kugelblitz* and *Donnerkeil*).[11]

### *Unternehmen Zauberflöte*: 17–24 April 1943

The *Druzhina SS-Brigade* took part in *Unternehmen Zauberflöte* (Operation Magic Flute). The operation was launched at exactly 4:00 a.m. on April 17, 1943 and involved the complete combing of the capital of White Russia, Minsk. The mission was for the city to be made partisan-free. With its 130,000 residents, ruins and the ghetto Minsk was a natural hiding place for partisans, agents and their supporters. Much valuable property had already been destroyed by arson and raids caused by these urban guerrillas. Partisan activity in Minsk had begun as early as 1941. The task of surrounding Minsk was given principally to the *SS Sonder Bataillon Dirlewanger*.[12] The mission of combing through the city of Minsk itself was left principally to *SS Polizeiregiment 13* and several Belarusian auxiliary battalions stationed in the city. The surrounding countryside was combed by other units.[13] The *141. Reserve Division* was based in Stolpce (Stolbtcy), about 72km south-west of Minsk. From January to November 1943, it was under *LXI. Armeekorps*, which was itself accountable to the *Wehrmacht Befehlshaber Ostland* command. The *390. Feldausbildungs Division* was at this time under held in reserve and listed as *zur Verfügung* – 'available' (for employment) – directly under the headquarters of the German Army High Command. The responsibility for coordinating the operation fell on *SS-Brigadeführer und Generalmajor der Polizei* Gerret Korsemann, who had been promoted in the summer of 1942 and transferred from Ukraine to White Russia. He now answered to his immediate boss, *SS-Obergruppenführer und General der Polizei* Erich von dem Bach-Zelewski, who held the *Höhere SS und Polizeiführer Russland Mitte* command. For Operation Magic Flute, the Germans would employ the following formations:

In Minsk:
SS *Polizeiregiment 13*
- *I. Bataillon*
- *II. Bataillon*

Surrounding Regions of Minsk:
*390. Feldausbildungs Division*
*141. Reserve Infanterie Division*
*Druzhina SS-Brigade* (one battalion)
*SS-Sonder Bataillon Dirlewanger*
*1. SS-Polizeiregiment*
*2. SS-Polizeiregiment*

Inside and in the surrounding region of the Belarusian capital 130,000 people were subjected to this drive. The entire city was cordoned off and searched. The surrounding countryside was also combed for people. The operation was to be ruthless and anyone not following instructions to the letter was to be shot. Those caught with no proper identification were to be shot. There was to be no looting permitted, on sentence of death.

## *Unternehmen Osterhase*: 29 April–3 May 1943

'Operation Eastern Bunny' was a small, local operation that was conducted by *45. Sicherungs Regiment*, led by *Oberst* Hans Wiemann, against the partisans threatening the Rogatschew–Dovsk and Gomel–Dovsk rail lines in the area of operations of *221. Sicherungs Division*. It began on Thursday, 28 April 1943 and lasted into Monday, 3 May. Towards the end of the operation, two companies from *Sicherungs Bataillon 242* of *Sicherungs Regiment 183* (belonging to *286. Sicherungs Division*) were employed, alongside one company of *Luftwaffe* field troops which was temporarily named '*Luftwaffen-Gefechtskompanie*'.[14] One other source says that for this anti-partisan drive, units of the now-disbanded *Einsatzgruppe D*, moving north from Ukraine to central Russia, also took part in the operation.[15] The troops included *GFP-724*,[16] two companies from *I. Bataillon* of *Sicherungs Regiment 45*[17] (*221. Sicherungs Division*), *I. Abteilung / Artillerie Regiment 221*, *Ost Reiter Schwadronen 203* and *221*, one company from *Sicherungs Regiment 613* (*203. Sicherungs Division*), and about ninety-five *Ordnungsdienst* men who were Eastern volunteers recruited to work for the SD. In April 1943, *Sicherungs Regiment 4* had been tasked with going against the partisans menacing the Rogatschew–Dowsk and Gomel–Dowsk rail lines in the central sector of the jurisdictional region of *221. Sicherungs Division*. *Osterhase* was a continuation of this attempt to keep these two lines open.

In spite of what appeared to be sufficient forces, the German command decided that it did not have enough troops to properly surround the enemy. Instead, units were directed to attack specific villages or important sites.[18] This small anti-partisan drive cost the lives of five members of *45. Sicherungs Regiment* but claimed that around 250 guerrillas had been killed. Only thirty-four rifles were recovered from the battlefield, leading again to speculation that innocent civilians may have been killed in order to swell the numbers of 'partisans' killed in this operation.[19] By 27 April the operation seemed to have been placed in and around the village of Kamenka, which the Germans claimed had been heavily fortified and was acting as a supply base for the partisan units in the region. Interestingly, it appears that the horses, cattle and other livestock which the security troops captured at Kamenka were kept by the troops themselves and not handed over to the local *Wirtschaftskommando* (Economic Command), whose closest unit was located in Gomel.[20]

The local *Wirtschaftskommando* unit was a part of the *Wirtschaftsorganisation Ost* organisation, which had been set up to exploit the East. The main goal was to procure grain and fuel, as well as to conscript the civilian population to work in Germany as forced labourers. For example, during *Unternehmen Osterhase*, the following crops and farm animals were captured by the Germans: 40kg of grain, 26 pigs, 200 sheep, 221 cows, and 95 horses.[21] The fighting next turned to a forest approximately 3km west of the village of Lossof. There the German security troops, with the aid of *Luftwaffe* infantry, were able to drive the guerrillas from the forest while capturing two partisan camps. The surviving partisans fled westward across a swampy region that lay west of the forest. According to an after-action report, the partisans took heavy losses. The report mentioned the great assistance that the *Luftwaffe* troops gave during this action on 29 April 1943. The nature of the anti-partisan war in 1943 intensified, but although the Germans were pouring in more troops to fight the increasing partisan threat, the sheer size of the USSR could never allow for most operations to take place with sufficient German forces that would guarantee that partisan units would not be able to escape these German attacks. As one can see, the amount of territory that German companies had to cover on average was about 16km$^2$ each.

It's no small wonder then, that some or all of the partisan troops targeted would invariably escape these traps. When you add the fact that beginning in the spring of 1943 the number of partisans behind the German lines increased dramatically, you get a recipe for the very results which many of these operations netted. The number of partisans had also significantly increased after the German debacle at Stalingrad. By the spring of 1943 there were about 102,000 guerrillas in the region of *Heeresgruppe Mitte* alone. Simply by comparing three relatively small operations that took place in 1943, we can see that these German anti-partisan drives would almost invariably leave a sufficient amount of territory unguarded, due to lack of sufficient forces, for partisan units to escape through:

Table 11. Example of the Average Number of Inadequate Anti-Partisan Forces per Area of Operation Covered[22]

| Operation | Date | Duration | Area Covered (sq. km.) | No. of Troops (companies and numbers of men) |
|---|---|---|---|---|
| *Ankara I* | Dec 1942 | 6 days | 160 | 10/800 |
| *Ankara II* | Jan 1943 | 5 days | 160 | 15/1200 |
| Average both *Ankara I* and *II* | n/a | 5½ days | 160 | 12.5/1000 |
| *Osterhase* | Apr–May 1943 | 5 days | 125 | 9/720 |

### *Unternehmen Maigewitter:* 5–21 May 1943

A report came into *2. Panzerarmee* in mid-March that from 3–11 March 1943, a great battle had been fought between Kaminski's militia battalions and about 3,000 partisans in the Komaritchi area. It was also noted by the liaison officer of *2. Armee* that Kaminski's men were doing more to aggressively search for and eliminate the guerrillas than the Hungarian security units in the rear of *2. Armee.* Following this action, a major anti-partisan sweep was ordered and planned for May 1943. For this operation, elements of the Hungarian 101st and 102nd Security Divisions, and the *216. Infanterie Division* were to participate. This operation would also include Kaminski's collaborationist brigade. Kaminski's base of operations was the town of Lokot. The first mention of *Maigewitter* (May Thunderstorm) was on 17 May, or a day before the start of the offensive.[23]

The operation was to be launched in the region of *3. Panzerarmee.* Specifically, the areas in and around Surash, Drosdy, Mesha, Vyshodki, Gorodok, and the areas west of the city of Vitebsk. The forces employed during this operation included units from *87. Infanterie Division,* parts of *8. Panzer Division* and several *Ost* battalions under *Korück 582,* as well as *Kosaken Gruppe von Renteln,* a combat group led by *Major der Reserve* (later *Oberstleutnant*) Ewert von Renteln. Renteln's headquarters controlled two *Plastun* (Cossack infantry) battalions.[24] These were *Kosaken Bataillon 623* and *Kosaken Bataillon 625.*[25] Later, *Kosaken Bataillon 622* and *Kosaken Bataillon 623* would be formally grouped under another regimental headquarters, *Ost Regiment Stab 750,*[26] which would become the basis for *(Kosaken) Festungs Grenadier Regiment 360* in the spring of 1944.[27]

In the meantime (mid-1943), *Major* von Renteln led *Kosaken Bataillon 623* and *Kosaken Bataillon 625.* He would later be given control of *Kosaken Bataillon 622* and *Kosaken Bataillon 623* when *Festungs Grenadier Regiment 360* was formed and he would be assigned as the regimental commander.[28] The OKW War Diary for 17 May 1943 mentions a *'Gruppe Hartmann'* which was part of the anti-partisan operation and was moving into positions west of the guerrilla region.[29] This is an obvious reference to *87. Infanterie Division,* whose divisional commander at this time was *Generalleutnant der Artillerie* Walter Hartmann.[30] The forces gathered for the operation from *8. Panzer Division* were grouped into four *Jagdkommandos,* or 'hunter groups'. These groups were mixed in with Eastern troops who knew the language, customs and the countryside. These four *Jagdkommandos* were divided as follows:[31]

*Gefechtsgruppe Oberstleutnant* Abel
- Staff headquarters of *Panzergrenadier Regiment 28*
- *Panzer Aufklärungs Abteilung 8*

One battalion from *Luftwaffe Feld Division 6*[32]
Two platoons from *Pionier Bataillon 59*

*Gefechtsgruppe Oberstleutnant* Neise
*Panzergrenadier Regiment 8*
Four 'Alarm' companies from *8. Panzer Division*
Two platoons from *Pionier Bataillon 59*
*Ost Kompanie 59* (*Oberleutnant* Anton)

*Gefechtsgruppe Major* von Renteln
*Kosaken Bataillon 623*
*Kosaken Bataillon 625*
*Kosaken Kompanie 638*
One platoon from *Pionier Bataillon 59*

*Gefechtsgruppe Oberst* von Scotti
*Jäger Bataillon 1*
*Kosaken Bataillon 631*
*Ost Bataillon Hensen*
Two platoons from *Pionier Bataillon 59*

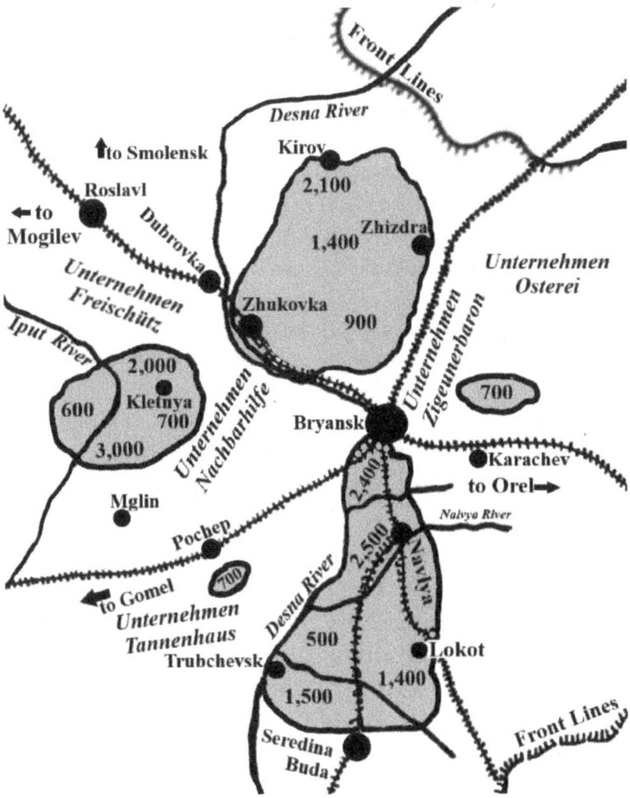


Figure 27. Location of the major anti-partisan operations in the Bryansk region. The partisan strengths and partisan-controlled areas are for the summer of 1943.

On 18 May the Germans reported that Antonyenko, the guerrilla commander of the Alexiev Partisan Brigade, had been killed after *Gruppe Hartmann* had broken through the partisan defences on the western side of the partisan region.[33] On 20 May the Germans took stock of their losses and those of the partisans. Up until then, Axis losses had been twenty-one dead (including five non-Germans), seventy-six wounded (including eighteen non-Germans) and two missing (including one non-German). Partisan losses included 398 enemy dead, 78 taken prisoner, 14 who had deserted, plus 1,679 people who had been apprehended as partisan suspects. Further information was also forthcoming regarding the Alexiev Partisan Brigade which contained five battalions. According to the OKW, one of Antonyenko's commanders by the name of Minikov had killed himself shortly after being captured. The Brigade Adjutant, Sacharov, had been found dead of a self-inflicted bullet wound when the partisan headquarters was secured.[34] Captured booty included 22 machine guns, 78 rifles, 21 machine-pistols, 3 bazookas, 5 mortars, 20,000 rounds of rifle ammunition, 44 horses, 223 cows, and 30 sacks of grain. The operation was concluded on 21 May 1943, but as the following reports indicates some units had to be returned to battle to mop up remaining pockets of resistance:

> Operation May Thunderstorm was concluded on 21 May for the combat groups of the division, the Jagdkommandos attacked into the middle of the pocket by Belikovo, around which the last resistance nests of the partisan lay. Their fighting morale there was low. All four combat groups returned to the original positions after the operation, only the Combat Group Major von Renteln was put back into action to mop up the last partisan vestiges. The Combat Group Lieutenant-Colonel Neise, with Panzer Aufklärungs Abteilung 8, had to be recommitted once again on 22 May in order to storm a strong resistance nest on height 179.5, where the Soviets stubbornly defended with heavy machine guns. During the fight, 50 partisans and their commander were able to escape.[35]

At that time, final German losses were twenty-three killed, eighty wounded, and two missing. Final captured items included 24 machine guns, 95 rifles, 21 machine-pistols, 3 bazookas, 5 mortars, 2 pistols, and 20,000 rounds of rifle ammunition. Animals and foodstuffs included a grand total of 292 cows, 45 horses and 150 sacks of grain. On 26 May the German Armed Forces High Command listed the final partisan losses for the operation. Eight hundred guerrillas were listed killed in battle, while 21 had deserted and 2,195 partisan suspects or supporters had been apprehended. In addition, seventy-seven bunkers and fifteen partisan camps had been destroyed while numerous hand grenades and other munitions were captured.[36] In June 1943, shortly after the conclusion of the drive, some of the partisan brigades in the region began to move out of the Vitebsk area and to take up new positions south of the Dvina River.[37] This may have occurred as a result of a lack of available supplies, since a serious food shortage developed in the region where the operation was launched shortly after it was concluded. Ponomarenko, the Chief of Staff of the Partisan Movement, ordered that food supplies be flown into the area but the importance of the region eventually diminished for the following reasons:

> The German anti-partisan operations, the food shortage, and the westward movement of the front combined to reduce the importance of the Velizh–Vitebsk partisan complex. The partisan brigades west of the Vitebsk–Nevel line, reinforced partly by the remnants of the brigades of the Velizh–Vitebsk sector, now assumed greater importance.[38]

The combination of operations *Kugelblitz* and *Maigewitter* combined to greatly reduce the partisan threat in the Vitebsk–Velizh region. While *Kugelblitz* did most of the damage against the estimated 6,000 partisans there, *Maigewitter* finished the job. Partisan attacks continued however, to target the rail lines in particular. The *Kaminski Brigade* had been responsible for a good number of those partisan losses. So effective was the unit from 1941–3 that the Soviets had placed a bounty on Bronislav Kaminski's head.

## *Unternehmen Zigeunerbaron:* 16 May–6 June 1943

'Operation Gipsy Baron' is considered to be the largest anti-partisan operation conducted in the region of Bryansk during the war.[39] Preparations by way of unit deployments began as early as 12 May 1943. The manoeuvre involved a total of six divisions: five infantry and one tank, plus other supporting forces. The higher headquarters elements which were to control all of these Axis forces were the staff and units of *XLVIII. Panzerkorps* and *Korück 532*. The divisions and other forces were as follows:[40]

*4. Infanterie Division*
*7. Infanterie Division*
*292. Infanterie Division*
*10. Panzer Grenadier Division*
*18. Panzer Division*
*102. (leichte) Ungarische Infanterie Division:* two infantry regiments

*Kaminski Brigade*:[41] four regiments, one artillery battalion and a tank company
*Ost Bataillon z.b.V.* : three companies
*Kosaken Kavallerie Sicherungs Abteilung III. / 57*: four cavalry squadrons[42]
*Ost Bataillon 615*: four rifle companies
*Ost Bataillon 616*: four rifle companies
*Ost Bataillon 617*: four rifle companies
*Ost Bataillon 620*: four rifle companies
*Ost Artillerie Abteilung 621*: three artillery batteries.
*Armenisches Infanterie Bataillon II. / 9*: five rifle companies
*Aserbeidschanische Infanterie Bataillon 807*: five rifle companies

The initial forces also could count on elements of the *XLVII. Panzerkorps*, which had their own Eastern units attached to the corps headquarters command and were employed as well in this operation.

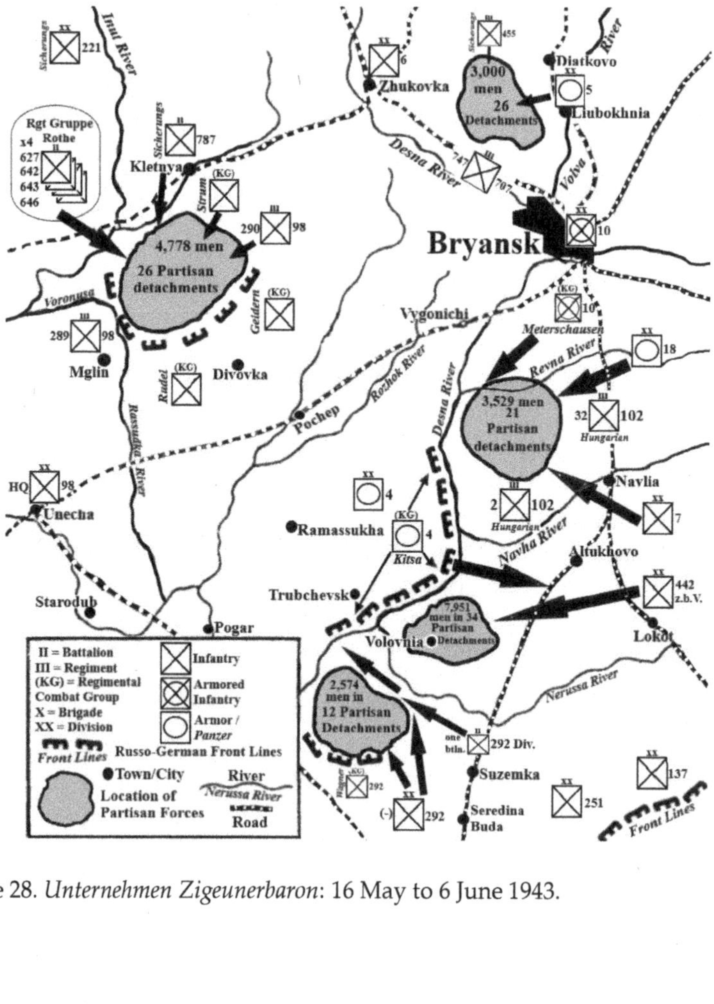


Figure 28. *Unternehmen Zigeunerbaron*: 16 May to 6 June 1943.

These forces included:[43]

*Kosaken Kavallerie Schwadron 1. / 137*: one Cossack cavalry squadron
*Kosaken Kavallerie Schwadron 2. / 137*: one Cossack cavalry squadron
*Ost Kompanie 45*: one rifle company
*Ost Kompanie 102*: one rifle company

The Germans did not wish to let the Soviets find out that the *18. Panzer Division* was to be employed against the partisans, so they referred to the unit during the operation as the *318. Infanterie Division*'.[44] This region contained about 6,000 guerrillas. It was well and good that the Germans employed an armoured unit since they quickly discovered to their consternation that the partisans not only possessed heavy artillery pieces, but a few tanks as well. The sweep was wide in its use of troops and eventually netted 15,812 civilians evacuated from the area, 1,584 partisans killed, 207 camps destroyed, 2,930 bunkers destroyed, 1,568 captured, while an additional 869 deserted to the Germans and collaborationist forces. The desertion rate for the partisans had been high and a German after-action report had attributed this to the approximately 840,000 leaflets dropped in the area before and during the war, urging guerrillas to desert by promising that not everyone in the region would be killed.[45]

Weapons captured included 55 mortars, 14 anti-tank guns, 28 bazookas, 1 T-34 tank and two light tanks, 2 armoured cars, 2 tractors, 1 locomotive, 2 planes, 124 machine guns, 88 machine-pistols, 1 revolver, 1 light pistol, 1,117 rifles (of which 181 were automatic rifles and 26 were sniper rifles), 165,720 rounds of rifle ammunition, 30,000 rounds of machine-pistol ammunition, 1,900 mortar rounds, 1,000 artillery rounds, 562 bazooka projectiles, 660lbs of explosives, 380 cows, 316 horses, 30 harnesses, 717 *panje* wagons, 183 sleds, 25 parachutes, and 110 pair of skis.[46]

## *Unternehmen Nachbarhilfe*: 19–27 May 1943

In preparation for their summer offensive of 1943, the Germans had planned several major anti-partisan drives in the Bryansk region. This was an area with vitally important rail lines and communications centres which would be of paramount important in the coming offensive. The elimination of the estimated 24,000–26,000 guerrillas in the Bryansk area, or their suppression, was the aim of these anti-partisan drives.[47] In the rear area of *2. Panzerarmee* alone, there was an estimated 16,000 partisans hiding in about 4,000 square miles.[48] It was by far the biggest concentration of the Bryansk region. By neutralising the guerrilla threat, the Germans would thus be assured a safe line of communication and supply line which would benefit their upcoming offensive. On 19 May 1943, the Germans launched *Unternehmen Nachbarhilfe* ('Good Neighbour') just west of the city of Bryansk. This was an area bordering the town of Kletnya. This operation was aimed at the estimated 6,500–7,000 guerrillas in this area. The primary German formation used in this operation was the *98. Infanterie Division.*

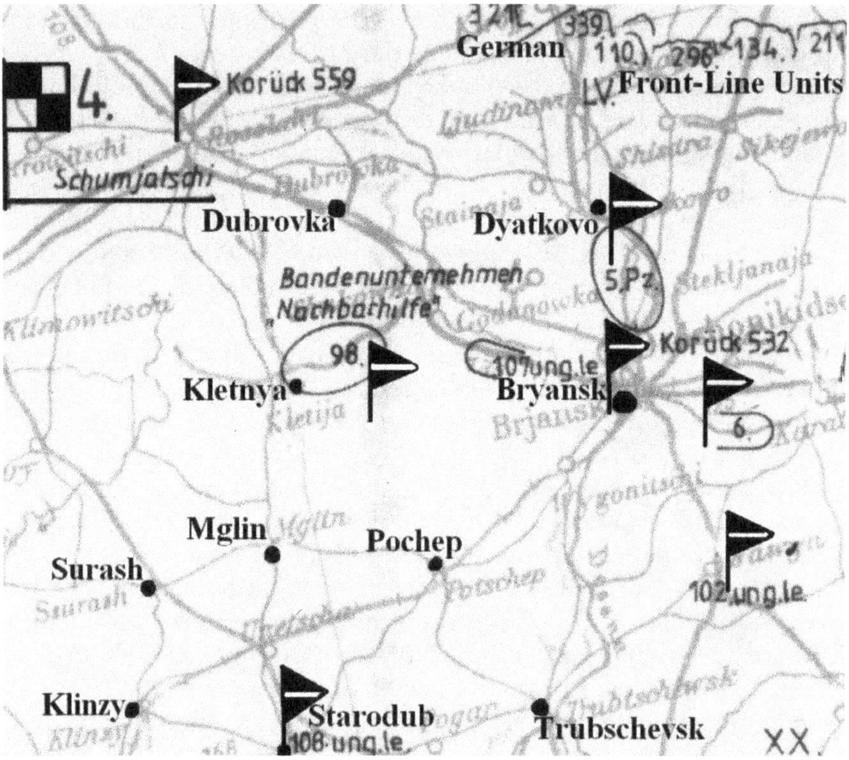


Figure 29. Area of operations for *Unternehmen Nachbarhilfe*, May 1943.

Up until March 1943, it had been holding the front line along the Spass–Demensk–Dorogubusch line. Now it was withdrawn from the front line and ordered to the Mamayevka forest, located roughly between Bryansk and Roslavl, and north of Pocher. The thickness and almost inaccessibility of the Mamayevka forest made it a perfect hiding place for partisan camps. This was especially true with regard to motorised vehicles, even tracked vehicles like tanks, that would find it difficult to traverse such a thick forest.[49] A distance of some 140km separated Bryansk from Roslavl. This is why it was the perfect location for many partisan bands. For example, the Grishin Partisan Brigade (1,000–2,000 men) had several well-equipped camps which they could use to rest, refit, and rearm.[50]

The *98. Infanterie Division* was split up into three combat groups, code-named 'Sturm', 'Rothe', and 'Reidel'. *Korück 559* would also help to coordinate the drive. The town of Kletnya was completely surrounded by this partisan region which was to be swept clean of guerrilla units. At the time, the headquarters of the *98. Infanterie Division* was in that town. The Hungarian 108th Security Division, stationed in Starodub, about 43km south-south-east of Kletnya, was to act as a blocking force but was not to advance against the partisans. The *5. Panzer Division,* which had seen some heavy action in February and early March, was withdrawn from the front lines in April and took part in this drive.[51] The contribution to this operation by the *Kaminski Brigade* was strictly limited to supplying interpreters, guides, and translators for the German combat groups. No 'People's Army' militia battalions were employed. It is interesting to note that the SD sent specialised sections to each of the three regimental combat groups (i.e., 'Sturm', 'Rothe', and 'Reidel') which would help screen and coordinate the speedy evacuation of the entire male population in the area in question. The SD platoons attached to each regiment had the specific duty of evacuating all of the males between the ages of 16–55.[52]

It was stressed in their orders that persons deemed to not be members of the partisans were to be released and sent home immediately, but they would have to identify their home village or town for future reference. On 24 May the OKW recorded that twenty-one 'bandit camps' had so far been discovered and destroyed by the German units performing the drive.[53] A further twenty-five bunkers were destroyed on 27 May 1943.[54] At the end of the operation a total of 16,900 'suspects' were evacuated. The plunder taken by the *Wirtschaftskommando* was relatively meagre: 171 horses, 15 cows, 9 cattle, and 2 sheep. Guerrilla suspects were to be sent directly to Kletnya where the *98. Infanterie Division* would forward the 'suspects' to the *707. Infanterie Division (bodenständig)* for further interrogation.[55] Kletnya was therefore the combat collection point for *98. Infanterie Division*.[56] *Nachbarhilfe II* was a follow up which was launched on 28 May and lasted until 3 June 1943. In this secondary drive, the Germans cleared out an area 18km north-east of Kletnya. Booty in this mopping up operation included 1,000 pairs of skis and

206 sacks of grain.[57] The final tally sheet for *Nachbarhilfe* was 571 partisans killed and 368 taken prisoner, 24 partisan deserters, and 16,990 'partisan suspects' and people apprehended and evacuated from the region. A total of 65 forest camps containing 833 bunkers were destroyed. Captured enemy weapons included 2 anti-tank guns, 6 mortars, 7 submachine guns, 21 light machine guns, 69 machine-pistols, 10 pistols, 11 anti-tank rifles, 231 rifles, 98 hand grenades, 64 land mines, 2,200 pounds of explosives, 10,000 rounds of ammunition, 1 aircraft plus a replacement engine, 1,700 pairs of skis, 100 *panje* wagons, and 171 horses.

German losses were 66 killed, 143 wounded, and 24 missing while pro-German indigenous losses were 64 killed, 124 wounded, and 24 missing.[58] Three tanks and 21 artillery pieces were captured during the drive. In addition, 15,812 civilians were evacuated from the region, while 2,930 bunkers and 207 guerrilla camps were destroyed. During this operation, the *Kaminski Brigade* also assisted in the creation of railway security units attached to the German Army in the Bryansk region.[59] A comparison of the number of partisans in the area before the drive (6,000 men) with the number of guerrillas which remained in the region after the drive (4,000–5,000 men) and those listed as killed or captured (3,152 men) would lead us to believe that once again the local Russian peasant population was made to suffer for the actions of the guerrillas. Here again was the tactic of *Kollektive Gewaltmassnahmen* (collective punishment).[60] This is confirmed by the following statement:

> In mid-May 1943 *18. Panzer Division* was pulled out of the line and sent to the forest area south of Bryansk. It was assigned the codename '*318. Infanterie Division*' while moving to the new intended positions. Together with other German, Hungarian, and Russian and Cossack volunteer units, they were ordered to 'purge' this forest region of an estimated 3,000–3,500 guerrillas. The troops about to take part in this operation, codenamed *Ziegeunerbaron*, were ordered to evacuate all of the civilians unfit for military service and to allow them to take only enough food for fourteen days. The rest of the property was to be confiscated by the Army. Men between the ages of 15 and 65 were to be treated as POWs. Red Army officers and commissars were to be taken to the intelligence section, while soldiers, party functionaries and Jews were to be used as guides or to clear mine fields. All villages in the area were to be burned down.[61]

It appears that the Army and police units had been forewarned to try and completely clean out the region of life. The plan was to try and deny the local partisan units any food or base of support. While this tactic was beginning to have effects, these tactics alienated that part of the population which had up until then remained neutral or friendly to the Germans. It was also a losing method since the partisan command would begin supplying its units by air and were thus able to keep its guerrilla forces in the regions which were devastated by these 'scorched earth' drives. In fact, partisan forces were getting air drops even before the operation was concluded. One inventive German regiment, mimicking how the guerrillas were signalling the Red Air Force for supply drops, received Red Army supplies for four consecutive nights during the anti-partisan drive. On the fifth night bombs were dropped and the German regimental commander realised that the partisans had informed the Red Air Force of the ruse.[62]

On 28 May the OKW reported that *XLVII. Panzerkorps* experienced good advances in spite of the difficult terrain in which its units were operating.[63] On 3 June a partisan group was reported to have been caught 27km north-east of Seredina Buda. On 5 June the OKW reported that *7. Infanterie Division* and *292. Infanterie Division* had made further gains during the operation by breaking through partisan lines to the east and south-west. On 6 June the operation was concluded. On that final day numerous camps were located by units of the *292. Infanterie Division* and destroyed.[64]

## *Unternehmen Freischütz:* 20–30 May 1943

*Unternehmen Freischütz* was an operation against the forest-massif north and north-west of Bryansk. The German *LV. Armeekorps* was employed as a higher command headquarters to manage part of the operation, including units of *5. Panzer Division* and the *6. Infanterie Division,* as well as *Ost Regiment Stab 455* which would control the *807. Aserbeidschan Infanterie Bataillon.*[65] Other forces earmarked for 'Operation Fire-at-Will' included the *1. Volksarmee Bataillon* and *2. Volksarmee Bataillon* belonging to the *1. Regiment* of the *Kaminski Brigade.* These two RONA battalions were to operate under *6. Infanterie Division.*[66]

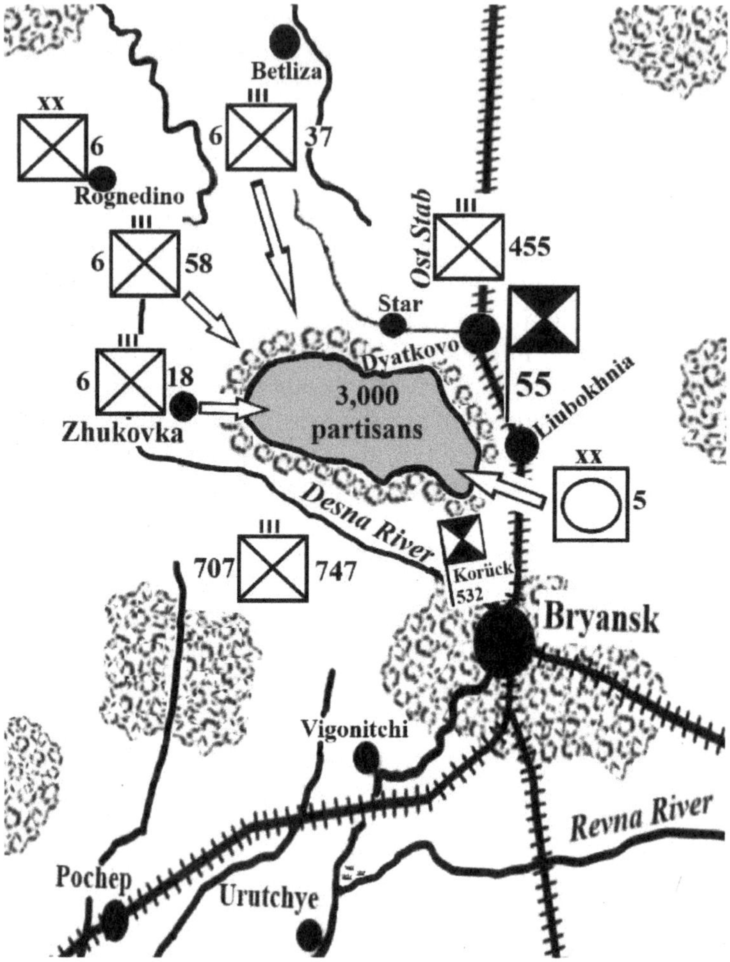


Figure 30. Area of operations and line of attack for *Unternehmen Freischütz*, May 1943.

Other forces for the drive included *Infanterie Regiment 747* of the *707. Infanterie Division,* which would act as 'Security Group South', as well as the *3. Volksarmee Bataillon* of the *1. Regiment, Kaminski Brigade,* and the *11. Volksarmee Bataillon* of the *4. Regiment, Kaminski Brigade*. German security forces included *Sicherungs Bataillon 587* and *Sicherungs Bataillon 791*. Finally, *Panzerzug Nr. 4* (Armoured Train No. 4) was also employed as a blocking force. The operation was one of many preliminary operations undertaken by the Germans as part of their preparations for Operation *Zitadelle* (launched on 5 July 1943).

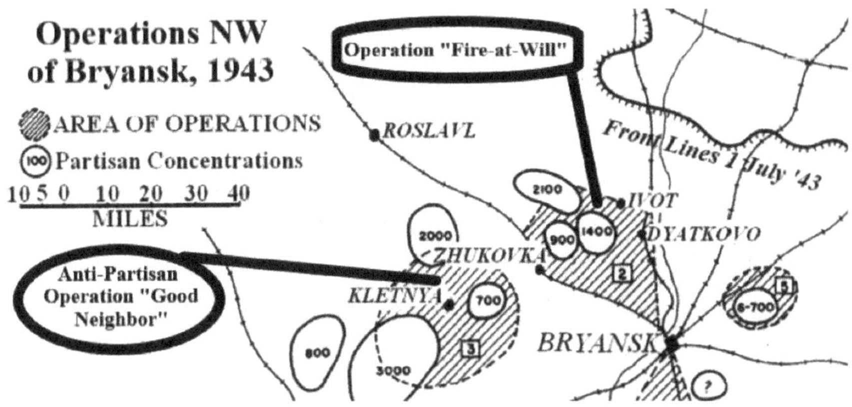


Figure 31. General location where *Nachbarhilfe* and *Freischütz* were launched.

The operation was targeting three principal partisan formations that together numbered about 4,400 guerrilla fighters. The operation proved only a partial success, as only 1,459 partisans were killed. The remaining 2,521 guerrillas managed to escape, with 420 taken prisoner. Axis losses were reported to have been about 100 killed and an unknown number of wounded. Although the operation was judged a success, by mid-June 1943 the area in question was once again threatened by about 2,000 Soviet partisans. It was during this operation that members of *Grenadier Regiment 39* (*6. Infanterie Division*), committed a war crime. There, on 21 May 1943, German soldiers from this regiment marched through one of many villages that covered the region. The village was called Belev by the locals. In that village, the population had barricaded themselves in their homes and refused to come out when ordered to do so by the Germans. After a few minutes of waiting for the villagers to comply, the soldiers broke into the homes and found a significant amount of ammunition.[67] The fifty-nine inhabitants of this village, which lay just north of Matrenovka, were executed on the spot, and the village was burned down.[68] Because this action on the part of the German soldiers went against the orders given, which banned the burning of villages and the random shootings of civilians, it was immediately reported to higher command: '*Grenadier Regiment 37* encountered resistance from the residents who had barricaded themselves in the houses and refused entry. Ammunition was found. According to corps orders, the entire population is massacred and the village itself is completely destroyed.'[69]

In April 1943 the area of responsibility for *Korück 532* (behind *9. Armee* lines), was expanded to now include the regions of Novgorod–Severskij–Seredina Buda. These areas would now remain in the permanent care of *Korück 532*. In order to reduce the size of the region that this rear-area command had to control, in June 1943 the northermost part, Kletnya, Südrognedino and Dubrovka, were given over to *4. Armee* control. However, this only happened after the conclusion of *Unternehmen Nachbarhilfe* and *Freischütz*.[70]

## *Unternehmen Tannenhauser*: 14–24 June 1943

The next anti-partisan operation launched in the Bryansk region during the May-June 1943 period was an anti-guerrilla sweep in the area east of Starodub, south-east of the Pochep rail line and west of the Desna River line. It was code-named *Unternehmen Tannenhauser* (also spelled 'Tannhäuser'), after a three-act opera that was written by the composer Richard Wagner between 1842–5. The area where the operation was to take place had an estimated 700 Partisans that the Germans hoped could be destroyed. The word 'Tannenhaus' (without the *umlaut* over the letter 'a'), means 'fir house'. This has led some historians calling this anti-partisan drive as 'Operation Fir House'. The Axis security units employed for this drive included the following forces:

*Sicherungs Bataillon 587.*
*II. Bataillon* of *Infanterie Regiment 727, 707. Sicherungs Division.*
*Kavallerie Verbände 'Trubtschevsk'.*[71]
*Armenisches Feld Bataillon II/9.*
*Ost Bataillon 618.*
Part of *Ost Bataillon 617.*
Two companies each of *Sicherungs Bataillon 304* and *Sicherungs Bataillon 757.*
The *12. Volksarmee Bataillon* of the *4. Regiment, Kaminski Brigade.*

*Unternehmen Tannenhauser* was finally concluded on 24 June 1943, without any enemy contact.[72] Apparently, the partisans had been able to extricate their units from the encircling native and German security troops. Again, we see that insufficient German forces worked in favour of the guerrillas, as these anti-partisan encirclements were never completely escape-proof. The region in and around the city of Bryansk was the subject of numerous major and minor German anti-partisan drives. A total of fifty took place between 1942 and 1943, but the following table lists thirty-eight of them:[73]

Table 12. Major and Minor Anti-partisan Operations in the Bryansk Region, 1942–1943

| Codename | Date | Region |
|---|---|---|
| *Fuchs* | 6 Feb 1942 | Around Kolodnya |
| *Anton I–III* | 3–6 Mar 1942 | East of Žukovka |
| *Jobst* | 20 Mar 1942 | West of Žuriniči |
| *Vogelsang I* | 18 May–18 Jun 1942 | Forest-massif by Dyat'kovo |
| *Louisenthal* | 29–30 May 1942 | West of Desna |
| *Vogelsang II* | 25 Jun–3 Jul 1942 | Between Reka Vet'ma and the Desna River |
| *Graf Strachwitz* | 20 Jun–6 Jul 1943 | Trubčevsk |
| *Waldkater*[74] | 16 Jul 1943 | Forest-massif by Kletnya |
| *Grünspecht I–VIII* | 9 Jul–21 Aug 1942 | Forest-massif west of Lokot |
| *Waldesruhe* | 20–26 Jul 1942 | West of the Desna River |
| *Karl May* | 31 Jul–2 Aug 1942 | Around the municipality of Gigant |
| *Adler* | 16–18 Aug 1942 | West of Star |
| *Hirschtod I* | 20–27 Aug 1942 | Between Počep and Trubčevsk |
| *Passau* | 24 Aug 1942 | South of Starja Lavšina |
| *Hüsecken I* | 31 Aug–2 Sep 1942 | North of Deryugino |
| *Erntefest I und II* | 6–10 Sep 1942 | North of Fošnja |
| *Hüsecken II*[75] | 17 Sep 1942 | North of Deryugino |
| *Dreieck* | 17–20 Sep 1942 | Region south of Brjansk up to Revna River |
| *Viereck* | 20 Sep–3 Oct 1942 | Region south of the Revna River and up to Navlja |
| *Michael* | 24 Sep 1942 | North of Ržanica |
| *Hirschtod II* | First week of Nov 1942 | Ramasucha Forest |
| *Klette I* | 12–25 Oct 1942 | North of Kletnya |
| *Hubertus*[76] | 3–13 Nov 1942 | South of Dmitrovsk |
| *Eisvogel I und II*[77] | 19–24 Nov 1942 | West of Navlya |
| *Zeisig* | 22–28 Nov 1942 | West of Bytoš |
| *Eisvogel*[78] | 15–20 Dec 1942 | N Kletnja |

| Codename | Date | Region |
|---|---|---|
| *Bärenfang* | 18–20 Dec 1942 | Area between Navlya and Bach Dumča |
| *Eisbär I–III* | Jan 1943 | East of Dmitriev-L'govskiy |
| *Klette II* | 22 Jan–9 Feb 1943 | Forest area around Mamayevka, south-east of Kletnya |
| *Bärenfang I–IV* | Feb 1943 | Forest between Seredina-Buda and Trubčevsk |
| *Eisrose* | 25 Mar 1943 | South of the road between Bryansk and Karačev |
| *Waldweben* | Apr 1943 | Region under *Korück 532* |
| *Panzergrenadier* | 17–24 Apr 1943 | Ramasucha Forest |
| *Finkenfang* | 1–8 May 1943 | Rail line between Vitemlja and Šuravka |
| *Zwischenspiel* | 10 May 1943 | West of Peklina |
| *Maiglöckchen* | 10 May 1943 | South-east of Bryansk |
| *Osterei* | May 1943 | North and north-west of Karačev |
| *Tannenhauser* | 14–24 Jun 1943 | East of Starodub, and south-east of the Pochep rail line |

## *Unternehmen Draufgänger I und II*: 26 April–10 May 1943

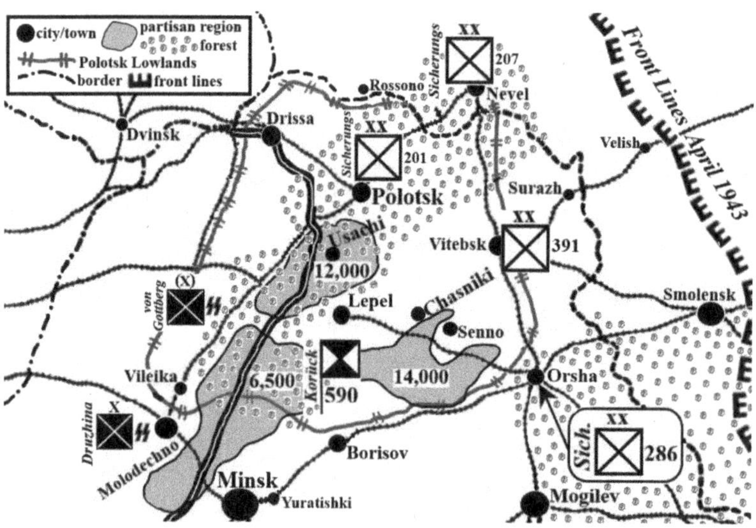


Figure 32. Area of operations for *Unternehmen Draufgänger*, April 1943.

All of the previous operations were to pale in comparison to the next few operations, however. *Draufgänger I* and *II* ('Daredevil I and II') were launched in the area surrounding Borisov–Lepel–Molodechno and were in actuality preparatory operations for the larger, more important anti-partisan drive, *Kottbus*. The main goal of *Draufgänger I* and *II* was the elimination of the approximately 6,000–7,000 partisans in the region bordering Molodechno, Vileika, Lepel and Borisov.[79] *Draufgänger I* began on 28 April 1943, and lasted until 30 April. *Draufgänger II* began on 1 May and lasted until 12 May.[80] The officer in overall command of both operations was *SS-Obergruppenführer und General der Polizei* Kurt von Gottberg, although for operational purposes *Oberst der Schutzpolizei* Hans Griep would command the actual combat units.[81] The units involved in the two 'Daredevil' drives were the following:

*SS-Druzhina Verbände*
*SS-Sonder Bataillon Dirlewanger*[82]
*SS-Polizeiregiment 2*
*Schutzmannschaft Bataillon 118*
*Polizei Panzer Kompanie 1*
*Polizei Panzer Kompanie 12.*[83]

The *Dirlewanger* battalion would take prominence during the operation for employing the harshest tactics. No locality in which the unit visited during the operation remained unscathed. Dirlewanger himself set the tone for his unit's actions:

> Dirlewanger demanded that his battalion force the villagers to walk on mined roads. He argued 'Roadblocks and artificial obstacles are almost always mined . . . Therefore, as a general rule: never remove barriers yourself, but always have them removed by natives. Blood saved justifies loss of time'. Dirlewanger himself came forward with his car. He ordered that all the people from the surrounding towns had to be rounded up. These people had to walk forward along these paths, tied together in a row, and behind them came another row . . . these people were completely blown apart and included women and old men.[84]

### *Unternehmen Seydlitz*: 26 June–27 July 1943

This drive was a local operation launched in the Ovruch–Mosyr region. Ovruch is located about 48km (some 30 miles) from Korosten, and 133km from Zhytomyr. It lies about 92km from Mosyr. In the course of the operation, the *SS-Kavallerie Division 'Florian Geyer'* destroyed 96 villages, killed 5,106 people, took 606 prisoners, deported 9,166 people for forced labour in Germany, and confiscated 19,941 head of cattle. The *5. Regiment* of the *Kaminski Brigade* as well as units of *Korück 582* and parts of *35. Infanterie Division* and *252. Infanterie Division* took part in this operation.

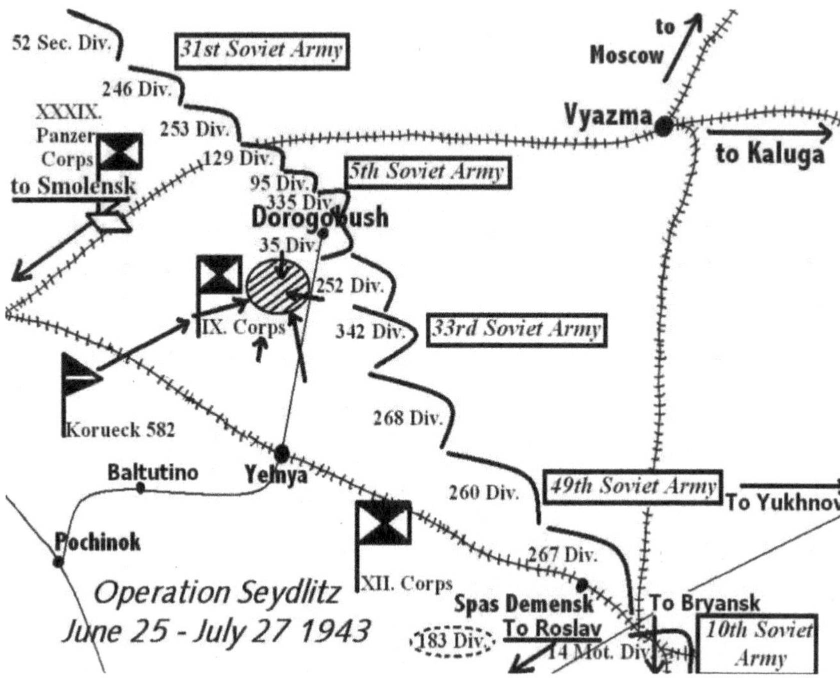


Figure 33. Area of operations for *Unternehmen Seydlitz*, 25–27 July 1943.

The *252. Infanterie Division* contributed one reinforced battalion of 1,300 men for the drive.[85] In addition, *SS-Polizeiregiment 11* and *Polizei Panzer Kompanie 10* were also employed.[86] *Jäger Bataillon 4* and *Radfahr Sicherungs Regiment 2*, both stationed in Smolensk, were also utilised. The operation was almost anti-climactic due to the events which were occurring between Orel and Belgorod.[87] The actions there would overshadow this drive and its final outcome in mid-July would make this anti-partisan operation superfluous.

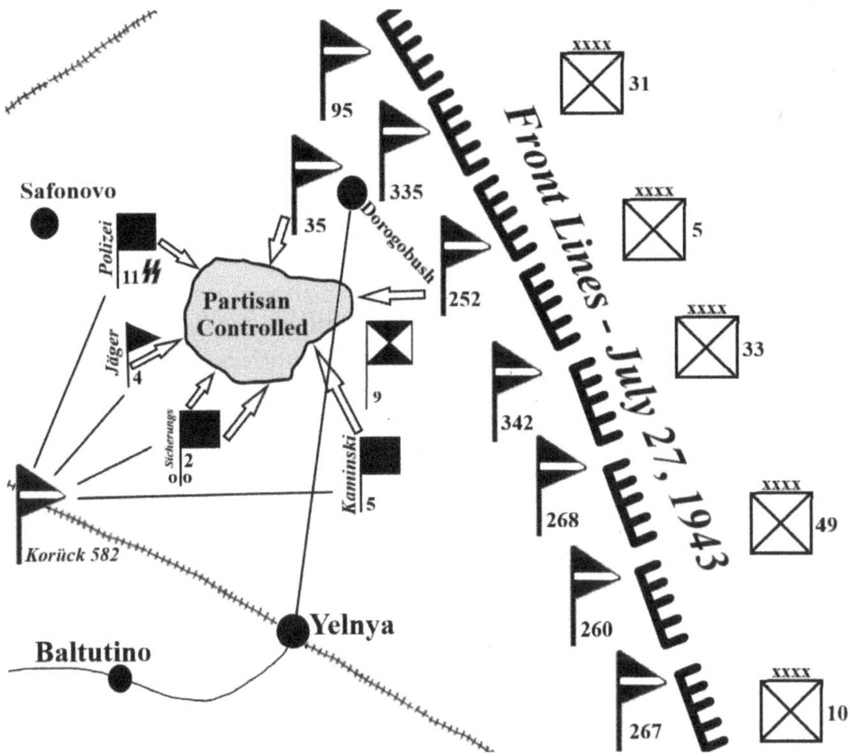


Figure 34. Detail view of *Unternehmen Seydlitz.*

## *Unternehmen Hermann:* 15 July–5 August 1943

Operation Hermann took place in July and August 1943 around the Naliboki forests west of Minsk. The principal forces deployed for the operation included *1. SS Infanterie Brigade (motorisiert), Polizeiregiment 2, (Gendarmerie) Einsatzgruppe Körner* and *Gendarmerie Kommando z.b.V. Kreikenbom,*[88] *Polizei Schutzenregiment 31* and *SS-Sonder Bataillon Dirlewanger,* as well as an *SD-Kommando* from the *Kommandeur der Sicherheitspolizei in Weißrussland.*[89] This was to simultaneously target the liquidation of the ghetto in Glebokie, while also aiming to destroy the Bielsky partisan unit in the Naliboki forest. The forest was located in the Novogrudok region and encompassed the areas surrounding Slutsk, Baranovichi, and Novogrudok.[90] The partisan unit had been singled out for their actions in trying to save Jews from the region before, during, and after the fourth *Aktion* against the ghetto Jews in Novogrudok on 7 May 1943.

Other non-Jewish partisan units were also targeted. The fact that the Bielski partisan *Otriad* (led by Tuvia Bielski) was Jewish-run and manned completely by Jews made it a target of special attention for the Germans. In fact, this partisan unit was so active that even during this German anti-guerrilla operation aimed at the brigade, the partisan commander found time to seek vengeance on a local farmer who had informed on the unit and was responsible for the deaths of at least fourteen Jews.[91] Many authors are unsure about this operation's start and finish date. For example, one author states that the drive began on 7 July 1943.[92] Another author affirms that the drive began on 12 July and ended on 11 August.[93] Still another author states that the operation began on 15 July and ended on 5 August 1943.[94] One other source says that the drive began on 13 July and only lasted until 19 July 1943.[95] What is sure is that the offensive was a major one, employing numerous German and collaborationist forces with an equivalent strength of four or five brigades. The Bielski partisan *Otriad* fought hard although admittedly, the Jewish battalion-sized 'brigade', along with the local non-Jewish Russian partisan unit was forced to withdraw further into the Naliboki forest as the operation progressed:

> The party seized the roads and planted mines. At a distance we could see military vehicles. Before the first German vehicle reached the first road-block, a bullet was fired at it by a Russian partisan. It was later found out that he was a traitor, although he pleaded that his shot was an accident. The truck stopped as well as the entire convoy. The soldiers jumped out of the vehicles and started to shoot in all directions. The partisans did not want to come out and fight on the open battlefield, and retreated. The ambush failed. The mines remained in the roads. Our comrades told me the details of the ambush. They complained that all of them could have been killed because of one traitor. In the meantime, we went deeper into the forest.[96]

This operation had included some Belarusian units as attested to the following statement from a member of the Bielski Partisan Brigade in early August 1943:

> We turned back. We didn't go into the swamp but walked along a path that Michlis found. We came close to a road along which the Germans were supposed to appear. We went out to the road and our spirits rose. We were still walking when we heard the shot of a cannon and a shell exploding with force. We heard the piercing whistle and saw from which direction the shot had come. We fell to the ground and crawled among the bushes; then another shell, and another. A cannon was probably

> shooting from the turret of a tank, shooting without let-up. I was certain the Germans were beginning to advance after the bombardment, as was customary. But we were mistaken. The Germans were very close to us; only half a kilometre separated us from them. We hurried and advanced several hundred meters toward our group; suddenly a hail of rifle shots burst in our vicinity. I thought we were lost. We stretched out in the ground. We distinguished White Russian voices: 'Hurry. Grab the Jews'. This was an attack on our deserted camp. We were very close and heard the crack of dry twigs under the feet of Germans and the police, but we didn't see a thing. The forest was very thick. 'Grab the cow. Grab this, grab that'. I understood that they were shouting to scare us, thinking that we might be lying in ambush. The Germans would always walk behind; the first would always be local police.[97]

The operation also involved German planes which paved the way by bombing suspected partisan positions. A Fiesler Fi 156 Storch scout plane would fly as low over the forest as was possible. When a suspected camp was discovered, the ground units would be alerted but would not attack on the ground until the German bombers could drop bombs on the camp. There were several instances during the drive that have been documented by partisan witnesses who saw German planes bombing the forest. Given the location of this anti-partisan drive (just west of Minsk), the Ju 87 Stuka dive bombers were almost certainly those from *Sonder Schwadron Gamringer* (led by *Luftwaffe Major* Johann Gamringer), which was a part of *Luftflotte 6* (6th Air Fleet). This fleet had created a special wing specifically for operations against partisan forces.[98] *Sonder Schwadron Gamringer* was a part of that wing.

When we look at the German order of battle, the drive included the following units:[99]

*1. SS-Infanterie Brigade*
*SS-Polizeiregiment 2*
SS *Sonder Bataillon Dirlewanger*
*Polizei Schutzenregiment 31*
*(ukrainische) Schutzmannschaft Bataillon 57*
*Polizei Panzer Kompanie 12*
*Polizei Panzer Kompanie 1*
*(litauische) Schutzmannschaft Bataillon 15*
*(lettische) Schutzmannschaft Bataillon 271*
*(weissruthenische) Schutzmannschaft Bataillon 47*
*(weissruthenische) Schutzmannschaft Bataillon 46*
*(ukrainische) Schutzmannschaft Bataillon 118*[100]
*1. Batterie der Schutzmannschaft Artillerie Ersatz Abteilung 56*
*Gendarmerie Zug (mot.) 21*[101]
*Stuka Gruppe* (Stuka dive bomber group)

The majority of the ground forces were under the command of *SS-Kampfgruppe von Gottberg*. The commander of *(ukrainische) Schutzmannschaft Bataillon 57, Hauptmann der Schutzpolizei* Hans Siegling, won notable mention in a post-operative report:

> During Operation 'Hermann' in the area of Naliboki Forest–Novogrudok from July 13–19 1943, Hauptmann Siegling again distinguished himself with his exemplary model bravery and daring. The 57th Schuma Battalion, reinforced by several companies from the Schutzmannschaft units in Baranovichi, Turets, and Mir occupied the switch position in the Nieman River on July 15, 1943.[102]

During the advance, partisan forces attempted, with the 'Mischka' partisan band leading the way, to cross the river with superior forces on rafts. According to the after-action report written by the Germans, only through the 'sensible, courageous and adroit leadership of *Hauptmann der Schutzpolizei* Siegling was the enemy breakout thwarted with severe losses to the partisan bands'. That proved vital to the overall success of the operation. Planning ahead had also proved helpful to the Germans, as they had emptied out and burned down villages that surrounded the area to be attacked. This greatly limited any assistance that the encircled guerrillas would receive during the operation. The remnants of the Bielski *Otriad* withdrew into the swampy areas around Krasnaya Gorka.[103] One other source state that both Ukrainian manned *Schutzmannschaft Bataillon 115* and *Schutzmannschaft Bataillon 118* were also employed in this operation.[104] The exact number of partisans killed during this drive is unknown, but it cost the lives of at least 4,280 people, while another 20,954 were arrested, out of which about 5,000 were deemed fit and sent to the *Reich* as forced labourers.[105] The local *Wirtschftskommando* confiscated 1,064 cows, 283 horses, and 1,146 sheep.[106] As stated previously, the *SS-Sonder Bataillon Dirlewanger* was responsible for driving hundreds of Russian peasants from their villages and sending them to the rear for transport to Germany.[107] The *Dirlewanger* formation reported killing '1,617 bandits' and arresting 2,955 people for slave labour in the *Reich*. Oskar Dirlewanger was promoted to SS *Obersturmbannführer* on 1 July 1943.[108] This was shortly before the start of Operation Hermann. Five days after the end of the drive, on 10 August 1943 the order came through to expand SS *Sonder Bataillon Dirlewanger* into a regiment. The reward for such brutality was clear: promotion and expansion. The order was signed by *SS-Obergruppenführer* Hans Jüttner.[109] However, the actual expansion

Two female members of the partisans, some time in 1943. Women partisan fighters were active in many guerrilla units. They were particularly useful because, dressed in peasant attire, they would be less conspicuous than a man traveling through the countryside. (*Minsk State Archive*)

Interesting photo of four well-armed partisans. One is using the DP-27 light machine gun which uses the 7.62×54mm cartridge. The other three guerrillas are armed with the PPSh 41 submachine gun. (*Minsk State Archive*)

Spring 1943, somewhere in the marshlands of the Pripet Marshes (also known as the Pinsk Marshes). Here we see the leadership of a partisan Otriad preparing for a raid. Although the photo was most likely staged for propaganda purposes, it nevertheless depicts the reality of the war behind the lines. The only exception is that they are seen preparing out in the open. In actuality, this type of planning would have occurred at the base camp just before departing for the operation. (*Minsk State Archive*)

A German patrol trudges through one of hundreds of Russian swamps, hunting for partisans in the summer of 1943. (*SA-kuva*)

A scene repeated all too often during the war: a village goes up in flames. (*SA-kuva*)

An *SS-Untersturmführer* supervises the destruction of weapons, some time in 1943. (*Bundesarchiv*)

German army troops hanging two partisan suspects. They appear satisfied with themselves for what they've done. (*United States Library of Congress*)

Russian partisans prepare to blow up a rail line, some time in 1943. (*Minsk State Archive*)

An Axis-allied patrol marches past the wreckage of a train that has been derailed by a guerrilla bomb planted on the tracks, some time in 1943. (*SA-kuva*)

A German armoured train in Dorogobuzh station, some time in 1943.

A German NCO with members of the *Druzhina SS-Brigade* during an anti-partisan operation. Until its defection, the *Druzhina SS-Brigade* (also referred to as the Russian National Liberation Army) was one of the most effective anti-guerrilla units in the German arsenal. (*Minsk State Archive*)

German SS men and Russian volunteers of the *Druzhina SS-Brigade*, some time in early 1943. When the brigade defected to the partisans in the summer of 1943, most of the German cadre personnel were murdered. (*Minsk State Archive*)

Another Belarusian village goes up in flames, sometime in 1943. Villagers were often killed during these German anti-partisan sweeps. (*Bundesarchiv*)

Two Russian villagers are led away by a member of the anti-partisan forces, sometime in the summer of 1943. Their fate was likely a bullet on the back of the neck after interrogation. (*Bundesarchiv*)

A Russian child has been discovered in the woods by SS troops during an anti-partisan operation. The forests of the USSR offered protection for not only the partisan forces but citizens seeking to hide from the Germans. Jews in particular would hide in the vast forests, swamps and marshes of the USSR, as a way of surviving the war. It is unlikely that this child lasted the war. (*Bundesarchiv*)

A German patrol in search of the enemy. (*Bundesarchiv*)

of the unit took place over the autumn of 1943 and winter of 1944. By February 1944 the formation was regimental in size.

## *Unternehmen Skank*: 13–15 August 1943

The name of this operation is a vulgar term in either English or German. It refers to a woman of 'negotiable virtue'. This was a fairly small operation aimed at a partisan unit located south-east of Kodianov. The town of Kodianov lay just south-west of Minsk and in the Slutsk region.[110] This drive lasted only two days and employed *SS-Polizeiregiment 2, Polizei Panzer Kompanie 1* and *SS-Kampfgruppe Bielhack*. *SS-Kampfgruppe Bielhack* was led by *SS-Sturmbannführer* Armin Bielhack, who was the commander of the 2nd SS Recruit Training Battalion of SS Recruit Training Depot 'Bobruisk'.[111] This SS recruit battalion, therefore, took part in this drive.[112] These recruit battalions were eventually referred to as *Jäger* (hunter) battalions. No other information has been forthcoming on this rather small and ultimately insignificant anti-guerrilla drive.[113]

## *Unternehmen Orloff*: 16 August–29 September 1943

On the night of 7 August 1943, the 13th Partisan Regiment, commanded by Major Sergei Vladimirovich Grishin, blew up 650 rails.[114] This was a particularly troublesome partisan unit which was operating in the region of the Mogilev district. A report from this partisan commander on 25 August clearly showed that a Cossack regiment under Colonel Kononov was operating in the region of Smolensk and would be employed against the guerrillas:

> On 25 August, 500 infantry troops occupied a camp next to the airfield. A concentration camp adjoining the Dmitrov Factory contains about 500 people, including 276 Jews. A small troop training area, which can accommodate about 1,500 men, is located behind the automobile repair shop, and there is another [training] area in Chapaev for about 1,000 men. A security regiment of the 'People's Army' is billeted on the grounds of an artillery regiment near the Mogilev No. 2 railway station. This regiment is fighting against the partisans. Colonel Kononov commands this regiment. A pigeon station containing about 500 pigeons is located on the road to Vidrista. A vegetable storage area has been established adjoining the overpass near the railway station. Locomotives are being repaired in the automobile repair shop. The meat combine is functioning, and the sausage department is located in the former newspaper building. Aircraft parts are being manufactured in the pipe foundry. There are about 1,000 troops in Mogilev, excluding those in the training areas.

> There are no armoured units. Anti-aircraft batteries are stationed on the bridges. At the present time, there are about 500 motor vehicles in Mogilev.[115]

The statement regarding a security regiment under *Oberst* Kononov was an obvious reference to the pro-German *Kosaken Abteilung 600* of *Oberst* Ivan Kononov, which was in reality a two-battalion regiment. Adolf Hitler had decreed that no volunteer units be larger than battalion size. In order to get around this rule, the Germans had initially referred to Kononov's regiment as *I und II / Kosaken Hundertschaft 102*. Later this changed to *I und II / Kosaken Abteilung 600*. These titles were later changed to *Kosaken Abteilung 600* and *Kosaken Abteilung 631*.[116] This Cossack formation was so effective that it was prized by *Heeresgruppe Mitte*.[117] The Grishin Regiment was a good partisan unit that, together with two other guerrilla formations, consisted of about 2,000 men. Their destruction would help to ease the pressure against the Vitebsk–Mogilev rail and road link. The area where the operation would be launched was under the operational control of *221. Sicherungs Division*.

The principal unit employed by the Germans for this operation therefore, was *221. Sicherungs Division*. In May 1943 it was taking part in anti-partisan operations around Semenovka, Pogar, Starodub, Klintsy, Unecha, Mglin, Akulichi, and Khotimsk. It later regrouped in July by Surazh and Kostyukovichi, doing security there while reorganising.[118] In August and September 1943 the division operated near Gomel, Voronezh, Stary Oskol, Koryukovka, and Radul. The units employed under *221. Sicherungs Division* included the following formations, grouped together under one battlegroup:[119]

*Kampfgruppe Kopf:*
- *SS Polizeiregiment 24*[120]
- *Polizei Panzer Kompanie 9*
- *Stab (Staff) / Sicherungs Regiment 34*
- *2. Kompanie der I. Bataillon, Feldausbildungs Gren. Regt. 636*
- *Ost Bataillon 642*
- *Ost Bataillon 643*
- *Kompanie der I. Bataillon / Sicherungs Regiment 930*
- *Ost Kompanie der I. Bataillon / Sicherungs Regiment 930*
- *15. (Ost) Kompanie der Sicherungs Regiment 45*
- *Kompanie der 286. Sicherungs Division*
- *Flak Zug von der Kommandeur der Flaktruppen*
- *Batterie der 4. Artillerie Gruppe Boehme*
- *'Enke' Artillerie Batterie*
- *Ost Artillerie Batterie 614*

It was thus that at the end of August 1943 that a serious attempt was made by the Germans to destroy this partisan regiment. The operation proceeded as follows:

> The troops marched out to begin the operation on August 29, 1943, and the operation began on August 30th. The 'Kopf' Group took up their blockade line and as planned, advanced with four armoured scout cars of the 9th Police Armoured Company as its spearhead, west of the Pronya through Rabovici and Uluki, took the crossing of the Resta and, by 7:00 A.M. reached, as ordered, the regiment's left boundary near Ushar. Troops of the 221st Security Division were able, on August 30, 1943, to surround the Grishin band completely, but the band broke out during the night of August 30th–31st. Attacks of the 221st Security Division on August 31st found no one. Because of a transfer of the division, a planned continuation of Operation 'Orloff' was called off.[121]

Because the operation was called off almost when it began, the partisans were able to escape the German net. It would not be until two months later, in October, that the Grishin Regiment was finally cornered and badly mauled in another anti-partisan drive which was conducted near Mogilev.[122] This occurred during *Unternehmen Entenjagd* (Operation Duck Hunt), which lasted 15–17 October 1943, and was centred on the regions of Orsha–Voloshin–Belinichi–Mogilev.

### *Unternehmen Fritz*: 24 September–6 October 1943

This was an operation launched in the region of Glebokie, north of Minsk, which employed the various units attached to *Kampfgruppe von Gottberg* plus an SD company under the command of *SS-Hauptsturmführer* Artur Fritz Wilke. The operation was specifically targeted at the battalions that had formerly made up the *Druzhina* SS formation. The final tally for 'Operation Fritz' included 327 partisans killed and 227 captured. On top of those numbers, a German SD report states that an additional 182 people were given 'special treatment'.[123] The report continued listing the tally of the operation thusly:

> Our losses: 11 dead Germans, 32 wounded German, 1 dead foreign volunteer, 9 wounded foreign volunteers. Captured items: 2 heavy machine guns, 1 light machine gun, 28 rifles, 16 machine pistols, 6 anti-tank rifles, 5 pistols, 18 hand grenades. Destroyed Bandit Areas: 19 Bandit camps, 45 bunkers, 50 foxholes, 87 homes. Work force apprehended: 6,752 men, 3,264 women, 1,708 children. Captured livestock: 11,146 reindeer, 2,367 pigs, 1,284 horses, 18,087 sheep, 3,059 small cattle.[124]

Once again, it is apparent from the disparate number of weapons captured (76) and the number of partisans killed (over 550) that the civilian population was most likely added to the tally sheet of dead guerrillas in order to swell the report. The mass drafting of all human life in the area, coupled with the confiscation of livestock, ensured that the region in question would be devoid of any life and sustenance. The razing of entire regions in order to deny the guerrillas any form of support was a brutal tactic employed throughout the war behind the German lines.

## *Unternehmen Entenjagd*: 15–17 October 1943

Units employed in this drive came from *286. Sicherungs Division* (in particular, *Sicherungs Regiment 45*) and the *SS und Polizeiführer Mogilev*, using *I.* and *II. Bataillon der* SS *Polizeiregiment 24* and *Polizei Panzer Kompanie 9*. In early October 1943 Major Grishin had received an order for him to temporarily leave his command so that he could re-enter Soviet-held territory for an important palaver. However, events on the ground prevented his departure when his unit was caught by German Army and *SS/Polizei* forces and surrounded near the town of Propoist on 11 October 1943. Reports from the 13th Partisan Regiment stated that the unit had been surrounded by the Germans and was heavily attacked:

> 11 October 1943
>
> We are encircled. The exits from the forest are blocked. The Red Army will be here tomorrow or the day after. You can hear for yourself that the front is approaching. Today's artillery preparation tells us that the Red Army is attacking. It is our task to hold out for two or three more days; after this time contact with the Red Army will have been made. Therefore, we must hold our positions. Retreat would mean extinction. There must be no cowards or panic raisers among us. Every honest patriot of our fatherland must shoot such people on the spot. Just a few more days, Comrades, and we will be among our own people. Hold on to your positions and thwart every attempt of the enemy to break through. We are strong and we will be victorious.
>
> Commander of the 13th Partisan Regiment<br>
> Signed: Grishin<br>
> Chief of Staff of the 13th Partisan Regiment<br>
> Signed Uzlov[125]

Grishin's regiment, although decimated, survived the encounter and even managed to temporarily replenish its ranks to continue its operations behind the German lines into the spring and summer of

1944. In July 1944 it was taken into the ranks of the Soviet 5th Army under 3rd Belarusian Front.

## Employment of armoured trains in the anti-partisan war: one example

When Germany invaded the Soviet Union in the summer of 1941, they went into the Russian campaign with only six armoured trains. Two armoured trains were assigned to each of the three army groups (North, Centre, and South). By 1942 however, the number of armoured trains being employed behind the lines in the USSR had jumped to twenty-nine, increasing to forty-two in 1943 and then fifty-five by 1944. One such armoured train was *Gepanzerter Zug Nr. 66*. On 18 August 1943, it arrived in Orsha around 2:30 p.m.[126] Together with *122. Sicherungs Regiment*, it was supposed to patrol the Orsha–Borisov rail line between Tolochin and Krupki. The headquarters of *Sicherungs Regiment 122* was located in Krupki, while its *I. Bataillon* was stationed in Tolochin. On 24 August 1943, a *kampfgruppe* consisting of two French tanks, plus a platoon of infantry and an engineer platoon was employed in reconnaissance in the direction of Volosova.

The *kampfgruppe* was attacked at Volosova by partisans who employed mortars and heavy machine guns. German losses were minimal (only wounded), while the partisans withdrew after taking casualties. On the return to Tolochin, one of the French tanks ran over a mine that had been created from a 150mm artillery shell. Losses included one killed, two seriously wounded and three lightly wounded. The remainder of the battlegroup was ordered to support a company of *Sicherungs Regiment 122* in the Vlatigovka–Chernotovichi area. On 27 August 1943, *Panzer Zug 66* departed Volosova and headed towards Borisov to patrol the rail line. The armoured train returned at 7:45 p.m. that same night with no attacks reported. That same day the commander of *Sicherungs Regiment 122* ordered that a platoon of soldiers from his *I. Bataillon* be placed on guard duty over the damaged French tank that had hit a mine on 24 August. That platoon was soon attacked by guerrillas, causing four casualties: one seriously wounded and three lightly wounded.

On 28 August the commander of *286. Sicherungs Division* noted that the employment of the armoured train had significantly reduced the activities of the partisans between Orsha and Borisov. On 4 September the armoured train departed towards Trasilovo, where it was reported that a large partisan band was preparing to attack the rail line. The arrival of the armoured train at Trasilovo delayed the partisan attack long enough to bring up a battery of artillery which began to pound the woods. By coincidence one shell apparently hit the ammunition depot of the guerillas, which exploded, lighting up the night sky. On 8 September at 6:00 a.m. *Panzer-Zug Nr. 66* departed for Kavrishino. The orders were to secure the hay harvest in the area. The security division tasked with protecting this was *286. Sicherungs Division.* This security formation had anticipated that the partisans were going to try and disrupt the harvest, so had also positioned infantry and artillery forces nearby. The entire forest east of Dudaki from Brevleki to Lyubihsche was fired upon by the divisional artillery. The partisans were prevented from disrupting the harvest and at 5:00 p.m. the armoured train returned to Tolochin. The employment of German trains, both armoured and un-armoured, was led by *Feldbahnkommando 2 der Heeresgruppe Mitte,* which was based in Smolensk. It was responsible for all rail operations up to the city of Orel. The command also oversaw a little over 2,000 miles of tracks and controlled 261 locomotives and 1,599 rail wagons. In July 1943 the Soviet partisan movement stepped up its attacks against the German rail system behind the lines. In the region of Bryansk alone, guerrilla activity against the rail and road system increased as spring gave way to summer.[127] The biggest Soviet partisan attacks occurred during the summer of 1943, and coincided with the battle of Kursk. This was not by chance. The Russians asked that the partisan efforts be concentrated on disrupting Nazi rail transport to prevent the Germans from bringing up reinforcements or fresh equipment and supplies. For example, in March 1943 there were around 400 attacks on the rail lines. By July that figure had risen to 1,100. In August 1943 it jumped astronomically, to about 21,300.

Table 13. Rail and Road Disruptions in the Bryansk Region, April–July 1943

| | *Korück 532* | | *2. Panzerarmee* | |
|---|---|---|---|---|
| | Rail | Road | Rail | Road |
| Apr | 76 | 16 | 55 | – |
| May | 62 | 32 | 20 | – |
| Jun | 31 | 40 | 39 | |
| Jul | 690 | 17 | – | |

Chapter 7

# ANTI-PARTISAN FORCES AND SS KILLING UNITS IN UKRAINE, 1941–1943

Perhaps we have gone too far.
*Reichsführer-SS* Heinrich Himmler, January 1944

## Collaborationist forces in Ukraine

The history of the Holocaust in the USSR cannot be discussed without discussing the collaboration that took place there. This is because collaborationist forces became a part of the killings which were perpetrated by the SS *Einsatzgruppen*. At the start of the Russian campaign, various German police units were assigned to the region of Ukraine. For operations in the rear of *Heeresgruppe Süd* the police forces assigned included several formations that were later reinforced.[1] In addition to these police units, the *Abwehr*, the German Armed Forces Secret Service, had formed two battalions of Ukrainian volunteers prior to the invasion of the Soviet Union. The *Roland* Battalion had been created at a base camp in Saubersdorf near Vienna, Austria, while the *Nachtigall* ('Nightingale') Battalion had been established at Neuhammer Training Camp in upper Silesia.[2] According to earlier instructions from the RSHA, these Ukrainian volunteers, although under the direction of the *Abwehr*, 'were also to be used for self-purging operations'.[3] These Ukrainian nationalist battalions took part in the initial advance into Ukraine and the *Nachtigall* Battalion was one of the first Axis units to enter L'viv in early July 1941.[4] These two battalions were later disbanded in August 1941. The men were merged into *Schutzmannschaft Bataillon 201* in March 1942.[5] This *Schuma* battalion was sent to White Russia in late March or early April 1942 to fight the partisans.[6] It was led by Ukrainian Major Ievhen Bobihushchy and his assistant, Captain Roman Shukhevych, who later left the unit to become Commander-in-Chief of the UPA, the Ukrainian Insurgent Army.[7] The initial Ukrainian collaborationist units were (*ukrainische*) *Nachtigall Bataillon*,[8] and (*ukrainische*) *Roland Bataillon*.[9] One source state that it was actually Roman Schuchevytch (also spelled 'Shukhevych'), and not Sconprynka,[10] who was the Ukrainian commander of the 'Nightingale' Battalion.[11] To these two Ukrainian battalions must be added the 10,000-man Ukrainian militia under *Oberst* Borovets, whose *nom de guerre* was 'Taras Bulba'.[12] The militia was anti-communist, so for a time it operated in conjunction with German requests. This situation changed in 1943, when the UPA decided to distance itself from the Germans. They continued to fight Soviet partisan forces and when the Soviets advanced into western Ukraine, they fought the Red Army as well. As it happened in the Baltic States, these anti-communist Ukrainian guerrillas fought a low-intensity guerrilla war in western Ukraine until NKVD forces overwhelmed them in the early 1950s. The *213. Sicherungs Division* officially recognised this Ukrainian guerrilla force in 1941 as a legitimate militia, known as the '*Polissia Sich*' in the Polesie region of Galicia. In fact, it was this Ukrainian militia which assisted the Germans in their anti-partisan operations in the district of Wolyn (Volhynia) in the autumn of 1941.[13] Recruitment of further Ukrainian volunteers by the Germans increased soon after the invasion of the USSR in June 1941. Although the enrolment of these men was principally as auxiliaries to the German police and SS and SD, it was actually the German army garrison commands which usually outfitted them with weapons and clothing and on occasion, also employed them on anti-partisan operations:

> There was area, however, in which all agencies consistently cooperated and dedicated their resources: 'security' measures. To this end, agencies shared manpower, materiel, and information. For example, Himmler's police leaders trained the Ukrainian police, and the individual recruits were checked by the SD; but the *Wehrmacht* village commanders actually enlisted them, outfitted them, and assigned them to their routine tasks of guarding buildings, roadways, and transports of prisoners. For the largest 'cleansing' campaigns in the northern Pripiat' marshland, *Wehrmacht* commanders called in the First SS Brigade to assist in the joint SS–army raids. District agricultural leaders, economic units, and armed Ukrainians in the Polisian Sich also worked closely with the army field commanders and police by patrolling the rural areas and reporting the presence of 'suspicious' persons hiding in the forests and fields.[14]

Because *Wehrmacht* rear-area garrison commands armed and often employed these men, especially the basically stationary local defence formations called the *Ordnungsdienst*, any criminal actions on the part of these formations should be attributed to the German command under which they operated. In most cases, this was either the German *Ordnungspolizei* or *Sicherheitspolizei* headquarters. However, when an anti-partisan operation or anti-Jewish action was to be performed and *Wehrmacht* troops were lacking, the local *Feldkommandantur* or *Ortskommandantur* would employ these auxiliaries as well. Any crimes committed by these volunteers should, therefore, be attributed to the respective German police, SS or Army command because they had ultimate jurisdiction and control. More recruiting drives were followed in early 1942 in the East with the establishment of the first Ukrainian *Schutzmannschaft* battalions. The Germans would end up recruiting Lithuanian, Latvian, Estonian, Belarusian, Russian, Ukrainian, Cossack, Turkic, Tartar, Armenian, Azerbaijani, Georgian, and other peoples of the USSR into combat battalions. In fact, the need for soldiers became so great that by 1944, one out of every five men wearing the uniform of the German Army in the East was actually a citizen of the USSR. In the Galician part of western Ukraine, a collaborationist police force was established when in August 1941 that province was detached and added to the *Generalgouvernement* in Poland. This police force was exclusively made up of Ukrainian volunteers and wore a special blue uniform with red trimmings, plus a cap badge depicting the Ukrainian emblem in blue on a yellow background. This force was said to number about 3,000 men.[15] Other units were raised in 1941 in the region of *Heeresgruppe Süd.* In the Crimea, in October 1941 a militia was formed which initially numbered eight Tartar local defence companies:

> Six Crimean Tartar battalions were recruited for police and anti-partisan duties largely under the direction of the SD. While the German command found them helpful, the extreme nationalists looked upon them as a future 'Crimean Army'. Among the rank and file their formation appears to have evoked neither enthusiasm nor violent hostility.[16]

These battalions had been formed originally as companies with the assistance of the SD detachment of *Einsatzgruppe D.* General Erich von Manstein attested as much when he stated to Dr. Laternser before the International Military Tribunal at Nuremberg that:

> We got a number of auxiliaries for combating partisans. In the Jaila mountains of the Crimea there were small inaccessible parts of the mountains where there were partisans. We could not get at them because we had no mountain troops. All we could do was to try to starve out these bands by preventing them from raiding Tartar villages and thereby maintaining their food supplies. For that reason, we armed Tartars in order to make sure that these villages were reliable in our sense; the SD assisted us. They also worked with us to discover the food depots. We had to do this because German troops were not available.[17]

After the withdrawal of the Germans from the Crimea, these Tartar battalions were brought back to Germany, then sent to northern Italy where they were to establish a Tartar SS brigade. The end of the war came before the unit became fully operational. The following is a case study of one Ukrainian *Schutzmannschaft* battalion. This unit was selected because it is a perfect paradigm for all such battalions which were raised in the East.

## Case study: *Schutzmannschaft Bataillon 118*

The history of *Schutzmannschaft Bataillon 115* and *Schutzmannschaft Bataillon 118* are very much linked to one another. *Schutzmannschaft Bataillon 115* was raised first in July 1942 while *Schutzmannschaft Bataillon 118* was created later, in November.[18] However, one source claims that the 118th was organised in the spring of 1942.[19] Approximately 100 men from *Schutzmannschaft Bataillon 115* were used to create the core of *Schutzmannschaft Bataillon 118*. Apparently, a good number of the Ukrainian recruits were drawn for the region in and around Bukovina. The 3rd Company of *Schutzmannschaft Bataillon 115* was drafted en masse to become the 1st Company of *Schutzmannschaft Bataillon 118*.[20] The rest of the companies in *Schutzmannschaft Bataillon 118* were created from Russian POWs. In total 500 men were organised into three rifle companies. In November 1942 *Schutzmannschaft Bataillon 118* was taken by trucks to Minsk, from where the battalion was re-directed to the town of Plesenichi (Pleszczenice) just north-east of Minsk. Troops were also stationed in the village of Evye.

There was a German staff within the battalion. When *Schutzmannschaft Bataillon 118* was created in the spring of 1942, *Major der Schutzpolizei* Erich Körner was the German commander designated to lead the unit. *Hauptmann der Schutzpolizei* Emil Sass was his second in command. Another member of the German staff was a Pole, *Oberleutnant* Konstantine Smowski, who would apparently act as substitute commander whenever Körner was away. In the autumn of 1943, the Ukrainian (titular) commander of the battalion was said to have been *Hauptmann der Schutzmannschaft* Vasilii Andreevich Meleshko.[21] *Oberleutnant* Hryhoryi Mykytovych Vasiura was Meleshko's second in command.[22] By late 1943 however, Vasiura, who was a former Red Army officer, had been promoted and was supposedly the leading Ukrainian officer in the battalion. It seems rather improbable to me, given the pattern of behaviour by the Germans, that this *Schutzmannschaft* battalion would have a dual German and Ukrainian command; or that a Polish national would lead the battalion while the German commander was away. The more likely scenario is that the Ukrainian companies in this battalion had a German commander, while a Ukrainian officer was assigned as adjutant.

The battalion as a whole was led by *Hauptmann der Schutzpolizei* Erich Körner whose (titular) Ukrainian counterpart, as stated earlier, was *Hauptmann der Schutzmannschaft* Meleshko. His presence was to show that the Ukrainian battalion was not led completely by the Germans. Nevertheless, the Germans were in charge. For example, we know that the *1. Kompanie* of this unit was led by *Hauptmann der Schutzpolizei* Hans Wölke. His company adjutant was a Ukrainian, *Leutnant* Vinnitsky. *Hauptmann der Schutzpolizei* Hermann led the *2. Kompanie,* while his adjutant was *Oberleutnant* Franczuk, another Ukrainian. The *3. Kompanie* of the battalion was led by *Hauptmann der Polizei* Müller. His adjutant was another Ukrainian, *Leutnant* Naradko. The unit remained stationed in Plesenichi for about one year, from the spring of 1943 until the time of the Russian advance in the spring of 1944.[23] With regard to the activities of *Schutzmannschaft Bataillon 118* while in Belarus, it appears that it performed duty guarding the harvesting of crops in their region, with particular attention to protecting the wheat mill in the village of Kyiv, as well as guarding the livestock of the village of Yewa.

This might indicate that *Schutzmannschaft Bataillon 118* may not have taken part in the drive however the likelihood that part of the unit may have been involved while another part was involved in guard duties is also a possibility. During this drive hundreds of people were pressed into service for forced labour in Germany. On 22 March 1943 *Schutzmannschaft Bataillon 118* surrounded, then entered the village of Khatyn, in Belarus. They were assisted by SS *Sonder Bataillon Dirlewanger,* which they had called on for support. There they would set the village ablaze and kill the occupants. A total of 149 villagers died that day. This tally sheet included 75 children under the age of 16. The people were first rounded up, then locked in homes whose roofs were set on fire. Anyone who managed to escape the blaze was machine-gunned. This murder was done in retaliation for the ambush by partisans of the headquarters unit belonging to *1. Kompanie* of *Schutzmannschaft Bataillon 118.*

The commander of *1. Kompanie, Hauptmann der Schutzpolizei* Hans Wölke, and three other officers had been killed in the ambush. It had occurred near the village of Kozyri, which lay about 6km from the village of Khatyn. After the war several leading figures in this massacre were tried and executed, like ex-Soviet Second Lieutenant Vasyl Andreevich Mereshko, who was supposed to be the commander of the battalion, former Red Army Senior Lieutenant Frikhor Vasiula, and *Oberleutnant der Schutzmannschaft* Bruno Pavel, who had apparently ordered the executions. The last trial regarding this massacre occurred in the 1980s in the former USSR.

## Willing Partners: GFP, *Ordnungspolizei, Feldgendarmerie*

To these SS killing units, we must also include the numbers of motorised *Geheime Feldpolizei* (GFP), *Feldgendarmerie* (Military Field Police), and *Ordnungspolizei* units attached to the security divisions which were sent behind the lines of the advancing German armies and were employed in the region of Army Group South and Ukraine in 1941. These units were militarised police formations and belonged to the *Wehrmacht*. Some regular German *Ordnungspolizei* battalions were also attached to the security divisions. Usually, one German *Ordnungspolizei* battalion was attached to each security division. The security divisions, which were basically horse-drawn formations and comprised two infantry regiments instead of the usual three, employed *Feldgendarmerie* and *Ordnungspolizei* units as their principal leading element during an anti-partisan drive, given that they were fully motorised. While the army *Feldgendarmerie* battalions usually performed traffic control duties, they also took part in anti-guerrilla operations, screening partisan suspects, interrogating captured guerrillas and 'suspicious persons', as well as performing disciplinary functions like arresting deserters, black marketeers, etc. Their motorisation also allowed them to patrol suspected partisan border regions, in an attempt to prevent guerrilla units from escaping a German anti-partisan drive. They also assisted the various GFP units as well as aiding the SS *Einsatzgruppen* when called upon. Their role in the Russian campaign, as defined by the criminal orders, would also include their participation in shooting of these same partisan suspects, Jews, Romani and just about anyone else deemed an enemy of the *Reich*. Their general location, therefore, becomes extremely important to scholars who are trying to track their movements and actions when trying to tie them to specific crimes.[24] Since army cooperation as between the SS occurred on a regular basis, assistance that was comprehensively shown in this study, a detailed listing of these SS forces which operated in the region of Ukraine and southern Russia should be presented.

## The SS *Einsatzgruppen*

The principal German SS killing groups in southern Russia included *Einsatzgruppe C* and *Einsatzgruppe D. Einsatzgruppe C* numbered 700–800 personnel and included a headquarters contingent which began the campaign with twenty men on staff. These killing units contained not only SS and SD personnel, but *Ordnungspolizei* members as well.[25] The following *Einsatzgruppen* commands in the region of *Heeresgruppe Süd* were split up as follows:[26] *Einsatzgruppe C,* with *Sonderkommando 4a, 4b, 5, 6; Einsatzgruppe D,* with *Sonderkommando 10a, 10b, 11a, 11b,* and *12. SS-Brigadeführer* Otto Ohlendorf led *Einsatzgruppe D.* Ohlendorf's unit was the smallest of the SS murder *Kommandos.* Like all of the other *Einsatzgruppen,* Ohlendorf's killing unit was to receive support and supplies from the German Army. Food, rations, fuel, maps, technical and medical assistance, as well as vehicle maintenance and repair were to be provided by the *Ostheer.* His unit initially traversed Bessarabia, where the initial killings by the unit began, then moved into Ukraine and the Crimea.

In the summer of 1942, the formation reached the Caucasus Mountains during the German 1942 summer offensive. In this the formation was assisted, first by Romanian security forces in Bessarabia, and then by Ukrainian volunteers when they entered the USSR. The killing spree for *Einsatzgruppe D* would be close to 92,000 lives. The final tally sheet for *Einsatzgruppen A, B, C* and *D* would be 1,152,731. In the Soviet Union, around 4,500,000 civilians died directly as a result of the war. Another 8,000,000 were killed due to famine and disease related to the conflict. Those figures do not include Red Army losses. Of the approximately 3,200,000 Jews in the USSR at the start of the Russo-German war, approximately 1,500,000 escaped the clutches of the Nazis by withdrawing to or living in Russian-controlled areas. Of that number, somewhere in the neighbourhood of 400,000 served in the Red Army. With the assistance of ancillary forces outside of the SS, the *Einstazgruppen* managed to murder 1,152,731 Jews in the USSR. Given how many Jews were living in the Soviet Union before the war, how many were killed by the SS killing units, and how many escaped the clutches of the Nazis, it appears that an additional 547,269 Jews who lived in the USSR at the time also died. We can attribute a good portion of that figure to Jews who died from famine or disease related to the war, but a percentage would have to be attributable to the SS, police and auxiliary police forces that operated behind the German lines. We must also include the *Ostheer* in this culpability, given that on numerous occasions, the German Army on the Eastern Front deployed rear area, as well as front-line troops for anti-partisan sweeps that killed tens of thousands of people, a good number of them Jews. These figures related to the genocide of the Jewish population could not have been achieved without substantial support from the German Army. Blame for these murders therefore, should also go to the *Wehrmacht*.

## *Einsatzgruppen* commanders

*SS-Standartenführer* Paul Blobel. Leader of *Sonderkommando 4a*. He held this post from June 1941 until 13 January 1942. Thereafter *SS-Standartenführer* Dr. Erwin Weinmann assumed command until 27 July 1942. Later officers included *SS-Standartenführer* Eugen Steimle (August 1942 until 15 January 1943), and *SS-Sturmbannführer* Theodor Christensen (beginning of March 1943 until the autumn of that year). *Sonderkommando 4a* ended the year 1941 headquartered in the city of Kharkov. This *Sonderkommando* was disbanded at the end of 1943.

*SS-Standartenführer* Günther Herrmann. Leader of *Sonderkommando 4b*. He held this post until September 1941. *SS Obersturmbannführer* Fritz Braune assumed command on 2 October 1941, and held this post until 21 March1942. Thereafter *SS-Obersturmbannführer* Walter Haensch held this post until the middle of June 1942. Then *SS-Obersturmbannführer* August Meier took control of the *Sonderkommando* from July to November 1942. The last CO was SS-*Sturmbannführer* Waldemar Krause, who held this post from August 1943 until January 1945. This *Sonderkommando* ended the year 1941 headquartered in the city of Poltava. This unit was disbanded in January 1944.

*SS-Oberführer* Erwin Schulz. Leader of *Einsatzkommando 5*. Schulz was later promoted to *SS-Brigadeführer*. Schulz held this post from June until August 1941 when *SS-Sturmbannführer* August Meier assumed control. Meier himself commanded this unit beginning 20 September 1941. It ended the year 1941 stationed just east of Kiev. The *Einsatzkommando* was disbanded in January 1942.

*SS-Standartenführer* Erhard Kröger. Leader of *Einsatzkommando 6*. He led this unit from June to October 1941. Thereafter *SS-Obersturmbannführer* Robert Mohr held this post until the middle of September 1942. *SS-Sturmbannführer* Ernst Biberstein briefly commanded the unit during the last two weeks of September 1942. The last commander of *Einsatzkommando 6* was *SS-Obersturmbannführer* Friedrich Suhr, who held this post from August until November 1943 when the unit was disbanded. At the end of 1941 *Einsatzkommando 6* was headquartered in Stalino.

*SS-Gruppenführer* Otto Ohlendorf.[27] Leader of *Einsatzgruppe D*. He held this post from June 1941 until the beginning of July 1942. Thereafter *SS-Standartenführer* Dr. Walter Bierkamp led *Einsatzgruppe D* from July 1942 until May 1943.

*SS-Standartenführer* Heinrich Seetzen. Leader of *Einsatzkommando 10a*. He led this unit from June 1941 until July 1942. On 20 October 1941, his unit shot 8,000 Jews in the city of Mariupol. Thereafter *SS-Obersturmbannführer* Dr. Kurt Christmann led *Einsatzkommando 10a* from August 1942 until July 1943. One source states that this unit was disbanded in July 1942, yet another insists that it was still operational until a full year later, in July 1943. At end of 1941, the unit was located in Taganrog.

*SS-Obersturmbannführer* Alois Persterer. Leader of *Sonderkommando 10b*. He held this command from June 1941 to December 1942. The last commander was *SS-Sturmbannführer* Eduard Jedamzik, who held this post from December 1942 until February 1943. However, it appears that the unit was not disbanded until May 1943. At the end of 1941 this unit was quartered in Skadovsk, just outside the 'neck' of the Crimean Peninsula.

*SS-Obersturmbannführer* Paul Zapp. Leader of *Sonderkommando 11a*. He led the unit from June 1941 to July 1942. In October 1942 a *'Teilkommando'* from this unit, under the command of *SS-Sturmbannführer* Reinhard Maurach, was sent to the Caucasus and titled *'Teilkommando Astrachan'*. It was disbanded in January 1943. The next SS officer to lead *Sonderkommando 11a* was *SS-Sturmbannführer* Dr. Gerhard Bast, who led this unit from November to December 1942. *SS-Sturmbannführer* Werner Hersmann was the last officer to lead *Sonderkommando 11a*, from December 1942 until May 1943. At the end of 1941, *Sonderkommando 11a*, like the other units of the *Einsatzgruppen*, was disbanded and served as the basis for the *Sicherheitspolizei* and *Sicherheitsdienst* command in Simferopol, in the Crimea. The *Sipo* and SD command structure in the USSR was manned by former *Einsatzgruppen* members.

*SS-Obersturmbannführer* Bruno Müller. Leader of *Sonderkommando 11b*. He led the unit from July until October 1941. *SS-Sturmbannführer* Dr. Werner Braune led this group from October 1941 until the beginning of September 1942. Braune's highest rank would be that of *SS-Obersturmbannführer*, which he attained on 21 June 1943. The last officer to hold this command was *SS-Sturmbannführer* Paul Schultz, who took over for Braune in September 1942 and remained commander until about February 1943. His new posting came with a promotion, since he attained the higher rank of *SS-Obersturmbannführer* on 1 September 1942. At the end of 1941 *Sonderkommando 11b* was stationed in Odessa.

*SSObersturmbannführer* Gustav Nosske. Leader of *Einsatzkommando 12*. He held this post from June 1941 to mid-February 1942. *SS-Standartenführer* Dr. Erich Müller held this post from mid-February until October 1942. *SS-Obersturmbannführer* Günther Hermann was the last commander of this unit, taking over for Müller in October 1942 and holding this post until March 1943 when this *Einsatzkommando* was disbanded. At the end of 1941, this killing unit was located in Donetsk.

## Security duties in Ukraine and Army Group South

As previously stated, at the start of the invasion of the Soviet Union, the *444.* and *454. Sicherungs Division* were at first attached to *17. Armee,* while *213. Sicherungs Division* would serve under *6. Armee.*[28] However, by 27 June 1941, *444.* and *454. Sicherungs Division* were listed under a new rear-area command, the *Befehlshaber Heeresgebiet Süd 103* command staff (see appendix for a full table of organisation of these divisions).[29] The *213. Sicherungs Division* was later attached to the *Befehlshaber Heeresgebiet Süd 103* command, beginning in August 1941.[30] The *403. Sicherungs Division,* which up until August 1941 had been serving in the region of *Heeresgruppe Mitte,* was transferred to *Heeresgruppe Süd* that same month and attached to the *Heeresgebiet Süd* command.[31] So by September 1941 the Germans were employing a total of four security divisions in Ukraine and southern Russia. According to a German document dated 18 May 1941, nine (fully motorised) *Ordnungspolizei* battalions were assigned to the nine security divisions which began the campaign in the Soviet Union:[32]

Table 14. Police Battalions Attached to Security Divisions, May 1941

| Security Division | Police Battalion | Date Attached |
|---|---|---|
| *207. Sicherungs Division* | *Polizei Bataillon 105* | 15 Jun 1941 |
| *213. Sicherungs Division* | *Polizei Bataillon 318* | 20 May 1941 |
| *221. Sicherungs Division* | *Polizei Bataillon 309* | 1 Jun 1941 |
| *281. Sicherungs Division* | *Polizei Bataillon 2* | 15 May 1941 |
| *285. Sicherungs Division* | *Polizei Bataillon 65* | 15 Jun 1941 |
| *286. Sicherungs Division* | *Polizei Bataillon 317* | 20 May 1941 |
| *403. Sicherungs Division* | *Polizei Bataillon 131*[33] | 15 Jun 1941 |
| *444. Sicherungs Division* | *Polizei Bataillon 311* | 1 Jun 1941 |
| *454. Sicherungs Division* | *Polizei Bataillon 82* | 1 Jun 1941 |

It is clear from this table that a lot of thought was placed on employing sufficient occupation forces for what was to be a 6–8-week campaign in Russia. That is to say, based on the calculation of the length of the campaign, there were sufficient rear area security forces. However, no preparations had been made if the campaign were to last longer than 9–17 weeks.[34] Adolf Hitler expected to destroy the Soviet Union within this time frame, so the OKW had apparently allocated enough security forces which would safeguard the rear of the advancing German armies for this time period. Accordingly, German estimates of the number of rear area forces allotted for the period was, in theory, sufficient for the length of time which the campaign was estimated to last. It appears however, that even that calculation was too low. Edward Westermann states that the sheer expanse of the Soviet Union and the speed of the initial German advance created such large areas behind the German front, that even the assigned police battalions working in conjunction with their respective security divisions, could not properly control all of the land taken:

> The police forces assigned to the security divisions could not adequately supervise or even patrol the large areas delegated to them. In addition, a large amount of police manpower was tied up in the other occupied territories extending from Serbia in the south to Holland in the west and to Norway in the north.[35]

The Germans attempted to augment their rear-area forces by recruiting volunteers from the local population. The result netted a substantial indigenous force, organised into battalions that would serve either as security and guard duty, or take part in combination with German forces in anti-partisan operations. That the Russian campaign would last three years was never anticipated. This problem was worse in the area of operation for *Heeresgruppe Süd*, that is, the region of Ukraine and southern Russia. Although the Germans experienced shortages of rear area security forces in the Baltic States as well as north and central Russia and Belarus, these deficiencies were not as great simply because the areas taken and conquered by *Heeresgruppe Süd* were much larger. In spite of these shortages of rear-area forces in the summer and autumn of 1941, the destruction of the Jewish population in the USSR proceeded quickly.

A possible factor in this may have been the criminal orders which labelled all Jews as partisans – thus allowing any front-line or rear-area formation, whether it was an SS, police or army unit, to murder them on sight. It goes a long way to explain how these police battalions, as well as army security and garrison formations assigned to control the rear areas of the advancing German armies and to combat the partisans, were again and again used to directly or indirectly assist in the policy of extermination which the SS *Einsatzgruppen* murder *Kommandos* were principally charged with from 1941 to 1943. As can be seen, *Heeresgruppe Süd* was to have comparatively fewer security divisions than in the areas controlled by *Heeresgruppe Nord* and Centre. This was simply because of the larger territories that made up Ukraine and southern Russia. However, it appears that the murder of the Jewish population in Ukraine and southern Russia was actually greater than all other areas. One reason for this was the fact that two entire SS killing units had been assigned to this region. Another reason has to be the policy of shooting all Jews on sight which, as we shall see, *Wehrmacht* forces appear to have followed. From 22 June 1941, until December 1942 the various SS *Einsatzgruppe* totals for the murder of the Jewish population in the USSR stood as follows:

Region of *Heeresgruppe Nord* (*Einsatzgruppe A*) – 363,337.
Region of *Heeresgruppe Mitte* (*Einsatzgruppe B*) – 134,000.
Region of *Heeresgruppe Süd* (*Einsatzgruppe C*) – 118,341.
Region of *Heeresgruppe Süd* (*Einsatzgruppe D*) – 91,728.
Forces Directly Under the Higher-SS and Police Leaders – 82,114.
Higher-SS and Police Leader South – 363,211.[36]
Grand Total: 1,152,731[37]

As the figures above indicate, the region of *Heeresgruppe Süd* experienced a total number of 573,280 Jews killed. This is quite a significant number of victims. The German Army operating in this southern region of the USSR was, like the rest of the regions of the Russian front, not free of implication in the murder of the Jewish population or, for that matter, in the murder of innocent Ukrainian and Russian civilians or captured Red Army soldiers. Killing of civilians is illegal and immoral, but the murder of captured soldiers who have surrendered is equally reprehensible and is considered a war crime. This was also true of the behaviour of most armies, especially European armies in the 1940s. It matters not that the Germans were operating 'under orders', since it is up to individuals to decide if an act is moral or immoral.[38] Most Germans serving in the *Wehrmacht* had lived in pre-Nazi times and knew what was morally right and what was morally wrong. Christopher Browning has already pointed to the fact that men, who refused to take part in these killings were ostracised but not really punished.[39] Browning instead blames peer pressure from what he terms the 'immediate community', which was the particular unit which the German soldier was attached to, and the 'society at large', which was anti-Semitic and anti-communist Nazi Germany.[40] The war diary of army Corporal Rudolf Lange is an example of this unity of purpose regarding the murder of Jews which pervaded the German armed forces on the Eastern Front. On 1 July 1941, he wrote that sixty prisoners were shot at the regimental headquarters. The entry for the next day simply read: 'Jews shot'.[41] Historian Raul Hilberg states that the ideological struggle which was waged in the USSR pervaded the manner in which the Germans' thought processes worked regarding the war in the East and in particular, the way they viewed and treated the Jews:

> A striking example of how the theory invaded German thinking is furnished in the format of portions of two reports by the army's Secret Field Police (*Geheime Feldpolizei*) in occupied Russia: Punishable Offenses by Members of the Population-
> Espionage: 1
> Theft of ammunition: 1
> Suspected Jews (*Judenverdacht*): 3
> Punishable Offenses by Members of the Population –
> Moving about with Arms: 11
> Theft: 2
> Jews: 2[42]

In the culmination of this theory, to be a Jew was a punishable act (*strafbare Handlung*). Thus, it was the function of the rationalisation of criminality to turn the destruction process into a kind of judicial proceeding.[43] Another example of the *Weltanschauungskrieg* being put into practice was the murder of forty-two wounded Red Army soldiers by members of the *62. Infanterie Division* on 2 July 1941. At this time the front line was about 25 miles to the north-east,[44] so these Russian prisoners were well behind it.[45] The significance of this fact is that the shootings could not have possibly taken place in the heat of battle, as sometimes occurs shortly after a battle has taken place and the soldier's blood is up. Since the front lines were far from the area where the massacre took place, the excuse that these wounded soldiers were killed during the fog of war is inadmissible. But this massacre was not an aberration. It was the end result of the criminal orders issued shortly before the start of the Russian campaign, coupled with the infectious racist nature of Nazism that was prevalent in the regime. The ideological struggle that was being waged – the *Weltanschauungskrieg* – in the East was another principal factor, as Raul Hilberg states, and a direct result of Nazi ideology being put into practice. An ethical society knows what is morally right and what is morally wrong. The Nazis tried to turn morality on its head by making their annihilationist policy 'moral' while making any act of pity taken by a German towards the enemy as treason to his own people. By doing so, it made killers out of men who normally would not be murderers. Nazi racist policies reinforced and encouraged sadistic and malevolent tendencies in men while ostracising those who showed mercy to their enemies, real or perceived. They even went a step further by making soldiers feel that if they avoided unpleasant duties like shooting women and children, they were in a way failing their comrades in the front-line units and their families at home. We must therefore conclude that those orders issued shortly before the start of the Russian campaign and affirmed by further decrees once the campaign got underway, were illegal commands because they were immoral. For example, in October 1941 *Generalfeldmarschall* Walter von Reichenau, who was leading the *6. Armee* under *Heeresgruppe Süd*, wrote a memo that was released to the troops. In it, he justified the *Einsatzgruppen* murder of the Jewish population as justified in fighting the partisan menace.[46]

A month later, on 20 November, even General Erich Manstein, who at the time was leading the *11. Armee* in the Crimea, wrote in an order released to the troops: 'The Jewish-Bolshevist system must be eradicated once and for all'.[47] What all of this indicates is that the rules of chivalry did not apply to the fighting in the Soviet Union. This campaign was indeed unique from all the other operations fought by the *Wehrmacht* – not only for the sheer size and magnitude of the campaign, but the manner in which it was waged. It is therefore unthinkable that the war against the partisans behind the lines of the advancing German armies would not be fought as ruthlessly and as uncompromisingly as it was being fought in the front lines. Given all of these factors, it is no surprise that so many Jews were killed since not only were SS and police units hunting them, but no mercy could be expected from army forces as well. Wolfram Wette said as much when he wrote: 'the campaign against the Soviet partisans was also seized upon to a considerable extent as a pretext for murdering Jews'.[48]

Chapter 8

# ANTI-PARTISAN WARFARE IN UKRAINE, 1941–1943

Guerrilla warfare is used by the side which is supported by a majority.

Che Guevara

## Partisan warfare begins in Ukraine

From the start of the German invasion, Joseph Stalin and his commanders understood the importance of establishing a partisan army behind the enemy's front line. Stalin wanted the enemy's supply lines and lines of communication to be disrupted. He therefore ordered the establishment of the partisan movement. In particular, Stalin considered it a high priority that a strong partisan presence should exist in the region of Belarus and Ukraine. Initially, the core of partisan units came from bypassed Red Army soldiers who had refused to surrender, or had been captured by the advancing panzer forces and told to move to the German rear. They had then fled when the advance elements of the panzers had moved on, and before the German infantry had reached them. Another fountain for recruits were the die-hard Komsomol members and Communist Party officials who had decided to remain behind the German lines in order to establish a guerrilla presence. During 1941 party members, workers and soldiers established what were termed 'destruction battalions'. These militia units were organised in every area where the advancing enemy threatened a valuable installation, whether it was a munitions dump, factory or collective farm. Members of the destruction battalions were to (1) safeguard these facilities, and (2) in case of the approaching enemy, destroy everything so the enemy could not use it. Afterwards, if the battalion survived the German advance, (3) they were to take to the woods and begin guerrilla operations. Aside from the destruction battalions, partisan units were created in the rear of the advancing German armies.

## Bread and salt

When the Germans entered Ukraine in the summer of 1941, most of the Ukrainian population greeted the invaders with bread and salt, the traditional Ukrainian welcome gift. On 20 August Adolf Hitler established the *Reichskommissariat Ukraine*. Twelve days later, on 1 September, Hitler appointed Erich Koch as *Reichskommissar* for Ukraine. With this title came the power to decide not only civil administrative duties, but also to administer, control, and employ the *Ordnungspolizei* and the *Geheimstaatspolizei* in Ukraine. Koch's primary goal was the exploitation of the people and the extraction of the region's resources for the Third Reich. The very first official act which Koch signed was an order closing all Ukrainian schools. When he was asked if the decision was imprudent, he was quoted as having said: 'If I meet a Ukrainian worthy of being seated at my table, I must have him shot'.[1] With this kind of attitude towards the very people he was supposed to rule, it didn't take long before many Ukrainians began reconsidering whether they had acted too hastily in welcoming the Germans.

## Winning over the population

By the end of 1941 a fair estimate of the number of guerrillas that were operating behind the German lines on the Eastern Front was roughly 60,000–70,000.[2] Of that number, approximately 15,750 partisans were operating in Ukraine.[3] For the period 1941–2, the Central Headquarters for the Partisan Movement in Moscow made targeting local collaborator forces, whether policemen, civilian spies, or town mayors, the principal goal. Killing German soldiers, destroying petrol and ammunition dumps and disrupting the rail lines were to also take place, but as a secondary priority. The political implication of this was clear. Stalin knew that many of his citizens hated him and hated the communist system as a whole. By targeting collaborators, he wished to remind those people who were now under German rule that Stalin and the communist party had not gone away completely. He understood very clearly that the key to defeating his regime was the confidence and support of the population. This vital point is something that few in power in the Third Reich ever contemplated or realised. Those Germans who understood this were never in a position to reverse Nazi state policies. Policies that eventually assured the loss of support by most of the people in the East. To have offered the people of Poland

and the Soviet Union a real partnership in a post-war Europe was anathema to the Nazis. This guaranteed that Germany would never win over the Eastern peoples to their cause.

## The German command structure in Ukraine

As for German preparations against resistance to their rule, the OKW had anticipated that the rear areas of the advancing German armies would need to be secure. The Germans had prepared what they believed would be sufficient forces. As in the rest of the Eastern Front, the *Korück* commands would be brought in, with their *Feldkommandanturen* and lower *Ortskommandanturen* headquarter commands. These would be in direct contact with the security divisions that had been assigned to operate in Ukraine and southern Russia. These were initially *213.*, *444.*, and *454. Sicherungs Divisionen* which have already been discussed in the previous chapter.

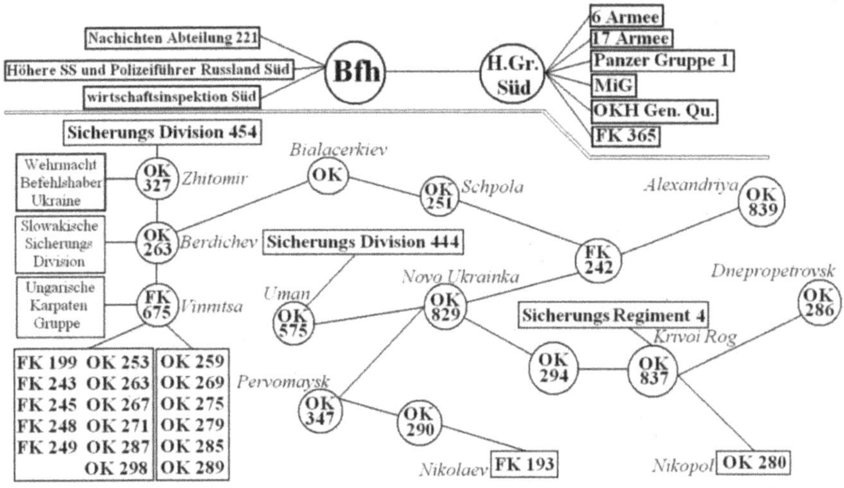


Figure 35. Organisation of the Rear Area Commands in Ukraine and Army Group South.

These commands, as Figure 35 indicates, were the connection between the front-line armies, the rear area security forces and even the higher SS commands. This allowed for the proper assembly of available *Heer*, SS, *Polizei*, and indigenous (*Hilfspolizei*, *Selbstschutz*, *Schutzmannschaft*, etc.) anti-partisan forces, in order to deploy them as effectively as possible.

In addition to the security divisions and the *Korück* commands, the Germans created three *Befehlshaber der Rückwartigen Heeresgebiete* headquarters, one for each of the three Army Groups, North, Centre, and South. The OKH also numbered these commands so the full titles were as follows:

*Befehlshaber der Rückwartigen Heeresgebiet Nord 101*
*Befehlshaber der Rückwartigen Heeresgebiet Mitte 102*
*Befehlshaber der Rückwartigen Heeresgebiet Süd 103*

The SS and *Ordnungspolizei* were also represented in Ukraine and southern Russia. The following were the *Ordnungspolizei* commands and their respective commanders:

Command: *Befehlshaber der Ordnungspolizei Ukraine und Russland Süd*
CO: *SS-Gruppenführer und Generalleutnant der Polizei* Otto von Oelhafen
5 September 1941 to 10 October 1942
CO: *SS-Brigadeführer und Generalmajor der Polizei* Paul Scheer
30 January 1942 to 1 March 1942
CO: *SS-Gruppenführer und Generalleutnant der Polizei* Adolf Theodor von Bomhard
1 November 1942 to 30 October 1943
CO: *Oberst der Gendarmerie*Werner Lorge
31 October 1943 to 15 December 1943
CO: *SS-Gruppenführer und Generalleutnant der Polizei* Karl Heinrich Brenner[4]
15 December 1943 to 1 June 1944
CO: *Oberst der Gendarmerie* Werner Lorge
6 June 1944 to September 1944

These were the *Befehlshaber der Ordnungspolizei Ukraine und Russland Süd* sub-commands:

*Kommandeur der Ordnungspolizei Charkow* (Kharkov)
*SS-Brigadeführer und Generalmajor der Polizei* Eberhard Herf
28 February 1942 to 2 August 1943

*Kommandeur der Ordnungspolizei Dnjepropetrowsk* (Dnepropetrovsk)
*Oberstleutnant der Schutzpolizei* Albert von Gayl
25 October 1941 to October 1943

*Kommandeur der Ordnungspolizei Kiew* (Kiev)
*SS-Brigadeführer und Generalmajor der Polizei* Paul Scheer
1 March 1942 to 19 February 1943
*Oberst der Schutzpolizei* Oskar Knofe

19 February 1943 to 22 December 1943[5]

*Kommandeur der Ordnungspolizei Krim* (Simferopol)
*SS-Brigadeführer und Generalmajor der Polizei* Ernst Konrad Hitschler
August 1943 to April 1944

*Kommandeur der Gendarmerie Mosyr* (Mazyr)
*Oberstleutnant der Gendarmerie* Hans Lebenrecht von Bredow
25 October 1941 to March 1943
*Major der Gendarmerie* Hirsch
March 1943 to October 1943

*Kommandeur der Ordnungspolizei Nikolajew* (Nikolayev)
*Oberstleutnant der Schutzpolizei* Hermann Weiberg
25 October 1941 to December 1943

*Kommandeur der Ordnungspolizei Rostow* (Rostov)
*SS-Standartenführer und Oberst der Schutzpolizei* Hermann Crux
December 1942 to February 1943

*Kommandeur der Ordnungspolizei Schitomir* (Zhitomir)
*Oberstleutnant der Gendarmerie* Gotthilf Oemler
25 October 1941 to November 1943

*Kommandeur der Ordnungspolizei Tschernigow* (Chernigov)
*Oberstleutnant der Schutzpolizei* Johann Klepsch
25 October 1941 to October 1942
*Oberst der Schutzpolizei* Georg Asmus
17 November 1942 to 22 December 1943

*Kommandeur der Ordnungspolizei beim SS und Polizeiführer Kaukasien-Kuban*
(Stavropol, then in Krasnodar)
*Oberstleutnant der Gendarmerie* Claus
September 1942 to January 1943

The SS command was organised as follows:

Command: *Höhere SS Polizeiführer Ukraine und Rußland Süd* – Rovno[6]
Commander: *SS-Gruppenführer und Generalleutnant der Polizei* Hans Adolf Prützmann
In March 1944 the title of this SS headquarters was changed to:
*Höherer SS Polizeiführer Rußland Süd und Höchster SS Polizeiführer Ukraine*
The sub-commands under this SS headquarters were the following:

SS *und Polizeiführer Volhynia* (Brest-Litovsk)[7]
*SS und Polizeiführer Shitomir* (Zhitomir)
*SS und Polizeiführer Kiew* (Kiev)
*SS und Polizeiführer Nikolajew* (Nikolaev)
*SS und Polizeiführer Dnjepropetrowsk* (Dnepropetrovsk)
*SS und Polizeiführer Tschernigow* (Chernigov)
*SS und Polizeiführer Charkow* (Kharkov)
*SS und Polizeiführer Taurien-Krim-Simferopol)* (Simferopol)
*SS und Polizeiführer Stalino* (Stalino)
*SS und Polizeiführer Rostow* (Rostov)
*SS und Polizeiführer Awdejewka* (Avdeevka)
*SS und Polizeiführer Pripjet (Pinsk)* (Pinsk)

***SS und Polizeiführer Kiew*** – with:
*Kommandeur der Ordnungspolizei* (October 1941)
*SS-Brigadeführer und Generalmajor der Polizei* Paul Scheer
1 March 1942 to 19 February 1943
*Oberst der Ordnungspolizei* Oskar Knofe
20 February to 22 December 1943
*Oberst der Ordnungspolizei* Georg Asmus
23 December 1943 to 14 February 1944
*Oberst der Gendarmerie* Werner Lorge
6 June 1944 to September 1944
*Kommandeur der Gendarmerie*
*Oberst der Gendarmerie* Dr. Eregger.
*SS und Polizei Standortführer Kiew*:
*SS-Brigadeführer und Generalmajor der Polizei* Haltermann.
*SS und Polizei Standortführer Poltawa*:
*SS-Sturmbannführer und Oberstleutnant der Schutzpolizei* Möller.
SS *und Polizei Standortführer Krementschug*:
*Major der Schutzpolizei* Georg Fischer.
Headquarters: Kiev
Commanders:
CO: *SS-Brigadeführer und Oberstleutnant der Polizei* Hans Haltermann.[8]
1 October 1941 to 29 January 1943
CO: SS-*Gruppenführer und Generalleutnant der Polizei* Paul August Ernst Hennicke[9]
May to December 1943
Temporary Forces:[10]
*Schutzmannschaft Bataillonen 112, 113, 114, 115, 116, 118, 119, 120* and *121* through the *Kommandeur der Ordnungspolizei Kiew*
Permanent Forces:
*Kommandeur der Schutzpolizei Kiew*
*Kommandeur der Schutzpolizei Poltawa*
*Schutzpolizei Dienstabteilung Krementschug*

*Gendarmerie Hauptmannschaften Kiew Poltawa, Lubny* and *Bila-Cerkwa* (Kiev Poltava, Lubny, and Bila-Cerkva)
*Gendarmerie Zug (mot) 5 Bila-Cerkwa* (Bila-Cerkva)
*Gendarmerie Zug (mot) 22 Kiew* (Kiev)
*Gendarmerie Zug (mot) 51 Poltawa* (Poltava)
*Gendarmerie Zug (mot)* 57 Lubny (Lubny)
*Fliegergruppe z.b.V. 7*[11]

**SS *und Polizeiführer z. b. V.***
(under the command of *Höheren* SS *und Polizeiführer Rußland Süd*)
Headquarters: Kiev, Ukraine
Commanders:
*SS-Brigadeführer* Hermann Harm[12]
July 1942 to 1 July 1943
Task: Used as a headquarters staff for anti-partisan operations.

***SS und Polizeiführer Wolhynien-Podolien-Luzk*** (Volhynia-Podolia) with:
*Kommandeur der Ordnungspolizei Wolhnien*: *Oberstleutnant der Gendarmerie* Oelmler
*Kommandeur der Ordnungspolizei Luzk*: *Oberstleutnant der Schutzpolizei* Helmut Ribstein
*Kommandeur der Gendarmerie*: *Major der Gendarmerie* Rohse
*SS und Polizei Standortführer Brest-Litovsk*: *Major der Schutzpolizei* Rohde
Headquarters: Brest-Litovsk, then Rovno, then Pinsk
Commanders:
*SS-Oberführer* Ernst Hartmann (Brest-Litovsk)
22 June 1941 to August 1941
*SS-Brigadeführer* Gerrett Korsemann (Rovno)
1 September 1941 to August 1942
*SS-Brigadeführer und Generalmajor der Polizei* Waldemar Wappenhans (Brest-Litovsk)
4 September 1941 to 1 September 1942
*SS-Brigadeführer* Wilhelm Günther (Rovno)
September 1942 to January 1944
*SS-Oberführer* Ernst Hartmann (Pinsk)
10 February 1944
Temporary Forces:
*Schutzmannschaft Bataillonen 101, 102,* and *(polnische) 202.*
Permanent Forces:
*Gendarmerie Hauptmannschaften Luzk, Brest, Rowno,* and *Proskurow*
*Gendarmerie Zug (mot) 1*: Luzk
*Gendarmerie Zug (mot)* 2: Proskurow
*Gendarmerie Zug (mot) 47*: Rowno
*Gendarmerie Zug (mot) 48*: Brest

***SS und Polizeiführer Shitomir*** with:
*Kommandeur der Ordnungspolizei Shitomir*:
*Oberstleutnant der Gendarmerie* Gotthilf Oelmler
25 October 1941 to November 1943
*Kommandeur der Ordnungspolizei Chernigow*:
*Oberstleutnant der Schutzpolizei* Johann Klepsch (11 November 1941–7 August 1943)
*Oberst der Ordnungspolizei* Georg Asmus (8 August–22 December 1943)
*Kommandeur der Gendarmerie*:
*Oberstleutnant der Gendarmerie* von Bredow
*SS und Polizei Standortführer Shitomir*:
*SS-Obersturmbannführer und Oberst der Polizei* Otto Hellwig.
*SS und Polizei Standortführer Winniza* (Vinnitsa):
*SS-Obersturmbannführer und Kriminal Rat* Bock
Headquarters: Kharkov, Chernigov, Zhitomir, then finally Chernigov
Commanders:
*SS-Standartenführer* Otto Hellwig
22 October 1941
SS *Brigadeführer und Generalmajor der Polizei* Willy Tensfeld (Kharkov)
19 April 1943
*SS-Brigadeführer* Willy Schmelcher (Chernigov)
5 May 1943
*SS-Brigadeführer* Willy Schmelcher (Zhitomir)
20 May 1943
*SS-Obersturmbannführer* Hans Traupe (Zhitomir)
25 September 1943
*SS-Oberführer* Ernst Hartmann (Chernigov)
31 October 1943
*SS-Brigadeführer* Christoph Diehm (Chernigov)
25 January 1944
Temporary Forces:
*Schutzmannschaft Bataillonen 108, 109, 110, 136, 137, 138, 139, 140* and *159,(lettische) Polizei Bataillon 25* through the *Ordnungspolizei Shitomir*
Permanent Forces:
*Schutzpolizei Dienstabteilung Shitomir, Schutzpolizei Dienstabteilung Berditschew, Schutzpolizei Dienstabteilung Winniza*
*Gendarmerie Hauptmannschaften Winniza, Berditschew, Korosten* and *Mosyr*
*Gendarmerie Zug (mot) 3 Winniza*
*Gendarmerie Zug (mot) 4 Korosten*
*Gendarmerie Zug (mot) 24 Shitomir*
*Gendarmerie Zug (mot) 58 Mosyr*
*K-Außenstelle Zwiahel*

**SS *und Polizeiführer Pripjet*** (Zhitomir)
*SS-Oberführer* Ernst Hartmann (Zhitomir)
18 December 1943

***SS und Polizeiführer Nikolajew*** – with:
*SS und Polizeiführer Nikolajew* (Nikolaev)
Commanders:
*SS-Brigadeführer* Fritz Tittmann
22 October 1941
*SS-Brigadeführer* Waldemar Wappenhans
1 September 1942
*SS-Brigadeführer und Generalmajor der Polizei* Paul Zimmermann
15 April 1943
*SS-Brigadeführer und Generalleutnant der Polizei* Rudolf Weiss
16 April 1944
*Kommandeur der Ordnungspolizei*:
*Oberstleutnant der Schutzpolizei* Hermann Weiberg
25 October 1941 to December 1943
*Kommandeur der Gendarmerie*:
*Oberstleutnant der Gendarmerie* Ernst Köllner
25 October 1941 to 9 March 1942
*Major der Gendarmerie* Franz Gansinger
10 March 1942 to October 1942
*Oberstleutnant der Gendarmerie* Ernst Köllner
October 1942 to 13 May 1943
Temporary Forces:
*Schutzmannschaft Bataillonen 122, 123* and *124* through the *Kommandeur der Ordnungspolizei Nikolajew*
Permanent Forces:
*SS und Polizei Standortführer Cherson,*[13] *Kommandeur der Schutzpolizei Nikolajew, Schutzpolizei Dienstabteilung Kirowograd, Schutzpolizei Dienstabteilung Chersson*
Gendarmerie Hauptmannschaften Nikolajew, and *Kirowograd*
*Gendarmerie Zug (mot) 8 Kirowograd*
*Gendarmerie Zug (mot)14 Nikolajew*

***SS und Polizeiführer Dnjepropetrowsk-Kriwoi Ro*** – with:
*Kommandeur der Ordnungspolizei*:
*Oberstleutnant der Schutzpolizei* Albert von Gayl
25 October 1941 to October 1943
*Kommandeur der Gendarmerie*
Headquarters: *Dnjepropetrowsk*
Commanders:
*SS-Oberführer* Georg Graf von Bassewitz-Behr (Dnjepropetrowsk)
11 November 1941 to 1 August 1942
*SS-Brigadeführer* Hermann Harm (Dnjepropetrowsk)
1 August 1942 to 3 October 1942
*SS-Brigadeführer und Generalmajor der Polizei* Waldemar Wappenhans (Nikolajew)[14]
4 October 1942 to October 1943

*SS-Brigadeführer und Generalmajor der Polizei* Karl Schäfer (Kriwoirog)
October 1943 to 1944
Temporary Forces:
*Schutzmannschaft Bataillonen 117* and *130, (lettische) Polizei Bataillon 22* and *268* through the *Kommandeur der Ordnungspolizei Dnjepropetrowsk*
Permanent Forces:
*Kommandeur der Schutzpolizei Dnjepropetrowsk, Kamenskoje, Kriwoj-Rog,* and *Saporoshje*
*Schutzpolizei Dienstabteilung Nikopol, Schutzpolizei Dienstabteilung Berdjansk*
*Gendarmerie Hauptmannschaften Kriwoj-Rog, Pawlograd* and *Saporoshje*
*Gendarmerie Zug (mot) 15 Kriwoj-Rog*
*Gendarmerie Zug (mot) 16 Dnjepropetrowsk*
*Gendarmerie Zug (mot) 53 Saporoshje*
*Einsatz Stab Gieseke*[15]

***SS und Polizeiführer Taurien-Krim-Simferopol***
*Kommandeur der Ordnungspolizei Krim*:
*SS-Brigadeführer und Generalmajor der Polizei* Ernst Konrad Hitschler
August 1943 to April 1944
*Kommandeur der Gendarmerie*:
*Oberst der Gendarmerie* Lorge
Headquarters: Taurien, Simferopol, Nikolajew
*SS-und Polizeiführer Taurien-Krim-Simferopol*
Commanders:
*SS-Brigadeführer* Ludolf von Alvensleben (Taurien)
19 November 1941
*SS-Oberführer und Oberst der Polizei* Heinz Roch (Simferopol)
3 March to 6 October 1943
*SS-Obergruppenführer* Ludolf von Alvensleben (Taurien)
10 October to 24 December 1943
*SS-Obergruppenführer* Richard Hildebrandt (Nikolajew)
25 December 1943
*SS-Brigadeführer* Rudolf Weiß (Simferopol)
11 February 1944
Temporary Forces:
*Schutzmannschaft Bataillonen 147, 148, 149, 150, 151* and *154* through *Kommandeur der Ordnungspolizei Simferopol*
Permanent Forces:
*Schutzpolizei Dienstabteilung Melitopol, Schutzpolizei Dienstabteilung Kertsch*
*Gendarmerie Hauptmannschaften Simferopol, Melitopol* and *Feodosia*
*Gendarmerie Zug (mot) 41 Melitopol*
*Gendarmerie Zug (mot) 42 Simferopol*

*Gendarmerie Zug (mot) 54 Feodosia*

***SS und Polizeiführer Charkow*** – with:
*Kommandeur der Ordnungspolizei*
*Kommandeur der Gendarmerie*
Headquarters: Kharkov
*SS und Polizeiführer Charkow*
Commanders:
*SS-Brigadeführer und Generalmajor der Polizei* Willi Tensfeld[16]
4 August 1941 to 29 January 1943[17]
*SS-Brigadeführer und Oberstleutnant der Polizei* Hans Haltermann
30 January 1943
Temporary Forces:
*Schutzmannschaft Bataillonen 143, 144, 145* and *146*
Permanent Forces:
*Kommandeur der Schutzpolizei Charkow*
*Schutzpolizei Dienstabteilung Kursk, Schutzpolizei Dienstabteilung Orel, Schutzpolizei Dienstabteilung Briansk*
*Gendarmerie Hauptmannschaften Charkow, Belgorod, Kursk, Orel* and *Liwny*
*Gendarmerie Zug (mot) 25 Charkow*
*Gendarmerie Zug (mot) 26 Kursk*
*Gendarmerie Zug (mot) 27 Orel*
*Gendarmerie Zug (mot) 60 Belgorod*
*Gendarmerie Zug (mot) 61 Liwny*

***SS und Polizeiführer Krim und Simferopol*** – with:
*Kommandeur der Ordnungspolizei*
*Kommandeur der Gendarmerie*

***SS und Polizeiführer Stalino*** with:
*Kommandeur der Ordnungspolizei*:
*Oberstleutnant der Schutzpolizei* Albert Loose
*Kommandeur der Gendarmerie*
Headquarters: Stalino
Commanders:
*SS-Standartenführer und Oberstleutnant der Polizei* Johannes Rudolf Georg Hans Döring[18]
19 November 1941 to 18 May 1943
*SS-Brigadeführer und Generalmajor der Polizei* Willi Tensfeld
19 May to 4 September 1943
Temporary Forces:
*Schutzmannschaft Bataillonen 157, 158, 159, 160, 161, 162, 163, 164* and *165* under the *Kommandeur der Ordnungspolizei Stalino*

Permanent Forces:
*SS und Polizei Standortführer Mariupol, Kommandeur der Schutzpolizei Stalino, Kommandeur der Schutzpolizei Mariupol, Kommandeur der Schutzpolizei Gorlowka*
*Gendarmerie Hauptmannschaften Stalino, Mariupol,* and *Nikitowka*
*Gendarmerie Zug (mot) 43 Stalino*
*Gendarmerie Zug (mot) 44 Sslawjansk*
*Gendarmerie Zug (mot) 52 Krassny-Lutsch*
*Gendarmerie Zug (mot) 59 Starobelskv*

***SS und Polizeiführer Rostow-Awdejewka*** (then Sarny) – with:
*Kommandeur der Ordnungspolizei Rostow:*
*SS-Standartenführer und Oberst der Schutzpolizei* Hermann Crux
September 1942 to February 1943
*Kommandeur der Gendarmerie*
Headquarters: Rostov
Commanders:
*SS-Gruppenführer und Generalleutnant der Polizei* Gerret Korsemann
27 July to 1 October 1942
*SS-Gruppenführer und Generalleutnant der Polizei* Paul Hennicke
2 October 1942 to 30 April 1943
Temporary Forces:
*Schutzmannschaft Bataillonen 166, 167, 168* and *169*
Permanent Forces:
*Kommandeur der Schutzpolizei Rostow, Kommandeur der Schutzpolizei Taganrog, Kommandeur der Schutzpolizei Schachty, Schutzpolizei Dienstabteilung Nowotscherkassk, Schutzpolizei Dienstabteilung Nachitschewan*
*Gendarmerie Hauptmannschaften Rostow* and *Kamensk*
*Gendarmerie Zug (mot) 45 Kamensk*
*Gendarmerie Zug (mot) 46 Rostow*

***SS und Polizeiführer Nord-Kaukasien*** – with:[19]
*Kommandeur der <Ordnungspolizei:*
*Oberstleutnant der Gendarmerie* Claus
September 1942 to January 1943
*Kommandeur der Gendarmerie*:
Headquarters: Stavropol (Voroshilovsk)
Commanders:
*SS-Standartenführer und Oberst der Polizei* Karl-Heinz Bürger
21 August 1942 to 5 January 1943

In November 1943, the *Höhere SS Polizeiführer Schwarzes Meer* headquarters was created and stationed in Simferopol, in the Crimea. This SS command was assigned to *Heeresgruppe A*,[20] but was answerable to the *Höhere SS Polizeiführer Ukraine und Rußland Süd* headquarters.

## An intensification of the anti-partisan war

On 18 August 1942, the *Führer* issued *Kriegsanweisung Nr. 46* (War Directive No. 46), *Richtlinien für die verstärkte Bekämpfung des Bandenunwesens im Osten* (Instructions for Intensified Action against the Bands in the East). This order had six principal goals:

> 1. The fight against banditry is as much a matter of strategy as the fight against the enemy at the front. It will therefore be organised and carried out by the same staffs.
> 2. The destruction of the bandits calls for active operations and the most rigorous measures against all members of gangs or those guilty of supporting them. Operation orders for action against bandits will follow.
> 3. The confidence of the local population in German authority must be gained by handling them strictly but justly.
> 4. A necessary condition for the destruction of bandit gangs is the assurance to the local population of the minimum requirements of life. Should this fail, or – what is particularly important – should available supplies not be fairly distributed, the result will be that more recruits will join the bandits.
> 5. In this struggle against the bandits the co-operation of the local population is indispensable. Deserving persons should not be parsimoniously treated; rewards should be really attractive. On the other hand, reprisals for action in support of the bandits must be all the more severe.
> 6. Misplaced confidence in the native population, particularly in those working for the German authorities, must be strictly guarded against. Even though the majority of the population is opposed to the bandits, there are always spies to be reckoned with, whose task is to inform the bandits of all action contemplated against them.[21]

It was clear, based on this new directive, that the *Wehrmacht* and SS had overlapping jurisdictional authority behind the lines. *Reichsführer*-SS Heinrich Himmler was named *Chef der Bandenkampfverbände* (Chief of the anti-Bandit Organisation), but the actual commanders in the field would be Erich von dem Bach Zelewski, who would be placed in charge of all anti-partisan operations in the East by Himmler. Von dem Bach's commanders were: Curt von Gottberg (Belarus, central Russia), Walter Schimana (Belarus, Ukraine), Friedrich Jeckeln (Ukraine, *Ostland,* north Russia, Belarus), Prützmann (*Ostland,* north Russia, Belarus, Ukraine, *Generalgouvernement*), Karl Knecht (*Ostland,* north Russia, Belarus), Walther Schröder (*Ostland,* north Russia) Hans Siegling (in Belarus, central Russia, *Generalgouvernement*) and others. In the case of Odilo Globocnik and Friedrich Wilhelm

Krüger (in the *Generalgouvernement* and Volhynia, western Ukraine), they had greater latitude and operated almost independently of Von dem Bach's command. The reason was their location in the *Generalgouvernement*.

## Reinforcements

The intensification of the anti-partisan war also involved sending additional forces into the USSR. In the spring, summer and autumn of 1942 several division-sized units reached Ukraine earmarked for rear area security duties. In July 1942 the *403. Sicherungs Division* arrived. Another was *Division Nr. 153*, which became *153. Reserve Division* on 12 September 1942.[22] It was in September that this division was sent to Ukraine. *143. Reserve Division* was established on 18 September 1942 through the reorganisation of *Division Nr. 143*. In that month it also left *Reich* territory and was sent to Ukraine. *Reserve Division 143* was stationed in and around Dubno, in eastern Ukraine, under the *Befehlshaber der Rückwartigen Heeresgebiet Süd* command. The recruits of *143. Reserve Division* needed to be trained as soldiers, but while this training was being performed, they were also expected to act as occupation troops. The men of this division were principally used for railway protection.[23] The division became responsible for rail security from Brest-Litovsk to Gomel (a little over 130 miles). The division was also responsible for rail security from Kovel to Sarny and then on to Kiev, which forced the division to protect another 87 miles of track. The following table below lists the available anti-partisan forces that the *Befehlshaber der Rückwartigen Heeresgebiet Süd* controlled from month to month beginning in June 1941:

Table 15. Forces Under the *Befehlshaber der Rückwartig Heeresgruppe Süd 103* Command

| Year | Date | Units |
|---|---|---|
| *Befehlshaber der Rückwartig Heeresgruppe Süd 103* | | |
| 1941 | 1 Jul | *444.* and *454. Sicherungs Division, LVII. Panzerkorps*: *100.* and *101. Infanterie Division*, Slovak Fast Brigade, *Sicherungs Regiment 4, Feldgendarmerie Abteilung 692.* |
| | 7 Aug | *213., 444.* and *454. Sicherungs Division, 1. SS Infanterie Brigade (mot.), Sicherungs Regiment 4, Feldgendarmerie Abteilung 692.* |
| | 3 Sep | *213., 444.* and *454. Sicherungs Division, 1. SS Infanterie Brigade (mot.), Sicherungs Regiment 4,* Slovak Fast Brigade, *Feldgendarmerie Abteilung 692.* |

| Year | Date | Units |
|---|---|---|
| | 2 Oct | *213.* and *444. Sicherungs Division,* part of *1. SS Infanterie Brigade (mot.),* Slovak Fast Brigade, 102nd and 108th Hungarian Light Division, *Sicherungs Regiment 4, Feldgendarmerie Abteilung 692.* |
| | 4 Nov | *213., 444.* and *454. Sicherungs Division,* Slovak Security Division, *62. Infanterie Division,* 102nd Hungarian Light Brigade / Division, 108th Hungarian Light Brigade / Division (until 27 Nov. 1941), *Sicherungs Regiment 4, Feldgendarmerie Abteilung 692.* |
| | 4 Dec | 102nd Hungarian Light Division, 105th and 108th Hungarian Light Brigades, *Sicherungs Regiment 4, Feldgendarmerie Abteilung 692.* |
| 1942 | 2 Jan | 102nd Hungarian Light Brigade / Division (until 30 Jan), 105th and 108th Hungarian Light Brigade / Division, *Sicherungs Regiment 4, Feldgendarmerie Abteilung 692.* |
| | Feb–March | Part of *454. Sicherungs Division,* main body of *444. Sicherungs Division,* 105th Hungarian Light Brigade / Division, *Sicherungs Regiment 4, Feldgendarmerie Abteilung 692.* |
| | Apr–Jun | Part of the *444. Sicherungs Division, Sicherungs Regiment 4,*[24] *Feldgendarmerie Abteilung 692.* |
| | 4 Jul | *213. Sicherungs Division* (one regiment only), *444. Sicherungs Division,* staff of *403. Sicherungs Division,* 105th Hungarian Light Brigade, *Feldgendarmerie Abteilung 692.* |
| | Aug–Sep | *213.* and *403. Sicherungs Division,* 105th Hungarian Light Brigade, *Feldgendarmerie Abteilung 692, Reserve Division 143.* |
| | Oct–Nov. | *213.* and *403. Sicherungs Division,* 105th Hungarian Light Brigade, Italian 'Vicenza' Division, *Feldgendarmerie Abteilung 692, Reserve Division 143.* |
| | 1 Dec | *213. Sicherungs Division,* 105th Hungarian Light Brigade, Italian 'Vicenza' Division, *Feldgendarmerie Abteilung 692, Reserve Division 143.* |
| 1943 | Jan–Feb | *213. Sicherungs Division* (partly), 105th Hungarian Light Brigade, *Feldgendarmerie Abteilung 692, Reserve Division 143.* |

| Year | Date | Units |
|---|---|---|
| *Befehlshaber Heeresgebiet Süd* | | |
| 1943 | 4 Mar | *213. Sicherungs Division* (partly), *403. Sicherungs Division, Feldgendarmerie Abteilung 692, Reserve Division 143.* |
| | Apr–May | *213. Sicherungs Division* (partly), *Feldgendarmerie Abteilung 692, Reserve Division 143.* |
| | Jun–Sep | *213.* and *454. Sicherungs Divisionen*, cadre staff of *444. Sicherungs Division, Feldgendarmerie Abteilung 692, Reserve Division 143.* |
| | 4 Oct | Cadre staff of *444. Sicherungs Division, Feldgendarmerie Abteilung 692, Reserve Division 143.* |

In addition to the above-listed units, the *Befehlshaber der Rückwartig Heeresgruppe Süd 103* command possessed troops that were permanently attached to its headquarters. Those included:[25]

*Ost Bau Bataillon 559* (three companies)
*Ost Ausbildungs Bataillon I* (four recruit cavalry squadrons)
*Ost Reiter Abteilung* (two cavalry squadrons)
*Ost Artillerie Abteilung* (3 batteries)

The principal operational employment for the *Befehlshaber der Rückwärtigen Heeresgruppe Süd 103* command in 1941 was as follows:[26]

22 June–5 July 1941: Following up the breakthrough by the San River.
6–26 July 1941: Following up the breakthrough by Kiev.
5–31 August 1941: Anti-partisan operations in the Pripet Marshes region.
31 October–8 November 1941: Anti-partisan operations in the Cherkassy region

In addition to the post of *Befehlshaber der Rückwärtigen Heeresgruppe Süd*, the Germans had a headquarters called the *Wehrmachtbefehlshaber Ukraine*. This headquarters was established on 1 September 1941 and was disbanded on 21 July 1944. Every region that was occupied by the Third Reich contained a *Wehrmachtbefehlshaber* (Supreme Commander of the Armed Forces). The task of the *Wehrmachtbefehlshaber* was the same in every occupied country: security and defence against invasion. In this, its command responsibility would naturally overlap with the

*Befehlshaber der Rückwärtigen Heeresgruppe Süd* headquarters, given that both were concerned with security. At the start of the invasion of the Soviet Union, the order of battle for the *Wehrmachtbefehlshaber Ukraine* was as follows:

Command Staff:
*CO: General der Flieger* Karl Kitzinger[27]
*Kommunikationschef*: *Generalleutnant* Rudolf Meltzer[28]
*O3: Hauptmann* Dschenfzig
*Chef der General Stabes*: *Oberst i.G.* Ernst von Krause
*O4*: *Leutnant* Karpf
*Verbindungsoffizier*: *Hauptmann* Dr. Schafferdt
*Ia*: *Oberstleutnant* Gais
*Quartermeister*: *Oberstleutnant i.G.* Sichting
*IIa: Major* Scipio
*Kdt. H. Qu.*: *Major* Graf Chamaré
*Veterinäroffizier*: Dr. Lindner
*Gericht*: Dr. Mellinghoff
*H.W. Nafü.*: *Oberst* Meltzer
*Ast.*: *Oberstleutnant* Neumerkel
*Kommandeur der Streifendientes*: *Major* Gebhardt
*Wehrmacht Inspekteur und Kommandeur der Kampfgruppe*: *Generalmajor* Feichtmeier
*Transportoffizier*: *Major* Kurek
Principal Headquarters and Combat Units:[29]
*Oberfeldkommandantur 393* – Zhitomir (later located in Kiev)[30]
*Oberfeldkommandantur 579* – Luck (later located in Rovno)[31]
*Ortskommandantur 899* – Brest-Litovsk
*Ortskommandantur 909* – Kovel
*Ortskommandantur 935* – Rovno
*Feldkommandantur 183 Kamenec* – Podolsk (19 October 1941)
  *Ortskommandantur 357* – Schepetovka
*Sicherungsdivision 454* – *Generalbezirk* – Zhitomir and Kiev
*Feldkommandantur 675*:
  *Ortskommandantur 261* – Berdichev
  *Ortskommandantur 275* – Gaissin
  *Ortskommandantur 269* – Uman
  *Ortskommandantur 285* – Pervomaisk
  *Ortskommandantur 298* – Bielaya-Zerkov
  *Ortskommandantur 251* – Schopola
*Feldkommandantur 811*:
  *Ortskommandantur 327* – Ovrutsch
  *Ortskommandantur 325* – Korosten

*Stadtkommandantur Kiev* with:
*Feldkommandantur 195*:
*Ortskommandantur 328* – Kiev
*Ortskommandantur 368* – Kiev
*123. Ungarische Infanterie Brigade* – Proskurov
*124. Ungarische Infanterie Brigade* – Staro-Konstantinov (later Schepetovka)[32]
*Landesschützen Regiment 102* – Korzec
*Landesschützen Bataillon 231* – Zwiahel
*Landesschützen Bataillon 988* – Rovno
*Landesschützen Bataillon 552* – Luck
*Landesschützen Bataillon 856* – Brest-Litovsk

Table 16. Forces Under the *Wehrmachtbefehlshaber Ukraine*, 1941–1943

| Year | Date | Units |
|---|---|---|
| | *Wehrmachtbefehlshaber Ukraine* | |
| 1941 | Sep | *Oberfeldkommandantur 393* and *579*. |
| | Nov | *Oberfeldkommandantur 393* and *579*, 108th Hungarian Light Division (from 27 Nov). |
| | Dec | *Oberfeldkommandantur 393* and *579*, 108th Hungarian Light Division (until 3 Dec). |
| 1942 | 2 Jan | *Oberfeldkommandantur 393* and *579*, *454. Sicherungs Division*, Slovak Security Division, 10th Romanian Infantry Division. |
| 1943 | Jun–Oct | *Oberfeldkommandantur 393* and *579*, *LXII. Reservekorps*, with *143. Reserve Division*[33] and *147. Reserve Divisionen.*[34] |
| | Nov | *Oberfeldkommandantur 393* and *579*, cadre staff of the *444. Sicherungs Division*, VIIth Hungarian Corps,[35] 18th, 21st, 24th, and 25th Hungarian Light Divisions, *LXII. Reservekorps*with *143.* and *147. Reserve Divisionen.* |
| | Dec | *Oberfeldkommandantur 393* and *579*, cadre staff of the *444. Sicherungs Division*, VIIth Hungarian Corps,[36] 18th, 21st, 24th, and 25th Hungarian Light Divisions, *LXII. Reservekorps*, with *147. Reserve Division.*[37] |
| 1944 | Jan | *Oberfeldkommandantur 393* and *579*, cadre staff of the *444. Sicherungs Division*, VIIth Hungarian Corps, 18th, 21st, 24th, and 25th Hungarian Light Divisions. |
| | Feb | *Oberfeldkommandantur 393* and *579*, VIIth Hungarian Corps, 18th, 21st, 24th, and 25th Hungarian Light Divisions, |

## *Geheime Feldpolizei* forces in the region of Ukraine and Army Group South

In the summer of 1941, *GFP-725* would see initial employment under the *6. Armee*. It would operate in the region of *Heeresgruppe Süd* well into 1944 when it would be attached to the *8. Armee* The first officer in charge of *GFP-725* was *Feldpolizeikommissar* Ignatz Roisel. Roisel would die in battle on 18 April 1942, fighting Red Army parachutists who had landed behind German lines to help organise a partisan group. On 14 June 1942, Kurt Arlt was the Field Police Director (with the army equivalent rank of 'Major') and head of all GFP units in the region of *Heeresgruppe Süd*. Previously he had been in charge of the GFP units assigned to the *213. Sicherungs Division*.[38] From February to April 1942 GFP superintendent Richard Sithof was in charge of *GFP-708*, *GFP-721* and *GFP-730*, all of which were currently performing security duties in the operational area of the 105th Hungarian Light Infantry Division. On 8 May 1942, Sithof's successor was *Feldpolizeikommissar* Karl Eschweiler. Eschweiler would end the war with the rank of *Leitender Feldpolizeidirektor*. The *Leitender Feldpolizeidirektor* in the *444. Sicherungs Division* was named Schmidt.[39] From September 1941 until October 1942 *Feldpolizeidirektor* Hans Stephainski was *Leitender Feldpolizeidirektor beim Heeresgruppe Süd* (Senior Field Police Director by Army Group South). From 1943–5 this position was taken by *Feldpolizeidirektor* Joachim Kaintzik. The leader of *GFP-730* in June 1943 was *Feldpolizeikommissar* Moll. The leader of *GFP-708* in April 1943 was *Feldpolizeikommissar* Forejtnik. Some GFP officials were made responsible for several GFP units within a higher divisional or army/rear area headquarters. These posts often had a large turnover of commanders as seen by the following listings:

*Leitender Feldpolizeidirektor für die Gruppen in den Ungarische 105. Infanterie Division,*
    *GFP-708, 721 u. 730*
    2 April 1942, *Leitender Feldpolizeidirektor* Sithoff
    May – July 1942, *Feldpolizeikommissar* Dr. Heinrichs
    27 August 1942, *Feldpolizeidirektor* Karl Eschweiler[40]
*Leitender Feldpolizeidirektor für die Gruppen GFP 706, 719 u. 725*
    February – July 1942: *Feldpolizeidirektor* Kurt Arlt
*Leitender Feldpolizeidirektor bei der 213. Sicherungs Division, GFP-706, 719, u. 725*
    From 30 August 1942, *Feldpolizeidirektor* Kurt Arlt
*Leitender Feldpolizeidirektor bei Befehlshaber Heeresgebiet Süd 103*

From 4 January 1943: *Feldpolizeidirektor* Friedrich Walz

*Leitender Feldpolizeidirektor bei der 444. Sicherungs Division, GFP-711, 720, u. 726*

*Feldpolizeidirektor* Schmidt

*Leitender Feldpolizeidirektor bei der 454. Sicherungs Division, GFP-708, 721, 726, u. 740*

*Feldpolizeidirektor* Sithoff, then *Feldpolizeidirektor* Hochgräbe

## Ukrainian reinforcements

The hatred that most Ukrainians had for Joseph Stalin and communism was the principal catalyst that explains why so many of them volunteered to serve alongside the Germans. The initial year and a half of the German occupation of Ukraine was the most productive vis-à-vis the recruitment of Ukrainians into pro-German forces. As Erich Koch's jackboot pressed harder and harder on the Ukrainians' necks, the number of volunteers began to dwindle. When the *Befehlshaber der Ordnungspolizei Ukraine* headquarters was established in Rovno in September 1941, it immediately began to work on recruiting Ukrainians as auxiliary policemen.[41] Not only did the *Ordnungspolizei* obtain volunteers for the *Gendarmerie* and *Schutzpolizei* units, but other Nazi organisations also began to recruit Ukrainians to serve as auxiliaries. These included the headquarters of the *Reichskommissariat Ukraine, Geheimstaatspolizei, Sicherheitspolizei, Sicherheitsdienst, Reichsarbeitsdienst, Deutsche Reichsbahn* (as auxiliaries in the service of the *Bahnschutzpolizei*), etc. By the end of 1941, Kurt Daluege, who was the current head of the *Ordnungspolizei,* claimed that there were 14,452 Ukrainian auxiliaries in the *Reichskommissariat Ukraine.*[42] The recruitment of Ukrainian volunteers did not occur only in western Ukraine, but also eastern Ukraine, as in the following quote:

> By November 1942, there were approximately 410 Gendarmes subordinated to the KdG Nikolajew, in charge of nearly 5,000 local policemen (Schutzmannschaft – Einzeldienst). In Generalkommissariat Dnjepropetrowsk, about 600 officials of the Schutzpolizei and 400 Gendarmes were responsible for some 6,000 Ukrainian auxiliaries. The Kommandeur der Ordnungspolizei (KdO) Dnjepropetrowsk was Colonel Gotthilf Hoffmann. Small outposts of the Security Police were established in major cities such as Nikolaev, Kirovograd, Dnepropetrovsk, and Zaporozh'e.[43]

The Ukrainian *Schutzmannschaft* was created under the control of the *Ordnungspolizei*, which was composed of the *Schutzpolizei* in the cities and the *Gendarmerie* in the towns and country areas. The following is a complete list of all *Schutzmannschaft* battalions that were raised from Ukrainian volunteers during the war:

*Schutzmannschaft Bataillon 101*. Raised in Lutsk on 6 October 1942. Operated against partisans in the region of Staro-Konstantinov in 1942 and 1943. Performed road security duty, then served as a replacement battalion for other Ukrainian *Schutzmannschaft* units. The battalion was disbanded in March 1944.
*Schutzmannschaft Bataillon 102*. Created in Kremianez (Kremenets), Volhynia District, in July 1942. In October 1942 it became a *Wach* (Guard) battalion and was stationed in Postavy, near Vilnius, Lithuania. Was renamed *Schutzmannschaft Bataillon 61* in January 1944.
*Schutzmannschaft Bataillon 103*. Created in Macieev (Makijeve), near Lutsk, Ukraine in July 1942. Performed road security duties along the roads Lutzk–Kovel, Lutzk–Rovno, Lutzk–Sarny.
*Schutzmannschaft Bataillon 104*. Established in Kobrin in July 1942. Training assignment in Kobrin, November 1942. Remained in the Lutsk area from 1942–4.
*Schutzmannschaft Bataillon 105*. Created in Macieev (Makijeve), near Lutsk, Ukraine in July 1942. Stationed in Sarny from 1942–4.
*Schutzmannschaft Bataillon 106*. Created in Rovno in November 1942. Remained there as a guard unit from 1942–3.
*Schutzmannschaft Bataillon 107*. Created in Lutsk in November 1942. Remained in Lutsk as a town garrison. Disbanded in March 1944.
*Schutzmannschaft Bataillon 108*. Created in Zhitomir in July 1942. Between July and November 1942, it was assigned to frontier guard duty along the Ukrainian-Romanian border region. Sometime in November 1942 it returned to Zhitomir and was given training tasks.
*Schutzmannschaft Bataillon 109*. Created in Berdichev (south of Zhitomir) in July 1942. Performed guard duty in Berdichev throughout 1942. In January 1943 it was tasked with continued guard duty in the town, but was also given the job of training recruits.
*Schutzmannschaft Bataillon 110*. Created in January 1943 in Zhitomir to act as a replacement battalion for other *Schutzmannschaft* units from 1943 until March 1944 when it was disbanded.
*Schutzmannschaft Bataillon 111*. Created in Zhitomir as a *Wach* (Guard) battalion in November 1942. Performed road security duty between Zhitomir-Korosten, and Zhitomir-Fastov. May have been formed of Cossacks or contained Cossack personnel. The battalion was listed in action in the *Generalgouvernement* in June 1944.

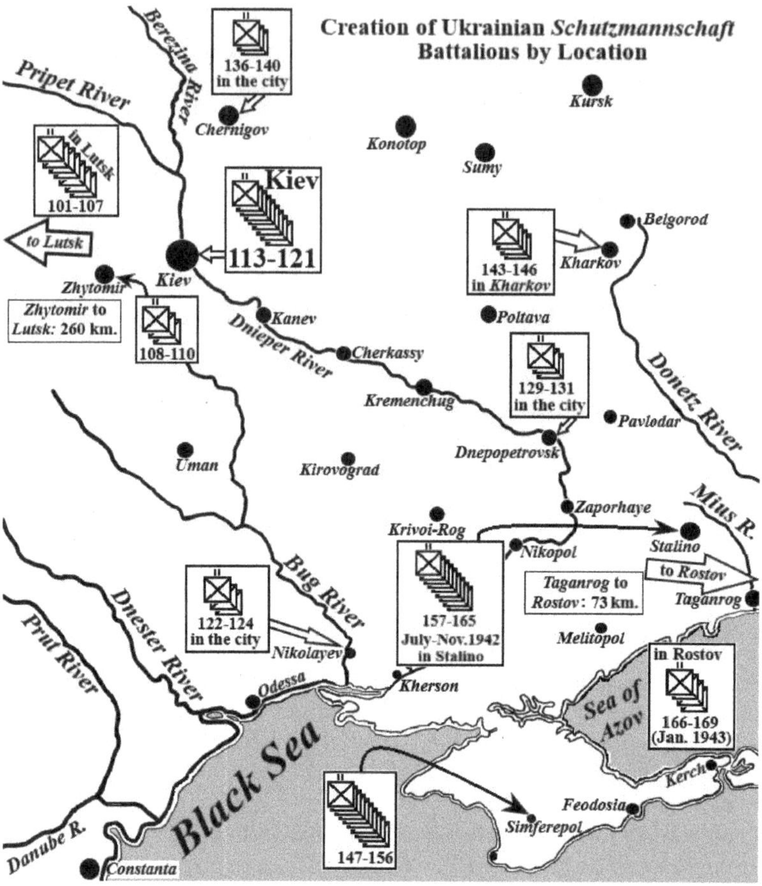


Figure 36. Principal locations where Ukrainian *Schutzmannschaft* battalions were raised.

*Schutzmannschaft Bataillon 112*. Never established.
*Schutzmannschaft Bataillon 113*. Created in November 1942 in the Kiev area. Transferred to Poltava in eastern Ukraine in January 1943. Fought partisan bands in the forests south of Poltava. Took part in the German defence of Poltava against the Red Army attack which began on 15 September 1943. Was destroyed in the process of the city being taken by the Russians between 15–18 September 1943.
*Schutzmannschaft Bataillon 114*. Established in Rovno in July 1942 as a guard battalion. Also served as a replacement battalion. In November 1941 the battalion was transferred to Lubny, about 121km north-east of Cherkasy. In July 1943 the battalion was shifted to Kiev. It remained there performing guard duty and supplying replacements to other battalions until it was disbanded in March 1944.

*Schutzmannschaft Bataillon 114*. Created in Rovno in July 1942 as a guard and replacement battalion. In November 1942 it was transferred to Lubny. In July 1943 it was stationed in Kiev. In March 1944 the battalion was disbanded.

*Schutzmannschaft Bataillon 115*. Established in Kiev in July 1942. In November 1942 it was renamed a *Wach* (Guard) battalion. It remained in Kiev until July 1943, when it was transferred to Minsk and renamed *Schutzmannschaft Bataillon 62* (renamed in December 1943). In July 1944 it was absorbed into *Polizei Brigade Siegling* in Minsk. This formation was led by *SS-Obersturmbannführer und Oberst der Schutzpolizei* Hans Siegling, the former commander of *(ukrainische) Schutzmannschaft Bataillon 57*. The brigade contained numerous *Schutzmannschaft* battalions (mostly Belarusian), *Ordnungspolizei*, SS and even SD personnel.

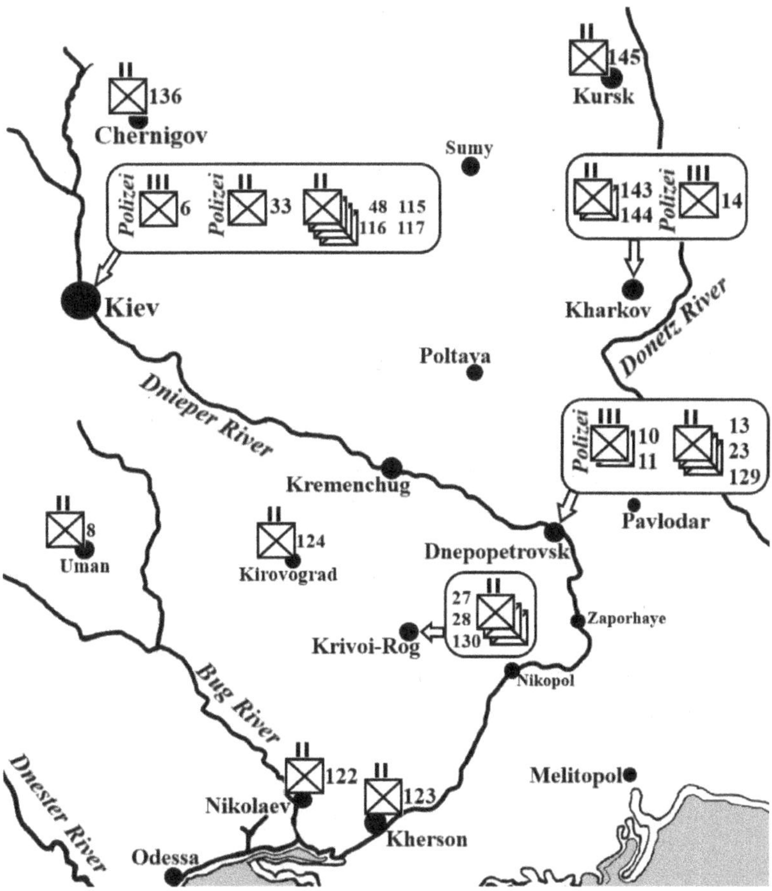


Figure 37. German police regiments and *Schutzmannschaft* battalions in central Ukraine, summer of 1943.

*Schutzmannschaft Bataillon 116*. Created in Belaya-Zerkov in July 1942. Belaya-Zerkov lies about 86km south-west of Kiev. Performed guard duty there. In July 1943 it was designated a *Wach* battalion. The battalion was disbanded in January 1944.

*Schutzmannschaft Bataillon 117*. Created in July 1942, in the town of Spola (Shpola), which lies about 73km south-west of Cherkasy. In October 1942 it was designated as a *Wach* battalion. In July 1943 the unit was sent to Krivoi-Rog (Kirovograd). There it performed guard duty. It was disbanded in March 1944.

*Schutzmannschaft Bataillon 118*. Created in Kiev in July 1942. Renamed as a *Wach* battalion in November 1942. In July 1943 it was transferred to Minsk. In December 1943 it was renamed as *Schutzmannschaft Bataillon 63*. In July 1944 it was absorbed into the *Polizei Brigade Siegling*.

*Schutzmannschaft Bataillon 119*. Created in Kremenchug in November 1942. In July 1943 it was designated a *Wach* battalion. The battalion was disbanded in March 1944.

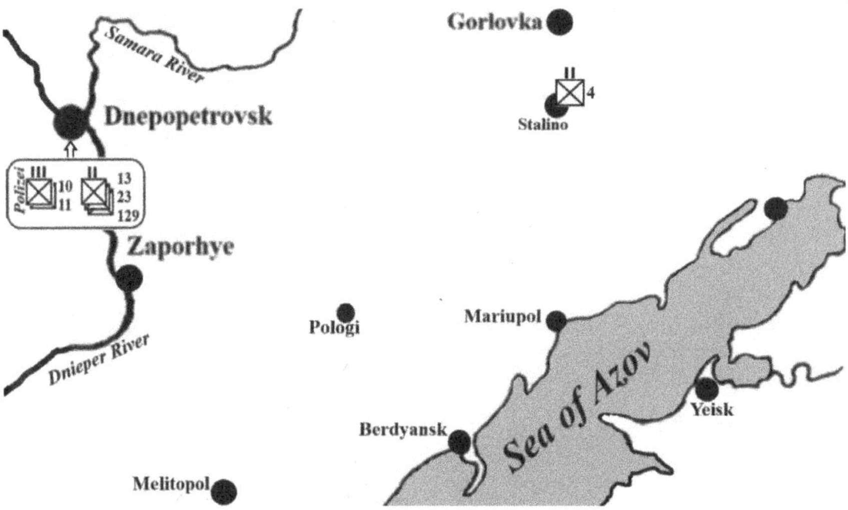


Figure 38. German police regiments and locally-raised volunteer battalions in south-eastern Ukraine, summer of 1943.

*Schutzmannschaft Bataillon 120*. Created in Kiev in November 1942. Transferred to Poltava in January 1943. Like *Schutzmannschaft Bataillon 113*, it battled the partisans whose base of operations was the forested region south of Poltava. The battalion was destroyed defending Poltava from the Red Army in September 1943.

*Schutzmannschaft Bataillon 121*. Established in Kiev in November 1942. In January 1943 it was ordered to Lubny. Like Poltava, Lubny was liberated by the Red Army on 18 September 1943. It is believed that this battalion was destroyed defending the town.

*Schutzmannschaft Bataillon 122*. Created in the city of Nikolaev in July 1942. Was renamed as a *Wach* battalion in July 1943. The battalion did not withdraw, but was destroyed in Nikolaev when the 88th Guards Division of the Red Army took the town on 28 March 1944.

*Schutzmannschaft Bataillon 123*. Created in Kherson in July 1942. Performed guard duty and was employed fighting the partisans in the surrounding woods. In July 1943 it was designated as a replacement battalion. In February 1944 the battalion was ordered to Krivoi-Rog. This was as a result of the Nikopol-Krivoi Rog offensive by the Red Army that ran from 30 January and 29 February 1944. It took part in the defence of the town. Krivoi-Rog was taken by the Red Army on 24 February 1944. The battalion withdrew with the rest of *6. Armee*. In September 1944 the battalion was disbanded.

*Schutzmannschaft Bataillon 124*. Formed in Kirovograd in July 1942. It was employed on guard duty in POW camps from the autumn of 1942 until May 1944 when it was disbanded.

*Schutzmannschaft Bataillon 125*. Created in November 1942. It was employed in guarding prisoner of war transit camps in the Ukraine. Dissolved in October 1943.

*Schutzmannschaft Bataillon 126*. Was actually a battalion composed of Cossacks in Ukraine. Created in November 1942 and employed guarding the roads. In July 1943 it was renamed *Kosaken Schuma Wach Bataillon 126*. Disbanded in March 1944.

*Schutzmannschaft Bataillon 127* and *128*. Never established.

*Schutzmannschaft Bataillon 129*. Created in Dnepropetrovsk in July 1942. Remained in this city as a guard battalion until disbanded in May 1943.[44]

*Schutzmannschaft Bataillon 130*. Created in in Dnepropetrovsk in July 1942. In June 1943 it was redesignated as a replacement battalion and sent to Krivoi-Rog. It remained in Krivoi-Rog until April 1944 when it was disbanded.

*Schutzmannschaft Bataillon 131*. Created in Dnepropetrovsk in November 1942. In spring 1942, a locally-raised partisan band began operating in the surrounding countryside, requiring the Germans to bring in more reinforcements. *Schutzmannschaft Bataillon 131* was transferred to Zaporozhe in January 1943 to act as guards. The hydroelectric plant and the steelworks were the two most important installations in the city.

*Schutzmannschaft Bataillon 132* and *133*. Never established.

*Schutzmannschaft Bataillon 134*. This battalion was composed of Cossacks from Ukraine. It was established as a *Wach* battalion in Krivoi-Rog in November 1942. In the months of January and July 1943 the battalion was sent on road security duty.

*Schutzmannschaft Bataillon 135*. Created in November 1942 employing Cossacks from Ukraine. Raised in Krivoi-Rog. The battalion was

renamed *Kosaken Schuma Wach Bataillon 135* and ordered to perform road security duty.
*Schutzmannschaft Bataillon 136*. Created in Chernigov in July 1942. In January 1943 the battalion was still located there.
*Schutzmannschaft Bataillon 137*. Created in Chernigov in October 1942. Stationed in Shostka in January 1943.
*Schutzmannschaft Bataillon 138*. Created in Chernigov in October 1942. For employment in anti-partisan warfare under the *Kommandeur der Ordnungspolizei Tschernigow*.
*Schutzmannschaft Bataillon 139*. Created in Chernigov in October 1942. For employment in anti-partisan warfare under the *Kommandeur der Ordnungspolizei Tschernigow*.
*Schutzmannschaft Bataillon 140*. Created in Chernigov in October 1942. For employment in anti-partisan warfare under the *Kommandeur der Ordnungspolizei Tschernigow*.
*Schutzmannschaft Bataillon 141* and *142*. Never established.

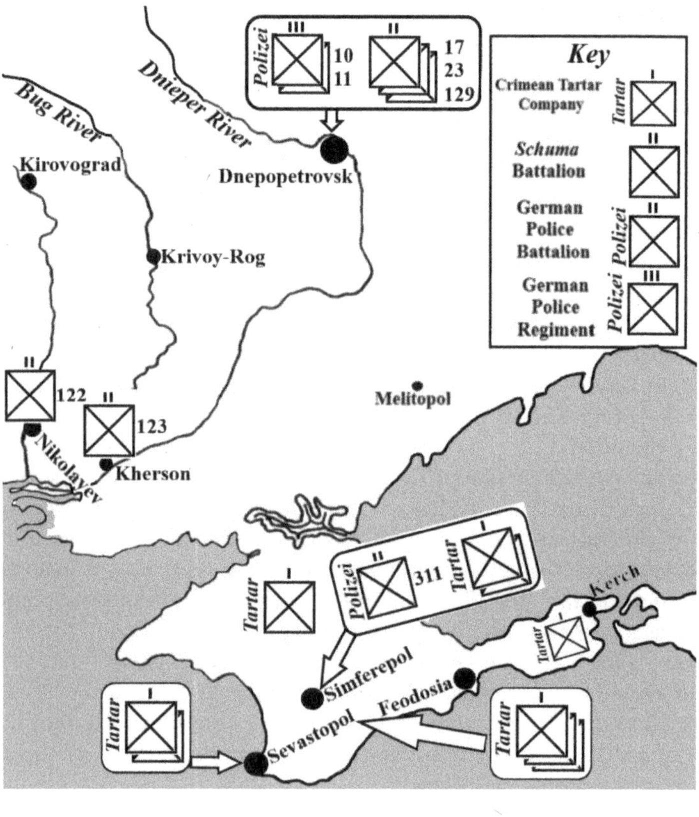


Figure 39. German police and locally-raised units in south-east Ukraine and Crimea, July 1942.

*Schutzmannschaft Bataillon 143*. Created in Kharkov in August 1942. July 1943 was designated as a replacement battalion.
*Schutzmannschaft Bataillon 144*. Created in Kharkov in August 1942. In January 1943 it was still located in Kharkov.
*Schutzmannschaft Bataillon 145*. Created in Kharkov in August 1942. In January 1943 the battalion was stationed in Kursk. The battalion remained active until May 1944 when it was disbanded.
*Schutzmannschaft Bataillon 146*. Created in Kharkov in August 1942. In January 1943 the battalion was part of the city garrison of Orel in central Russia.
*Schutzmannschaft Bataillon 147*. Raised in Simferopol in October 1942 by the *Kommandeur der Ordnungspolizei Simferopol* command from Tartar volunteers. It was designated as a *Wach* battalion in Simferopol. Withdrawn from Crimea in 1944 and sent to northern Italy to form the *Waffen Gebirgs Brigade der SS (Tatar Nr. 1)* which never completed training before the end of the war came.
*Schutzmannschaft Bataillon 148*. Raised in Simferopol in October 1942 by the *Kommandeur der Ordnungspolizei Simferopol* command from Tartar volunteers. Designated as a *Front* battalion in July 1943 and stationed in Karasubazar. Withdrawn from Crimea in 1944 and sent to northern Italy to form the *Waffen Gebirgs Brigade der* SS *(Tatar Nr. 1)* which never completed training before the end of the war came.
*Schutzmannschaft Bataillon 149*. Raised in Simferopol in October 1942 by the *Kommandeur der Ordnungspolizei Simferopol* command from Tartar volunteers. Designated as a *Front* battalion in July 1943 and stationed in Bakhchisarai. Withdrawn from Crimea in 1944 and sent to northern Italy to form the *Waffen Gebirgs Brigade der SS (Tatar Nr. 1)* which never completed training before the end of the war came.
*Schutzmannschaft Bataillon 150*. Raised in Simferopol in October 1942 by the *Kommandeur der Ordnungspolizei Simferopol* command from Tartar volunteers. Transferred to Yalta in July 1943 and redesignated as a replacement unit for other battalions. Disbanded in March 1944.
*Schutzmannschaft Bataillon 151*. Raised in Simferopol in October 1942 by the *Kommandeur der Ordnungspolizei Simferopol* command from Tartar volunteers. Designated as a *Front* battalion in July 1943 and stationed in Alushta. Withdrawn from Crimea in 1944 and sent to northern Italy to form the *Waffen Gebirgs Brigade der SS (Tatar Nr. 1)* which never completed training before the end of the war came.
*Schutzmannschaft Bataillon 152*. Raised in Simferopol in October 1942 by the *Kommandeur der Ordnungspolizei Simferopol* command from Tartar volunteers. Remained in Simferopol into 1943. Withdrawn from Crimea in 1944 and sent to northern Italy to form the *Waffen Gebirgs Brigade der SS (Tatar Nr. 1)* which never completed training before the end of the war came.

*Schutzmannschaft Bataillon 153.* Raised in Simferopol in October 1942 by the *Kommandeur der Ordnungspolizei Simferopol* command from Tartar volunteers. Disbanded in February 1944.
*Schutzmannschaft Bataillon 154.* Raised in Simferopol in October 1942 by the *Kommandeur der Ordnungspolizei Simferopol* command from Tartar volunteers. Remained in Simferopol. In July 1943 it was redesignated as a replacement unit for other battalions.
*Schutzmannschaft Bataillon 155.* Raised in Simferopol in November 1942 by the *Kommandeur der Ordnungspolizei Simferopol* command from Tartar volunteers. Disbanded in January 1943.
*Schutzmannschaft Bataillon 156.* Raised in Simferopol in November 1942 by the *Kommandeur der Ordnungspolizei Simferopol* command from Tartar volunteers. Disbanded in January 1943.
*Schutzmannschaft Bataillon 157.* Raised in Stalino in November 1942. In January 1943 it was still located in Stalino under the *Kommandeur der Ordnungspolizei Stalino* command. Took part in the German withdrawal from Stalino in early September 1943.
*Schutzmannschaft Bataillon 158.* Raised in Stalino in November 1942. In January 1943 it was still located in Stalino under the *Kommandeur der Ordnungspolizei Stalino* command. Took part in the German withdrawal from Stalino in early September 1943.
*Schutzmannschaft Bataillon 159.* Created from Cossacks in Ukraine in Stalino in the month of November 1942 and sent to Krivoi-Rog. It initially performed guard duty in the town, but also patrolled the local roads from Krivoi-Rog. The battalion was named *Kosaken Schuma Bataillon 159.* In July 1943 the battalion was stationed in Korosten, where it remained. In March 1944 it was disbanded
*Schutzmannschaft Bataillon 160.* Created from Cossacks in Ukraine in Stalino, in November 1942, and named *Kosaken Schuma Bataillon 160* in July 1943. In January 1943 the battalion was stationed in Stalino. Performed road security duty in and around Stalino.
*Schutzmannschaft Bataillon 161.* Created in November 1942 in Stalino. In April 1943 it became known as *(ukrainische) Schutzmannschaft Wach Bataillon 161.* Was redesignated a Cossack battalion in July when the title was changed to *Kosaken Schuma Wach Bataillon 161.* Performed road security duty in and around Stalino.
*Schutzmannschaft Bataillon 162.* Created in November 1942 in Stalino. In January 1943 it redesignated as a *Wach* battalion. Patrolled the surrounding areas of Stalino. In July 1943 the battalion was stationed in Mariupol.
*Schutzmannschaft Bataillon 163.* Created in November 1942 in Stalino. In July 1943 it redesignated as a *Wach* battalion. In March 1944 it was disbanded.
*Schutzmannschaft Bataillon 164.* Created in November 1942 in Stalino. In July 1943 it redesignated as a *Wach* battalion and transferred to Gorlovka.
*Schutzmannschaft Bataillon 165.* Created in November 1942 in Stalino. In January 1943 it was still located in Stalino performing guard duty.

An attempt was made to raise four more Schuma battalions in Stalino from Ukrainian volunteers. The new battalions were to be numbered '166–169'. These units were to be organised in the city by the *Kommandeur der Ordnungspolizei,* but there weren't enough men to establish them. In March 1943 they were stricken from the records and never raised. As can be seen, the Ukrainians contributed a substantial number of volunteer battalions for the German war effort. The Baltic States did as well by providing an equally large number of *Schutzmannschaft* battalions. Without the assistance of these volunteer battalions, the military situation for the *Ostheer* would have been worse than actually happened. Many of these *Schutzmannschaft* battalions also took part in the Holocaust across the wide expanse of the Eastern Front. Again, as with the military support, without their backing, the SS killing units would have found it harder to prosecute their murderous plan:

As already noted, following the large-scale massacres in major cities in September and October 1941, conducted mainly by mobile units of the SS and police, the remaining smaller ghettos were liquidated successively from February through the summer of 1942, mostly by the *Gendarmerie* and local Ukrainian *Schutzmannschaft*.[45]

## Local and major anti-partisan operations in Ukraine

### *147. Reserve Division*

147. Reserve Division was stationed from 1942 to 1943 in the regions of Novograd–Volynski (present-day Zviahel), Korosten, and Kiev. Between 10–30 October 1942 elements of the division fought partisan forces north of their region, around Ovruch. Men of the division also performed railway security duties, while also continuing their training. The division was spread out amongst the following localities: Novograd-Volynski, Korosten, Malin, Zhitomir, and Kiev. Between April and September 1943, the division was involved in safeguarding the harvest, continued rail security and training. It also took part in smaller anti-partisan drives in their area of control. Between 1 October and 31 December 1943, the division took part in *Unternehmen Himmelfahrt* ('Operation Ascension'), a local anti-guerrilla drive.

### *Feldkommandantur 509, Korück 558 and the Kirovograd partisans*

In 1942, *Feldkommandantur 509* was stationed in Kirovograd.[46] This rear area command was responsible for security for the town and important installations like depots, warehouses, the two main roads and the bridges over the Bug River, as well as the railway line. The year 1942 hardly saw any partisan attacks or sabotage. In March 1943 however, a guerrilla *Otriad* crossed over the frozen Dnieper River and undertook ambushes and demolitions in the area that lasted close to a month. This eventually forced the Germans to station in *Korück 558* in Kirovograd and to launch local anti-partisan drives in order to eliminate this partisan threat.[47] The headquarters of *Korück 558* consisted of 17 officers, 6 civil servants, 18 non-commissioned officers and 38 enlisted men, plus 7 Ukrainian volunteers. It controlled certain units that were employed against the partisans. The units temporarily attached at this time to *Korück 558* were *Pionier Regimentsstab z.b.V. 545, Armenisches Infanterie Bataillon 810,* and *II. Bataillon* of *Kuban Kosaken Regiment 5* (*Plastun:* Cossack infantry),[48] plus *Sicherungs Regiment 46* and *Sicherungs Regiment 602.* Both of these security regiments were on loan from *444. Sicherungs Division.* This *Korück* command did not remain in Kirovograd for the entire year. On 1 October 1943 *Korück 558* became the rear-area command for the newly reorganised *8. Armee* in southern Ukraine.[49]

***Background to the Weichsel ('Vistula') anti-partisan drives***

The first partisan units to be created in Ukraine in 1941 were located in the Sumy and Oblast regions. These turned out to be led by M. Popudrenko and Sydir Kovpak. There were four serious partisan units by the autumn of 1941 in Ukraine, but the Germans destroyed two of them before the end of the year. Only the Kovpak and Popudrenko *Otriad* survived into 1942. In the spring of 1942, the partisans in Ukraine were finally able to establish radio communication with the partisan command in Moscow. They were sent specialists, arms and special equipment via air drops that spring and summer. By the summer of 1942 there were four major partisan units operating in Ukrainian territory: The Federov, Kovpak, Saburov and Popudrenko partisan brigades. In May 1943, Kovpak, Federov and Saburov were ordered to enter western Ukraine and to try and reach the district of Volhynia and, hopefully, the Carpathian Mountains. Their movements westwards led the Germans to launching the three 'Vistula' anti-partisan drives. The decision to move these partisan unit's westward was an attempt by the Soviet command to show that in 1943 the guerrilla war had reached the borders of Poland. Although these brigades took some heavy losses, they were never completely destroyed. In 1944 an important partisan unit was organised in western Ukraine. The 1st Ukrainian Partisan Division was established in early 1944. It was led by Colonel Peter Vershigora. Between January and July 1944 this partisan formation took part in raids from the district of Volhynia on through to north-western Galicia.

***Unternehmen Weichsel I: 12 May–8 June 1943***

This operation was led by *Generalmajor der Polizei* Walter Schimana, who had been one of SS General Curt von Gottberg's assistants between July

1942 and July 1943. Apparently, Schimana was one of the officers who led SS and police forces on the ground when General von Gottberg could not be present. He had commanded *Polizeiregiment Mitte*[50] and an emergency battlegroup of the *137. Infanterie Division* during the crisis-winter at the front from January–February 1942.[51] 'Operation Vistula' was directed at partisan forces in the so-called 'Wet Triangle': the area between Pinsk–Mozyr–Sarny. Although this drive was actually under the control of the *Wehrmacht Befehlshaber Ukraine.* Given that the operation also included SS and police units from Belarus, this operation is an example of cooperation between two separate commands two separate and distinct regions of the USSR. After *SS-Brigadeführer und Generalmajor der Polizei* Walter Schimana had been relieved of his duties commanding the mixed *Heer* and police battlegroup at the front, he was reassigned to Bach-Zelewski's anti-partisan staff. His new duties entailed leading a mixed *kampfgruppe* against the growing guerrilla menace. His first *kampfgruppe* had been formed in late March 1943. Its table of organisation and strength stood as follows:[52]

SS *und Polizei Kampfgruppe Schimana,* 31 March 1943
SS *Polizeiregiment 2*
*III. Bataillon der SS Polizeiregiment 13*
*I. Bataillon der SS Polizeiregiment 23*
*Polizei-Panzer-Kompanie 12*
SS *Sonder Bataillon Dirlewanger*
*(ukrainische) Schutzmannschaft Bataillon 57*

By 25 April that structure had been expanded to include the following forces:

*SS Kavallerie Division 'Florian Geyer'*
*SS Polizeiregiment 10*
*Sturm Bataillon 'Süd'*
*Polizei-Panzer-Kompanie 10.*[53]

In July 1943 Schimana left this *kampfgruppe* and went on to become the first commander of the forming *14. Waffen Grenadier Division der SS (ukrainische Nr. 1).*[54] Schimana's SS and police battlegroup was taken over by another officer on Bach-Zelewski's anti-partisan staff. The results of the drive forced the Saburov, Fedorov and other partisan units to retreat westwards. The constant pressure by German anti-partisan forces on the Saburov Brigade eventually caused its destruction in a later anti-guerrilla drive. During the anti-partisan drive, the partisans saw the attack from their own vantage point thusly:

> After we had returned from the vicinity of Pinsk, I was sent to the landing strip along with a company of ground scouts in order to protect the planes that were to be flying in a great deal of military equipment, including 76mm field guns. Immediately after the planes had taken off with the wounded, the Germans started a combined operation against the landing strip, from the air and with tanks. The bombardment continued for twenty-four hours. The Germans then entered the village, but they found it in ruins. All the inhabitants had gone into the woods. In retaliation Nikolaevich Fedorov decided to strike at the German garrison in Rakitnoya, which to my knowledge numbered 300 men. We shelled them all night, but their positions were well fortified. At dawn we were severely attacked by German planes. We had to withdraw. Under a heavy barrage of fire we crossed, the river Goryn in the direction of the village of Velyun, but here too we could find no rest.[55]

The partisans gave battle where they could and on the move. By the time they reached the Rovno region, they had inflicted a heavy toll on German convoys and garrisons along the way:

> At this time, we attacked an armoured train on the railway tracks running between Kovel and Brest. Our 45mm gun succeeded in a second shot to set the train on fire. This forced the Germans, about thirty soldiers, to jump off it. Being mounted, I attacked them with my ground scouts and finished them off. As a result of all the battles, all the German garrisons along the way to Rovno were wiped out.[56]

***Unternehmen Weichsel II*: 27 May–10 June 1943**

The continuation of this anti-partisan drive was 'Vistula II', which included the *SS Kavallerie Division 'Florian Geyer'* as an integral part of it. It was launched within the Dnieper River and Pripet Marshes region, just south-west of Gomel. The principal partisan forces that the Germans were seeking to destroy were the Kovpak, Federov and Saburov partisan brigades. During this operation, *SS Kavallerie Division 'Florian Geyer'* alone was responsible for the killing of 4,018 'partisans and partisan suspects'. In addition, the drive netted 18,860 people who were apprehended and sent as forced labourers to the *Reich*. Of these 18,860, some 10,422 were apprehended by the SS cavalry division alone. In addition, the anti-partisan drive was able to confiscate around 21,000 head of cattle. When the operation concluded, the Germans left sixty-one villages completely destroyed. The following units were employed in this drive:

*SS Kampfgruppe Schimana:*
- SS *Polizeiregiment 2*
- *III Bataillon der SS Polizeiregiment 13*

*I Bataillon der SS Polizeiregiment 23*
*12. Polizei-Panzer-Kompanie*
*SS Sonder Bataillon Dirlewanger*
*(ukrainische) Schutzmannschaft Bataillon 57*
*SS Polizeiregiment 10*
*Sturm Bataillon 'Süd'*
*Polizei-Panzer-Kompanie 10*
*SS Kavallerie Division 'Florian Geyer'*
*Ortskommandantur 760* (Pinsk)
*Sicherungs Bataillon 242*
*Reserve Grenadier Regiment 208* (Kovel)
*Reserve Grenadier Regiment 323* (Sarny)
*Landesschützen Bataillon 988*
*Feldkommandantur 619* (Mozyr)
*Feldkommandantur 280* (Rovno)
*Landesschützen Bataillon 439* (Rovno)
*Landesschützen Bataillon 842* (Rovno)
*143. Reserve Division* (Korosten)
*271. Schutzmannschaft Bataillon* (Slutsk)
*SS und Polizeiführer Rovno*
*Polizei Sicherungs Kompanie Rovno*

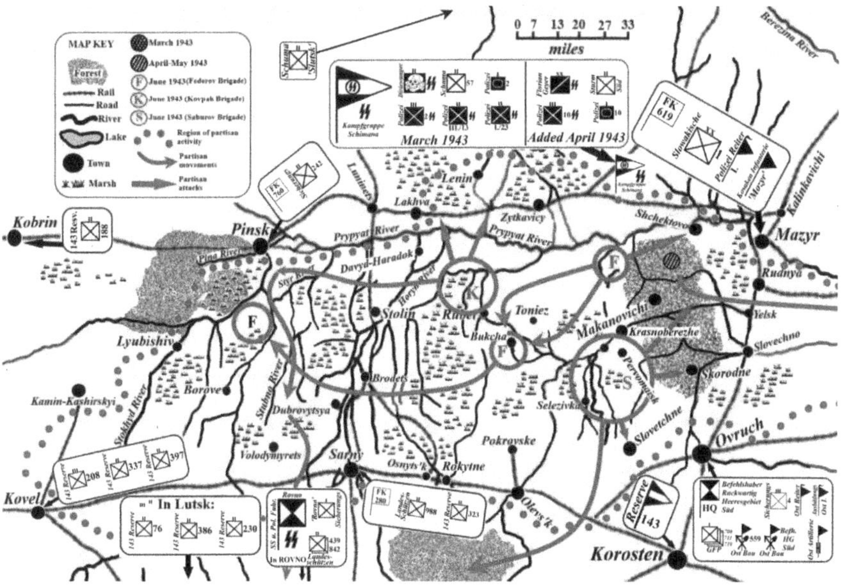


Figure 40. Throughout the period from March–May 1943, the Germans had been hunting the three principal Russian partisan brigades in the region of the Pripet Marshes, between Mazyr (also spelled Mozyr) and Korosten. These turned out to be the Kovpak, Federov, and Saburov brigades. May and June would see several anti-partisan drives launched against these three guerrilla bands.

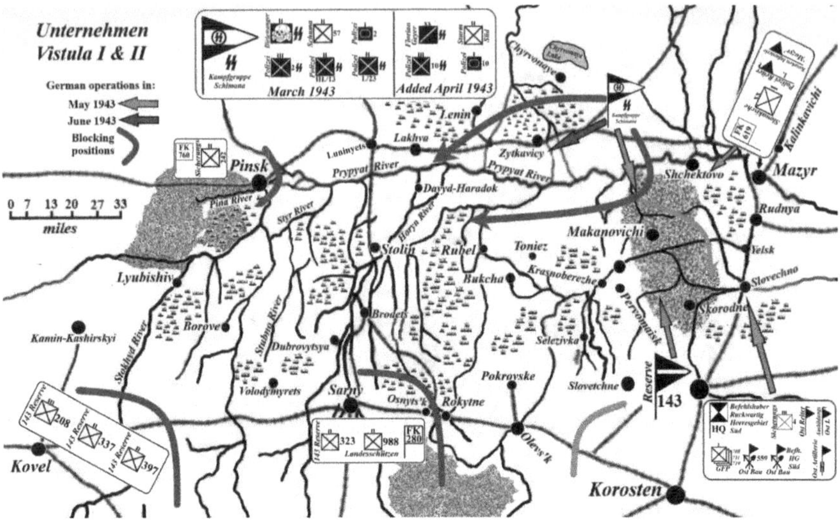


Figure 41. Operation Vistula I and II, May–June 1943. The operation was aimed at trying to destroy the Kovpak, Federov, and Saburov partisan brigades.

### *Unternehmen Ziethen: 13–16 June 1943*

This was a local anti-guerrilla drive launched by *SS Kavallerie Division 'Florian Geyer'* west of the town of Retsiza (Reçyca). It was an afterthought operation that had not been planned before, but was formulated based on the results of *Unternehmen Weichsel I* and *II*. Before the operation concluded, sixty-three hamlets were destroyed. The area in question which this SS cavalry division was tasked with neutralising the partisans encompassed an area about 150km by 200km.

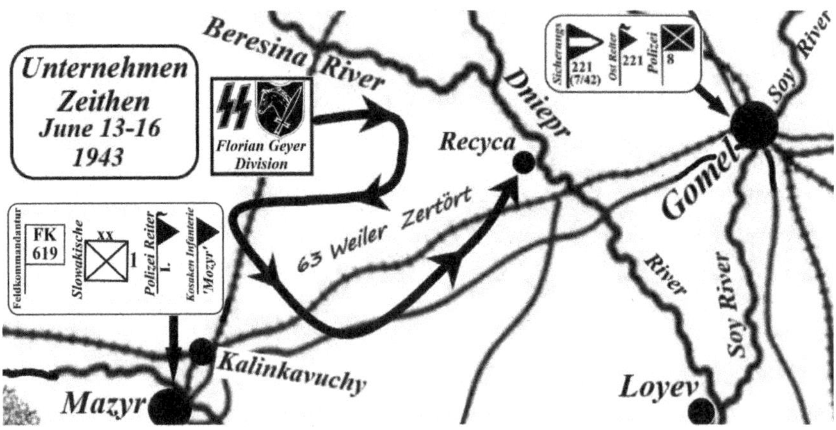


Figure 42. Movements of the *SS Kavallerie Division 'Florian Geyer'* during *Unternehmen Zeithen*, 13–16 June 1943.

***Unternehmen Weichsel III: 1–10 August 1943***

This anti-guerrilla drive was conducted in the region of Volhynia, Ukraine. The two major towns there are Lutzk and Rovno. Units which took part in this operation included:

*Volga-Tatar Bataillon 825*
*1. Kosaken Kavallerie Division*
*SS Polizeiregiment 4*
*SS Polizeiregiment 12*
*SS Polizeiregiment 13*
*SS Polizeiregiment 26*

The drive was the third and final of the 'Vistula' anti-partisan offensives. The Germans had pushed the Saburov Partisan Brigade from the region west of Ovruch. Now it was situated in the triangle Sarny-Rovno–Lutsk. The German command had managed to harass and reduce the Saburov, Federov, and Kovpak Partisan Brigades but they never did succeed in completely destroying them. By the start of *Unternehmen Weichsel III,* the Saburov Brigade was very near the border between Ukraine and the *Generalgouvernment.* The number of partisan units in Ukraine had only grown in number.

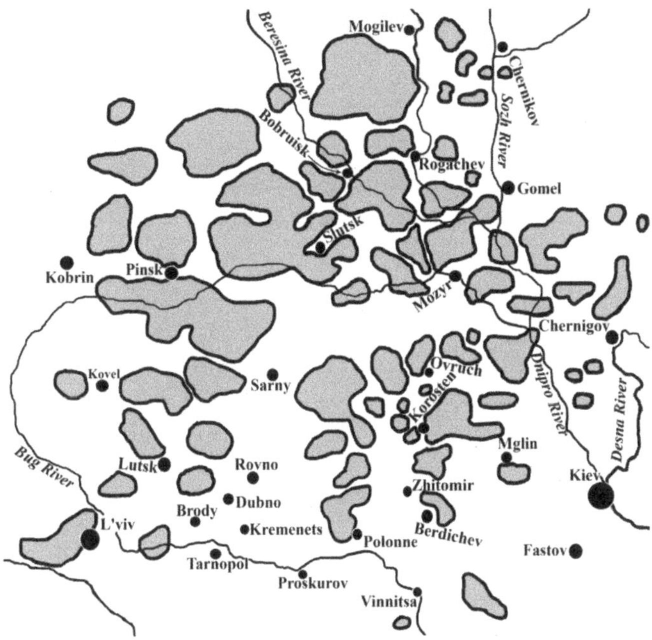


Figure 43. Soviet partisan forces in western and north-western Ukraine in August 1943. The areas shaded in grey were controlled by the partisans.

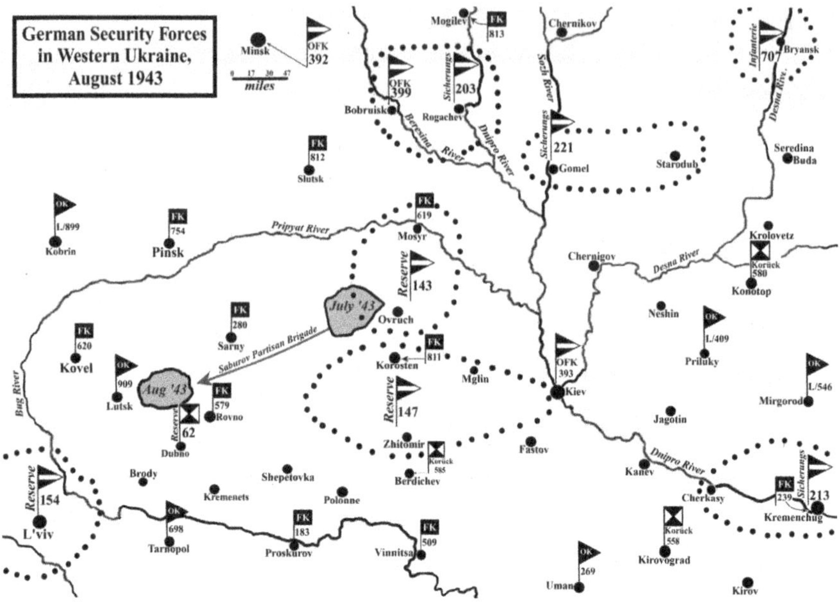


Figure 44. Anti-partisan and garrison forces in western Ukraine, August 1943.

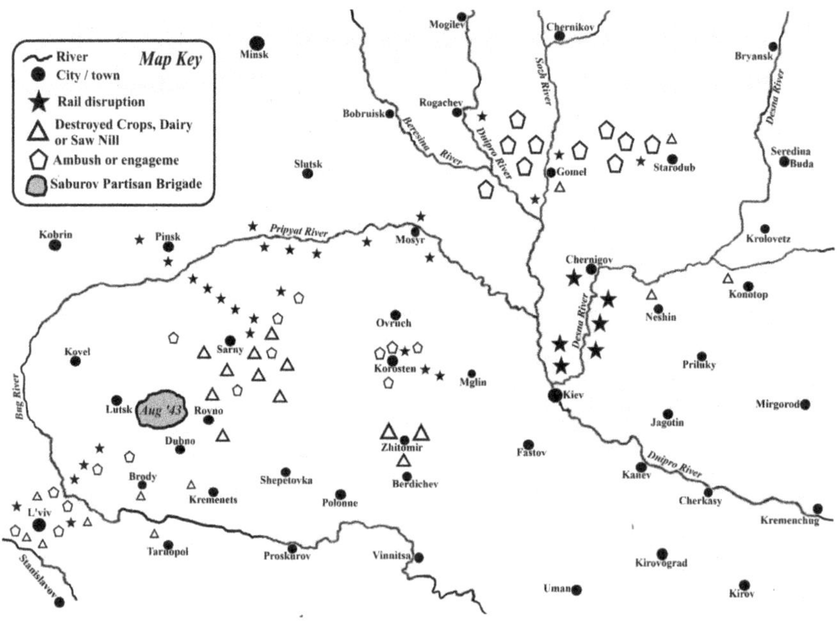


Figure 45. Partisan attacks in western Ukraine for the month of July 1943.

The German attempts to suppress the Soviet partisan movement in Ukraine was only partially successful. By 1943 wide areas of western Ukraine were covered with territories controlled or threatened by the guerrilla bands. At the end of 1942, the partisan movement in Ukraine barely had 13,000 men in its ranks. However, by the end of 1943 that number had risen to around 44,000. As elsewhere along the Eastern Front, the partisan movement was destroying valuable enemy equipment and facilities, as well as impeding the extraction of resources by destroying crops, dairy farms, blowing up miles of railway tracks, killing enemy soldiers and their collaborator forces, and preventing the smooth flow of enemy troops and supplies to the front. The partisan movement in Ukraine proved to be an impediment in facilitating the management of Germany's planned eastern empire.

As 1943 began to close, it was clear to all except the very naive or the very fanatical that Nazi Germany's back was against the wall. The disastrous *Zitadelle* offensive, launched on 4 July 1943, had squandered what armoured and infantry reserves Hitler had allocated to the *Ostheer*. On the German side, estimates suggest that around 250,000 men were lost, killed, wounded, and missing. In terms of tanks, the Germans lost hundreds of armoured vehicles, including many of their formidable Ferdinand, Tiger and Panther tanks. Soviet losses were also significant, with estimates that the Red Army suffered around 800,000–1,000,000 casualties, killed, wounded and missing. In terms of tanks, the Soviets lost thousands of armoured vehicles during the battle. However, while the Red Army could afford to take such losses, the *Wehrmacht* could not. For example, after the battle of Kursk the *18. Panzer Division* had been so devastated by tank losses that it could not even be rebuilt to a skeletal level. The Germans simply renamed the unit as *18. Artillerie Division,* and wrote off the armoured division as a complete loss. Beginning in August 1943 the Soviets went over to the offensive, beginning in the Orel region. Soon entire swathes of what had been German-held Soviet territory were recaptured by the Red Army. As December 1943 turned into January 1944, German forces along the Eastern Front braced for yet more Soviet offensives. In the rear areas, the writing was clearly on the wall. Entire regions of the German rear were covered with territory that no longer belonged to the German invader. The men of the *Ostheer,* both at the front lines and in the rear areas, braced themselves for yet another year of what had become a life and death struggle for Germany's very existence. Where would the Red Army strike next was anyone's guess.

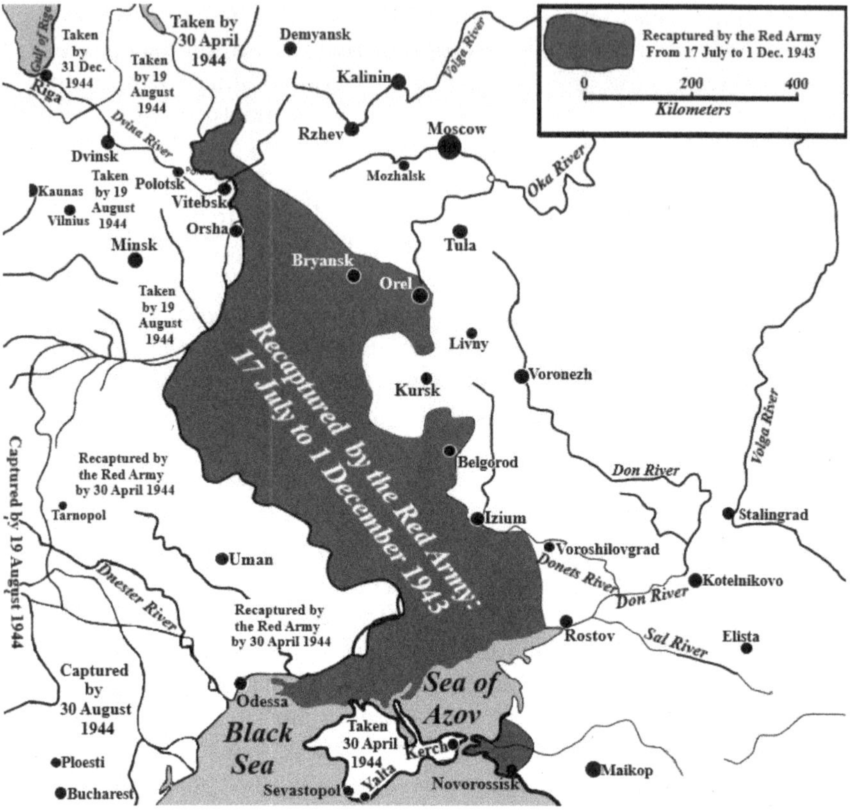


Figure 46. The defeat at Kursk in July 1943 opened the way for the Red Army to seize the initiative and go over to the offensive. The days of the German Blitzkrieg had come to an end. From now on, aside from some small minor tactical operations, the *Ostheer* was on the defensive. Instrumental in these territorial gains were the Soviet partisans, who coordinated their attacks to assist in upcoming Russian offensives.

Appendix I

# GLOSSARY OF GERMAN MILITARY AND POLITICAL TERMS

**A**

| | |
|---|---|
| *Abteilung* | Battalion. It could also mean Section or Department. |
| *Abschnitt* | Sector, district. |
| *Abwehr* | The Intelligence and Clandestine Warfare Service of the German Armed Forces High Command. |
| *Abzeichen* | Insignia, badge of rank, appointment or distinction. |
| *Adlerhorst* | Eagle's Nest. The name given by British intelligence to Hitler's mountain-top retreat located in Berchtesgaden, in the Bavarian Alps. |
| *Afrika Korps* | The German military force, led by Erwin Rommel, which fought in North Africa, 1941–3. |
| *Amt* | Office, Bureau, or Department. |
| *Anwärter* | Cadet, or candidate. |
| *Angriff* | Attack. |
| *Angriffspunkt* | Attack point. |
| AOK | *Armee-Oberkommando* – An army headquarters (HQ). |
| *Arbeit* | Work. |

| | |
|---|---|
| *Arbeitsdienst* | Literal translation is work service but was meant as labour service. |
| *Arbeitskommando* | Work commando or work group. |
| *Arbeitslager* | Work camp. |
| *Armee* | Army. |
| *Armeegebiet* | Army region or district. |
| *Armeekorps* | Army corps. |
| *Artillerie* | Artillery. |
| *Aufklärung* | Reconnaissance. |
| *Ausbildung* | Training. |

**B**

| | |
|---|---|
| *Bahnlinie* | Railway line. |
| *Bahnschutzpolizei* | Railway security police. |
| *Banditen* | Bandits. The Germans referred to the partisans behind the front lines as bandits. |
| *Bandengebiet* | Bandit region (partisan-controlled region). |
| *Barbarossa* | Codename for the German invasion of the USSR. |
| *Bataillon* | Battalion. |
| *Bataillonsführer* | Battalion commander. |
| *Bataillonskommandeur* | Battalion commander. |
| *Batterie* | Battery |
| *Bau* | Construction. |
| *Baudienst* | The national labour service of the Reich. |
| *Baupionier* | Construction engineer. |
| BdO | *Befehlshaber der Ordnungspolizei* (Supreme Commander of the Order Police). |
| BdS | *Befehlshaber der Sicherheitspolizei* (Supreme Commander of the Security Police). |
| *Befehl* | Command. The plural form of the word is *Befehle*. |
| *Befehlshaber* | Commander. |
| *Begleit* | Escort, usually denoting an elite unit. |
| *Belarus* | White Russia. |
| *Beobachter* | Artillery or air observer. |

| | |
|---|---|
| *Beutepanzer* | Captured tank or armoured vehicle. |
| *Bewachungsmannschaft* | The literal translation is 'security crew', but in Third Reich era terminology, it referred to an SS guard detachment in a concentration camp. |
| *Bezirk* | A district or administrative unit of the German civilian government. |
| *Brigade* | A brigade of troops. |
| *Brigadeführer* | *Generalmajor* in either the SS or Police. |
| *Brücke* | Bridge. |
| *Brücken* | Bridging. |
| *Bürgermeister* | The mayor of a town or community. |

**C**

| | |
|---|---|
| *Chef* | Commander of a unit, or sub-unit. |
| *Chef des Generalstabes* | Chief of the General Staff. |

**D**

| | |
|---|---|
| *der SS* | Belonging to the SS. Usually a Germanic SS unit was prefixed with the title 'SS' while the non-Germanic formations were referred to as *'der SS'* (of the SS). |
| *Dienst* | Service. |
| *Dienstgrad* | Rank. |
| *Dienststelle* | An administrative department, or administrative office. |
| *Division* | A division-sized military unit. |
| *Dnjepr* | German spelling for Dnieper, as in Dnieper River. |
| *Dorpat* | German spelling for the town of Tartu, in Estonia. |
| *Drang nach Osten* | Spread to the East, or Push to the East. It was the nineteenth-century German nationalist zeitgeist for a desire to expand German territory into Eastern European lands. |

**E**

| | |
|---|---|
| *Eingeschlossen* | Surrounded, trapped, encircled. |
| *Eingreifgruppe* | The literal translation is 'response group', but in military terms it meant 'assault group'. |
| *Einheit* | A detachment or a unit. |
| *Einsatz* | Mission, action. |
| *Einsatzgruppen* | An operational group made up of the *Sipo* (Security Police), SD (Security Service), and *Ordnungspolizei* units used for special missions, initially for liquidation of the Jewish population, communist commissars etc., but later used to fight the partisans. One *Einsatzgruppe* could have as many as six *Einsatzkommando*. |
| *Einsatzkommando* | A sub-group detachment of the *Einstazgruppen*. |
| *Ersatz* | Replacement. |
| *Ersatzhee* | Replacement army. |
| *Estland* | Estonia. |
| *Estnische (est.)* | Estonian, with the German abbreviation of the word in parenthesis. |

**F**

| | |
|---|---|
| *Fallschirmjäger* | Paratrooper. |
| *Feind* | Enemy. |
| *Feldausbildungs* | Field training. |
| *Feldheer* | Field Army. |
| *Feldkommandantur* | Field Command: A German Army military administration headquarters. |
| *Feldwebel* | Sergeant. |
| *Feldzug* | Military campaign. |
| *Fellin* | The German spelling for the Estonian town of Viljandi. |
| *Festung* | Fortress. |
| *Feuerpolizei* | Fire Police. |
| *Finnische* | Finnish. |

| | |
|---|---|
| *Flak* | Anti-aircraft. |
| *Fluss* | River |
| *Frankreich* | France |
| *Freiwilliger* | Volunteer. The plural form of the word is *Freiwillige*. |
| *Front* | Referring to the front line, or a front-line unit. Example: *(estnische) Front Bataillon 38*. |
| *Frontkämpfer* | Front-line soldier. |
| *Führer* | Leader; specifically, to the Second World War, referring to Adolf Hitler. |
| *Führungshauptamt* | Leadership Head Office. |

## G

| | |
|---|---|
| *Gau* | The main territorial division of the Nazi Party. Germany was divided into forty-two *Gau*. The conquered territories also had this system. |
| *Gauleiter* | The highest-ranking Nazi Party official in a *Gau*. The *Gauleiter* was responsible for all political and economic activity, mobilisation of labour and civil defence in his area. |
| *Gefreiter* | Enlisted rank. It was senior to the rank of private, but was not considered an NCO. |
| *Geheimfeldpolizei* | Secret Field Police of the *Heer* (Army). |
| *Geheimstaatspolizei* | State Secret Police. The abbreviation of the word was *Gestapo*. Was *Amt IV* (Department IV) of the *Reichssicherheitshauptamt* (RSHA); the Reich Main Security Office. |
| *Gemeindepolizei* | Municipal police. |
| *Generalkommando* | General command. Refers to a corps-sized unit in the military. |
| *Genesenden* | Convalescent. Example: *Genesendenbataillon* (convalescent battalion). |

| | |
|---|---|
| *Generalgouvernement* | The General Government – i.e., German-occupied Poland administered by a German civilian governor with its headquarters in the city of Cracow. It was classed as an appended territory (*Nebenland*, meaning outlying) of the Reich. |
| *Generalleutnant* | Lieutenant-General. |
| *Gendarmerie* | The rural police, including motorised units for traffic control. |
| *Goldfassanen* | 'Golden Pheasants'. It was basically the way the representatives of Alfred Rosenberg's Office for the Eastern Occupied Territories were referred to pejoratively. They wore the Nazi Party brown uniform with gold epaulets (shoulder insignia). The term was derogatory and it represented Nazi opportunists who sought their fortune by exploiting the captured Eastern territories, with no regard for the people they ruled. |
| *Grenadier* | Elite infantrymen of the seventeenth and eighteenth centuries. In 1943, Hitler redesignated most of his infantry units as '*Grenadier*' – thus elevating them to the status of elite troops, if only in name. |
| *Grenzpolizei* | Border police. |
| *Grenzschutz* | Frontier or border guards. |
| *Gruppenführer* | The SS equivalent to *Generalleutnant* (Lieutenant-General). |
| *Gulag* | Soviet penal camp for political dissidents and others considered enemies of the state. The concentration camps were usually located in Siberia. Very few ever left these camps.[1] |

**H**

| | |
|---|---|
| *Hauptamt* | Main office. |
| *Hauptmann* | Captain. |
| *Hauptmann der Polizei* | Captain of the police. |
| *Hauptsturmführer* | The SS rank equivalent of Captain. |
| *Heer* | Army. |
| *Heeresgebiet* | Army Region. It usually referred to an army rear area. |
| *Heeresgruppe* | Army Group. |
| *Heimat* | Homeland. |
| *heimatwehr* | The uncapitalised version of home guard. |
| *Heimwehr* | Home Guard (capitalised). |
| *Hilfswilliger* | Helper or assistant. |
| *Hilfsdienst* | Auxiliary service. |
| *Höhere SS und Polizeiführer* (abbreviated to HSSPF) | Higher SS and Police Commander. Also referred to as Senior SS and Police Commander. These staffs represented *Reichsführer-SS* Heinrich Himmler's personal representatives in the Reich military districts, and in the occupied territories. |
| *Hundertschaft* | Century, equivalent to a company or more of men. |

**I**

| | |
|---|---|
| *im Dienst* | In service. |
| *Infanterie* | Infantry. |
| *Inspekteur* | Inspector. |
| *Iwan* | Ivan, the German slang term used to denote a Red Army soldier. |

**J**

| | |
|---|---|
| *Jagdkommando* | Hunting commando. In Second World War terms, a German anti-partisan unit of between a platoon and company in size. |
| *Jäger* | Hunter, but in military terms it meant light infantry. |
| *Jagdpanzer* | Tank destroyer. |

**K**

| | |
|---|---|
| *Kaukasische* | Caucasian. In the Second World War the Germans recruited Caucasian volunteers from the Caucasus mountains in southern Russia. |
| *Kavallerie* | Cavalry. |
| *Kollektive Gewaltmassnahmen* | Collective violence, but meaning 'collective punishment'. |
| *Kommandeur* | Commander. |
| *Kommandeur der Ordnungspolizei* | Commander of the uniformed police. Abbreviated as KdO, it was a subordinate command to the BdO. |
| *Kommandeur der Sicherheitspolizei* | Commander of the security police. Abbreviated as KdS, it was a subordinate command to the BdS. |
| *Kommissarbefehl* | Commissar Order – the infamous command which ordered that all Red Army political officers were to be shot, even if they surrendered. |
| *Kompanieführer* | Company commander. |
| *Konzentrationslager* (KZL) | Concentration camp. |
| *Korporal* | Corporal. |
| *Korps* | Corps. |
| *Korpsabteilung* | Army detachment. |
| *Korück* | Abbreviation for *Kommandeur des Rückwartige Heeresgebiete* (Commander of the Army Rear Area). |
| *Kriegsgefangener* | POW – prisoner of war. The plural of the word is *Kriegsgefangene.* |
| *Kriegsmarine* | The German Navy, as it was referred to between 1935 and 1945. |
| *Krim* | Crimea. |
| *Kriminalpolizei* | Criminal Police. |
| *Krimtatar* | Crimean Tartar. A Turkic people that live in the Crimea. |

**L**

| | |
|---|---|
| *Landesschützen* | The literal term is 'provincial shooters', but for the Nazi period, it refers to older-age men who were members of regional defence battalions. Like the Army security forces, these battalions were employed behind the lines. They guarded important geographical structures, like bridges and railway lines, and physical structures vital to the war effort. They also took part in anti-partisan drives. |
| *Landkreis* | A rural administrative district. |
| *Landrat* | A district administrator. |
| *Lebensunwertes Leben* | Life unworthy of life. In Nazi thinking, a person who does not deserve to exist. |
| *Lebensraum* | Living space. The Nazi belief that Germans needed land upon which to grow and expand. |
| *Leichte* | Light. |
| *Lettische* (*lett.*) | Latvian. The abbreviation of the word is in parenthesis. |
| *Leutnant* | Lieutenant. |
| *Litauische* (*lit.*) | Lithuanian. The abbreviation of the word is in parenthesis. |
| *Luftwaffe* | The German Air Force, as it was referred to between 1935 and 1945. |

**M**

| | |
|---|---|
| *Major* | Major, a rank between captain and colonel. |
| *Massenmörder* | Mass murder. |
| *Militär* | Military. |
| *Mitte* | Centre, as in *Heeresgruppe Mitte* (Army Group Centre). |
| *Mörser* | Mortar. |

**N**

| | |
|---|---|
| *Nachricht* or *Nachrichten* | Communication, signals, or even intelligence. |
| *Nachrichtendienst* | Intelligence service. |
| *Nebelwerfer* | Rocket artillery |
| *Nachschub* | Supply. |
| *Nord* | North. |
| NSKK | The abbreviation for *Nationalsozialisten Kraftfahrkorps* (National Socialist Motor Corps). |

**O**

| | |
|---|---|
| *Oberbaustab* | The higher military construction staff. This headquarters usually controlled several construction regiments. |
| *Oberbürgermeister* | Lord Mayor. |
| *Oberführer* | SS rank below *Brigadeführer*. There was no equivalent rank in the British or US Army. |
| *Obergruppenführer* | SS rank equivalent to Lieutenant-General. |
| *Oberstleutnant* | Lieutenant-Colonel. Example: *Oberstleutnant der Polizei* (Lieutenant-Colonel of the Police). |
| *Obersturmbannführer* | SS rank equivalent to Lieutenant-Colonel. |
| *Oberstgruppenführer* | Like *Obergruppenführer*, the SS rank equivalent to Lieutenant-General. |
| OKH | Abbreviation for *Oberkommando des Heeres* (Army High Command). |
| OKW | Abbreviation for *Oberkommando der Wehrmacht* (Armed Forces High Command). |
| *Omakaitse* | Estonian term meaning 'self-defence'. |
| *Ordnungsdienst* | The auxiliary service made up of foreign volunteers, that assisted the German police. |
| *Ordnungspolizei* | Order Police. |

| | |
|---|---|
| *Organisation Todt* | This was a semi-military Nazi government agency established in 1933, and used mainly for the construction of strategic highways and military fortifications and installations. |
| *Ortskommandantur* | Local Command: they were local army headquarters below the *Feldkommandantur*. |
| *Ost* | East. |
| *Ostbataillon* | A battalion of foreign volunteers from Eastern Europe, including the USSR. |
| *Ostfront* | Eastern Front. |
| *Ostheer* | 'Eastern Army'. It refers to the German Army fighting on the Eastern Front. |
| *Ostland* | A title given by the Germans to the Baltic region encompassing the Baltic countries of Lithuania, Latvia, and Estonia, and part of Belarus (Belorussia, or White Russia). |
| *Ostministerium* | The (Nazi) Ministry for the Occupied Eastern Territories. |
| *Osttruppen* | Eastern troops that served in either the *Heer*, SS, or Police forces of the Third Reich. |
| *Ostvolker* | Eastern people. |

**P**

| | |
|---|---|
| *Panzer* | Armoured. |
| *Panzerfaust* | Literally 'armoured fist'. It was a disposable, hand-held, one-shot anti-tank weapon. |
| *Panzerschreck* | German name for Bazooka – a hand-held, reusable anti-tank weapon. |
| *Partisan* | Partisan. The plural form of the word is *Partisanen*. |
| *Partisanenjäger* | Partisan hunter. |

| | |
|---|---|
| *Partisanhelfer* | Partisan helper. |
| *Pferd* | Horse. |
| *Pionier* | Engineer. |
| *Pleskau* | German spelling for the Russian city of Pskov. |
| *Polizei* | Police. |
| *Prepjet-Sümpfe* | German spelling for the Pinsk (Pripyat) Marshes. In English the spelling is Pripet. |
| *Putsch* | An internal uprising against an existing government, like a *coup d'etat.* |

**Q**

| | |
|---|---|
| *Quartiérmeister* | Quartermaster. |

**R**

| | |
|---|---|
| RAD | Abbreviation for *Reichsarbeitsdienst*, the (Nazi) National Labor Service. |
| *Radfahr* | Bicycle. |
| *Regiment* | Regiment. |
| *Reich* | Nation. |
| *Reichskommissar* | National Commissioner. |
| *Reichsführer-SS* | National Leader of the SS. |
| *Reichskommissariat Ostland* | The civilian occupation government in the Baltic states led by Hinrich Lohse |
| *Reichskommissariat Ukraine* | The civilian occupation government in Ukraine headed by Erich Koch. |
| *Reichsministerium für die besetzten Ostgebiete* | Reich Ministry for the Occupied Eastern Territories. |
| *Reiter* | Horse, cavalryman. |
| *Reserve* | Reserve |
| *Reval* | German spelling for the Estonian capital of Tallinn. |
| RNNA | *Russkaya natsional'naya narodnaya armiya* (Russian National People's Army) |

| | |
|---|---|
| RSHA | Abbreviation for *Reichssicherheitshauptamt* (Reich Security Main Office). |
| *Rückwärtig* | Behind, as in the rear of the front lines. |
| *Russische* (*russ.*) | Russian. The abbreviation of the word is in parenthesis. |

**S**

| | |
|---|---|
| SA | *Sturmabteilung* (Storm Detachment). The militarised members of the Nazi Party. |
| *Schlachtfliegerstaffel* | Attack squadron. |
| *Schule* | School. |
| *Schutzmannschaft* (*Schuma*) | Self Defence Guard. These men, organised into battalions, assisted the SS and Police. The abbreviation of the word is in parenthesis. |
| *Selbstschutz* | Self-defence. Referring to Eastern-raised militia units of volunteers from the USSR and other Eastern countries. It was originally to have consisted of ethnic Germans from these territories, but also included large numbers of non-German people. |
| *Sicherheitsdienst* | (SD) The SS Security Service. |
| *Sicherung* | Security. |
| *Sipo* | Abbreviation for the word *Sicherheitspolizei* (Security Police). |
| *Sonderdienst* | Special Service. This organisation was a part of the German occupation force in Poland. It was made up of ethnic German Poles serving as guards. |
| *Sonderkommando* | Sub-group detachment of the *Einsatzkommando*. |
| *Sonder* | Special. In Third Reich terminology, it could refer to a special detachment or even a penal formation. |

| | |
|---|---|
| *Sonderstab* | Special staff. |
| SS (*Schutzstaffel*) | The SS originated as a small corps of bodyguards for Adolf Hitler, while he travelled the country giving speeches. This paramilitary branch of the Nazi Party expanded exponentially beginning in 1933, creating numerous seperate departments, in much the same way that an octopus has many tentacles. They included such branches as the *Allgemeine-SS, Waffen-SS,* and *SS-Totenkopfverbände.* |
| SSPF | Abbreviation for *SS und Polizeiführer* (SS and Police Leader) |
| *SS-Waffengruppe* | An armed group, usually of regimental or brigade size, serving in the *Waffen* SS. |
| *Stabsoffizier* | Staff officer. |
| *Staffeln Flieger Gruppe* | Squadron Air Group. |
| *Stamm* | Cadre. |
| *Standarte* | Basically another way to say regiment. The formation so named was equal to a regiment in size. |
| *Standartenführer* | SS Colonel. |
| *Strafe* | Penal, referring to a penal (punishment) formation, such as *Strafbataillon* (penal battalion). |
| *Sturmbannführer* | SS Major. |
| *Sturmkompanie* | Assault company. |
| *Süd* | South. |

**T**

| | |
|---|---|
| *Technische Nothilfe* | The Technical Emergency Corps, an auxiliary police force of the ORPO consisting of engineers, technicians and specialists concerned with communications, construction work, public utilities, |

salvage and recovery, etc. Each police regiment that entered the USSR in 1941 had one TN company attached. Later on, these companies were detached and expanded into battalions.

*Teilkommando* — A sub-unit of a special force, such as a *Teilkommando* of an SS *Sonderkommando*

*Totenkopfstandarte.*Any one of a series of SS Death's Head (*Totenkopfstandarte*) regiments.

*Truppenübungslager* — Troop Training Camp.

*Truppenübungsplatz* — Troop Training Ground.

**U**

*Ukrainische* (*ukr.*) — Ukrainian. The abbreviation of the word is in parenthesis.

*Und* (*u.*) — And. The abbreviation of the word is found in parenthesis.

**V**

*Verband* — Formation. Could also mean a military unit of brigade size.

*Verbindungsoffizier* — Liaison officer.

*Vernichtungskrieg* — War of extermination.

*Vernichtungslager* — Extermination camp.

V1/V2 — These were designations for two types of missiles that the Nazis employed, mainly against the city of London.

**W**

*Wach* — Guard.

*Wachbataillon* — Guard battalion.

*Waffen-SS* — Armed SS. The SS ground combat formations that fought in the field.

*Wehrkreis* — A German military district.

*Wehrmachtbefehlshaber* — The Armed Forces Commander for a military region or area. Example: *Wehrmachtbefehlshaber der Rückwärtig Heeresgebiet*

| | |
|---|---|
| | (Armed Forces Commander of the Army Rear Area). |
| *Weissruthenische* | White Russian. Properly spelled using the *eszett*: *Weißruthenische*. It refers to Belarus. |
| *Weltanschauungskrieg* | Ideological war. |
| *Wirtschaftskommando* | Economic Command. Referring to a paramilitary unit responsible for organising and managing economic exploitation in the occupied territories (in this case, the USSR). |
| *Wolga* | Volga. |

**XYZ**

| | |
|---|---|
| *z.b.V.* | Abbreviation for *zur besondere Verwendung* (for special use, or special employment). |
| *Zug* | Platoon. |
| *Zugführer* | Platoon leader. |

Appendix II

# 1942: GERMAN CONDUCT BEHIND THE LINES OF ARMY GROUP NORTH

## Case sample: *Korück 583*

By 1942 the rounding up of the indigenous population in entire villages and towns had become routine for German security forces fighting behind the front lines. The following excerpts, taken directly from the War Diary of *Korück 583* (*18. Armee*) for the period from 1 April to 31 December 1942, is a perfect paradigm for German comportment behind the lines. One interesting item here is that while the SS and police forces would refer to the insurgents as 'bandits' (see previous chapter), the *Wehrmacht* commander in charge of *Korück 583* called them either partisans or guerrillas. Only two months are listed here: April and May 1942:

> On 1 April 1942 two partisans were picked up in Lipovo and were arrested after a thorough interrogation by the local police. *Ortskommandantur I 315* later ordered that they be shot. Active enemy air movements over Luga and Andruchskiy (see attachment 743, 744) of the official order Nr. 319, as per the daily report of *Korück 583*. *Generalmajor* Knuth was promoted to *Generalleutnant* on 2 April 1942. Also on this day, enemy planes dropped bombs on Kingiseps without causing any damage (see attachment 745), official order Nr. 320, as per the daily report of *Korück 583* (see also attachment 746). As per the daily report of *Korück 583* (see attachment 747), on 3 April 1942 a group of four enemy parachutists landed south of the village of Ivenitza. *Sicherungs Gruppe 182* killed two parachutists in firefight, while the rest were captured (see attachment 747 and 748), service order. Nr. 321 issued by *Korück 583*.

Daily report issued by *Korück 583* (attachment 748 and 749), activity report from Department III for 4 April 1942, *Feldkommandantur 189* (Narva) reports that major enemy troop movements were observed from the Oranienbaum Pocket towards the island of Saiskari (see attachment 750).

Daily report *Korück 583* (attachments 750-51) for 5 April 1942 about property damage caused by fire bombs in the homes in Siverskaya where the men of *Wach Bataillon 571* are billeted. Official order Nr. 322 for the daily report for *Korück 583* (attachment 752) for 6 April 1942, stating six men were killed and two were wounded by a bomb that hit members of *Wach Bataillon 531* in Krasnovardeisk (see attachment 753).

Daily report for *Korück 583* (attachment 753) for 6 April 1942 notifying that Typhus has broken out in the Veimarn Evacuee Camp. Official order Nr. 323.

Daily report for *Korück 583* (attachments 754) for 7 April 1942: no special incidents occurred on this day. Official Order Nr. 324 (attachment 756) as part of the daily report from *Korück 583* discussing the task of securing the area between Lake V'yele and Lake Orlino to protect the Luga–Krasnovardeisk railway line. *Major der Schutzpolizei* Hans Hellwes, the commander of *Reserve Polizei Bataillon 105*, assumed control of *1. Wach Kompanie / Wach Bataillon 571*, as well as the *2. Kavallerie Schwadron / Kosaken Hundertschaften 38*, both of which were quartered in Grigun in the Lake Orlino area.[1] (see attachment 758). In the period from 1–6 April 1942, *Reserve Polizei Bataillon 105* and its attached elements killed 121 partisans and destroyed 10 bandit camps. Our own losses amounted to 14 dead (attachment 759).

Daily report for *Korück 583* for 8 April 1942, stating that at Terbinka (10km south-east of Narva), two Russian parachutists were arrested by the Estonian self-defence (see attachment 760).

Daily report for *Korück 583* for 9 April 1942, official order Nr. 385 issued (see attachment 761), states that a female parachutist was captured by *V-Leute* near Gusinska, approximately 35km south of Volossovo.[2]

Daily report for *Korück 583* for 10 April 1942 (see attachment 762-763), official order Nr. 326 regarding the activity report from Department III (see attachment 764); On the night of 9/10 April the bridge over the Yakhera River near the town of Dolgovka was attacked by around 150–200 Red Army soldiers. While trying to blow it up, the enemy was able to partially destroy the bridge. An immediate pursuit of the bandits was carried out by *Major der Schutzpolizei* Hans Hellwes's *kampfgruppe* but it proved unsuccessful.

Daily report for *Korück 583* for 11 April 1942, (attachment 765), stated that no special incidents had taken place that day. Daily report for *Korück 583* as per official order Nr. 327 (attachment 767-768), is a statement to *18. Armee* about the deployment of security forces. The report said that on 12 April 1942, *Kampfgruppe* Hellwes encountered 20–30 partisans south of the town of Chashcha, and that further pursuit to the east was immediately started (attachment 769). Daily report for *Korück 583* for 13 April 1942, regarding *Kampfgruppe* Hellwes. Group Hellwes reported that the enemy has withdrawn from the town of Pelkovo and is moving in a northerly direction (see attachment 770).

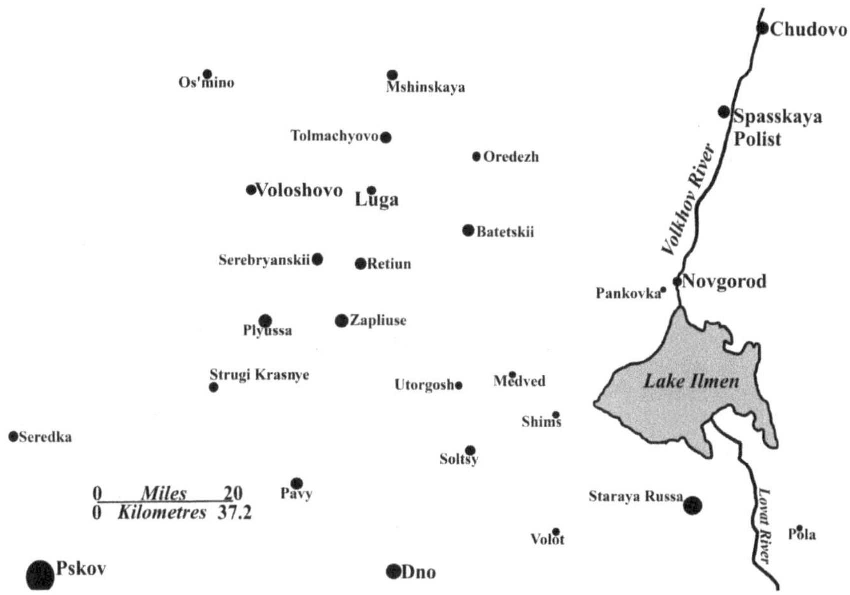


Figure 47. General reference map with place names for the region from Lake Ilmen to Luga.

Daily report for *Korück 583* for 14 April 1942, official order Nr. 328 (see attachments 771-774) regarding the fact that *Kampfgruppe* Hellwes reports that the enemy has retreated east, via the Vitebsk railway line (see attachment 772). *Sicherungs Gruppe 187* assumed security duties for the Grigorovo–Batetskaya railway line (see attachment 773), and activity report from Department IVa (see attachment 774).

Daily report for *Korück 583* for 15 April 1942, (see attachment 775), order Nr. 330 stated that a soldier from *Sicherungs Gruppe 182* was killed by partisans while on duty. Further, that *Sicherungs Gruppe 182* could count on 90 men, 20 of whom were foreigners (see attachment 776).

Daily report for *Korück 583,* as per official orders Nr. 331 for 17 April 1942. The Hellwes combat group reports from Nisovskaya that the section west and north to Lake Vyelye is enemy-free (see attachment 777-778). The Hellwes combat group fought on the Vitebsk railway line with 5 to 7 partisans, whose tracks led freshly eastwards from

Lake Mochaleshche. Two partisans were shot. The area around Lake Mochaleshche is reported to be impassable. (see attachment 780). Daily report for *Korück 583,* as per official order Nr. 332 for 18 April 1942 (see attachment 779-780). During a 10-day operation by *Sicherungs Gruppe 182* in the area south of Masana Gorka, five partisans were killed and one partisan was wounded (see attachment 782).

Daily report for *Korück 583,* as per official order Nr. 333 (see attachment 783) for 19 April 1942. Typhus broke out in *Durchgangslager 134* (see attachment 784). *Korück 583* established a train repair workshop (see attachment 785) in order to service locomotives.

Daily report for *Korück 583,* as per official order Nr. 334 for 20 April 1942. The staff and *11. Kompanie* of *Sicherungs Gruppe 183* are ordered to be relocated to Krasnoye Selo (see attachments 784, 785, and 786).

Daily report for *Korück 583,* as per official order Nr. 335 for 21 April 1942 is issued (see attachment 788). The sawmill at the lime works in Vol'sovo burned down, apparently due to a short circuit (see attachment 789 and 790).

Daily report for *Korück 583,* as per official order Nr. 336 are issued (see attachment 791) for 22 April 1942. No special incidents occurred on this day.

Daily report for *Korück 583,* as per official order Nr. 337 (see attachment 791) for 23 April 1942. No special incidents occurred on this day.

Daily report for *Korück 583,* as per official order Nr. 338 (attachment 793) for 24 April 1942. No special incidents occurred on this day.

Daily report for *Korück 583,* as per official order Nr. 339 (see attachment 796) for 25 April 1942. No special incidents occurred on this day. On the orders of *18. Armee,* a security staff was established for the foreign units subordinate to *Korück 583* (see attachment 797). Creation of a regimental staff for the foreign units to serve as part of the security forces for the *Korück.*

Daily report for *Korück 583,* as per official order Nr. 340 for 26 April 1942. The action against partisans in the area around Masana Gorka by *Sicherungs Gruppe 182* ended on 24 April 1942. Two partisan groups were destroyed (see attachment 798).

Daily report for *Korück 583,* as per official order Nr. 342 for 28 April 1942. The *29. Kompanie* of *Sicherungs Gruppe 187* is relocated to the town of Volosovo, to help cover the Volosovo–Moloskovitsy railway line (see attachments 801 and 802).

Daily report for *Korück 583,* (see attachment 801). The operational order for *Sicherungs Gruppe 187* is to relieve the *6. Kompanie* of *Sicherungs Gruppe 182* with *15. Kompanie* from *Sicherungs Gruppe 164* in the Feodosino area (see attachment 803). On 29 April 1942 no special incidents were reported.

Daily report for *Korück 583*, official orders Nr. 343 and 344 for 30 April 1942 (see attachments 804 and 805). On order from *18. Armee, Korück 583* will assume control of five former Russian state properties for management (see attachment 806). Inspection of the roads in the army rear area shows that overall, they are in good condition (see attachment 807). Order to the local commanders about the repair and care of the German heroes' graves (see attachment 809).

Signed this 30 April 1942
Signature
Hans Knuth, *Generalleutnant*,
*Kommandeur – Korück 583*[3]

Daily report for *Korück 583*, as per official order Nr. 345 (see attachment 810) for 2 May 1942. Activity report for Department III. A patrol from *Ortskommandantur I/315* encountered two partisans about 8km west of Mchi. One partisan was killed and one was wounded. The wounded partisan managed to escape (see attachment 811).

Daily report for *Korück 583*, as per official order Nr. 346 (see attachment 812) for 3 May 1942. No special incidents occurred on this day.

Daily report for *Korück 583*, as per official order Nr. 346 for 4 May 1942. A three-man patrol from *Sicherungs Gruppe 182* encountered a group of seven men near Verdzhest, about 60km south of Volosovo. During the arrest attempt, they opened fire on the patrol who, lacking sufficient firepower, were wounded and had to let the men escape. There was an enemy air raid south of Tigoda station with a direct hit that killed four horses and caused some property damage (see attachment 813).

Daily report for *Korück 583*, as per official order Nr. 347 (see attachment 814) for 5 May 1942. The *33. Kompanie* of *Sicherungs Gruppe 188* is hereby relocated to Kingisepp (Estonia), and is to be used as a *Jagdkommando* against partisan groups north and south of Veymarn (see attachment 817).

Daily report for *Korück 583*, as per official order Nr. 348 (see attachment 816) for 6 May 1942. *Gefreiter* Görgens is to be promoted to *Unteroffizier* as of 1 May 1942. *Obergefreiter* Fröck is also promoted to *Unteroffizier* (see attachment 818).

Daily report for *Korück 583*, as per official order Nr. 349 for 6 May 1942. No special incidents occurred on this day (see attachment 820).

Daily report for *Korück 583* for 7 May 1942 (see attachment 819), as per official order Nr. 350, reports that *Ortskommandantur I 864* reports the capture and shooting of two partisans (see attachment 821). *Korück 583* has created a *Bandenkampf Sonderkommando* and deployed the unit in the area around Verdzhest, in order to destroy partisans in the area (see attachment 823). A report was sent to the *Höhere* SS *und Polizeiführer Russland Nord* command listing the strengths of the Estonian security battalions (see attachment 824). The report was generated after a visit by *Hauptmann* Förster from Quartermaster General. In particular, the replacement situation of the Estonian units was discussed (see attachment 825).

Daily report for *Korück 583* for 8 May 1942, as per service order Nr. 351. *Ortskommandantur II 362* reports that the old Russian minefield near Pillovo was cleared and around 500 mines were blown up (see attachment 826 and 827). Activity report from Department III (see attachment 828). The order was made to set up another *russische Hundertschaft Kompanie* (see attachment 829). As of 8 May 1942, a Russian construction unit (*Pionier Hundertschaft*) was also set up.

Daily report for *Korück 583* for 9 May 1942, as per service order Nr. 352 and 353 (see attachment 831 and 832). One platoon from *21. Kompanie* of *Sicherungs Gruppe 185*, which was part of the *254. Infanterie Division* was deployed for anti-partisan duty. It skirmished with the partisans, suffering 11 killed and 26 wounded (see attachment 830). The telephone communication unit previously led by *Armee Nachrichten Regiment 520* is hereby transferred to *Korück 583* (see attachment 818). On 9 May 1942 *Ortskommandantur II 351* is again subordinated to *Korück 583*.

Daily report for *Korück 583* for 10 May 1942. It is reported by our undercover operatives within the civilian population that a *Politruk* (communist political leader) is a member of the *32. Kompanie* of *Sicherungs Gruppe 188*. An order for his arrest has been issued (see attachment 833).

Daily report for *Korück 583* for 11 May 1942. No special incidents occurred on this day.

Daily report for *Korück 583* for 12 May 1942. A railway patrol belonging to *Ortskommandantur I 315* removed an explosive charge of 25–30 kilograms south of the town of Mchi (see attachment 834).

Daily report for *Korück 583* for 13 May 1942. As per *Feldkommandantur 189*, coastal watch duty has been assigned as part of the various security tasks of *225. Infanterie Division* (see attachment 835).

Daily report for *Korück 583* for 14 May 1942. No special incidents occurred on this day.

Daily report for *Korück 583* for 15 May 1942. The *3. Kompanie* of *Sicherungs Gruppe 181* lost one truck due to a direct hit, and all of the equipment and clothing in the vehicle were lost. (see attachment 836, 837, and 838). Service order Nr. 359 is issued (see attachment 839). Activity report section IIa (see attachment 818), activity report Department III (see attachment 840) activity report Department Ic (see attachment 841). Current strength of *3. Kompanie* is 85 men.

Daily report for *Korück 583* for 16 May 1942, service order Nr. 360 is issued (see attachment 843). Enemy airmen dropped 2 high-explosive bombs 30 metres south of the Volosovo railway station. Two more bombs were dropped in the area around Isvara, but no damage was sustained (see attachment 842). *Radfahr Wach Bataillon 620*[4] was withdrawn and returned to the *Korück 583* command.

Daily report for *Korück 583* for 17 May 1942. The *21. Kompanie* of *Sicherungs Gruppe 185* has lost a total of 64 men who were either wounded in combat near Lipovik, or became ill (see attachment 844).

Daily report for *Korück 583* for 18 May 1942. No special incidents occurred on this day.

Daily report for *Korück 583* for 19 May 1942, as per service order Nr. 361 (see attachment 845). A report to *18. Armee* (see attachment 846) by *Wach Bataillon 571* stated that on 19 May men from the battalion discovered a downed Me 109 fighter plane about 1km north-west of Voronovo, whose on-board weapons and engine were not removed (see attachment 847).

Daily report for *Korück 583* for 20 May 1942, as per service order Nr. 362 (see attachments 847 and 848). One of our agents reports that a strong partisan group is approaching the town of Gussinka. A platoon from *Sicherungs Gruppe 187* has been sent there (see attachment 849).

Daily report for *Korück 583* for 21 May 1942. Today partisans fired upon our men near Gussinka. A partisan group west of Rozhdestvenno was reported. *Sicherungs Gruppe 188* initiated action against this group (see attachment 850). *Infanterie Ersatz Regiment 605* (*Feldkommandantur Narva*) is hereby made subordinate to *Korück 583* (see attachments 851 and 852).[5]

Daily report for *Korück 583* for 22 May 1942. No special incidents occurred on this day. A letter was sent to *18. Armee* from *Korück 583* about the deployment of the Estonian security battalions from Department III (see attachment 854). *Wach Bataillon 571* took over security duties with in the Kursk region.[6] Daily report for *Korück 583* for 23 May 1942 as per service order Nr. 364 (see attachment 855). Due to the risk of typhus, new entrances to *Durchgangslager 200* in the Weimarn camp are closed (see attachment 855). A letter was sent to *18. Armee* regarding the defence of Krasnovardeisk (see attachment 857) and the creation of three Cossack *Hundertschaften* (see attachment 858).[7]

Daily report for *Korück 583* for 24 May 1942. Action against partisans with a *sicherungs gruppe* in the area around Lyady was unsuccessful (see attachment 859). Relief order: *Feldkommandantur 189* [stationed in Narva] handed over control to the staff *Infanterie Ersatz Regiment 605* (see attachment 860). Operational order to *Sicherungs Gruppen 185, 187* and *Wach Bataillon 531* (see attachment 861). Daily report for *Korück 583* for 25 May 1942 (see attachment 859), as per service order Nr. 365 (see attachment 365). A locomotive hit three mines about 4km north of Batetskaya. Only minor material damage was caused. An Estonian battalion arrived by train to Batetskaya as railway security (see attachment 862).

Daily report for *Korück 583* for 26 May 1942. The railway line between Batetskaya–Grigorovo, Approximately 7km east of Batetskaya, was blown up by the partisans (see attachment 864). Service order No. 366

is issued (see attachment 865). Letter to *18. Armee* about administrative officials for the Estonian security battalions (see attachment 866).

Daily report for *Korück 583* for 27 May 1942. No special incidents occurred on this day. Service order No. 367 are issued (see attachment 868). A letter was sent to *Ortskommandantur I (V) 315* on Russian supply drops (see attachment 869). Army order on securing the railways in the army area was also issued (see attachment 870).

Daily report for *Korück 583* for 28 May 1942. Three escaped prisoners of war were picked up near Kotly by patrols from *20. Kompanie / Sicherungs Gruppe 185*. On 28 May 1942, *Durchgangslager 200* was under *Korück 583* command.

Daily report for *Korück 583* for 29 May 1942. No special incidents occurred on this day.

Daily report for *Korück 583* for 30 May 1942, as per service order Nr. 369 is issued from Department III (see attachment 873 and 874). An enemy bomb was thrown north of the Suida railway station, but no damage was caused (see attachment 876).

Daily report for *Korück 583* for 31 May 1942, as per service order Nr. 370 are issued (see attachment 877). An enemy air attack was reported in the town of Krasnovardeisk. Only minor material damage was caused (see attachment 878).

Signed this 31 May 1942
Signature
Hans Knuth, *Generalleutnant,*
*Kommandeur – Korück 583*[8]

Appendix III

# RUSSIAN VOLUNTEER FORMATIONS, MAY TO DECEMBER 1943

**May 1943**

*I. / Ost Bataillon 447.* Sent to *Heeresgruppe Süd* under *XLVII. Panzerkorps.* Note that because the German higher command prohibited volunteer formations being larger than battalion size, the staff of *XLVII. Panzerkorps* did as most other German commands did to get around that order: two battalions were created (*I.* and *II.*) named *Ost Bataillon 447.*

*II. / Ost Bataillon 447.* Sent to *Heeresgruppe Süd* under *XLVII. Panzerkorps.*

*Ost Bataillon 604 Pripjet.* Committed to front-line fighting this month.

*Ost Bataillon 308.* Formed in the region of *Heeresgruppe Mitte* under *Arko 308* (Artillery Commander No. 308). Interestingly enough the field post numbers were not assigned until March 1944. It contained only two rifle companies which were used as infantry protection for the artillery observers and batteries.

*Ost Bataillon 427.* This unit was finally committed to front-line fighting after almost five months of training and undertaking anti-guerrilla operations behind the lines of *XXVII. Armeekorps, 9. Armee, Heeresgruppe Mitte.*

*Ost Bataillon 268.* Formed from three rifle companies of Russian volunteers for service in the *268. Infanterie Division,* which was then serving under the *4. Armee, Heeresgruppe Mitte.*

*Kommandeur der Osttruppen z.b.V. 741.* Formed on 20 May 1943, for employment in controlling Eastern units under *Heeresgruppe A.* This month it was employed in the Kuban bridgehead of *Heeresgruppe Süd.*

## June 1943

*Ost Bataillon 82*. Still operating under *2. Panzer Division, 3. Panzerarmee, Heeresgruppe Mitte*. This two-company battalion received a much-needed influx of troops when a third company (*3. Kompanie*) and a 'headquarters' company were organised and added this month.

*Ost Nachschub Bataillon 574*. Formed using three supply companies. It was organised by the German *Heer Kommandeur Ventspils* in Courland, Latvia. It was later expanded to six companies. It was probably formed from Latvian volunteers, although it is possible Russians could have also served.

*Ost Bataillon 600*. Formed of four rifle companies under *Heeresgruppe Mitte*.

*Ost Bataillon 601 'Beresina'*. Returned to Bobruisk, Belarus which was its home base and began *pionier* (engineer) training this month. It would be redesignated as an engineer bridging unit in November 1943 when it was transferred to France. One reason why this battalion was no longer to be a rifle unit was that it was not considered fully reliable by the German command.

*Ost Bataillon 619*. Renamed this month as a cadre forming battalion for other Russian units.

*Ost Bataillon 646*. Formed this month using three rifle companies of Russian volunteers in the region of *Heeresgruppe Mitte*. It apparently never attained full operational strength. It was disbanded in February 1944.

*Ost Bataillon Weicker*. Formed under the staff of the *Kommandeur der Osttruppen 711* (Commander of Eastern Troops 711).

*II. Ostvölk Genesenden Bataillon*. Formed in the *Generalgouvernment* (occupied Poland) on 1 June 1943.

(*Weiss.*) *Schuma Wachbataillon 47*. Still located in Minsk.

*4.–7. Ost Sicherungs Kompanie der Sicherungs Abteilung 456*. These four Russian security companies were formed and officially added to the German *Sicherungs Bataillon 456* this month. The *1.-3. Kompanien* contained German personnel. This battalion was operating behind the lines of *2. Armee, Heeresgruppe Mitte*. Later in the summer, two additional Russian companies (numbered *8.* and *9.*) were added.

## July 1943[1]

*Regimentsstab z.b.V. 709*. Formed on 9 July from *Kommandeur der Osttruppen z.b.V. 709* in the region of *9. Armee, Heeresgruppe Mitte*. As all of the other HQ staffs like them, this staff was used to control Eastern battalions.

*Ost Ersatz Regiment Mitte.* This was simply a redesignation of *Kommandeur der Osttruppen 701.* It contained three Eastern volunteer recruit training battalions numbered *I., II.* and *III.*

## August 1943

*Ost Bataillon 412.* This month this *Ost* battalion was redesignated as the *III. Bataillon der Grenadier Regiment 578* of *305. Infanterie Division.* The unit was located in northern Italy.

*Bau Pioneer Bataillon 246.* This was merely a redesignation of *Bau Bataillon 246.* The new title became effective on 19 August 1943.

*Regimentsstab z.b.V. Klobe.* Formed by redesignating *Regimentsstab z.b.V. Findeisen.* As all of the other HQ staffs like them, this staff was used to control Eastern battalions.

*Regimentsstab z.b.V. 709.* This Eastern regimental staff headquarters was officially disbanded on 31 August after being wiped out.

*Regimentsstab z.b.V. Klobe.* Formed on 12 August 1943. It was simply a redesignation of *Regimentsstab z.b.V. Findeisen.*

*Kriegsgefangenen Bau und Arbeits Bataillon 1.* 'Prisoner of War Construction and Work Battalion No. 1'. Attached to *189. Infanterie Division* in Norway.

*Kriegsgefangenen Arbeits Abteilung 188.* Sent to Bergen and Stavanger in Norway this month after having been stationed in Holland.

## September 1943

*3. (Russ.) Bau Abteilung.* Under *702. Infanterie Division, XXXIII. Armeekorps,* in Norway.

*Kriegsgefangenen Bau und Arbeits Abteilung 180.* Under *702. Infanterie Division, XXXIII. Armeekorps,* Norway.

*Kommandeur der Osttruppen z.b.V. 712.* Ordered formed on 1 September 1943, in the region of *Heeresgruppe Nord,* although it is not known if it was ever fully organised. As all of the other HQ staffs like them, this staff was supposed to control Eastern battalions.

*Ost Bataillon 649.* Formed on 12 September from the *4.-7. Ost Kompanien* of the German *Wachbataillon 581.*

*Ost Bataillon 648.* Formed on 12 September in the region of *2. Armee, Heeresgruppe Mitte* from the *8.* and *9. Ost Kompanien* of the *456. Sicherungs Bataillon,* and the *8.* and *9. Ost Kompanien* of *Wachbataillon 581.*

*Ost Bataillon 680.* Formed on 12 September from the *4.-7. Ost Kompanien* of *456. Sicherungs Bataillon.*

*Ost Bataillon 647.* Formed on 12 September partly from *Wachbataillon 581* under *2. Armee, Heeresgruppe Mitte.*

*Ost Regimentsstab z.b.V. 753.* Formed on 12 September by simply re-designating *Regimentsstab z.b.V. Klobe.* As all of the other HQ staffs like them, this staff was used to control Eastern battalions.
*Weiss. Schuma Wachbataillon 45.* Formed this month in Baranovichi, Belarus. This original numerical designation ('45') had been assigned previously to an Estonian *Schuma* battalion.
*Ost Regimentsstab z.b.V. 752.* Formed in September in the area of *2. Armee, Heeresgruppe Mitte.* As all of the other HQ staffs like them, this staff was used to control Eastern battalions.

## October 1943

*Kommandeur der Osttruppen z. b.V. 702.* Sent to *19. Armee* in southern France on 2 October 1943.
*Ost Bataillon 648.* Attached to *Korück 580* on 20 October 1943.
*Ost Bataillon 649.* Attached to *Korück 580* on 20 October 1943.
*Ost Bataillon 654.* Sent from *Heeresgruppe Nord* to *19. Armee* in southern France and stationed initially in Chalons-sur-Marne.
*Kommandeur der Osttruppen 721.* Sent to *7. Armee* in France this month. As all of the other HQ staffs like them, this staff was used to control Eastern battalions.
*Ost Bataillon 627.* Sent to the St. Malo in the area of Brittany, France and placed under *7. Armee* this month.
*Ost Bataillon 674.* Formed by simply renaming *Ost Bataillon Weicker* on 21 October 1943.
*Ost Bataillon 661.* Sent to southern France towards the end of the month.
*Ost Regimentsstab z.b.V. 751.* Formed this month in the region of *9. Armee, Heeresgruppe Mitte.* As all of the other HQ staffs like them, this staff was used to control Eastern battalions.
*Kommandeur der Osttruppen z.b.V. 703.* Sent to France this month. As all of the other HQ staffs like them, this staff was used to control Eastern battalions.
*Ost Bataillon 615.* Sent to the town of Chatillon under the German Administrative Military Commander in France.
*Ost Reiter Abteilung 281.* Sent to *Truppenübungsplatz 'Coetquidan'* (Troop Training Ground) in France on 20 October 1943. It was now a part of *7. Armee.*
*Ost Reiter Abteilung 285.* Sent to *Truppenübungsplatz 'Coetquidan'* in France in October 1943. It now was a part of *7. Armee. Truppenübungsplatz 'Coetquidan'* had existed as early as the First World War, where it served the American Expeditionary Force (AEF) under General Pershing as an artillery training centre.

*Ost Bataillon 406*. Sent to the *326. Infanterie Division, 19. Armee* in southern France during the first week in October 1943.
*Ost Ausbildungs Regiment Mitte*. This cadre training regiment was sent to *Truppenübungsplatz 'Coetquidan'* in France in the area of *7. Armee* in this month.
*Ost Bataillon 439*. On its way to Bayeux, about 25km north-west of Caen in Normandy, France. It began arriving there on 28 October 1943.
*Ost Regimentsstab z.b.V. 750*. Located in Blaye and St. Lucie, north of Bordeaux under *1. Armee*. As all of the other HQ staffs like them, this staff was used to control Eastern battalions.
*Ost Bataillon 642*. Sent to *7. Armee* area in France on 30 October 1943.
*Ost Bataillon 669*. Sent to *7. Armee* area in France on 30 October 1943.
*Ost Bataillon 643*. On its way to *7. Armee* in France, arriving on 24 October 1943. It was stationed in Plancoët, a town north-west of Dinan in north-west France.
*Ost Bataillon 663*. Sent to *19. Armee* in southern France. It arrived around mid-October. It contained four rifle companies.
*Ost Bataillon 665*. Sent to France on 21 October 1943. It was attached to the *338. Infanterie Division* under *19. Armee* in France. On 29 October 1943 it arrived in the region of Aimarques, about 5km east of Lunel.
*Ost Bataillon 666*. Sent to *19. Armee* and attached to *338. Infanterie Division*. It was stationed in Rivesaltes, north of Perpignan, France.
*Ost Nachschub Bataillon 651*. This supply battalion was transferred to *15. Armee* in France in this month.
*Ost Artillerie Abteilung Befehlshaber Heeresgebiet Süd*. This unit was formed from Russian volunteers and captured guns. It contained three artillery batteries. It was now employed in the region of *Heeresgruppe Süd* where it had been raised this month.
*Ost Bataillon Hensel*. Arrived in southern France on 8 October 1943, and was placed under the *326. Infanterie Division* of *19. Armee*.
*Ost Bataillon 681*. Transferred to *19. Armee* in France on 23 October 1943. It was originally titled *Ost Bataillon Hansen*.
*Ost Bataillon 633*. Sent to France in late October.
*Ost Bataillon 634*. Sent to France in late October.
*Ost Bataillon 635*. Sent to north-west France in mid-October.
*Ost Bataillon 642*. Sent to north-west France and joined *7. Armee*.
*Ost Bataillon 618*. Sent to *15. Armee* in France this month.

## November 1943

*Kommandeur der Osttruppen z.b.V. 700*. Sent to *7. Armee* in France. As all of the other HQ staffs like them, this staff was used to control Eastern battalions.

*Ost Bataillon 669*. Sent this month to *7. Armee* in north-west France.
*Ost Bataillon 668*. Redesignated as *Ost Bataillon Schittenhel.*
*Ost Bataillon 339*. Sent to Italy and redesignated as the *III. Bataillon/ Grenadier Regiment 871* of the *356. Infanterie Division.*
*Ost Bataillon 600*. Sent to France on 16 November 1943. Stationed in Vannes and assigned directly under the 'German Military Commander France'.
*Ost Pioneer Brücken Bataillon 601*. Eastern Engineer Bridging Battalion. This was simply a redesignation of *Ost Bataillon 601*. This unit had been undergoing engineer training shortly before it was withdrawn from Russia. It was sent to *19. Armee* in southern France on 5 November 1943. It was stationed in Sorques, north-east of Avignon.
*Ost Bataillon 602 Dnjepr*. Sent to *7. Armee* in the Brittany region of north-west France. The battalion arrived on 27 November 1943, and stationed at St. Malo, in Brittany. It would later be destroyed in July 1944 but would not be officially dissolved until 14 October 1944.
*Ost Bataillon 603 Duna*. Left Russia for Denmark at the end of this month.
*Ost Bataillon 604 Pripjet*. Disbanded this month.
*Ost Bataillon 605 Wolga*. Sent this month to the town of Pont d'Ardres, in the Amiens area south-west of Calais, France. It was attached to *15. Armee*.
*Ost Bataillon 406*. Sent to France this month and stationed in Le Bourget, about 10km north of Chamberly. Under the direct control of the *Militär Befehlshaber Frankreich* (German Military Commander France).
*Ost Bataillon 412*. Sent to *14. Armee* in Italy, and stationed in and around Villa Nevoso, about 30km north-north-west of Fiume, Italy. It was redesignated as *III. Bataillon der Grenadier Regiment 578* of the *305. Infanterie Division*.
*Ost Ersatz Bataillon*. Located in Bologna, Italy. No apparent numerical designation. It was first listed this month. It is possible that it might have been created from excess Russian personnel from various other German units then stationed in that region of Italy.
*Ost Bataillon 669*. Sent to France this month. It was under the direct control of the German Military Commander. France.
*Ost Bataillon 618*. Arrived in late October in France and attached to *15. Armee*. On 2 November it was located in Caffiers, south-south-west of Calais. It was then moved to Valenciennes.
*Ost Bataillon 630*. Sent to Brittany, France this month. Located in Bayeux under *7. Armee*.
*Ost Bataillon 629*. Sent to *7. Armee* in France this month. On 25 November it was located in Lannion, Brittany.

*Ost Bataillon 633*. Sent to France this month. On 10 November it was located in Landerneau under *7. Armee*.
*Ost Bataillon 634*. Sent to France this month. On 10 November it was located in Quimperlé, Normandy under *7. Armee*.
*Ost Bataillon 635*. Sent to France in late October or early November. It was stationed in Landerneau on 8 November 1943.
*Ost Regimentsstab z.b.V. 750*. Sent to France on 8 November 1943, and arrived at Bordeaux in the region of *1. Armee* towards the end of the month. As all of the other HQ staffs like them, this staff was used to control Eastern battalions.
*Ost Bataillon 642*. On 1 November 1943, it was located in Beauregard, France about 5km north-north-east of Caen.
*Ost Bataillon 649*. Arrived on 17 November 1943, and stationed in Cherbourg, in the Brittany area of France. Attached to *7. Armee*.
*Ost Bataillon 654*. Attached to the *19. Armee* in southern France on 14 November 1943, but by 17 November it was attached directly to the *Militärbefehlshaber in Frankreich*, and stationed in Chaumont.
*Ost Bataillon 660*. On 18 November 1943, it was still on its way to Belgium, where it would be under the direct control of the *Militärbefehlshaber Belgien-Nord Frankreich*.
*Ost Bataillon 669*. On 18 November 1943 it was still on its way to Belgium, where it would be under the direct control of *Militärbefehlshaber Belgien-Nord Frankreich*.
*Ost Bataillon 661*. Located in Grasse, France under *19. Armee* as of 2 November 1943.
*Ost Bataillon 680*. Sent to France and initially stationed in Mezieres. On 1 November 1943, it was located in Sissone, about 20km east of Lyon. It was under the *Militärbefehlshaber in Frankreich*.
*Ost Bataillon 662*. Sent to Denmark this month.
*Ost Bataillon 620*. Sent to northern Italy towards the end of November.
*Ost Bataillon 617*. Sent to Italy this month. It became an independent unit of *LXXV. Armeekorps, Armeeoberkommando Ligurien*, which was then located on the Italian-French border region.[2]
*Ost Bataillon 619*. Disbanded this month but not officially removed from the German Field Post rolls until February 1944.
*Ost Bataillon 628*. Sent to Bruges, Belgium this month. Attached to the *712. Infanterie Division*.
*Ost Bataillon 616*. Sent to north-eastern Italy this month. It was attached to the *71. Infanterie Division* which was then operating in the Tarvisio-Gorizia-Trieste-Fiume areas. It would later be officially absorbed into this German division as an integral battalion in one of its regiments.

*Ost Bataillon 636*. Sent to north-west France under *7. Armee*. By 19 November it was located at Vannes.
*Ost Bataillon 268*. This battalion was sent to northern Italy after its parent German unit, *268. Infanterie Division*, was destroyed while operating under *41. Panzerkorps, 9. Armee, Heeresgruppe Mitte*.
*Weiss. Schuma Wachbataillon 47*. Attached to the *SS und Polizeiführer Weissruthenien* ('SS and Police Leader White Russia') for anti-partisan warfare.
*Weiss. Schuma Wachbataillon 48*. Attached to the *SS und Polizeiführer Weissruthenien* for anti-partisan warfare.
*Weiss. Schuma Wachbataillon 49*. Attached to the *SS und Polizeiführer Weissruthenien* for anti-partisan warfare.
*Weiss. Schuma Artillerie Abteilung 56*. Attached to the *SS und Polizeiführer Weissruthenien* for anti-partisan warfare.
*Weiss. Schuma Front Bataillon 60*. Attached to the *SS und Polizeiführer Weissruthenien* for anti-partisan warfare.
*Ausbildungs Schuma Bataillon*. Stationed in Uretschye, Belarus.

## December 1943

*Ost Ausbildungs Regiment Mitte*. Simply a redesignation of *Ost Ersatz Regiment Mitte*. Sent to Brittany, France this month and attached to *7. Armee*.
*Kommandeur der Osttruppen z.b.V. 711*. Disbanded on 8 December 1943. Its personnel were then transferred to *Ost Ausbildungs Regiment Mitte*.
*Kommandeur der Osttruppen z.b.V. 704*. Disbanded this month.
*Kommandeur der Osttruppen z.b.V. 720*. Disbanded this month in the region of *Heeresgruppe Süd*. It was removed from the Field Post rolls in February 1944.
*Ost Bataillon Schittenheim*. Destroyed on 17 December 1943. Not reformed.
*Ost Reiter Abteilung 207*. Disbanded this month after having incurred severe combat losses in Russia.
*Ost Radfahr Abteilung 285*. Simply a redesignation of *Ost Reiter Abteilung 285*. This new designation took effect beginning 4 December 1943. The new title implies that the unit was assigned bicycles instead of horses with which to move around on. It was operating under *XXV. Armeekorps* in western France.
*Ost Bataillon 449*. Formed by bringing together four independent company-sized units of Russian volunteers which had been in existence since May 1943.
*Ost Pioneer Brücken Bataillon 605*. A redesignation of *Ost Bataillon 605 Wolga* (Eastern Battalion 605 'Volga').

*Ost Artillerie Abteilung 752*. Formed on 23 December 1943 from four Russian artillery batteries under the control of the *Befehlshaber Heeresgebiet Süd*. These batteries had been formed using captured Russian 76mm and 122mm guns. The battalion was now sent to *7. Armee* in France. In France it was immediately placed under the control of *Kommandeur der Osttruppen 721*.

*Ost Bataillon 268*. On 1 December 1943 the remnants of this unit were on its way to the town of Cremona, Italy. It was to be assigned to the *14. Armee*.

*Ost Bataillon 339*. On 1 December 1943 this unit was stationed in Milano, Italy under *14. Armee*.

*Ost Bataillon 412*. 1 December 1943 this battalion was situated in the town of San Pietro, about 20km north-north-west of Udine, Italy. Udine was near the Italian–Slovene border. This region was north-eastern Italy.

*Ost Bataillon 427*. This battalion was disbanded this month from Russia.

*Ost Bataillon 556*. Sent to Italy from southern Russia this month.

*Ost Bataillon 600*. Located in Vannes, France under *7. Armee*.

*Ost Bataillon 616*. This *Ost* battalion was redesignated as the *III. Bataillon der Grenadier Regiment 194* of *71. Infanterie Division* this month. The *71. Infanterie Division* was currently located in and around the city of Fiume (Rijeka), near the Istrian peninsula.

*Ost Bataillon 627*. On 1 December 1943 it was located north-west of Plancoët, France under the *346. Infanterie Division, 7. Armee*.

*Ost Bataillon 628*. On 2 December 1943 this unit was stationed in Brue under *15. Armee*, but by 8 December it had been moved to Sluis, about 15km north-east of Bruges.

*Ost Bataillon 663*. On 5 December 1943 this battalion was listed under the command of the *338. Infanterie Division, 19. Armee* in southern France. It was assigned to coastal guard duty and its battalion headquarters was situated in Le Salin de Giraud, near Rhone Muendung, France.

*Ost Bataillon 633*. On 21 December 1943 this battalion was located in Ploudalmézeau, north-east of Brest, France.

*Ost Bataillon 642*. Located in Beauregard, France about 5km north-west of Caen. It was under the control of *7. Armee*.

*Ost Bataillon 653*. Arrived in Greve, Denmark this month from Russia.

*Ost Bataillon 662*. Located in Hump, Denmark. It contained four rifle companies.

*Ost Bataillon 666*. On 21 December 1943 this unit was listed attached to the *326. Infanterie Division, 19. Armee* in southern France.

*Ost Bataillon 667*. Arrived in Mosbjerg, Denmark this month from Russia.

*Ost Bataillon 681*. On 21 December 1943 this eastern battalion was listed as being attached to *326. Infanterie Division, 19. Armee* in southern France.

*Ost Bataillon 603 Duna*. Arrived in Denmark this month from Russia.

*Ost Artillerie Abteilung 621*. Sent to France and attached to the *15. Armee*. It was assigned coastal guard duty as part of the Atlantic Wall artillery defences.

*Ost Wachbataillon 555*. Sent to Italy from southern Russia this month.

# NOTES

## Author's Note

1 https://freedomhouse.org/report/freedom-world/2022/global-expansion-authoritarian-rule, accessed 13 June 2022.

2 Sebastian Ullrich, *Der Weimar-Komplex. Das Scheitern der ersten deutschen Demokratie und die politische Kultur der fruhen Bundesrepublik 1945-1959*, Göttingen: Wallstein Verlag, 2009, p. 120.

3 In 1926, Marshal Józef Pilsudski established a dictatorship in Poland. Pilsudski claimed that he was doing this for the good of the nation. However, it is no coincidence that the political party he helped to create won all four of the next national elections (1928, 1930, 1935, and 1938). Most historians agree that the elections were rigged. Therefore, Czechoslovakia was the only nation in central Europe which remained a true democracy by 1938.

4 There were many instances between 1934 and September 1938 when Hitler broke the Treaty of Versailles and the democracies of the West did nothing.

5 Putin wanted this *Oblast*, which belonged to Georgia, because it has vast deposits of oil.

## Introduction

1 The term literally translates as 'collective violence', but it was meant as collective punishment (*Kollektive Bestrafung*).

2 Christopher Browning, *Ordinary Men: Reserve Police Battalion 101 and the Final Solution in Poland*, New York: Harper Collins, 1992, p. 182.

3 Christian Streit, 'Wehrmacht, Einsatzgruppen, Soviet POWs and Anti-Bolshevism in the Emergence of the Final Solution', in David Cesarani (ed.), *The Final Solution. Origins and Implementation*, London: Routledge, 1994, p. 110.

4 For our purposes, the term USSR refers to those lands that in 1941 encompassed the Baltic States, European Russia, Belarus (White Russia), and Ukraine. European Russia covers an area roughly 3,960,000 km$^2$. Its eastern border is defined by the Ural Mountains and

(in the south) by the border with Kazakhstan. The Caucasus mountains and the region bordering Turkey and Persia define the southernmost boundary, while the northern edge covers the border area with Finland and Norway.

5 *Ostheer*: Eastern Army, the German military forces fighting on the Russian Front.

6 International Military Tribunal, *Trial of the Major War Criminals before the International Military Tribunal*, 42 vols, Nuremberg: Secretary of the Tribunal, Vol. 7, p. 59.

7 Matthew Cooper, *The Nazi War Against Soviet Partisans 1941-1944*, New York: Stein and Day, 1979, pp. 171–2.

8 Ben Shepperd, *War in the Wild East: The German Army and Partisans*, Cambridge: Harvard University Press, 2004, p. 130.

9 Ibid., p. 233.

10 The American edition of this book was released a year later, in 1957.

11 Although a bit dated, the book is still considered a must-read for anyone interested in the topic of the German occupation of the East.

12 Alexander Dallin, *German Rule in Russia 1941-1945: A Study of Occupation Policies*, London: MacMillan and Co. Ltd., 1957, p. 30.

13 Yitzhak Arad, 'The Holocaust of Soviet Jewry in the Occupied Territories of the Soviet Union', *Yad Vashem Studies XXI* (1991), p. 6.

14 Gerald Reitlinger, *The House Built on Sand: The Conflicts of German Policy in Russia*, New York: The Viking Press, 1960, p. 81.

15 Ibid., p. 81.

16 *Landser* is the German equivalent of 'G.I.'.

17 Omer Bartov, *The Eastern Front 1941-45: German Troops and the Barbarisation of Warfare*, New York: St. Martin's Press, 1986, p. 68.

18 Theo J. Schulte, *The German Army and Nazi Policies in Occupied Russia*, Oxford: Berg Publishers, 1989, p. 284.

19 Michael Geyer, 'Traditional Elites and National Socialist Leadership', in Charles S. Maier and Andrew Gould (eds), *The Rise of the Nazi Regime: Historical Reassessments*, Boulder: Westview Press, 1986, p. 71.

20 Edward Davies and Ronald Smelser, *The Myth of the Eastern Front: The Nazi-Soviet War in American Popular Culture*, New York: Cambridge University Press, 2007, pp. 22–4.

21 Ibid., p. 24.

22 Paul Kohl, *Der Krieg der deutschen Wehrmacht und der Polizei 1941–1944*, Frankfurt am Main: Fischer Taschenbuch Verlag, 1995, p. 333.

23 Walter Manoschek, *Die Wehrmacht Im Rassenkrieg: Der Vernichtungskrieg Hinter der Front*, Vienna: Picus Verlag, 1996, p. 142.

24 Willi Dreßen, 'The Role of the Wehrmacht and the Police in the Annihilation of the Jews, the Prosecution of Postwar Careers of Perpetrators in the Police Force of the Federal Republic of Germany', *Yad Vashem Studies XXIII* (1993), pp. 295–319.

25 Hannes Heer and Klaus Naumann, *Vernichtungskrieg: Verbrechen der Wehrmacht 1941 bis 1944*, Hamburg: Hamburger Edition, 1995, p. 14.

26 Hannes Heer and Klaus Naumann, *War of Extermination: The German Military in World War II, 1941–1944*, New York: Berghahn Books, 2000.

27 Wolfram Wette, *The Wehrmacht: History, Myth, Reality*, Cambridge: Harvard University Press, 2006, p. 296.

28 Wolfram Wette, *Die Wehrmacht: Feindbilder, Vernichtungskrieg, Legenden*, Frankfurt am Main: S. Fischer Verlag, 2002, p. 295.

29 Ibid., p. 296.

30 Ibid., p. 297.

31 Daniel J. Goldhagen, *Hitler's Willing Executioners: Ordinary Germans and the Holocaust*, New York: Alfred A Knopf, 1996, pp. 23–4.

32 Julius Schoeps (ed.), *Ein Volk von Mordern? Die Dokumentation zur Goldhagen-Kontroverse um die Rolle der Deutschen im Holocaust*, Hamburg: Hoffmann und Campe, 1996, pp. 1–5.

33 Dr. Fritz Stern, 'Book Review: *Hitler's Willing Executioners: Ordinary Germans and the Holocaust*', *Foreign Affairs*, Volume 75, No. 6 (November-December 1996), pp. 640–4.

34 Geoffrey P. Megargee, *War of Annihilation: Combat and Genocide on the Eastern Front, 1941*, New York: Rowman and Littlefield Publishers, Inc., 2006, p. 151.

35 *S.R. G. G. 1203 (c) v. 6. Mai 1945, P.R.O. WO 208/4170 Generalleutnant SIRY171 (Comd., 347ID), Captured Friedrichsroda 10. April 1945 Generalstabsintendant PAUER172* (Formerly of the OKH), Captured Kleinrinderfeld, 7. April 1945.

36 Sönke Neitzel, *Abgehört: Deutsche Generäle in britischer Kriegsgefangenschaft 1942–1945* (Berlin: Propyläen, 2005), 44.

37 Timothy Snyder, *Bloodlands: Europe Between Hitler and Stalin*, New York: Basic Books, 2010.

38 Mark Mazower, *Hitler's Empire: How the Nazis Ruled Europe*, New York: Penguin Books, 2008.

## Chapter 1: Reinforcements and Reorganisation in the East, 1942–1943

1 Georg Tessin, Norbert Kannapin and Brün Meyer, *Waffen-SS und Ordnungspolizei im Kriegseinsatz 1939–1945*, Biblio Verlag: Osnabrück, 2000, p. 632.

2 In 1940 *Polizei Bataillon 313* was referred to as *Polizei Battalion Zamosc* (because of where it was stationed). It became a part of *Polizeiregiment Lublin* in the *Generalgouvernement.* At the start of Operation Barbarossa, the battalion marched into the USSR via Brest-Litovsk and Bobruisk. In Belarus it performed occupation duties. In January 1942 it was sent to the front lines of *Heeresgruppe Nord,* to fight before Leningrad. The battalion was made subordinate to the *268. Infanterie Division.* The battalion was withdrawn to Germany in the spring of 1942 after taking heavy losses. In June 1942 the battalion completed its replenishing in Wismar, when it was once again deployed to the front. On 9 July 1942 the battalion became *III. Bataillon* of *Polizeiregiment 14.*

3 Antonio Muñoz, *The Druzhina SS Brigade: A History, 1941-1943,* New York: Europa Books, 1999, p. 30.

4 Belarus has also been referred to as White Russia.

5 French L. MacLean, *The Cruel Hunters: SS Sonderkommando Dirlewanger. Hitler's Most notorious anti-partisan unit,* Atglen: Schiffer Publishing Ltd., 1998, p. 69.

6 Having looked at his personnel file, I believe it would have been nearly impossible for Dirlewanger to have obtained his PhD degree, given that quite often he was behind bars for one offence or another. The only way that he could have possibly gotten his degree (based on the date it was issued) was, and I say this sarcastically, is if he had been taking a correspondence course from jail. Nevertheless, throughout his military career he was referred to as 'Dr. Oskar Dirlewanger' in official documents.

7 Antonio Muñoz, *Forgotten Legions: Obscure Combat Formations of the Waffen SS, 1943-1945,* Boulder: Paladin Press, 1991, p. 181.

8 Erich Hesse, *Der sowjetrussische Partisanenkrieg 1941 bis 1944,* Göttingen: Musterschmidt Verlag, 1969, p. 280.

9 Georg Tessin, *Verbände und Truppen der deutschen Wehrmacht und Waffen SS 1939-1945,* Osnabrück: Biblio Verlag, 1975–2002, 18 volumes, Vol. 1, p. 76.

10 This battalion was composed of convicted German Army officers, NCOs and enlisted men. It was later renamed *Grenadier Battalion z.b.V. 550.* Between 1943 and 1944 the unit was led by *Hauptmann* Albert Boeckmann, who was awarded the German Cross in Gold on 16 January 1944 for actions against the Belarusian partisans. Between 1942 and 1944 the battalion operated against partisans in the Vitebsk region. In the late summer of 1944, it took part in anti-partisan operations in the region of Varka, about 76km south of Warsaw. In August 1944 it was sent to Warsaw to help put down the uprising. In the autumn of 1944, it was attached to *551. Volksgrenadier Division* and fought with the division around Memel in 1945.

11 Franz W. Seidler, *Die Militärgerichtsarbeit der Deutschen Wehrmacht 1939-1945*, Münich: F. A. Herbig Verlagsbuchbuchandlung GmbH, 1991, p. 73.

12 It was later enlarged to division size in the summer of 1944 (June).

13 The title of the regiment is deceptive, given that a regiment in this period usually contained three battalions. The unit was created in the winter of 1941/42 using two companies of Air Force men. It was initially known as *Luftwaffe Bataillon Moskau*. In the spring of 1942, a third company was added to the battalion. A second battalion was added in the summer of 1942 by simply renaming *Luftwaffe Bau Bataillon 7/IV* as *II. Jäger Bataillon,* while the original battalion became *I. Jäger Bataillon*. The formation was then renamed as *Luftwaffe Regiment Moskau*. It saw stationed in Vitebsk. It saw service behind the lines fighting partisans in the Vitebsk and Rzhev areas of *Heeresgruppe Mitte*.

14 Kurt Mehner, *Die Waffen-SS und Polizei 1939-194*. Norderstedt: Militair-Verlag Klaus D. Patzwall, 1995, p. 331.

15 Tessin, *Verbände und Truppen*, Vol. 10, p. 61.

16 Ibid., p. 58.

17 US Military Intelligence Division, Chief of Military History, Washington D.C., *Order of Battle of the German Army*, op. cit., p. 315.

18 *Bandenlage Karte, 11-22.9.42 WfSt Op (H)*. German anti-partisan situation map, courtesy United States Holocaust Memorial Museum Collection.

19 Kurt Mehner, *Die Geheimen Tagesberichte Der Deutschen Wehrmachtführung Im Zweiten Weltkrieg 1939-1945*, Osnabrück Biblio Verla, 1989–1994, 12 volumes, Vol. 5, p. 332.

20 *Bandenlage Karte, 11-22.9.42 WfSt Op (H)*. German anti-partisan situation map, courtesy United States Holocaust Memorial Museum Collection.

21 Ibid.

22 This regiment was created by cannibalising one battalion from each regiment in the 141st and 151st Reserve Divisions

23 Tessin, *Verbände und Truppen*, Vol. 10, p. 76.

24 George Nafziger, *German Order of Battle: Waffen SS and Other Units*, Conshohocken: Combined Books, 2001, p. 300.

25 Mark Axworthy, *Axis Slovakia: Hitler's Slavic Wedge, 1938-1945*, New York: Europa Books, 2002, pp. 149. 150.

26 Ibid., p. 150.

27 This command was redesignated as *Kommandieren General und Befehlshaber der Sicherungstruppen Weissruthenien* on 8 October 1943.

28 Andris J. Kurseitis, *The Fallen Generals: The Destruction of the German Officer Corps in World War II and Its Aftermath*, Osceola: Ark Publications Co., 1994, p. 360.

29 Tessin, *Verbände und Truppen*, Vol. 14, p. 158.

30 Cooper, op. cit., p. 144.

31 John A. Armstrong (ed.), *Soviet Partisans in World War II*, Madison: The University of Wisconsin Press, 1964, p. 438.

32 Mehner, *Die Geheimen Tagesberichte*, Vol. 6, p. 548.

33 *707 Infanterie Division* was formed on 2 May 1941 as a *bodenständige* (static) infantry division of the 15th German recruitment wave.

34 Established in Thuringia on 15 December 1940 as a *bodenständige* (static) infantry division of the 14th German recruitment wave. On 2 November 1943, the division was merged with other divisions belonging to *4. Panzerarmee* in southern Russia, to form *Korpsabteilung* C (remnants of various shattered German divisions).

35 These divisions were simply the old *201. Sicherungs Brigade* and *203. Sicherungs Brigade* elevated to divisional status.

36 These units remained unchanged August–December 1942.

37 This battalion was led by *Oberst* (Colonel) Kononov. See: Hesse, op. cit., pp. 173–4.

38 The *Graukopf Brigade* was ordered disbanded by *Generalfeldmarshall* Günther von Kluge. The battalions were employed independently. Morale began to suffer when the men and officers in the unit saw first-hand the abysmal treatment of the local population at the hands of the Nazis. The disbandment of the brigade further lowered the morale of the volunteers.

39 Heinz Künrich, *Der Partisanenkrieg in Europa 1939-1945*, Berlin: Dietz Verlag, 1968, p. 157.

40 Leonid Grenkevich, *The Soviet Partisan Movement 1941-1944*, Frank Cass: Portland, 1999, p. 211.

41 Werner Haupt, *Die Schlachten Der Heeresgruppe Mitte. Aus der Sicht der Divisionen*, Friedberg: Podzun Pallas Verlag, 1983, p. 161.

42 At this time (June 1942), *221. Sicherungs Division* was organised as follows. Commander: *Generalmajor* Karl Freiherr von Lersner (from 18 June 1942). Operations officer: *Major* Friedrich. Component units: *Sicherungs Regiment 21* with *I. Bataillon, II. Bataillon,* and *III. Bataillon.* The *I. Bataillon* of *Sicherungs Regiment 44* (from 20 June 1942), *Sicherungs Regiment 45* (CO: *Oberst* Wiemann) with *I. Bataillon* and *II. Bataillon,* the *III. Bataillon* of *Französisches Infanterie Regiment 638,* and *Reserve Polizei Bataillon 91* (which would eventually be redesignated as *I. Bataillon* of *Polizeiregiment 8*).

43 Niehorster, op. cit. p. 163.

44 In 1941 *Feldkommandantur 197* controlled *454. Sicherungs Division* and was located in Zhitomir. In May 1942 it was made subordinate to

*Befehlshaber Heeresgebiet B*. However, by 1943 it was under *Befehlshaber Heeresgebiet Mitte*.

45 Krisztián Ungváry, 'Ungarische Besatzungskräfte in der Ukraine 1941-1942', in *Ungarn Jahrbuch Nr. 26, 2002-2003*, Munich: Ungarisches Institut, p. 127.

46 Activated in May 1943 and sent to Ukraine, to act as the headquarters for Hungarian occupation forces operating west of the Dnieper River.

47 This division was formerly known as the 102nd Hungarian Light Division.

48 This division was formerly known as the 105th Hungarian Light Division.

49 This division was formerly known as the 108th Hungarian Light Division.

50 The *Wehrmacht Befehlshaber Ukraine* command was created on 1 September 1941 to control two lower headquarters: *Oberfeldkommandantur 393* in Zhitomir (later Kiev), and *Oberfeldkommandantur 579* in Rovno.

51 Actually a part of Poland, although 'absorbed' into Belorussia in early 1944.

52 This headquarters served in Beresino in 1944.

53 This headquarters served in Mogilev, then Smolensk in 1942 and Gomel in 1943.

54 This command was stationed in Gorki in 1942.

55 Actually a part of Poland, although 'absorbed' into Belorussia in early 1944.

56 This unit was stationed in Dobryn in 1943.

57 This command was located in Vitebsk in 1941.

58 This town was decreed a part of Belorussia in early 1944.

59 This headquarters was officially disbanded in 1942.

60 In early 1944, this town was officially assigned to.

61 This town bordering Belorussia was located in February 1944 in the *Generalbezirk Weissruthenien*.

62 Part of the Bialystok District.

63 Actually a part of Poland, although 'absorbed' by a German decree into Belarus in early 1944.

64 Actually a part of Poland, although 'absorbed' by a German decree into Belarus in early 1944.

65 From *Ortskommandantur 354*.

66 This headquarters was stationed in Kurzenice in 1944.

## Chapter 2: Operations in the Baltic States and the Polish-Russian-Latvian Border Region

1 Colonel of the Municipal Police.

2 Led by *SS-Brigadeführer und Generalmajor der Polizei* Walther Schröder.

3 By all accounts, Friedrich Jeckeln had a low opinion of Schröder. He believed that Schröder lacked the necessary toughness that most SS officers were supposed to have. He also thought that Schröder was not a very good soldier, and that politics suited him better than combat.

4 BA MA, R 20, *Chef der Bandenkampfverbände, Andere Einheiten der Ordnungspolizei – Kriegstagebüch und Tätigkeitsberichten der Kampfgruppe Knecht, 4 Februar bis 3 April 1943,* 54, *Alt-/Vorsignatur 172-d-10-10/ 2.*

5 *Gendarmerie Zug Nr. 10 (motorisiert)* arrived in Riga in August 1942. Initially it contained thirty-six men. On 1 February 1943 it contained one officer and twenty-nine men. From 16 February and 31 March 1943 the motorised platoon was employed under *SS und Polizei Kampfgruppe Knecht*. Between 1–10 November 1943 the platoon was under *SS und Polizei Kampfgruppe Schröder*. At the time, this battlegroup was operating as a sub-unit of *SS und Polizei Einsatzgruppe Jeckeln*. During this time, Jeckeln's command was taking part in *Bandenkampf Unternehmen Heinrich.*

6 This regional defence company was only employed with the battlegroup for two days: 18–20 February 1943.

7 This battalion was only added to the battlegroup on 27 March 1943.

8 BA R 20/54, *Chef der Bandenkampfverbände und Polizei Schulen,* Folio 1-58, F. 22.

9 BA R 20/54, *Chef der Bandenkampfverbände und Polizei Schulen,* Folio 1-58, F. 24. The order of battle lists this battalion incorrectly as a 'Ukrainian' unit, when in fact, it was an Estonian volunteer police battalion.

10 NARA T 172, Roll, Frames 2512851-2.

11 The *(lettische) Schutzmannschaft Bataillon 275* was established in Riga on 16 October 1942. It was created using men from *(lettische) Schutzmannschaft Bataillon 266E*. It never went above company in strength. At its height, it contained 4 officers, 14 NCOs and 148 enlisted men. It was eventually disbanded and merged with *(lettische) Schutzmannschaft Bataillon 276* on 7 December 1942. Throughout its existence, the commander was Captain Fridrichs Kuģinieks. Similarly, *(lettische) Schutzmannschaft Bataillon 273,* which had been formed in the eastern region of Latvia, was merged into *(lettische) Schutzmannschaft Bataillon 276* on 15 July 1943. That battalion, in turn, became the *IV. Bataillon* in *(lettische) Freiwilligen Polizei Regiment 1.*

12 BA R 20/54, *Chef der Bandenkampfverbände und Polizei Schulen,* Folio 1-58, F. 24.

13 BA R 20/54, *Chef der Bandenkampfverbände und Polizei Schulen,* Folio 1-58, F. 27.

14 On 15 February two *panje* drivers were killed and two were wounded by snipers.

15 Including *Leutnant* Veldraum.

16 Including *Oberleutnant* Sarinsch.

17 This figure includes five men of the *SD Einsatzkommando*, plus another man wounded due to his own carelessness.

18 These were Latvian volunteers.

19 BA R 20/54, *Chef der Bandenkampfverbände und Polizei Schulen*, Folio 1-42, F. 28.

20 The *panje* was a light, open-air, four-wheeled horse-drawn wagon common in Eastern Europe during this period. It was usually pulled by just one or two horses and were used to carry any number of things. The Red Army, partisans as well as the German Army employed hundreds of thousands of these wagons during the war.

21 The Horch 901 type 40 KfZ.15 car which they had used to get to Daugavpils had developed a problem with its carburetor. Carburetors from this time period were less efficient at mixing air and fuel in extremely cold temperatures.

22 The description of this anti-partisan operation comes word for word from the war diary of *Kampfgruppe Knecht*. The Germans employed terminology in describing the operation that was pejorative of the partisans. For example, they used the term 'bandit' or 'bandits' instead of referring to these fighters in the proper context of being guerrillas or partisans. I have employed single quotation marks when repeating these pejorative words to indicate that these terms were employed by the Germans and not by the author of this work. In addition, the Germans employed terms like 'cleansing operation' to indicate elimination of people in certain areas where the anti-partisan sweeps occurred. Those terms have also been placed in single quotation marks to indicate its ulterior (more sinister) meaning.

23 Tessin, *Verbände und Truppen*, op. cit., Vol. 16, p. 201.

24 At this time, this battalion formed the group reserve.

25 Also known as Lake Osveya.

26 Russian translation of *Beloje See* is 'Beloye ozero' (Lake White).

27 Isserstedt had served as a *Hauptmann der Schutzpolizei* while stationed in Lodz from 15 May to 23 July 1941. He then served as 'censorship officer' for the *Kommandostab Reichsführer SS* until December 1941. He was born in Greußen on 20 October 1900 and was killed in Budapest on 4 January 1945, while serving in the newly reconstituted SS *Polizeiregiment 1*. Since 1940 he also held an SS grade equivalent to his police rank.

28 i.e.- SS *und Polizei Kampfgruppe Knecht*.

29 The mention of an Armenian formation operating in the region of *Heeresgruppe Nord* is highly unusual and suspect. I am convinced that the author of this report was mistaken regarding the ethnicity of the volunteer battalion that *(lettische) Schutzmannschaft Bataillon 279* encountered.

## Chapter 3: Partisan and Anti-Partisan Activity in the Region of Army Group North

1 The Germans referred to this region as *Weissruthenien* (White Ruthenia).

2 Anton Grasser used the staff of *Wehrmacht Befehlshaber Ostland* and incorporated this command with *Armeeabteilung Narva,* which was created on 2 February 1944 using the headquarters staff of *LIV. Armeekorps.* This occurred when he assumed command of the 'Narva' Army Detachment.

3 *BA RH 26-123/240, Geschichte der 123. Infanterie Division.*

4 Werner Regenberg, *Panzerfahrzeuge und Panzereinheiten der Ordnungspolizei 1936–1945,* Friedberg: Podzun Pallas Verlag, 1996, p. 66.

5 Rolf Michaelis, *The SS-Sonderkommando Dirlewanger: A Memoir,* Atglen: Schiffer Publishing, 2013, p. 48.

6 Rolf Michaelis, *Der Weg zur 36. Waffen Grenadier Division der SS,* Rodgau: Verlag fuer Militaerhistorische Zeitgeschichte, 1991, p. 58.

7 Wolf Keilig, *Rangliste Des Deutschen Heeres 1944/45,* Friedberg: Podzun Pallas Verlag, n.d., p. 73.

8 Tessin, *Verbände und Truppen,* Vol. 3, op. cit., p. 199.

9 Mehner, *Die Waffen SS und Polizei,* op. cit., p. 323.

10 Regenberg, op. cit., p. 66.

11 Antonio Muñoz, *Göring's Grenadiers: The Luftwaffe Field Divisions 1942-1945,* New York: Europa Books, 2002, p. 71.

12 Ziemke, Earl, *Stalingrad to Berlin: The German Defeat in the East,* Washington DC: Center of Military History, United States Army, 1986, p. 203.

13 Edgar M. Howell, et al., *The Soviet Partisan Movement 1941-1944,* Washington DC: Center of Military History, United States Army, 1956, p. 176.

14 Seven battalions and four police tank companies.

15 Tessin et al, *Waffen SS und Ordnungspolizei,* op. cit., p. 620.

16 Thirteen battalions.

17 Antonio Muñoz, *Hitler's Eastern Legions, Volume I – The Baltic Schutzmannschaft 1941-1945,* New York: Europa Books, 1996., p. 35.

18 Regenberg, op. cit., p. 83.

19 Ziemke, *Stalingrad to Berlin*, p. 204.

20 Howell, op. cit., p. 177.

21 *Heeresgruppe Mitte, Ia. Nr.14550/43 g.Kdos.,8.XII.43., Anlage zur Kriegstagebuch, Heeresgruppe Mitte, Führungsabteilung, Akte XXIII, Heft 12, 1.X.-31.XII.43. 65002/24.*

22 Ernst Percy Schramm, *Kriegstagebuch des Oberkommandos*, Bonn: Bernard & Graefe, 1982, 8 volumes, Vol. 6, p. 910.

23 Leo G. Niehorster, *The Royal Hungarian Army, 1920-1945*, New York: Europa Books, 1998, pp. 243 and 248.

24 Steven H. Newton, *Retreat from Leningrad. Army Group North, 1944/1945*, Atglen: Schiffer Publishing, 1995, p. 40.

25 Muñoz, *Göring's Grenadiers*, op. cit., p. 74.

26 *Polizeiregiment 26* had arrived in Poland (from Norway) in May 1943. It took part in anti-partisan operations there, until it was sent to *Heeresgruppe Nord* in December 1943.

## Chapter 4: The Central Sector

1 Antonio Muñoz, *Hitler's Eastern Legions, Volume II: the Osttruppen*, New York: Europa Books, 2003, p. 26.

2 Burkhard von Grafenstein, 'From a Coup Plan to a Military Experiment: The Graukopf Operation', *Journal for Intelligence, Propaganda and Security Studies* Vol. 4, No. 2, 2010, pp. 108–27.

3 Oleg V. Romanko, S. I. Drobyazko, and K. K. Semyonov, *Иностранные формирования Третьего рейха (Foreign Formations of the Third Reich)*, Moscow: Act Publishing, 2011, pp. 444–6.

4 Antonio Muñoz, *Hitler's War Against the Partisans During the Stalingrad Offensive. June 1942 to Spring 1943*, London: Frontline Books (Pen & Sword), 2025.

5 Antonio Muñoz, *The Druzhina SS-Brigade: A History, 1941-1943. A Study of German Occupation Policies and Russian Collaboration During the Second World War*, New York: Europa Books, 2000, p. 29.

6 Colonel Aimé Costantini, *L'Union Soviétique En Guerre (1941-1945)*, Paris: Imprimerie Nationale, 1968, 3 vols, Vol. 2, p. 255.

7 Muñoz, *The Druzhina SS-Brigade*, op. cit., p. 65.

8 NARA T-78, Roll 413, Frames 000314-320.

9 At this time, *330. Infanterie Division* was located in the region of *Heeresgruppe Mitte.*

10 In late 1943 this battalion began receiving Russian replacements as the Finnish volunteers dwindled.

11 Unfortunately, this practice is not as uncommon as one would want to believe. For example, the American Army in Vietnam and the Russian Army in Afghanistan both employed inflated statistics based on civilian as well as guerrilla deaths.

12 BA MA RH 22/31, Mai 1942, BA MA RH 22/60, BA MA RH 22/86, BA MA RH 22/100, BA MA RH 22/173, and BA MA WF 0315831, *Feldpolizeidirektor beim Befehlshaber Heeresgebiet Süd.*

13 Hesse, op. cit., p. 281.

14 Nazi Conspiracy and Aggression (Washington, DC: Government Printing Office, 1946), 8:205–8. R-135; and: Trials of War Criminals before the Nuremberg Military Tribunals under Control Council Law No. 10, October 1946-April 1949 (Washington, DC: Government Printing Office, 1949), 13:516-22. NO-3028.

15 Timothy Patrick Mulligan, *The Politics of Illusion and Empire. German Occupation Policy in the Soviet Union, 1942-1943*, Westport: Praeger Publishing, 1988, p. 121.

16 *Chef der Bandenkampfunternehmen,Verteiler über Unternehmen Kottbus, 23 Juni, 1943*. Document NO-2608, NMI, XII, 305-9. Yad Vashem Archive, Israel.

17 Hesse, op. cit., p. 209n.

18 Armstrong, op. cit., p. 538.

19 Helmut Krausnick, *Hitlers Einsatzgruppen. Die Truppen des Weltanschauungskrieges 1938-1942*, Frankfurt am Main: Fischer Taschenbuch Verlag, 1985, pp. 346–7.

20 Dallin, op. cit., p. 28.

21 Ibid.

22 Steenberg, op. cit., p. 107.

23 NARA Microfilm T-175, Roll 225, Frames 2764396-420.

24 *Schutzmannschaft Bataillon 12* and *Schutzmannschaft Bataillon 51* were in the process of forming into the 2nd and 3rd Battalions of *Polizei Schützen Regiment 31* (Police Rifle Regiment 31).

25 Mulligan, op. cit., p. 142.

26 Dallin, op. cit., p. 29n.

27 Armstrong, op. cit., p. 538; and Cooper, op. cit., p. 156.

## Chapter 5: The Soviet Partisans in Belarus and Russia, 1943

1 Bernhard Chiari, *Alltag Hinter Der Front: Besatzung, Kollaboration und Widerstand in Weissrussland, 1941-1944*, Düsseldorf: Droste Verlag, 1998. p. 176n.

2 Hesse, op. cit., pp. 207–08.

3 Howell, op. cit., p. 147.

4 Armstrong et al, op. cit., p. 464.

5 Ibid, p. 471.

6 Armstrong et al, op. cit., p. 465.

7 Grenkevich, op. cit., p. 227.

8 Martin K. Sorge, *The Other Price of Hitler's War: German Military and Civilian Losses Resulting from World War II*, New York: Greenwood Press, 1986, p. 56.

9 Howell, op. cit., p. 226.

10 Ibid., p. 154.

11 Ibid., op. cit., p. 242.

12 Ibid., p. 244.

13 Ibid., p. 162.

14 Costantini, op. cit., Vol. II, p. 244.

15 Theo Schülte, *The German Army and Nazi Policies In Occupied Russia 1941-1944*, New York: Berg Publishers, 1989, p. 312.

16 *Heeresgruppe Mitte, Ia. Nr.14550/43 g.Kdos.,8.XII.43., Anlage zur Kriegstagebuch, Heeresgruppe Mitte, Führungs-abteilung, Akte XXIII, Heft 12, 1.X.-31.XII.43.*

17 Costantini, op. cit., Vol. II, p. 268.

18 Muñoz, *The Druzhina* SS *Brigade*, p. 65.

19 This figure is for 1 August 1943. According to Soviet sources, these men were split up into five partisan detachments and one guerrilla regiment operating behind the lines of *Heeresgruppe Nord.*

20 These figures are for April 1943 and included the major partisan units there: Kovpak's 1,929 men split up into seven battalions; Saburov's 3,333 men into nineteen battalions; and Fyodorov's 1,777 men into eight guerrilla battalions. According to another, more reliable source, the strength figures for the Saburov, Fyodorov and Kovpak formations are a Soviet overestimation. The actual number should be 5,568 men for Ukraine region. The true figures (dated 25 August 1943) should be 1,728 men for Kovpak, 1,862 for Saburov, and 1,978 men for Fyodorov.

21 *Stab Bfh. rückw.H.Geb. Mitte, 'Vorschläg zur Vernichtung der Partisanen im rückw. Heeresgebiet und in den rückw. Armeegebietes', 1 Marz 1942,* T-501, Roll 15, Frame 312.

22 According to the document the figure of 500 locals appointed by the Germans, and later assassinated, is an estimate.

23 Ziemke, *Stalingrad to Berlin*, p. 304.

## Chapter 6: Major Anti-Partisan Operations in 1943

1 Peter Lieb, 'Täter aus Überzeugung? Oberst Carl von Andrian und die Judenmorde der 707. Infanteriedivision 1941/42', in: Hartmann/ Hürter/Lieb/Pohl, *Der deutsche Krieg im Osten 1941-1944, Facetten Einer Grenzuberschreitung*, Oldenbourg: De Gruyter, 2009, pp. 271–306.

2 Dieter Pohl, *Die Herrschaft der Wehrmacht: Deutsche Militärbesatzung und einheimische Bevölkerung in der Sowjetunion 1941-1944* (Quellen und Darstellungen zur Zeitgeschichte, Band 71), Oldenbourg: De Gruyter, 2009, p. 290.

3 BA-MA: RH 23-25, s. 63, *'Befehl Nr. 1 für Unternehmen 'Dreieck', 11 September 1942'.*

4 BA-MA: RH 23-25, s. 25, *'Gefechtsbericht über Unternehmen 'Dreieck' und 'Viereck' vom 17.9-2.10.1942, 19 October 1942'.*

5 Hamburger Institut für Sozialforschung (ed.), *Verbrechen der Wehrmacht: Dimensionen des Vernichtungskrieges 1941-1944*, Hamburg: Hamburger Edition HIS, 2002, p. 490.

6 Ibid, p. 491.

7 Michaelis, *Der Weg zur 36. Waffen-Grenadier-Division*, op. cit., p. 53.

8 MacLean, *The Cruel Hunters*, op. cit., p. 280.

9 Ibid., p. 114.

10 NARA Microfilm T-78, Roll 413, Frame 357, *Schematische Kriegsgliederung der landeseigenen Verbände, stand vom 5.5.43,* OKH/*Gen.St.d.H. General der Osttruppen Nr. 402/43 gKdos.*

11 Christian Gerlach, *Kalkulierte Morde. Die deutsche Wirtschafts- und Vernichtungspolitik in Weißrußland 1941 bis 1944*, Hamburger Edition, Hamburger Institut für Sozialforschung, 2000, pp. 826–8.

12 Phillip W. Blood, *Hitler's Bandit Hunters: The* SS *and the Nazi Occupation of Europe*, Sterling: Potomac Books, 208, p. 185.

13 NARA, RG242, T354, roll 649, Frames 357-61.

14 NARA Microfilm T-315, Roll 1685, file 36509/13. *Sich. Btl. 242, 4.5.43. 'Erfahrungsbericht aus dem Unternehmen 'Osterhase' vom 27.4. – 30.4.43'.*, pp. 1–2.

15 Timothy Snyder, *Into the Bloodlands: Europe Between Hitler and Stalin*, New York: Basic Books, 2022, p. 247.

16 *Geheime Feldpolizei Gruppe 724* (Secret Field Police Group 724).

17 At this time, the commander of *Sicherungs Regiment 45* was *Oberst* Hans Wiemann.

18 NARA T-315, Roll 1685, file 36509/13, op. cit., p. 5.

19 Ibid., p. 1.

20 NARA T-315, Roll 1685, file 36509/13. Op. cit., p. 2.

21 NARA T-315, Roll 1685, file 36509/13. *221. Sich.-Div. Abt. la, 2.5.43. Betr.: Bericht über Unternehmen Osterhase.*

22 NARA T-315, Roll 1678, file 29380/1. Sich.-Div. 221 Ia KTB, 22.12.42; T-315/1682, file 36509/1. Sich.-Div. 221 Ia KTB, 19.1.43; T- 315/1685, file 36509/11. Sich.-Rgt. 36 Ia, 26.12.42. Betr.: *Unternehmen Ankara. Gefechtsbericht, 19.-24.12.42, 1; Verlauf des Unternehmen Ankara I* (map; no date); *Sich.-Div. 221 Ia, 16.1.43, 1; Geplanter Verlauf des Unternehmens Ankara II* (map; no date); T- 315/1685, file 36509/12. Sich.-Rgt. 36 Ia, 25.1.43. Betr.: *Unternehmen Ankara II. Gefechtsbericht,* 17.-21.1.43; T-315/1685, file 36509/13. Sich.-Div. 221 Ia, 2.5.43. Betr.: *Bericht über Unternehmen Osterhase.*

23 Schramm, *Kriegstagebuch des Oberkommandos,* op. cit., Vol. 5, p. 490.

24 Peter Schuster and Harald Tiede, *Die Uniformen und Abzeichen der Kosaken in der Deutschen Wehrmacht,* Norderstedt: Verlag Klaus D. Patzwall, 1999, p. 86.

25 NARA Microfilm T-78, Roll 413, Frame 1302. (H 1/153), OKH/*Gen.St.d.H. General der Osttruppen Nr. 402/43 gKdos. Stand vom 5. Mai .43.*

26 Tessin, *Verbände und Truppen,* op. cit., Vol. 12, p. 254.

27 Ibid, Vol. 9, p. 289.

28 Schuster et al, op. cit., p. 86.

29 Mehner, *Die Geheimentagesberichte,* op. cit., Vol. 6, p. 417.

30 Werner Haupt, *Die Deutschen Infanterie-Divisionen,* Friedberg Podzun Pallas Verlag, 1992, Vol. 2, p. 52; and Kurseitis, *The Fallen Generals,* op. cit., p. 128.

31 Werner Haupt, *Die 8. Panzer Division im Zweiten Weltkrieg,* Friedberg: Podzun Pallas Verlag, 1987, p. 267.

32 Muñoz, *Göring's Grenadiers,* op. cit., p. 69.

33 Mehner, *Die Geheimentagesberichte,* op. cit., Vol. 6, p. 424.

34 Ibid., Vol. 6, p. 427.

35 Haupt, *Die 8. Panzer Division,* op. cit., p. 268.

36 Mehner, *Die Geheimentagesberichte,* op. cit., Vol. 6, p. 537.

37 Armstrong et al, op. cit., p. 174.

38 Ibid., p. 371.

39 Schramm, *Kriegstagebuch des Oberkommandos,* op. cit., Vol. 5, p. 464.

40 Rolf Michaelis, *Die Russische Volksbefreiungsarmee 'RONA' 1941-1944,* Erlangen: Selbstspubliziert, 1992, pp. 18–19.

41 By mid-1943 the Kaminski Brigade had grown to five infantry regiments, an artillery battalion, two tank companies of twenty-four tanks and tank destroyers and a brigade headquarters staff.

42 NARA Microfilm T-78, Roll 413, Frame 1302. *Schematische Kriegsgliederungen der landeseigenen Verbände;* OKH / *Gen.St.d.H. General der Osttruppen Nr. 402/43 gkdos. Stand von 5.5.43.*

43 NARA Microfilm T-78, Roll 413, Frames 1320-04.

44 Bartov, *The Eastern Front, 1941-1945. German Troops and the Barbarisation of Warfare,* op. cit., p. 124.

45 Armstrong et al, op. cit., p. 513.

46 NARA T-313, R-172, *Erfahrungsbericht of Pz.AOK 2 hinsichtlich Unternehmen Ziegeunerbaron,* pp. 14–15.

47 Cooper, op cit., p. 112.

48 Ibid, p. 150.

49 Karl Drum, et al., *Airpower in Russian Partisan Warfare,* USAF Historical Study No. 177, New York: Arno Press, 1968, p. 9.

50 Ibid.

51 Rolf Stoves, *Die Gepanzerten und Motorisierten Deutschen Grossverbände 1935-1945,* Podzun Pallas Verlag: 1986, p. 51.

52 Norbert Müller, *Deutsche Besatzungspolitik in der UdSSR 1941-1944,* Köln: Pahl-Rugenstein Verlag, 1980, p. 102.

53 Schramm, *Kriegstagebuch des Oberkommandos,* op. cit., Vol. 5, p. 525.

54 Ibid, p. 543.

55 *707. Sicherungs Division* was composed of *Infanterie Regiment 727, Infanterie Regiment 747, Pionier Bataillon 707, Signal Kompanie 707* and *Artillerie Abteilung 657.*

56 Müller, op. cit., p. 102.

57 Schramm, *Kriegstagebuch des Oberkommandos,* op. cit., Vol. 5, p. 585.

58 Mehner, *Die Geheimentagesberichte,* op. cit., Vol. 7, p. 59.

59 Cooper, op. cit., p. 112.

60 The literal translation is 'collective violent measures'.

61 Bartov, op. cit., pp. 123–4.

62 Armstrong et al, op. cit., p. 376.

63 Schramm, *Kriegstagebuch des Oberkommandos,* op. cit., Vol. 5, p. 549.

64 Ibid., p. 600.

65 *Ost Regiment Stab 455:* 455th Eastern Regimental Staff.

66 RONA: Russkaya Narodno-Osvoboditel'naya Armiya (*Russische Volksbefreiungsarmee*), or Russian People's Liberation Army.

67 BA-MA, RH 21-2/500, Bl. 5. Report from *Generalkommando LV. Armee-Korps zum Unternehmen Freischütz vom 07.06.1943, Seite 7.*

68 Ibid.

69 BA-MA, RH 26-6/47. Entry of 21 May 1943 from *Kriegstagebuch Nr. 7 der 6. Infanterie-Division vom 01.01. bis 30.09.1943.*

70 BA-MA, RH 21-2/570, Bl. 5. *Panzer-AOK 2 an Korück 532 vom 02.06.1943,* and BA-MA, RH 21-2/570, Bl. 3ff. as well as an order from *Oberkommandos der Heeresgruppe Mitte vom 18.06.1943.*

71 Also spelled 'Trubchevsk'. This unit was established in the town of Trubschevsk, which lies about 100km south-west of the city of Bryansk.

72 Howell, op. cit., p. 160.

73 Artium Sebastian Stoppe,. *Das Brjansker Gebiet unter der Besatzungsherrschaft der Wehrmacht 1941 to 1943.* Dissertation for obtaining the academic degree of Doctor of Philosophy. Humboldt University, 2012, pp. 196–7.

74 This operation never took place.

75 This operation never took place.

76 This was a 2. *Panzerarmee* operation.

77 This was a 2. *Panzerarmee* operation.

78 This was a 4. *Armee* operation.

79 Cooper, op. cit., p. 155.

80 Michaelis, op. cit., p. 56.

81 MacLean, *The Cruel Hunters,* op. cit., p. 119.

82 The *Dirlewanger* SS battalion would be expanded to regimental size on 19 March 1944.

83 Michaelis, op. cit., p. 55.

84 Hans-Peter Klausch, *Antifaschisten in SS-Uniform. Schicksal und Widerstand der deutschen politischen KZ-Häftlinge, Zuchthaus- und Wehrmachtgefangenen in der SS-Sonderformation Dirlewanger* Bremen: Edition Temmen 1993, p. 66.

85 Mehner, *Die Geheimentagesberichte,* op. cit., Vol. 7, p. 82.

86 Regenberg, op. cit., p. 119.

87 Carrell, *Scorched Earth,* op. cit., p. 13.

88 This *Gendarmerie* formation was led by led by *Major der Gendarmerie* Kurt Kreikenbom.

89 The commander of the security police and SD in Belarus.

90 Regenberg, op. cit., p. 129.

91 Albert Nirenstein, *A Tower from the Enemy: Contributions to a History of Jewish Resistance in Poland,* New York: The Orion Press, 1959, p. 364.

92 MacLean, *The Cruel Hunters,* op. cit., p. 281.

93 Regenberg, op. cit., p. 66.

94 Hesse, op cit, p. 282.

95 Mark W. Yerger, *Waffen SS-Commanders: The Army, Corps and Divisional Leaders of a Legend. Krüger to Zimmermann*, Atglen: Schiffer Military History, 1999, p. 229.

96 Nirenstein, op. cit., pp. 364–5.

97 Ibid., pp. 368–9.

98 Drum, op. cit., p. 37.

99 Michaelis, *Der Weg zur 36. Waffen Grenadier Division der-SS*, op. cit., p. 58.

100 Per Anders Rudling, 'Terror and Local Collaboration in Occupied Belarus: The Case of the *(ukrainische) Schutzmannschaft-Bataillon 118*', in Romanian. Bucharest: Academy Nicolae Iorga History Institute Historical Yearbook, Vol. VIII, 2011, p. 204.

101 Regenberg, op. cit., p. 129.

102 *Vorschlag für die Verleihung des Deutschen Kreuzes in Gold, 02.03.44-Billigung an 11.04.44.*

103 Nechama Tec, *The Bielski Partisans*, Oxford: Oxford University Press, 1993. p. 163.

104 MacLean, *The Cruel Hunters*, op. cit., p. 130.

105 Gerlach, op. cit., p. 907.

106 Blood, op. cit., p. 199.

107 Ibid., pp. 130–1.

108 Michaelis, *Der Weg zur 36. Waffen Grenadier Division der-SS*, op. cit., p. 13.

109 NARA Microfilm T-175, Roll 225, Frame 2763980.

110 Regenberg, op. cit., p. 66.

111 This SS recruit training depot had been established in 1942 as a forest camp near the village of Kissyelevichi, which lay about 8km south-east of the city of Bobruisk. Its commander was initially SS *Standartenführer* Georg Martin. Later, SS *Standartenführer* Rudolf Pannier assumed command. This SS recruit training regiment mainly processed *Volksdeutsche* (ethnic Germans) from the USSR and other parts of Eastern Europe, especially from Romania.

112 Muñoz, *Forgotten Legions*, op. cit., p. 181.

113 Ibid., p. 112.

114 Grenkevich, op cit., p. 251.

115 Armstrong et al, op cit., p. 350.

116 Tessin, *Verbände und Truppen*, op. cit., Vol. 12, p. 1.

117 Samuel J. Newland, *Cossacks in the German Army 1941–1945*, London: Frank Cass and Company, Ltd., 1991, p. 114.

118 NARA Microfilm T-315, rolls 1665-1687.

119 *Generalmajor* Karl Böttger became the commander of *221. Sicherungs Division* on 1 August 1943.

120 Tessin et al, *Waffen SS und Ordnungspolizei*, op. cit., p. 625.

121 Regenberg, op. cit., p. 113.

122 Armstrong et al, op. cit., p. 352.

123 Dr. Reinhard Rürup and Dr. Peter Jahn, eds., *Der Krieg gegen die Sowjetunion 1941-1945. Ein Dokumentation*, Berlin: Argon Verlag, 1991, p. 139.

124 Ibid., p. 140.

125 Rürup and Jahn, eds, op. cit., p. 738.

126 *Gepanzerter Zug Nr. 66*: 'Armoured Train No. 66'.

127 BA-MA, RH 21–2/725, RH 21–2/725 and RH 21–2/727; and BA-MA, RH 21–2/521 auf Bl. 68, Report for May 1943 found on p. 107 and total number of successful attacks in June 1943 on p. 121.

## Chapter 7: Anti-Partisan Forces and SS Killing Units in Ukraine, 1941–1943

1 These police battalions and regiments included the following principal formations: *Polizei Technische Nothilfe Kompanie* of *Polizeiregiment Süd, Polizeiregiment Süd, Reserve Polizei Bataillon 82 – Major der Schutzpolizei* Ebert. *Polizeiregiment z.b.V. – Oberstleutnant der Schutzpolizei* Gresser. *Polizei Reiter Abteilung I – Major der Schutzpolizei* Hahn, *Polizei Bataillon 304 – Major der Schutzpolizei* Deckert, *Polizei Bataillon 311 – Major der Schutzpolizei* Danz, *Polizei Bataillon 315 – Major der Schutzpolizei* Gewehr, *Polizei Bataillon 320 – Hauptmann der Schutzpolizei* Dall, *Polizei Bataillon 45 – Major der Schutzpolizei* Besser, *Polizei Bataillon 303 – Oberstleutnant der Schutzpolizei* Heinrich Hannibal, *Polizei Bataillon 314 – Major der Schutzpolizei* Severt, *1. SS Infanterie Brigade (mot.)* – this unit operated in the region of *Heeresgruppe Süd* until it was moved to *Heeresgruppe Mitte* in November 1941. The *3. Kompanie der Bataillon der Waffen SS z.b.V.* was led by *SS-Obersturmführer* Bernhard Grafhorst. Note: From July to October 1941, it served under *Einsatzgruppe* C. In addition, *Polizei Bataillonen 82, 311* and *318* made their appearance in July 1941.

2 Hans Werner Neulen, *An deutscher Seite: Internationale Freiwillige von Wehrmacht und Waffen SS*, Munich: Universitas Verlag, 1985, pp. 308–09.

3 Horst Boog, Jürgen Förster, Joachim Hoffmann, Ernst Klink, Rolf-Dieter Müller and Gerd R. Ueberschär, *Germany and the Second World War: Volume IV: the Attack on the Soviet Union*, Oxford: Clarendon Press, 1998, p. 496.

4 Reitlinger, *The House Built on Sand*, op. cit., p. 167.

5 David Littlejohn, *Foreign Legions of the Third Reich, Volume IV – Poland, Ukraine, Bulgaria, Rumania, Free India, Estonia, Latvia, Lithuania, Finland and Russia*, San Jose: R. James Bender Publishing, 1987, p. 42.

6 Neulen, op. cit., p. 309.

7 Tadeusz Piotrowski, *Poland's Holocaust: Ethnic Strife, Collaboration with Occupying Forces and Genocide in the Second Republic, 1918-1947*, Jefferson: MacFarland and Company, Inc., 1998, p. 213.

8 *Hauptmann* (Captain) Sconprynka, Ukrainian commander; *Oberleutnant* Professor Dr. Theodor Oberländer, German commander; *Hauptmann* Roman Schuchevytch, Adjutant. It had 400–500 Ukrainian volunteers.

9 *Hauptmann* Iarii, Ukrainian commander; *Hauptmann* Polihucher, German commander.

10 The confusion comes from the fact that Schuchevytch's pseudonym was 'Taras Chuprynka', who was also referred to as 'Sconprynka'; thus the mix-up in names.

11 Yuriy Tys-Krokmaliuk, *UPA Warfare in Ukraine*, New York: Vantage Press, 1972, p. 25.

12 Piotrowski, op. cit., p. 207.

13 Ibid., p. 206.

14 Wendy Lower, *Nazi Empire Building and the Holocaust in Ukraine*, Chapel Hill: The University of North Carolina Press, 2005, pp. 52–3.

15 Piotrowski, op. cit., p. 226.

16 Antonio Muñoz (ed.), *The East Came West: Muslim, Hindu, and Buddhist Volunteers in the German Armed Forces 1941-1945*, New York: Europa Books, 2001, p. 196.

17 Dixon, et al, op. cit., p. 129.

18 Tessin et al, *Waffen* SS *und Ordnungspolizei*, op. cit., p. 645.

19 Rudling, op. cit., p. 195.

20 Court transcripts; *The Canadian Government vs. Vladimir Katriuk*. Docket No.: T-2409-96, Date: 1999.01.29.

21 Rudling, op. cit., p. 206.

22 Ibid., p. 207.

23 Tessin, et al, *Waffen* SS *und Ordnungspolizei*, op. cit., p. 645.

24 Muñoz, et al, *Hitler's White Russians*, op. cit., p. 131.

25 These *Ordnungspolizei* forces included the *3. Kompanie / Polizei Bataillon 9* (until December 1941), and *2. Kompanie / Polizei Bataillon 3* (beginning in January 1942). By the end of the year, the number of men in the HQ staff of *Einsatzgruppe C* had increased to eighty, including a number of Ukrainian auxiliaries acting as guards and interpreters.

26 *SS Personalhauptamt, Dienstalterliste der Schutzstaffeln der NSDAP (SS-Obergruppenführer bis SS-Standartenführer) Stand vom 30. Januar 1942,.* Berlin: Herausgegeben vom Personalhauptamt: Gedruckt in der Reichsdruckerei, 1942, p. 15.

27 Otto Ohlendorf ended the war with the rank of *SS-Gruppenführer,* but when the Russian campaign began, his rank was *SS-Standartenführer.*

28 Dunnigan, et al, op. cit., p., 82.

29 Schramm, op. cit., Vol. 2, Part II, p. 1135.

30 Tessin, *Verbände und Truppen,* op. cit., Vol. 8, p. 63.

31 Ibid., Vol. 10, p. 92.

32 NARA Microfilm T-315, Roll 2215, Frame 512.

33 Tessin and Kannapin state that it was *Polizei Bataillon 111,* although they do not cite where they obtained that information.

34 *The German Campaign in Russia – Planning and Operations (1940-1942),* No. 20-261a. Washington D.C.: Department of the Army, March 1955, p. 12.

35 Westermann, op. cit., p. 319.

36 Ibid., pp. 309–29.

37 This figure includes thousands of Romani and Red Army political commissars, but the majority were Jews.

38 In other words, operating under the 'criminal orders'.

39 Browning, op. cit., p. 185.

40 Ibid, p. 186.

41 Manoschek, op. cit., p. 121.

42 Raul Hilberg, *Perpetrators, Victims, Bystanders: The Jewish Catastrophe 1933-1945,* New York: Harper Collins Publishers, 1992., p. 289.

43 Raul Hilberg, *The Destruction of the European Jews,* 3 vols, New York: Holmes and Meier, 1985, Vol. 3, pp. 1022–3.

44 Manoschek, op. cit., p. 95.

45 The killings occurred between Luck (Lutsk) and Kiverce, on the road to Rovno.

46 Wette, op. cit., p. 97.

47 Ibid, p. 96.

48 Wette, op. cit., p. 127.

## Chapter 8: Anti-Partisan Warfare in Ukraine, 1941–1943

1 Snyder, op. cit., p. 319.

2 This number is an honest estimate obtained by extrapolating figures from German, Russian, and other sources.

3 Alexander Gogun, *Stalin's Commandos: Ukrainian Partisan Forces on the Eastern Front*, London: I. B. Tauris, 2016, pp. 36–7. Based on figures provided by the author from August 1941 to March 1942. Gogun states that by March 1942, 30,000 partisans in 1,800 separate guerrilla units were operating in Ukraine.

4 Brenner was also deputy commander of *SS Polizei Kampfgruppe Prützmann*, beginning 10 February 1944. On 27 March 1944, Brenner established his own SS and police combat group, which he named *SS Polizei Kampfgruppe Brenner*. However, this battlegroup was disbanded two days later, on 29 March. It was reactivated under the title *Gruppe Brenner* on 17 April 1944. It was then made subordinate to *XIII. Armeekorps* of *4. Panzerarmee* (*Heeresgruppe Nordukraine*).

5 On 13 November 1943 Kiev was liberated by the Red Army. *Oberst der Schutzpolizei* Georg Asmus would have assumed command of this post in December 1943, but the loss of the Ukrainian capital ended this command.

6 This SS headquarters was established in September 1941. It was transferred from Rovno to Kiev in February 1942.

7 This SS command was moved to Lutsk in September 1942.

8 He was appointed to lead the *SS und Polizeiführer Charkow* command beginning 30 January 1943.

9 In January 1944 he was placed in the *Führerreserve*, pending a future post.

10 Temporary forces were units that tended to shift from command to command, as the need arose. Permanent forces were units that were endemic to the particular command.

11 Air reconnaissance and air support for anti-partisan operations.

12 In August 1942, Harm took over as commander of *SS und Polizeiführer Dnjepropetrovsk-Kriwoi Rog*, where he served until 4 October 1942. Upon which he returned to Kiev to hold his position as leader of *SS und Polizeiführer z.b.V.*

13 Led by *SS-Obersturmbannführer und Oberstleutnant der Schutzpolizei* Heinrich Hannibal from 1 January 1942 to 21 Aoril 1943.

14 In October 1943 Wappenhans was ordered to the anti-partisan staff of Hans Prützmann, where he served fighting the guerrillas in Ukraine. In April 1944 he was sent home on leave due to stress and anxiety. In January 1945 he was posted to Field Marshal Walter Model's command in the West. Towards the end of the war, he was ordered to report to Berlin, but instead deserted and returned to his home town.

15 This unit was tasked with coordinating the construction of a highway from Lviv–Vinnitsa–Dnepropetrovsk. The head of this command was *Oberstleutnant der Gendarmerie* Walter Gieseke, who would lead *Polizei Schuetzen Regiment 37* from 23 November 1943. *Verfahren gegen Friese u. a. (DG IV)*, in: *BA-Aussenstelle Lüdwigsburg*. See also: *Kaienburg H. Jüdische*

*Arbeitslager an der 'Strasse der SS'*, in *Zeitschrift für Sozialgeschichte des 20. und 21. Jahrhunderts*, 1999, Heft 1/96

16 Tensfeld was also the temporary commander of *SS und Polizeiführer Shitomir* from April to May 1943, when the incumbent, *SS-Gruppenführer* Otto Hellwig, was on leave.

17 Tensfeld may or may not have held this post until May 1943.

18 Promoted on 20 April 1942 to SS *Brigadeführer und Generalleutnant der Polizei.*

19 *Höhere SS und Polizeiführer Kaukasien*, six *SS und Polizeiführer* commands were designated to be under the *Höhere* SS *und Polizeiführer Kaukasien* headquarters, but only three were actually established: *SS und Polizeiführer Nordkaukasien, SS und Polizeiführer Kuban* and *SS und Polizeiführer Rostow.* Three others remained academic: *SS und Polizeiführer Bergvölker, SS und Polizeiführer Azerbaijan*, and *SS und Polizeiführer Georgien.* In his testimony, during his trial, Jürgen Stroop claimed he was to be assigned the *SS und Polizeiführer Georgien* command.

20 The *Höhere SS Polizeiführer Schwarzes Meer* was subordinate to the *Höhere SS Polizeiführer für Rußland Süd* command.

21 Der Reichsführer SS und Chef der Deutschen Polizei, *Bandenbekämpfung*, Berlin: Gedruckt im Reichssicherheitshauptamt, 1. Ausgabe, September 1942, pp. 21–4.

22 Beginning June 1942, the divisional commander was *General der Kavallerie* Diether von Böhm-Bezing.

23 On 18 September 1942 the divisional commander was *Generalleutnant* Paul Stöwer.

24 *Sicherungs Regiment 4* was transferred to *Kommandierender General der Sicherungstruppen und Befehlshaber im Heeresgebiet A* in May 1942. It was also re-designated as *Radfahr Regiment 4* at this time.

25 The original title was *Befehlshaber Heeresgruppe Süd* but was changed to *Befehlshaber der Rückwartig Heeresgruppe Süd 103* on 5 July 1941. This title was once again changed to *Kommandierender General der Sicherungstruppen und Befehlshaber im Heeresgebiet Süd* on 15 March 1942. On 9 July 1942, when *Heeresgruppe Süd* was divided into Army Group 'A' and 'B', this title was again redesignated as *Kommandierender General der Sicherungstruppen und Befehlshaber im Heeresgebiet B.*

26 NARA Microfilm T-315, Roll 2215, Frame 489.

27 Kitzinger had been *Befehlshaber des Luftgau Norwegen* until 26 June 1941, when he was transferred to Ukraine and placed in charge of combating the partisan movement behind the lines of *Heeresgruppe Süd.* He held this post until 1 August 1944, although a few sources say he left the post on 21 July 1944.

28 Meltzer held this post from 1 August 1941 to 1 November 1943.

29 NARA Microfilm T-315, Roll 2216, Frames 335-338.

30 The *Wehrmacht Befehlshaber Ukraine* command employed *Oberfeldkommandantur 393* as the principal battlegroup headquarters control when launching anti-partisan sweeps in Ukraine.

31 This headquarters command staff became operational on 19 October 1941.

32 Krisztlán Ungváry, 'Ungarische Besatzungskräfte in der Ukraine 1941-1942' in *Ungarn Jahrbuch* No. 26, Budapest (2002/2003), p. 126.

33 The headquarters of *143. Reserve Division* was located in Dubno.

34 On 25 September 1943 the official strength of 147. *Reserve Division* was 8,942 men, and 1,490 horses.

35 The headquarters for the VIIth Hungarian Corps was located in Korosten.

36 The headquarters for the VIIth Hungarian Corps was located in Korosten.

37 *The 143. Reserve Division* was disbanded in December 1943, while the *147. Reserve Division* was disbanded in January 1944.

38 Winter, *Die Geheime Feldpolizei*, op cit., p. 60.

39 Not to be confused with Cuno Schmidt.

40 BA-MA, RH 22/199 u. RH 22/200.

41 This main German police headquarters for Ukraine was transferred to Kiev in July 1942.

42 Edward B. Westermann, *Hitler's Police Battalions: Enforcing Racial War in the East*, Lawrence: University Press of Kansas. 2005, p. 290.

43 Christopher R. Browning, *Project Muse. Nikolaev and Dnepropetrovsk Regions*, The United States Holocaust Memorial Museum Encyclopedia of Camps and Ghettos, 1933-1945, Volume II: Ghettos in German-Occupied Eastern Europe. Indiana University Press, 2012, p. 1615.

44 The city of Dnipropetrovsk was not captured by the Red Army until 26 October 1943.

45 Ibid., p. 1615.

46 In the spring of 1943, *Feldkommandantur 509* would be transferred to Vinnitsa, along the Bug River.

47 NARA, RG-338, fiche D-157, *Schutz der Versorgungsleitungen in der Südukraine, Luftwaffe Generalleutnant* Ludwig Keiper.

48 During the war, there were two pro-German Cossack regiments bearing the ancillary number '5': *Kuban Kosaken Regiment 5*, and *Don Kosaken Regiment 5*.

49 *Korück 558* was formerly known as *Oberfeldkommandantur 787*. It had been stationed in Kharkov during 1942.

50 In July 1942 *Polizeiregiment Mitte* was renamed as *Polizeiregiment 13*.

51 Muñoz, *The Druzhina* SS *Brigade*, op. cit., p. 54.

52 NARA Microfilm T-175, Roll 225, Frames 2764132, and 2764136-7.

53 Yerger, *Waffen* SS *Commanders*, op. cit., p. 190.

54 Rolf Michaelis, *Ukrainer in der Waffen* SS: *Die 14. Waffen-Grenadier-Division der-*SS (*ukrainische Nr. 1*), Berlin: Michaelis Verlag, 2000, p. 120.

55 Jack Nusan Porter (ed.), *Jewish Partisans: A Documentary of Jewish Resistance in the Soviet Union During World War II* Washington DC: University Press of America, Inc, 1982, pp. 149–50.

56 Porter, op cit., pp. 150–1.

## Appendix I: Glossary of German Military and Political Terms

1 For example, when the German 6th Army surrendered at Stalingrad, the Red Army captured approximately 91,000 soldiers. They were forced-marched to Siberian *gulags*. Many died along the way. From these camps, only about 3,000 survived to return to Germany between 1953–6.

## Appendix II: German Conduct Behind the Lines of Army Group North

1 Hans Hellwes would continue to be in command of *Reserve Polizei Bataillon 105* until relieved in March 1944. *Reserve Polizei Bataillon 105* was under the immediate control of *Sicherungs Division 207*, which was itself under the *Korück* command.

2 *V-Leute*: 'V-people'. This refers to agents within the local civilian population, who were actings as agents (spies) for the German command.

3 *Kriegstagebücher Kdt. rückw. Armeegeb. 583 für die Zeit vom 1.4.42-31.12.42.* War Diary of Army Rear Area Command 583 (*18. Armee*) for the period from 1–30 April 1942.

4 This guard battalion became the *II. Bataillon* of *Sicherungs Regiment 3* on 29 May 1942.

5 Stationed in Narva were *Infanterie Ersatz Regiment 605* (which became *Sicherungs Regiment 605* in October 1943) and *Estnisches Ersatz Bataillon Narwa.* At one time or another, the following commands were also stationed in Narva: *Korück Narwa, Ortskommandantur 852, Ortskommandantur (I) 257 Narwa, Feldkommandantur Narwa, Feldkommandantur 189, Feldkommandantur 247, Wehrwirtschaftskommando Narwa, Wirtschaftskommando 308,* and *Außenstelle 48 des Rüstungskommandos Reval.*

6 The battalion was transferred to *Heeresgruppe Mitte* in May 1942. In the winter of 1942/43, the battalion added a *4. und 5. ukrainische Kompanie*, a *6. turkestanische Kompanie* and a *7. georgische Kompanie*. In February 1943 it was made subordinate to the *Höheren Kommandeur der*

*Nachschubtruppen 3* in Southern Russia. On 15 July 1943, the battalion was renamed *Nachschub Bataillon 571,* becoming a supply battalion. *Nachschub Bataillone 119* and *151* contributed to its reorganisation.

7 The *Hundertschaft* (singular form) was equivalent to a company in size. Three to four *Hundertschaften* would make a battalion.

8 *Kriegstagebücher Kdt. rückw. Armeegeb. 583 für die Zeit vom 1.4.42-31.12.42.* War Diary of Army Rear Area Command 583 (*18. Armee*) for the period from 1–31 May 1942.

## Appendix III: Russian Volunteer Formations, May to December 1943

1 Kursk offensive launched at the beginning of this month.

2 BA RH 20-28, 14 AE0.3 lfm, *Armeeoberkommando Ligurien, 1 Jan. – 31 Dez. 1944.*

# BIBLIOGRAPHY

## Primary Source Material


***Belarus Central State Archives, Minsk, Records 1941–1949***

Records Group RG-53.002M, Reels 3, 5, 11, and 13.

Belarusian State Minsk Archives, USHMM RG-53.002M (1993.A.0082), Folder 1262 and 1265.

Grodno Oblast Archive Records, 1940–1944. RG-53.004M. Reel No. 2, Fond 1, Section 100 – Grodno Amtskommissar correspondence.

Grodno Oblast Archive Records, 1940–1944. Records Group RG-53.004M, Reel 5.

Grodno Oblast Archive Records, 1940–1944. RG-53.004M. Reel No. 2, Fond 1, Section 100 – Grodno Amtskommissar correspondence.

***Military Historical Institute (Prague), Records 1941–1944***

Records Group RG-48.004M, Reels 1, 2, 3, 4, and 6.

RG-48.004M, (1993.A.0019), Reel No. 3 – *1.* SS *Infanterie-Brigade (mot.)– 29.11.42, 'Aufmarsch Glebokie'.*

***Bundesarchiv, Koblenz***

BAK-N756/214a, SS *Kampfgruppe von Gottberg: Band Zwei. Vgl. BArch Bestand RS 4 Brigaden, Legionen, Standarten sowie Kampfgruppen und Einheiten der Waffen SS; Verschiedene Sperrverbände und Eingreifgruppen Fotografie von* SS *Hauptsturmführer Robert Ancans.*

BAK-NS19-13, *Reichsführer-SS Meldung an der Führer über Bandenbekämpfung. Feldkommandostelle, 8.10.1942.* Neldung Nr. 23.

BAK-NS19-03, *Reichssicherheitshauptamt Nachrichten Uebermittlung,* NR 162/42 (G) AUS 160 ZWEI/42. Pages 12–13.

BAK-NS19-11. 470.

*Bandenkampf Unternehmen* – Folio: NS19/1, 1500, 1671, 1463, 2661, 2835, 3140, and 3695.

*Meldung vom 06.06.1943 über die Personalstärke der landeseigenen Verbände (BA-MA, RH 21-2/509, Bl. 78 und 78r). Vgl. Tabelle im Anhang auf Seite 405f. Der Arbeit.* Operations Abteilung, NO. 5645/42, Heeresgruppe Mitte. 15.07.42.

RH 22-229. Berück, Kriegstagebuch 07.04.42.

***Bundesarchiv, Freiburg***

*Reichssicherheitshauptamt. Höhere SS und Polizeiführer Ostland. 7.8.42. BAF, NS–19/1, 1500, 1671, 1463, 2661, 2835, 3140 and 3645.*

*Heeresgruppe Mitte, Ia. Nr.14550/43 g.Kdos.,8.XII.43., Anlage zur Kriegstagebuch, Heeresgruppe Mitte, Führungsabteilung, Akte XXIII, Heft 12, 1.X.-31.XII.43. 65002/24. Bundesarchiv, Frieburg. Chef der Sicherungstruppen—Rückwartigen Heeresgebiet 102, Operationsabteilung Nr.272/43, 25.1.43. 23).*

***Bundesarchiv / Militärarchiv Berlin-Lichterfelde***

BA-MA WF 01/2151, Bl. 816.

BA-MA WF 03/15831, *Feldpolizeidirektor beim Befehlshaber Heeresgebiet 103.*

BA-MA RH–19 VII/2, Bl. 2.

BA-MA RH 19 XI/37, *Bericht des GFP-Angehörigen Georg Koch,* 37.

BA-MA RH 22/31, *Meldung Direktor GFP, Mai 1942.*

BA-MA RH 22/60, *Bericht GFP für Heeresgebiet B, August 1942.*

BA-MA RH 22/86, 27.

BA-MA RH 22/173, *Meldung Direktor GFP, Juli 1942.*

BA-MA RH 22/199, *Befehlshaber rückwärtiger Heeresgebiete Tätigkeitsberichte der Geheimen Feldpolizeigruppen 1, 708, 719, 725, 730, 739, 721. – Stärkemeldungen Laufzeit: Jan.–Aug. 1942.*

BA-MA RH 22/200, *Befehlshaber rückwärtiger Heeresgebiete Tätigkeitsberichte der Geheimen Feldpolizeigruppen 1, 708, 719, 725, 730, 739, 721. – Stärkemeldungen Laufzeit: Sept.–Dez. 1942.*

BA-MA: RH 23-25, *'Befehl Nr. 1 für Unternehmen 'Dreieck', 11 September 1942'.*

BA-MA: RH 23-25, *'Gefechtsbericht über Unternehmen 'Dreieck' und 'Viereck' vom 17.9-2.10.1942, 19 October 1942'.*

BA-MA RH-24-22/21, folio 88-89.

BA-MA RH 24-22/23, *Jäger – Gen.Kdo.22 AK, 14 May 1944, Ic – Aussenstelle Korfu – Korpsgruppe Joannina / Ic, 25 April 1944.*

BA-MA RH-24, 23-24.

BA-MA RH-26 / 117/16.

BA-MA RH-40, 10.

BA-MA RH-40, 11.

BA-MA RH 48, *Dienststellen und Einheiten der Ordnungstruppen, der Geheimen Feldpolizei, der Betreuungs und Streifendienste des Heeres. RW 40/170: Fester Platz Kreta, Sept. 1944 RW 40/172: Tätigkeitsbericht, Juli – Aug. 1944; Bundesarchiv. Wi. Kdo. Witebsk, 'Monatsbericht', 23 November 1942* (GMDS, *Wi/ID 2.779*).

***National Archives, College Park, Maryland***

NARS Microfilm T-78.

Roll 413, 645.

NARS Microfilm T-175.

Roll 16, 111, 129, 140, 141, 174, 191, 225, 233.

NARS Microfilm T-315.

Roll 1665, 1687, 2213, 2214, 2215, 2216.

NARS Microfilm T-580.

Roll 88.

NARA RG-238 Working Conference on 23 April 1940, Service Diary of Governor General Hans Frank, Vol. 9.

***National Archives, Kew, Richmond, Surrey, United Kingdom***

C.S.D.I.C. (U.K.) S.I.R. (Special Interrogation Report) 730 (8 Aug 1944) 'Geheime Feldpolizei Gruppe 644'.

C.S.D.I.C. (U.K.) S.I.R. (Special Interrogation Report) 818 (20 Aug 1944) 'Geheime Feldpolizei in Greece 1942'.

C.S.D.I.C. (U.K.) S.I.R. (Special Interrogation Report) 1675 (24 May 1945) 'Notes on the GFP and Other Security Services in the Area of Army Group Nord (Later Kurland)—1942–1 Jan 45'.

C.S.D.I.C. (U.K.) S.I.R. (Special Interrogation Report) 1676 (24 May 1945) 'Notes on the GFP and Other Security Services in the West—1939–42'. CAB / 129 / 28, *Kommandobefehl, den 18 Okt. 1942.*

***German Armed Forces War Diary***

Schramm, Percy, *Kriegstagebuch Des Oberkommandos Der Wehrmacht 1939-1945,* 8 Vols. Herrsching: Manfred Pawlak, 1982.

Supreme Headquarters Allied Expeditionary Force, Office of Assistant Chief of Staff G-2, Counterintelligence Sub-Division Evaluation, and Dissemination Section

E.D.S. Report No. 15 – *Geheime Feldpolizei* (Secret Field Police) January 8, 1945, Supreme Headquarters Allied Expeditionary Force, Office of Assistant Chief of Staff G-2, Counter-intelligence Sub-Division Evaluation and Dissemination Section.

*Geheime Feldpolizei* (GFP) Vol. I XE 019650 Par 43, SR 380-20-10. General Staff, US Army G2 Central Records Facility, Fort Holabird, Baltimore 19, Maryland.

*Geheime Feldpolizei* – EI (GFP) G-2 Department of the Army, Volume II, XE 019650.

Office of Strategic Services Research and Analysis Branch, R and A N, 2500.15, 'German Military Government Over Europe: Economic Controls in Occupied Europe', Washington. D.C., August 28, 1945.

Box No. 4 – No. XE003923 German Police System in Occupied Czechoslovakia.

Box No. 5 – NND 881019, File No. XE019650 *Geheime Feldpolizei* (GFP) Volume I and Volume II.

*Records of the Army Staff (Record Group 319) – CIC Collection – Declassified Files*

Box No. 4 – No. XE003923 German Police System in Occupied Czechoslovakia.

Box No. 5 – NND 881019 File No. XE019650 *Geheime Feldpolizei* (GFP) (Secret Field Police) Vol. I and Vol. II.

*Military Intelligence Service Centre/US Forces European Theater CI*

Final Interrogation Report No. 98 (14 Mar 1946) 'Reg.-u.Krim.Dir. Philipp GREINER, Leitender FP Direktor, Mil.Befh. Frankreich'.

***The Seventh Army Interrogation Centre***

Final Interrogation Report No. 20 (8 Aug 1945) 'Secret Military Police Unit 712'.

***French Army Military Archive, Paris***

*Ordre De Bataille II – A – Etat-Major de la 30ěme Division d'Infanterie des Waffen*-SS (*Russe Nr.* 2) (*plustard*): *Stab, Waffen-Grenadier-Brigade der SS* (*Weissruthenien*).

***Legal Court Cases***

Innsbruck Court Case: GG Innsbruck 10 Nr. 415170-23 10 H 7170: 1–43.

Nuremberg Trial: NOKW 1382, Directive of the Quartermaster of the *Kommandant rückwärtiges Armeegebiet* 560 (Army Groups A, Twelfth Army, 560th Army Rear Area Security Command), May 21, 1941.

The Minister of Canadian Citizenship and Immigration vs. Vladimir Katriuk Court transcripts, Docket No.: T-2409-96. Date: 1999/01/29.

Court transcripts: *The Canadian Government vs. Vladimir Katriuk*. Docket No.: T-2409-96, Date: 1999.01.29.

Nazi Conspiracy and Aggression (Washington, DC: Government Printing Office, 1946), 8:205–8. R-135.

Trials of War Criminals before the Nuremberg Military Tribunals under Control Council Law No. 10, October 1946–April 1949 (Washington, DC: Government Printing Office, 1949), 13:516-22. NO-3028.

***Court Trial Testimonials***

Testimony of Heinz Hermann Schubert, Office of Chief of Counsel for War Crimes. APO 696 A, US Army, Document No. 4816, pages 3–4, 18).

Testimony of Private Albert Rodenbusch, Grenadier (Feldausbildungs) Regiment 635 given during court proceedings of the Minsk war crimes trials held in 1946 a, 1947. Belarusian SSR, 15-19 January 1946 (Minsk Trial), Minsk (1947), pp. 262–3.

*Testimony of Erich von dem Bach-Zelewski at the Nuremberg War Crimes Trials: The Trial of German Major War Criminals*. His Majesty's Stationery Office: London, 1946–52. Twenty-four volumes.

*The Trial of Major War Criminals.* His Majesty's Stationery Office: London, 1946–52. Twenty-three volumes.

### *Other Primary Sources*

Krüger to Gunst, November 14, 1939, W. Gunst SS Officer file (formerly Berlin Document Centre), RGp-242, A3343/SSO/043A/321, NARA; judgment in proceedings against Friedrich Paulus, May 26, 1977, p. 6, file 4 Ks 1/74, State Prosecutor's Office in Frankfurt am Main.

Meyer, Brünn, *Dienstalterliste der Waffen-SS: SS Obergruppenführer bis SS Hauptsturmführer; Stand vom 1 Juli 1944.* Osnabrück Biblio Verlag: 1987.

Telex:General Löhr to the *Befehlshaber Südost,* dated October 1, 1944 - RH 19 VII/37, Part 1, Annex 12.

'*Generalkommando LIV.A.K., Abt.Ic/A.O. vom 2.8.41, An den Führer des Sonderkommandos XIa Herrn* SS *Sturmbannführer Zapp.*', MAP, microfilm 56748, fr. 954; '*Geheime Feldpolizei 647, Koat II beim LIV.A.K., Tgb.-Nr. 77/41 vom 2.8.1941, An den Stab der Geheimen Feldpolizei 647 beim A.O.K. 11.,*' Ibid, fr. 945.

'*Der Beauftragte des Chefs der Sicherheitspolizei und des* SD *beim Befehlshaber des rückwartigen Heeresgebiet Süd, Sonderkommando 11a, Tgb. 83/41 vom4.8.1941, Betrifft: Bericht über die Tätigkeit des Sonderkommandos in der Zeit vom 17. Juli bis 3. August und die Einsatzplanung für die erste Augusthalfte 1941*'. On the concentration of Jews in labour camps in Bessarabia, see '*Die Gesandschaft in Bukarest an das Auswartige Amt,*' August 6, 1941, Nuremberg Doc. NO-2067, reproduced in ADAP, Series D, vol. XIII/1, 23839.

Roosevelt, Franklin D. 'No Peace with Hitler: Eight Common Principles for a Better World', in *Vital Speeches of the Day*. Vol. 7 Issue 22 (September 1, 1941).

'Central Registry of War Criminals and Security Suspects' (CROCASS Allied Control Authority, Part 1 and 2, US Army, APO 742, 1947).

### *Publications of the Third Reich Printing Office, Berlin*

*Der Reichsführer-SS und Chef der Deutschen Polizei, Banden-bekämpfung.* Berlin: Gedruckt im Reichssicherheitshauptamt, 1. Ausgabe, September 1942.

*Dienstalterliste der Schutzstaffel der NSDAP (SS Obergruppenführer bis* SS *Standartenführer) Stand vom 30. Januar 1942, Herausgegeben vom Personalhauptamt,* Berlin: Gedruckt in der Reichsdruckerei, 1942.

*Dienstalterliste der Schutzstaffel der NSDAP (SS Obersturmbannführer und SS Sturmbannführer) Stand vom 1. Oktober 1944. Herausgegeben vom Personalhauptamt.* Berlin: Gedruckt in der Reichsdruckerei, 1944.

*Dienstalterliste der Schutzstaffel der NSDAP* (SS *Obergruppenführer bis* SS *Standartenführer) Stand vom 1. Oktober 1944. Herausgegeben vom Personalhauptamt,* Berlin: Gedruckt in der Reichsdruckerei, 1944.

*Befehlsblatt des Chefs der Sicherheitspolizei und der SD, Nr. 14/44 Berlin, 1. April 1944. Herausgegeben vom Reichssicherheitshaupt-amt,* Berlin: Gedruckt in der Reichsdruckerei, 1944.

*Dienstalterliste der Schutzstaffel der NSDAP, Stand vom 1. Oktober 1934,* Berlin: Gedruckt in der Reichsdruckerei, 1934.

*Dienstalterliste der Schutzstaffel der NSDAP, stand vom 30 Januar 1942,* Berlin: Gedruckt in der Reichsdruckerei, 1942.

*Dienstalterliste der Schutzstaffel der NSDAP, stand vom Oktober/November 1944,* Berlin: Gedruckt in der Reichsdruckerei, 1944.

*Dienstalterliste der Schutzstaffel der NSDAP, stand vom 1 Juli 1944,* Berlin: Gedruckt in der Reichsdruckerei, 1944.

## Secondary Source Material

### *Doctorate of Philosophy Works Cited*

Birn, Ruth Bettina, *Die Höheren SS und Polizeiführer: Himmlers Vertreter im Reichs und in den besetzten Gebieten,* Droste Verlag, 1986.

Gordon, Gary Howard, *Soviet Partisan Warfare, 1941–1944. The German Perspective,* University Microfilms: Ann Arbor, 1972.

Porter, Jack Nusa, *Jewish Partisans: A Documentary of Jewish Resistance in the Soviet Union during World War II,* Volume II, University Press of America, Inc.: Washington D.C., 1982.

Pronin, Alexander, *Guerrilla Warfare in the German Occupied Soviet Territories 1941–1945,* Georgetown University Graduate School: Georgetown, 1965.

Sheppard, Ben, *German Army Security Units in Russia, 1941-1943: A Case Study.* A thesis submitted to the Faculty of Social Science and Commerce of The University of Birmingham for the degree of Doctor of Philosophy, Institute for German Studies Faculty of Social Science and Commerce: The University of Birmingham, June 2000.

Stopper, Artium Sebastian, *Das Brjansker Gebiet unter der Besatzungsherrschaft der Wehrmacht 1941 to 1943.* Dissertation in partial completion for obtaining the academic degree of Doctor of Philosophy. Humboldt University, 2012.

### *Pamphlets and journals*

*German Anti-Guerrilla Operations in the Balkans, 1941-1944.* DA Pamphlet 20-243, August 1954, Washington, DC: Centre of Military History, US Army,

Grafenstein, Burkhard von, 'From a Coup Plan to a Military Experiment: The Graukopf Operation', *Journal for Intelligence, Propaganda and Security Studies,* Vol. 4, No. 2, 2010.

Kowalska, Magdalena, *A Polish heart in a feldgrau uniform – complicated journeys from the Wehrmacht to the Polish Army in Exile* in 'Polish Scientific Society Abroad in London', Poznań: Adam Mickiewicz University, Humanities Education No. 2 (33), 2015.

Krichbaum, Wilhelm, *The Secret Field Police,* MS # C-029. Edited by George Vanderstadt. Translated by M. Franke. Washington, DC: Centre for Military History, US Army Historical Division, 18 May 1947.

*The Case Against General Heusinger. Documents Illustrating the Charges of the USSR Against Former Lieutenant-General Adolf Heusinger, Former Operations Chief of the Wehrmacht High Command.* Soviet Government. New York: Translation World Publishers, 1961.

Ungváry, Krisztlán, 'Ungarische Besatzungskräfte in der Ukraine 1941-1942', *Ungarn Jahrbuch* No. 26, Budapest (2002/2003).

### *Internet*

Grabowski, Jan, *The Polish Police: Collaboration in the Holocaust,* United States Holocaust Memorial Museum: Washington, D.C. https://www.ushmm.org/m/pdfs/20170502-Grabowski_OP.pdf. 2017.

### *Published Works*

Adair, Paul, *Hitler's Greatest Defeat. The Collapse of Army Group Centre,* New York: Sterling Publishing, 1994.

Albrecht-Carrié, René, *A Diplomatic History of Europe Since the Congress of Vienna,* New York: Harper and Row, Publishers, 1958.

Anders, Wladyslaw, *Hitler's Defeat in Russia,* Chicago: Henry Regnery Company, 1953.

Anders, Wladyslaw, *Russian Volunteers in Hitler's Army, 1941-1945,* New York: Europa Books. 1997.

Andrew, Christopher, *Defend the Realm: The Authorized History of MI5,* New York: Knopf Doubleday, 2009.

Andreyev, Catherine, *Vlasov and the Russian Liberation Movement. Soviet Reality and Émigré Theories,* Cambridge: Cambridge University Press, 1987.

Angolia, Lieutenant-Colonel John R., *Cloth Insignia of the* SS, San Jose: R. James Bender Publishing, 1983. 2nd (updated) edition.

Angrick, Andrej, *Besatzungspolitik und Massenmord: Die Einsatzgruppe D in der Sowjetunion 1941-1943,* Hamburg: Hamburger Edition, 2003.

Applebaum, Ann, *Red Famine: Stalin's War on Ukraine,* New York: Doubleday, 2018.

Arad, Yitzhak, 'The Holocaust of Soviet Jewry in the Occupied Territories of the Soviet Union', in Aharon Weiss (ed.), *Yad Vashem Studies XXI,* Jerusalem: The Holocaust Martyrs' and Heroes' Remembrance Authority, 1991.

Arico, Massimo, *Ordnungspolizei Volume 1: Encyclopedia of the German Police Battalions September 1939-July 1942,* Stockholm: Leandoer and Co. Forlag, 2016.

Armstrong, John A. (ed.), *Soviet Partisans in World War II,* Madison: University of Wisconsin Press, 1964.

Armstrong, John A., *Ukrainian Nationalism,* Englewood: Ukrainian Academic Press, 1990.

Aschenauer, Rudolf, *Krieg Ohne Grenzen: Der Partisanenkampf gegen Deutschland 1939-1945,* Leoni am Starnberger See: Druffel Verlag, 1982.

Axworthy, Mark W. A., *Axis Slovakia: Hitler's Slavic Wedge, 1938-1945*, New York: Europa Books, 2002.

Banach, Jens, *Heydrich's Elite: Das Führerkorps der Sicherheitspolizei und des SD 1936-1945*, Paderborn: Ferdinand Schöningh, 1998.

Baker, Gabriel, *Spare No One: Mass Violence in Roman Warfare*, New York: Rowman & Littlefield, 2021.

Bartov, Omer, *The Eastern Front 1941-1945: German Troops and the Barbarisation of Warfare*, New York: St. Martin's Press, 1986.

Bartov, Omer, *Hitler's Army: Soldiers, Nazis, and War in the Third Reich*, Oxford: Oxford University Press, 1992.

Bartov, Omer, *Mirrors of Destruction: War, Genocide, and Modern Identity*, Oxford: Oxford University Press, 2000.

Bartov, Omer, *Germany's War and the Holocaust: Disputed Histories*, Cornell: Cornell University Press, 2003.

Bauer, Eddy, *The History of World War II*, London: Galley Press, 1984.

Bayer, Hanns, *Die Kavallerie Der Waffen SS*, Heidelberg: Selbstverlag der Truppenkameradenschaft der SS Kavallerie Divisionen, 1980.

Bayer, Hanns, *Kavallerie Divisionen der Waffen-SS im Bild*, Osnabrück: Munin Verlag, 1982.

Becker, Hans, *Devil on My Shoulder*, London: Jarrolds Publishers, 1955.

Beevor, Anthony, *Crete: The Battle and the Resistance*, New York: Penguin Books, 2014.

Bennett, Rab, *Under the Shadow of the Swastika: The Moral Dilemmas of Resistance and Collaboration in Hitler's Europe*, New York: New York University Press, 1999.

Bergen, Doris L., *War and Genocide: A Concise History of the Holocaust*, New York: Rowman and Littlefield Publishers, Inc., 2009.

Berthel, Hans Dieter, *Die Feldgendarmerie im Zweiten Weltkrieg und ihre Teilnahme an völkerrechtswidrigen Aktionen 1939–1945*, Norderstedt: Herstellung und Verlag, 2006.

Bethell, Nicholas, *The Last Secret. The Delivery to Stalin of Over Two Million Russians by Britain and the United States*, New York: Basic Books Inc., 1974.

Birn, Ruth Bettina, *Die Sicherheitspolizei in Estland, 1941-1944: Eine Studie zur Kollaboration im Osten*, Paderborn: Ferdinand Schöningh, 2006.

Bischof, Günther, Fritz Plasser, and Eva Maltschnig (eds), *Austrian Lives: Contemporary Austrian Studies Vol. 21*, New Orleans: University of New Orleans Press, 2012.

Blood, Philip W., *Hitler's Bandit Hunters: The SS and the Nazi Occupation of Europe*, Washington, D.C.: Potomac Books, Inc., 2006.

Bonn, Keith E. (ed.), *Slaughterhouse: The Handbook of the Eastern Front*, Bedford: The Aberjona Press, 2005.

Boog, Horst, et al., *Germany and the Second World War. Volume IV, the Attack on the Soviet Union*, Oxford: Clarendon Press, 1998.

Boshyk, Yury (ed.), *Ukraine during World War II: History and its Aftermath*, Edmonton: Canadian Institute of Ukrainian Studies, 1986.

Brandon, Ray and Wendy Lower, *Shoah in Ukraine: History, Testimony, Memorialization*, Bloomington: Indiana University Press, 2008.

Browning, Christopher, *Ordinary Men: Reserve Police Battalion 101 and the Final Solution in Poland*, New York: Harper Collins Publishers, Inc., 1992.

Browning, Christopher, *The Origins of the Final Solution: The Evolution of Nazi Jewish Policy, September 1939-March 1942*, Lincoln: University of Nebraska Press, 2004.

Browning, Christopher R., *Project Muse. Nikolaev and Dnepropetrovsk Regions. The United States Holocaust Memorial Museum Encyclopedia of Camps and Ghettos, 1933-1945, Volume II: Ghettos in German-Occupied Eastern Europe*, Indiana University Press, 2012

Bruns, Friedrich, *Die Brücke von Neuenburg: Eine Dokumentation über den Endkampf der 19 Armee in Elsaß 1945*, Celle: Self-published, 1990.

Buchanan, Patrick J., *Churchill, Hitler, and The Unnecessary War: How Britain Lost Its Empire and the West Lost the World*, New York: Crown Press, 2008.

Buchner, Alex, *Ostfront: The German Defensive Battles on the Russian Front 1944*, West Chester: Schiffer Military History, 1991.

Campbell, Bruce, *The* SA *Generals and the Rise of Nazism*, Lexington: The University Press of Kentucky, 1998.

Campbell, Stephen, *Police Battalions of the Third Reich*, Atglen: Schiffer Publishers, 2007.

Carell, Paul, *Hitler Moves East, 1941-1943*, Boston: Little, Brown, and Company, 1964.

Carell, Paul, *Scorched Earth. The Russo-German War 1943-1944*, Boston: Little, Brown, and Company, 1970.

Carnier, Pier Arrigo, *L'Armata Cosaca in Italia 1944-1945*, Milan: Mursia Editoriale, 1990.

Caroe, Olaf, *Soviet Empire. The Turks of Central Asia and Stalinism*, New York: MacMillan and Co. Ltd., 1954.

Chiari, Bernhard, *Alltag Hinter Der Front: Besatzung, Kollaboration und Widerstand in Weissrussland, 1941-1944*, Düsseldorf: Droste Verlag, 1998.

Cholawsky, Shalom, *The Jews of Belorussia during World War II*, Amsterdam: Harwood Academic Publishers, 1998.

Citino, Robert M., *The German Way of War: From the Thirty Years' War to the Third Reich*, Lawrence: University Press of Kansas, 2005.

Clark, Allan, *Barbarossa. The Russo-German Conflict, 1941-45*, New York: William Morrow and Company, 1965.

Clarke, Jeffrey J. and Robert Ross Smith, *United States Army in World War II. The European Theater of Operations: Riviera to the Rhine*, Washington, D.C.: Centre of Military History, 1993.

Conquest, Robert, *Harvest of Sorrow: Soviet Collectivization Methods and the Terror-Famine*, Oxford and New York: Oxford University Press, 1986.

Cooper, Matthew, *The Nazi War Against Soviet Partisans, 1941-1944*, New York: Stein and Day, 1979.

Costantini, Colonel Aimé, *L'Union Soviétique En Guerre* (*1941-1945*), Paris: Imprimerie Nationale, 1968, 3 volumes.

Coudry, Georges, *Les Camps Sovietiques. Les 'Russes' Livres a Staline en 1945*, Paris: Albin Michel, 1997.

Crankshaw, Edward, *Gestapo: Instrument of Tyranny*, London: Greenhill Books, 1990.

Cüppers, Martin, *Wegbereiter der Shoah: Die Waffen SS, der Kommandostab Reichsführer*-SS *und die Judenvernichtung 1939-1945*, Darmstadt: Wissenschaftliche Buchgesellschaft, 2005.

Curilla, Wolfgang, *Die deutsche Ordnungspolizei und der Holocaust im Baltikum und im Weißrußla, 1941-1944*, Paderborn: Verlag Ferdinand Schöningh GmbH, 2006.

Dallin, Alexander, *German Rule in Russia 1941-1945, A Study of Occupation Policies*, London: MacMillan and Co Ltd, 1957.

Dasnoy, Philippe, and Jean Leon Charles, *Les dossiers secrets de la police allemande en Belgique. La Geheime Feldpolizei en Belgique et dans le Nord de la France, Vols. 1 and 2*, Brüssel: Arts et Voyages / Lucien De Meyer, 1972.

Dawidowicz, Lucy S., *The War against the Jews 1933-1945*, New York: Holt, Reinhart and Winston, 1975.

Dean, Martin, *Collaboration in the Holocaust: Crimes of the Local Police in Belorussia and Ukraine, 1941-1944*, New York: St. Martin's Press, 2000.

Dixon, Brigadier C. Aubrey and Otto Heilbrunn, *Communist Guerrilla Warfare*, New York: Frederick A. Praeger, 1954.

Dorril, Stephen, *M.I.6*, London: Fourth Estate Publishing Ltd., 2000.

Dreßen, Willi, 'The Role of the Wehrmacht and the Police in the Annihilation of the Jews; the Prosecution of Postwar Careers of Perpetrators in the Police Force of the Federal Republic of Germany', *Yad Vashem Studies XXIII*, 1993: 295–319.

Drum, D. Karl, et al., *Airpower in Russian Partisan Warfare*, USAF Historical Study No. 177. New York: Arno Press, 1968.

Dunnigan, James F., David C. Isby, E. C. McCarthy, Stephen Patrick, and Trevor N. Dupuy (eds), *War in the East: The Russo-German Conflict, 1941-45*, New York: Simulations Publications Inc., 1977.

Eckmann, Lester, and Chaim Lazar, *The Jewish Resistance: The History of the Jewish Partisans in Lithuania and White Russia during the Nazi Occupation 1940-1945*, New York: Shengold Publishers, Inc., 1977.

Ehrenburg, Ilya, and Vasily Grossman, *The Black Book*, New York: Holocaust Library, 1981.

Erickson, John, *The Road to Berlin. Stalin's War with Germany*, London: Weidenfeld and Nicolson Ltd., 1983.

Evans, Richard J., *The Third Reich in Power*, New York: The Penguin Press, 2005.

Evans, Richard J., *The Third Reich at War*, London: Penguin Books Ltd., 2008.

Ezergailis, Andrew, *The Holocaust in Latvia 1941-1944*, Washington D.C.: The United States Holocaust Memorial Museum, 1996.

Faber, David, *Munich 1938: Appeasement and World War Two*, New York: Simon and Schuster, 2010.

Federov, Alexander, *Partisans d'Ukraine – 2. operations contre la Wehrmacht*, Paris: Editions J'ai Lu, 1951.

Fischer, George, *Soviet Opposition to Stalin: A Case Study in World War II*, Cambridge: Harvard University Press, 1952.

Fontaine, Thomas, 'Chronology of Repression and Persecution in Occupied France, 1940-44', in *The Encyclopedia of Mass Violence* (Philadelphia: Running Press, 2004).

Förster, Jürgen, 'The German Army and the Ideological War against the Soviet Union' in Gerhard Hirschfeld (ed.), *The Policies of Genocide: Jews and Soviet Prisoners of War in Nazi Germany*, London: Allen and Unwin, 1986, 15–29.

Franz, Hermann, *Gebirgsjäger der Polizei: Polizei-Gebirgsjäger-Regiment 18 und Polizei-GebirgsArtillerieabteilung 1942*, Bad Nauheim: Verlag Hans Henning, 1963.

Frei, Norbert. *Vergangenheitspolotik*. Einbeck: AHA-Buch GmbH, 1996.

Geldmacher, Thomas, *Wir als Wiener waren ja bei der Bevölkerung beliebt: Östtereichsische Schutzpolizisten und die Judenvernichtung in Ostgalizien 1941-1944*, Vienna: Mandelbaum Verlag, 2002.

Gellermann, Guenther W., *Moskau ruft Heeresgruppe Mitte. Was nicht im Wehrmachtbericht stand: Die Einsätze des geheimen Kampfgeschwaders 200 im Zweiten Weltkrieg*, Koblenz: Bernard and Graefe Verlag, 1988.

Gerlach, Christian, *Kalkulierte Morde: Die deutsche Wirtschafts- und Vernichtungspolitik in Weißrußland, 1941 bis 1944*, Hamburg: Hamburger Edition HIS, 2013.

Gerlach, Christian. 'Men of 20 July and the War in the Soviet Union', in Hannes Heer and Klaus Naumann (eds), *War of Extermination: The German Military in World War Two 1941–1944*, New York: Berghahn Books, 2000.

Geβner, Klaus, *Geheime Feldpolizei*, Berlin: Militarverlag der Deutschen Demokratische Republik, 1986.

Geβner, Klaus, *Geheime Feldpolizei: Die Gestapo der Wehrmacht*, Berlin: Militärverlag, 2010.

Geyer, Michael, Charles S. Maier and Andrew Gould (eds), 'Traditional Elites and National Socialist Leadership', 77–133, in *The Rise of the Nazi Regime: Historical Reassessments*, Boulder: Westview Press, 1986.

Gibson, Hugh, and Sumner Welles (eds), *Ciano Diaries 1939-1943, Complete, Unabridged Diaries of Count Galeazzo. Italian Minister for Foreign Affairs 1936-1943*, New York: Doubleday and Co., 1946.

Gilbert, Dr. Martin, *Atlas of the Holocaust*, London: Lester Publishing, Ltd., 1988. Revised edition, 1993.

Gilbert, Dr. Martin, *The Holocaust: A History of the Jews of Europe During the Second World War*, New York: Henry Holt And Company, 1985.

Gildea, Robert, Anette Warring and Olivier Wieviorka (eds), *Surviving Hitler and Mussolini: Daily Life in Occupied Europe*, New York: Bloomsbury Academic, 2006.

Glantz, David M. and Harold S. Orenstein, *Belorussia 1944: The Soviet General Staff Study*, London: Frank Cass, 2001.

Gogun, Alexander, *Stalin's Commandos. Ukrainian Partisan Forces on the Eastern Front*, London: I.B.Tauris, 2016.

Goldhagen, Daniel Jonah, *Hitler's Willing Executioners: Ordinary Germans and the Holocaust*, New York: Alfred A. Knopf, 1996.

Gooch, John, *Mussolini and His Generals: The Armed Forces and Fascist Foreign Policy, 1922-1940*, Cambridge: Cambridge University Press, 2007.

Görlitz, Walter, and David Irving (eds), *In the Service of the Reich*, New York: Stein and Day, 1979.

Grenkevich, Leonid, *The Soviet Partisan Movement 1941-1944*, London: Frank Cass Ltd, 1999.

Grundmann, Siegfried, *Die V-Leute des Gestapo-Kommissars Sattler*, Berlin: Hentrich und Hentrich Verlag, 2010.

Hamburger Institut für Sozialforschung (ed.), *Verbrechen der Wehrmacht: Dimensionen des Vernichtungskrieges 1941-1944*, Hamburg: Hamburger Edition HIS, 2002.

Hanusiak, Michael, *Lest We Forget*, Toronto: Progress Books, 1976.

Hartmann, Christian, Johannes Hürter, Peter Lieb and Dieter Pohl, *Der deutsche Krieg in Osten 1941-1944: Faceten einer Grenzüberschreitung*, Oldenbourg: Wissentschaftsverlag, 2009.

Hartmann, Christian, Johannes Hürter, and Ulrike Jureit, *Verbrechen der Wehrmacht: Bilanz einer Debatte*, Munich: Verlag C.H. Beck, 2005.

Haupt, Werner, *Army Group Centre: The Wehrmacht in Russia 1941-1945*, Atglen: Schiffer Publishing, 1997.

Haupt, Werner, *Die 8. Panzer Division im 2. Weltkrieg*, Friedberg: Podzun Pallas Verlag, 1987.

Haupt, Werner, *Die Schlachten Der Heeresgruppe Mitte 1941-1944*, Friedberg: Podzun Pallas Verlag, 1983.

Haupt, Werner, *Die Deutschen Infanterie-Divisionen*, Friedberg: Podzun Pallas Verlag, 1991. Three volumes.

Haupt, Werner, *Army Group North. The Wehrmacht in Russia 1941-1945*, Atglen: Schiffer Publishers, 1997.

Haupt, Werner, *Die Schlachten Der Heeresgruppe Süd. Aus der Sicht der Divisionen*, Friedberg: Podzun Pallas Verlag, 1985.

Haupt, Werner, *Army Group South. The Wehrmacht in Russia 1941-1945*, Atglen: Schiffer Publishers, 1997.

Haupt, Werner, *Leningrad: Die 900 Tage Schlacht 1941-1944*, Friedberg: Podzun Pallas Verlag, 1980.

Hausser, Paul, *Soldaten Wie Andere Auch. Der Weg der Waffen* SS, Osnabrück: Munin Verlag GmbH, 1966.

Hechelhammer, Bodo, and Susanne Meinl, *Geheimobjekt Pullach: Von der NS-Mustersiedlung zur Zentrale des BND*, Berlin: Christoph Links Verlag, 2014.

Heer, Hannes, and Klaus Naumann, *Vernichtungskrieg: Verbrechen der Wehrmacht 1941-1944*, Hamburg: Hamburger Edition, 1995.

Heer, Hannes and Klaus Naumann (eds), *The German Army and Genocide: Crimes Against War Prisoners, Jews, and Other Civilians in the East, 1939-1944*, New York: The New Press, 1999.

Heer, Hannes, and Klaus Naumann (eds), *War of Extermination: the German Military in World War II–1944*, New York: Berghan Books, 2000.

Heer, Hannes and Klaus Naumann (eds), *Verbrechen der Wehrmacht: Dimensionen des Vernichtungskrieges 1941–1944*, Hamburg: Hamburger Institut für Sozialforschung, 2002.

Herbert, Ulrich (ed.), *National Socialist Extermination Policies: Contemporary German Perspectives and Controversies*, New York: Berghan Books, 2000.

Herf, Jeffrey, *Reactionary Modernism: Technology, Culture, and Politics in the Third Reich*, New York: Cambridge University Press, 1984.

Hesse, Erich, *Der Sowietrussische Partisanenkrieg 1941 bis 1944*, Göttingen: Musterschmidt Verlag, 1969.

Hilberg, Raul, *Perpetrators, Victims, Bystanders: The Jewish Catastrophe 1933-1945*, New York: Harper Collins Publishers, 1992.

Hilberg, Raul, *The Destruction of the European Jews*, New Haven: Yale University Press, 2003, 3rd Edition.

Hill, Alexander, *The War Behind the Eastern Front: The Soviet Partisan Movement in North-West Russia, 1941-44*, New York: Frank Cass, 2005, Three volumes.

Hinsley, F. H., *British Intelligence in the Second World War*, London: His Majesty's Stationery Office, 1984, Volume 3, Part I.

Hinze, Rolf, *Der Zusammenbruch Der Heeresgruppe Mitte Im Osten 1944*, Stuttgart: Motorbuch Verlag, 1980.

Hinze, Rolf. *Rückzugskämpfe in der Ukraine 1943/44*, Meerbusch: Verlag Dr. Rolf Hinze, 1991.

Hinze, Rolf, *Das Ostfront-Drama 1944*, Stuttgart: Motorbuch Verlag: 1988.

Hinze, Rolf, *East Front Drama 1944. The Withdrawal Battle of Army Group Centre*, Winnipeg: J. J. Fedorowicz Publishing, 1996.

Hoffmann, Joachim, *Die Geschichte Der Wlassow-Armee*, Frieburg: Verlag Rombach, 1986.

Hoffmann, Joachim, *Kaukasien 1942/43. Das deutsche Heer und die Orientvölker der Sowjetunion*, Frieburg: Rombach Verlag, 1991.

Hoffmann, Joachim, *Deutsche und Kalmyken 1942 bis 1945*, Frieburg: Rombach Verlag, 1986.

Hoffmann, Joachim, *Die Ostlegionen 1941-1943*, Frieburg: Rombach Verlag, 1986.

Hogan, David J. (Editor in Chief), *The Holocaust Chronicle: A History in Words and Pictures*, Lincolnwood: Publications International Ltd., 2002.

Höhne, Heinz, *Der Orden unter dem Totenkopf. Die Geschichte der SS*, Frankfurt am Main: Fischer Bücherei, 1969.

Höhne, Heinz, *The Order of the Death's Head. The Story of Hitler's SS*, New York: Coward McCann, Inc., 1970.

Höttl, Wilhelm, *The Secret Front: The Story of Nazi Political Espionage*, New York: Praeger Publishers, 1954.

Howell, Edgar M. et al., *The Soviet Partisan Movement 1941–1944*, Washington DC: Centre of Military History, United States Army, 1956.

Hull, Isabel V., *Absolute Destruction: Military Culture and the Practices of War in Imperial Germany*, Ithaca: Cornell University Press, 2005.

Huxley-Blythe, Peter J., *The East Came West*, Caldwell: The Caxton Printers, Ltd., 1968.

Ignatov, P.K., *Partisans of the Kuban*, New York: Hutchinson and Co., 1944.

Ioanid, Radu, *The Holocaust in Romania: The Destruction of Jews and Gypsies under the Antonescu Regime, 1940-1944*, Chicago: Ivan R. Dee, 2008.

Jackson, Robert H., *Tyranny on Trial: The Evidence at Nuremberg*, Dallas: Southern Methodist University Press, 1954.

Jörgensen, Christer, *Hitler's Espionage Machine: The True Story Behind One of the World's Most Ruthless Spy Networks*, Guilford: The Lyons Press, 2004.

Jurado, Carlos Caballero, *Breaking the Chains. 14. Waffen Grenadier Division der* SS *and Other Ukrainian Volunteer Formations, Eastern Front, 1942-1945*, London: Shelf Books, 1998.

Jurado, Carlos Caballero, *Commandos En El Caucaso: La Unidad Especial Bergmann, Voluntarios Caucasianos En El Ejercito Aleman, 1941-45*, Granada: Garcia Hispan, 1995.

Jurado, Carlos Caballero, *Rompiendo Las Cadenas: La Division Ucraniana De Las Waffen*-SS, Granada: Garcia Hispan, 1992.

Jurado, Carlos Caballero and Nigel Thomas, *Germany's Eastern Front Allies* (2) *Baltic Forces*, London: Osprey Men-at-Arms Series, Osprey Publishing, 2002.

Jurs, August (ed.), *Estonian Freedom Fighters in World War II*, Printed with a grant from the 'New Horizons Program'. Ontario: Vôitleja Relief Foundation, n.d.

Kamenetsky, Ihor, *Hitler's Occupation of Ukraine* (*1941-1944*). *A Study of Totalitarian Imperialism*, Milwaukee: The Marquette University Press, 1956.

Kampe, Norbert, Wolfgang Schleffler and Gerhard Schoenberger (eds), *Die Einsatzgruppen in der besetzten Sowjetunion 1941/42. Die Tätigkeits und Lageberichte des Chefs der Sicherheitspolizei und des* SD, Berlin: Edition Hentrich, 1997.

Karashuk, A. (ed.), *Russkiya Osvobodetelnya Armia 1939-1945* (Russian Liberation Army, 1939-1945), Moscow: Act Publishers, 1999.

Keegan, John, *The Second World War*, Toronto: Key Porter Books, 1989.

Keilig, Wolf, *Rangliste Des Deutschen Heeres 1944/45*, Friedberg: Podzun Pallas Verlag, n.d.

Kershaw, Ian, *Fateful Choices: Ten Decisions That Changed the World, 1940–1941*, New York: The Penguin Press, 2007.

Kirchubel, Robert, *Operation Barbarossa 1941: Army Group South*, Westport: Praeger Illustrated Military History Series, 2004.

Kirchubel, Robert, *Hitler's Panzer Armies on the Eastern Front*, London: Pen and Sword, 2009.

Klausch, Hans Peter, *Antifaschisten in SS-Uniform*, Bremen: Edition Temmen, 1993.

Klee, Ernst, Willi Dressen and Volker Riess, *The Good Old Days*, Old Saybrook: Konecky and Konecky, 1991.

Kleitmann, Dr. K.G., *Die Waffen SS: eine Dokumentation*, Osnabrück: Verlag 'Der Freiwillige' GmbH, 1965.

Kliment, Charles and Bretislav Nakladal, *Germany's First Ally: Armed Forces of the Slovak State 1939-1945*, Atglen: Schiffer Publishing Ltd: 1997.

Knopp, Guido, *Die Wehrmacht – Eine Bilanz*, Munich: Wilhelm Goldmann Verlag, 2009.

Kohl, Paul, *Der Krieg der deutschen Wehrmacht und der Polizei 1941-1944*, Frankfurt am Main: Fischer Taschenbuch Verlag, 1995.

Krätschmer, Ernst-Günther, *Die Ritterkreuzträger der Waffen-SS*, Preussich Oldendorf: Verlag K. W. Schütz KG, 1955.

Krausnick, Helmut, *Hitlers Einsatzgruppen. Die Truppen des Weltanschauungskrieges 1938-1942*, Frankfurt am Main: Fischer Taschenbuch Verlag, 1985.

Krausnick, Helmut (ed.), *Anatomy of the* SS *State*, New York: Walker and Company, 1965.

Künrich, Heinz, *Der Partisanenkrieg in Europa 1939-1945*, Berlin: Dietz Verlag, 1968.

Kursietis, Andris J., *The Wehrmacht at War 1939-1945. The Units and Commanders of the German Ground Forces during World War II*, Soesterberg: Aspekt, 1999.

Kursietis, Andris J., *The Fallen Generals: The Destruction of the German Officer Corps in World War II and Its Aftermath*, Osceola: Ark Publications Co., 1994.

Kurowski, Franz, *Deadlock before Moscow: Army Group Centre 1942-1943*, Atglen: Schiffer Publishers, 1992.

Kurowski, Franz, *The Brandenburgers – Global Mission*, Winnipeg: J.J. Fedorowicz Publishing, 1997.

Kurowski, Franz, *The Brandenburger Commandos: Germany's Elite Warrior Spies in WWII*, Mechanicsburg: Stackpole Books, 2005.

Laar, Mart, *War in the Woods: Estonia's Struggle for Survival, 1944-1956*, Washington DC: The Compass Press, 1992.

Landwehr, Richard, *Fighting for Freedom: The Ukrainian Volunteer Division of the Waffen* SS, Silver Spring: Bibliophile Legion Books, 1985.

Laqueur, Walter, *The Holocaust Encyclopedia*, New Haven: Yale University Press, 2001.

Laub, Thomas J., *After the Fall: German Policy in Occupied France, 1940-1944*, New York: Oxford University Press, 2010.

Le Tissier, Tony, *Zhukov at the Oder: The Decisive Battle for Berlin*, Westport: Praeger Publishing, 1996.

Le Tissier, Tony, *The Battle of Berlin 1945*, New York: St. Martins Press, 1988.

Leide, Henry, *NS-Verbrecher und Staatssicherheit: Die geheime Vergangenheitspolitik der DDR*, Göttingen: Vandenhoeck and Ruprecht GmbH and Co., 2007.

Lemkin, Raphael, *Axis Rule in Occupied Europe: Laws of Occupation, Analysis of Government. Proposals for Redress*, Washington, D.C.: Carnegie Endowment for International Peace, 1944.

Leumi, Vaad (ed.), *The Black Book: The Nazi Crime Against the Jewish People*, New York: The Jewish Black Book Committee, 1946.

Lichtenstein, Heiner, *Himmlers grüne Helfer: Die Schutz-und-Ordnungspolizei im Dritten Reichs*, Bund Verlag: Berlin, 1996.

Lieb, Peter, *Konventioneller Krieg oder NS-Weltanschauungskrieg? Kriegfürung und Partisanenbekämpfung in FrankReichs 1943/44*, Munich: R. Oldenbourg Verlag, 2007.

Lieb, Peter: 'Täter aus Überzeugung? Oberst Carl von Andrian und die Judenmorde der 707. Infanteriedivision 1941/42', in Christian Hartmann, Johannes Hürter, Peter Lieb and Dieter Pohl,, *Der deutsche Krieg im Osten 1941 – 1944*, Oldenbourg: De Gruyter, 2009.

Linck, Stephan, *Der Ordnung verpflichtet: Deutsche Polizei 1933-1949*, Paderborn: Ferdinand Schöningh Verlag, 2000.

Littlejohn, David, *The Patriotic Traitors: The History of Collaboration in German Occupied Europe, 1940-45*, Garden City: Doubleday and Company, 1972.

Littlejohn, David, *Foreign Legions of the Third Reichs, Volume IV- Poland, Ukraine, Bulgaria, Rumania, Free India, Estonia, Latvia, Lithuania, Finland and Russia*, San Jose: R. James Bender Publishing, 1987.

Littman, Sol, *Pure Soldiers or Sinister Legion: The Ukrainian 14th Waffen*-SS *Division*, Montreal: Black Rose Books, 2003.

Loftus, John, *The Belarus Secret*, New York: Alfred A. Knopf, 1982.

Logusz, Michael O., *Galicia Division: The Waffen SS 14th Grenadier Division 1943-1945*, Atglen: Schiffer Publishing Ltd., 1997.

Longhardt-Söntgen, Rainer, *Partisanen, Spione und Banditen: Abwehrtätigkeit in Oberitalien 1943-1945*, Neckargemünd: Kurt Vowinckel Verlag, 1961.

Lower, Wendy, *Nazi Empire-Building and the Holocaust in Ukraine*, Chapel Hill: The University of North Carolina Press, 2005.

Lower, Wendy and Ray Brandon (eds), *The Shoah in Ukraine: History, Testimony, Memorialization*, Bloomington: Indiana University Press, 2008.

Lukas, Richard C., *The Forgotten Holocaust: The Poles under German Occupation 1939-1944*, Lexington: University Press of Kentucky, 1986.

Lumans, Valdis O., *Himmler's Auxiliaries: The Volksdeutsche Mittelstelle and the German National Minorities of Europe, 1933–1945*, Chapel Hill: The University of North Carolina Press, 1993.

MacLean, French L., *The Cruel Hunters. SS Sonderkommando Dirlewanger. Hitler's Most Notorious Anti-Partisan Unit*, Atglen: Schiffer Publishers, 1998.

MacLean, French L., *The Field Men. The SS Officers Who Led the Einsatzkommandos – the Nazi Mobile Killing Units*, Atglen: Schiffer Publishers, 1999.

MacLean, French L., *The Camp Men: The SS Officers Who Ran the Nazi Concentration Camp System*, Atglen: Schiffer Military History, 1999.

Mallmann, Klaus-Michael, Volker Rieβ, and Wolfram Pyta, *Deutscher Osten 1939-1945: Der Weltanschauungskrieg in Photos und Texten*, Darmstadt: Wissenschaftliche Buchgesellschaft, 2003.

Malthäus, Jürgen, *War, Pacification, and Mass Murder, 1939: The Einsatzgruppen in Poland*, Lanham: Rowman and Littlefield Publishers, 2014.

Manoschek, Walter, *Die Wehrmacht Im Rassenkrieg: Der Vernichtungskrieg Hinter der Front*, Vienna: Picus Verlag, 1996.

Mayer, Hermann Frank, *Blutiges Edelweiβ: die 1. Gebirgsdivision im Zweiten Weltkrieg*, Berlin: Christoph Links Verlag GmbH, 2008.

Megargee, Geoffrey P., *War of Annihilation: Combat and Genocide on the Eastern Front, 1941*, New York: Rowman and Littlefield Publishers Inc., 2006.

Mehner, Kurt, *Die Waffen-SS und Polizei 1939-1945*, Norderstedt: Militair-Verlag Klaus D. Patzwall, 1995.

Mehner, Kurt, *Die Geheimen Tagesberichte Der Deutschen Wehrmachtführung Im Zweiten Weltkrieg 1939-1945*, Biblio Verlag: Osnabrück, 1989–94. 12 volumes.

Mendelsohn, John (ed.), *Covert Warfare: Intelligence, Counterintelligence, and Military Deception during the World War II Era*, 18 volumes, Vol. 13: *The Final Solution of the Abwehr*, New York: Garland Publishing, Inc., 1988.

Mendelsohn, John (ed.), *The Holocaust. Selected Documents in Eighteen Volumes*, New York: Garland Publishing, 1982, 18 volumes.

Messenger, David A. and Katrin Paehler (eds), *A Nazi Past: Recasting German Identity in Postwar Europe*, Lexington: University Press of Kentucky, 2015.

Messerschmidt, Manfred, *Die Wehrmachtjustiz 1933-1945*, Paderborn: Ferdinand Schöningh Verlag, 2005.

Michaelis, Rolf, *Die Russische Volksbefreiungsarmee 'RONA' 1941-1944*, Erlangen: Selbstspubliziert, 1992.

Michaelis, Rolf, *Ukrainer in der Waffen SS: Die 14. Waffen Grenadier Division der SS (ukrainische Nr. 1)*, Berlin: Michaelis Verlag, 2000.

Michaelis, Rolf, *Die Kavallerie Divisionen der Waffen* SS, Erlangen: Selbstpubliziert, 1993.

Michaelis, Rolf, *The SS-Sonderkommando Dirlewanger: A Memoir*, Atglen: Schiffer Publishing, 2013.

Michaelis, Rolf, *Der Weg zur 36. Waffen Grenadier Division der* SS, Rodgau: Verlag fuer Militaerhistorische Zeitgeschichte, 1991.

Michaelis, Rolf, *Russen in der Waffen* SS, Berlin: Michaelis Verlag, 2002.

Miller, Norbert, *Deutsche Besatzungspolitik in der UdSSR 1941-1944*, Köln: Pahl-Rugenstein, 1980.

Milton, Sybil (transl.), *The Stroop Report*, New York: Pantheon Books, 1979.

Mitcham, Samuel W., *Hitler's Legions: the German Army Order of Battle, World War II*, New York: Dorset Press, 1985.

Mitcham, Samuel W., *Crumbling Empire: The German Defeat in the East, 1944*, Westport: Praeger Publishers, 2001.

Mitcham, Samuel W., *German Order of Battle, Volume One: 1st-290th Infantry Divisions in WWII*, Mechanicsburg: Stackpole Books, 2007.

Mitcham, Samuel W., *Hitler's Legions: The German Army Order of Battle, World War II*, New York: Dorset Press, 1985.

Mollo, Andrew, *Uniforms of the* SS. *Volume 5: Sicherheitsdienst und Sicherheitspolizei 1931-1945*, London: Windrow and Greene, 1992.

Müller, Norbert¸*Deutsche Besatzungspolitik in der UdSSR 1941-1944*, Köln: Pahl-Rugenstein Verlag, 1980.

Müller, Rolf-Dieter, and Gerd R. Ueberschaer, *Hitler's War in the East 1941-1945. A Critical Assessment*, Providence: Berghahn Books, 1997.

Müller, Rolf-Dieter, and Hans Erik Volkmann, *Die Wehrmacht: Mythos und Realität*, Oldenbourg: Wissenschaftsverlag, 1999.

Mulligan, Patrick Timothy, *The Politics of Illusion and Empire. German Occupation Policy in the Soviet Union, 1942-1943*, New York: Praeger Publishers, 1988.

Muñoz, Antonio (ed.), *The East Came West: Muslim, Hindu, and Buddhist Volunteers in the German Armed Forces, 1941-1945*, New York: Europa Books, 2002.

Muñoz, Antonio, *Göring's Grenadiers: The Luftwaffe Field Divisions 1942-1945*, New York: Europa Books, 2002.

Muñoz, Antonio, *Hitler's Eastern Legions, Volume I – The Baltic Schutzmannschaft 1941-1945*, New York: Europa Books, 1996.

Muñoz, Antonio, *The Last Levy: Waffen SS Officer Roster, March 1st 1945*, New York: Europa Books, 2000.

Muñoz, Antonio, *Hitler's Eastern Legions, Volume II – The Osttruppen*, New York: Europa Books, 1997.

Muñoz, Antonio, *The Druzhina* SS *Brigade: A History, 1941-1943*, New York: Europa Books, 2000.

Muñoz, Antonio, *The Kaminski Brigade: A History, 1941-1945*, New York: Europa Books, 1996.

Muñoz, Antonio, *The Kaminski Brigade: A History, 1941-1945*, New York: Europa Books, 2003, 2nd revised and expanded edition.

Muñoz, Antonio, *For Croatia and Christ: The Croatian Army in World War II, 1941-1945*, New York: Europa Books, 1996.

Muñoz, Antonio (ed.), *The German Police*, Supreme Allied Headquarters, G-2 Section, prepared jointly with British MI-14(d). US Army War Office: Washington, April 1945. Reprinted in revised and expanded format. New York: Europa Books, 1997.

Muñoz, Antonio, *Forgotten Legions: Obscure Combat Formations of the Waffen* SS, *1943-1945*, Boulder: Paladin Press, 1991.

Muñoz, Antonio, *Forgotten Legions Companion Booklet*, New York: Europa Books, 1995.

Nafziger, George F., *The German Order of Battle. Waffen SS and Other Units in World War II*, Conshohocken: Combined Publishing, 2001.

Neitzel, Sönke, *Abgehört: Deutsche Generäle in britischer Kriegsgefangenschaft 1942–1945*, Berlin: Propyläen, 2005.

Neufeldt, H.-J., J. Huck, and Georg Tessin, *Zur Geschichte der Ordnungspolizei: Die Stabe und Truppeneinheiten der Ordnungspolizei, 1936-1945*, Koblenz: Als Manuskript gedruckt. Bundesarchiv, 1957.

Neulen, Hans Werner, *An Deutscher Seite: Internationale Freiwillige von Wehrmacht und Waffen SS*, München: Universitas Verlag, 1985.

Newland, Samuel J., *Cossacks in the German Army, 1941-1945*, London: Frank Cass and Co. Ltd., 1991.

Newton, Steven H., *Retreat from Leningrad. Army Group North, 1944/1945*, Atglen: Schiffer Publishing, 1995.

Newton, Steven H., *German Battle Tactics on the Russian Front*, Atglen: Schiffer Publishing, 1994.

Niehorster, Leo W.G., *The Royal Hungarian Army, 1920-1945*, New York: Europa Books, 1998.

Niepold, Gerd, *Battle for White Russia: The Destruction of Army Group Centre June 1944*, New York: Brassey's Defense Publishers, 1987.

Nirenstein, Albert, *A Tower from the Enemy: Contributions to a History of Jewish Resistance in Poland*, New York: The Orion Press, 1959.

Overmans, Rüdiger., *Deutsche militärische Verluste im Zweiten Weltkrieg*, München: R. Oldenbourg Verlag, 1999.

Overy, Richard, *Russia's War: A History of the Soviet War Effort, 1941-1945*, New York: Penguin Putnam, Inc., 1998.

Padfield, Peter, *Himmler*, New York: Henry Holt and Company, 1990.

Perro, Oskars, *Fortress Cholm*, Toronto: Kurland Publishing, 1981.

Person, Katarzyna, *Warsaw Ghetto Police: The Jewish Order Service during the Nazi Occupation*, Ithaca: Cornell University Press, 2021.

Piotrowski, Tadeusz, *Poland's Holocaust: Ethnic Strife, Collaboration with Occupying Forces and Genocide in the Second Republic, 1918-1947*, Jefferson: MacFarland and Company, Inc., 1998.

Pohl, Dieter, et al., *Der deutsche Krieg im Osten 1941-1944*, Munich: De Gruytyer, 2009.

Pohl, Otto J., *Ethnic Cleansing in the USSR, 1937-1949*, Westport: Greenwood Press, 1999.

Poirier, Robert G. and Albert Z. Conner, *The Red Army Order of Battle in the Great Patriotic War*, Novato: Presidio Press, 1985.

Porter, Jack Nusan (ed.), *Jewish Partisans: A Documentary of Jewish Resistance in the Soviet Union During World War II*, Washington DC: University Press of America, Inc, 1982

Pottgeiser, Hans, *Die Reichsbahn in Ostfeldzug*, Neckargemünd: Kurt Vowinckel Verlag, 1960.

Präg, Werner and Wolfgang Jacobson, *Das Dienstagebuch des deutschen Generalgouverneurs in Polen 1939-1945*, Stuttgart: Deutsche Verlag Anstalt, 1975.

Prechtl, G.M., *Unsere Ehre Heisst Treue: Kriegstagebuch des Kommandostabes Reichsführer-SS; Tätigkeitsberichte der 1. und 2. SS Infanterie-Brigade und von Sonderkommandos der* SS, Zürich: Europa Verlag, 1965.

Preradovich, Nikolaus von, *Die Generale der Waffen*-SS, Berg Am See: Kurt Vowinckel Verlag, 1985.

Ramme, Alwin, *Der Sicherheitsdienst Der SS*, Berlin: Deutscher Militärverlag der DDR, 1970.

Ready, J. Lee, *The Forgotten Axis: Germany's Partners and Foreign Volunteers in World War II*, Jefferson: MacFarland and Company, Inc., 1987.

Redcliffe, Alexander, *Lessons Learned from the Partisan War in Russia*, MS No. P055C, Washington D.C.: Office of the Chief of Military History, Department of the Army, 1947.

Redelis, Valdis, *Partisanenkrieg: Entstehung und Bekämpfung der Partisanen und Untergrundbewegung im Mittelabschnitt der Ostfront 1941 bis 1943*, Heidelberg: Scharnhorst Buchkameradenschaft, 1958.

Regenberg, Werner, *Panzerfahrzeuge und Panzereinheiten der Ordnungspolizei 1936–1945*, Friedberg: Podzun Pallas Verlag, 1996.

Regenberg, Werner, *Armoured Vehicles and Units of the German Order Police (Ordnungspolizei) 1936-1945*, Atglen: Schiffer Military History, 2002.

Reinicke, Adolf, *Die 5. Jäger-Division 1939-1945*, Friedberg: Podzun Pallas Verlag GmbH, n.d.

Reitlinger, Gerald, *The House Built on Sand: The Conflicts of German Policy in Russia, 1939-1945*, New York: The Viking Press, 1960.

Reitlinger, Gerald, *The SS, Alibi of a Nation, 1922-1945*, London: William Heinemann Ltd., 1956.

Reitlinger, Gerald, *The Final Solution. The Attempt to Exterminate the Jews of Europe 1939–1945*, South Brunswick: Thomas Yoseloff, 1961.

Richter, Hans, *Einsatz der Polizei bei den Polizei Bataillonen im Ost, Nord, und West*, Berlin: Zentralverlag der NSDAP, 1943.

Romanko, Oleg and Antonio Muñoz, *Hitler's White Russians: Collaboration, Extermination and Anti-Partisan Warfare in White Russia, 1941-1944*, New York: Europa Books, 2002.

Romanko, Oleg V., S.I. Drobyazko, and K.K. Semyonov, *Иностранные формирования Третьего рейха (Foreign Formations of the Third Reich)*, Moscow: Act Publishing, 2011.

Rossino, Alexander B., *Hitler Strikes Poland: Blitzkrieg, Ideology, and Atrocity* (Modern War Studies), Lawrence: University Press of Kansas, 2003.

Rudling, Per Anders, 'Terror and Local Collaboration in Occupied Belarus: The Case of the Schutzmannschaft Battalion 118', in Romanian. Bucharest: *Academy Nicolae Iorga History Institute Historical Yearbook*, Vol. VIII, 2011.

Rürup, Dr. Reinhard and Dr. Peter Jahn (eds), *Der Krieg gegen die Sowjetunion 1941-1945*, Berlin: Berliner Festspiele GmbH, 1991.

Ryan, Cornelius, *The Last Battle*, New York: Simon and Schuster, 1966.

Scheibert, Horst, *Die Träger Der Ehrenblattspange Des Heeres Und Der Waffen* SS, Friedberg: Podzun Pallas Verlag, 1986.

Scheibert, Horst, *Die Träger Der Deutschen Kreuzes In Gold: Kriegsmarine, Luftwaffe, Waffen* SS, Friedberg: Podzun Pallas Verlag, n.d.

Schellenberg, Walter, *The Labyrinth. The Memoirs of Hitler's Secret Service Chief*, New York: Harper and Brothers, 1956.

Schmitz, Peter and Klaus-Jürgen Thies, *Die Truppenkennzeichen der Verbände und Einheiten der Deutschen Wehrmacht und Waffen SS und ihre Einsätze im Zweiten Weltkrieg 1939-1945*, Osnabrück: Biblio Verlag, 1987–94. Four volumes.

Schneider, Jost W., *Verleihung Genehmigt! Eine Bild und Dokumentargeschichte Der Ritterkreuzträger Der Waffen* SS *und Polizei 1940-1945*, San Jose: R. James Bender Publishing, 1993.

Schülte, Theo, *The German Army and Nazi Policies In Occupied Russia 1941-1944*, New York: Berg Publishers, 1989.

Schumann, Wolfgang and Ludwig Nestler, *Nacht über Europa: Band II: Die faschistische Okkupationspolitik in Polen* (*1939-1945*), Köln: Pahl-Rugenstein Verlag GmbH, 1989.

Schuster, Peter and Harald Tiede, *Die Uniformen und Abzeichen der Kosaken in der Deutschen Wehrmacht*, Norderstedt: Verlag Klaus D. Patzwall, 1999.

Seaton, Albert, *The Russo-German War 1941-45*, New York: Praeger Publishers, 1970.

Seewald, Dr. Heinrich, *Das toenende Erz: Deutsche Propaganda gegen die Rote Armee im Zweiten Weltkrieg*, Stuttgart: Seewald Verlag, 1978.

Seidler, Franz W., *Die Kollaboration 1939-1945*, München: F.A. Herbig Verlagsbuchhandlung, 1995.

Seidler, Franz W., *Die Militaergerichtsbarfeit der Deutschen Wehrmacht 1939-1945*, Munich: Herbig Verlag, 1991.

Seidler, Franz W., *Deutscher Volkssturm: Das letzte Aufgebot, 1944-1945*, München: F.A. Herbig Verlag, 1989.

Silgailis, Arthur, *Latvian Legion*, San Jose: R. James Bender Publishing, 1986.

Snyder, Timothy, *Into the Bloodlands: Europe Between Hitler and Stalin*, New York: Basic Books, 2022.

Steenberg, Sven, *Vlasov*, New York: Alfred A. Knopf, 1970.

Stein, George H., *The Waffen SS: Hitler's Elite Guard at War 1939-1945*, Ithaca: Cornell University Press, 1966.

Stöber, Hans, *Die Flugabwehrverbände der Waffen SS*, Preussiche Oldendorf: Verlag K. W. Schütz KG, 1984.

Stöber, Hans, *Die 22. Panzer Division; 25. Panzer Division; 27. Panzer Division; und die 233. Reserve Panzer Division*, Friedberg: Podzun Pallas Verlag, 1985.

Stockhorst, Erich., *5000 Köpfe: Wer War Was Im Dritten Reich*, Kiel: Arndt Verlag, 2000.

Stoves, Rolf, *Die Gepanzerten und Motorisierten Deutschen Grossverbände 1935-1945*, Friedberg: Podzun Pallas Verlag, 1986.

Strik-Strikfeldt, Wilfried, *Against Stalin and Hitler. Memoir of the Russian Liberation Movement 1941-1945*, New York: The John Day Company, 1973.

Tec, Nechama, *The Bielski Partisans*, Oxford: Oxford University Press, 1993.

Tessin, Georg, *Verbände und Truppen der deutschen Wehrmacht und Waffen SS 1939-1945*, Osnabrück: Biblio Verlag, 1975–2002. 18 volumes.

Tessin, Georg, Norbert Kannapin and Brün Meyer, *Waffen-SS und Ordnungspolizei im Kriegseinsatz 1939–1945*, Biblio Verlag: Osnabrück, 2000.

Tessin, Georg, with H. J. Neufeldt, and J. Huck, *Zur Geschichte der Ordnungspolizei, 1936-1945*, Koblenz: Bundesarchiv, 1956.

Thomas, Nigel and Carlos Caballero Jurado, *Wehrmacht Auxiliary Forces*, London: Osprey Publishing Ltd., 1992.

Thomas, Nigel, et al., *Partisan Warfare 1941-45*, London: Reed International Books Ltd., 1983.

Thorwald, Jürgen, *The Illusion: Soviet Soldiers in Hitler's Armies*, Harcourt Brace Jovanovich, 1975.

Thurston, Robert W. and Bernd Bonwetsch (eds), *The People's War: Responses to World War II in the Soviet Union*, New York: University of Illinois Press: Urbana, 2000.

Tieke, Wilhelm, *Das Ende Zwischen Oder Und Elbe: Der Kampf Um Berlin 1945*, Stuttgart: Motorbuch Verlag, 1994.

Tolstoy, Nikolai, *The Secret Betrayal 1944-1947*, New York: Charles Scribner's Sons, 1977.

Tys-Krokhmaliuk, Yuriy, *UPA Warfare in Ukraine: The Ukrainian Insurgent Army*, New York: Vantage Press, 1972.

Ullrich, Sebastian, *Der Weimar-Komplex. Das Scheitern der ersten deutschen Demokratie und die politische Kultur der frühen Bundesrepublik 1945-1959*, Göttingen: Wallstein Verlag, 2009,

Vakar, Nicholas P., *Belorussia: The Making of a Nation: A Case Study*, Cambridge: Harvard University Press, 1956.

Vizetelly, Frank H., Editor in Chief, *Funk and Wagnall's New Standard Encyclopedia of Universal Knowledge*, New York: Funk and Wagnall's Company, 1931. Volume 25.

Wegner, Bernd, *The Waffen-SS: Organisation, Ideology and Function*, Oxford: Basil Blackwell, 1990.

Werbizky, George G., *Ostarbeiters: Belarusian, Russian and Ukrainian Forced Laborers in Nazi Germany – World War II*, Endwell: Self Published, 2002.

Westermann, Edward B., *Hitler's Police Battalions: Enforcing Racial War in the East*, Lawrence: University Press of Kansas.

Westwood, David, *The Waffen SS: Higher formations, Divisions, Brigades 1939-1945*, Derbyshire: Privately Published, n.d.

Wette, Wolfram, *The Wehrmacht: History, Myth, Reality*, Cambridge: Harvard University Press, 2007.

Wicziok, Wilhelm, *Die Armee Der Gerichteten. Zur besonderen Verwendung – Bewaehrungsbataillon 500*, Essen: Heitz and Hoeffkes Verlag, 1992.

Wilhelm, Hans-Heinrich. *Die Einsatzgruppe A: der Sicherheitspolizei und des SD 1941/42*, Frankfurt am Main: Peter Lang Verlag GmbH, 1996.

Witte, Hans Joachim, and Peter Offermann, *Die Boeselagerschen Reiter: Das Kavallerie-Regiment Mitte die aus ihm hervorgegangene 3. Kavallerie-Brigade/ Division*, München: Schild Verlag, 1998.

Witter, Robert E., *Chain Dogs: The German Army Military Police of World War II*, Missoula: Pictorial Histories Publishing Company, Inc., 1994.

Yelton, David K., *Hitler's Volkssturm: The Nazi Militia and the Fall of Germany, 1944-1945*, Lawrence: University Press of Kansas, 2002

Yerger, Mark C., *Riding East. The SS Cavalry Brigade in Poland and Russia 1939-1942*, Atglen: Schiffer Publishers, 1996.

Yerger, Mark C., *Allgemeine SS*, Atglen: Schiffer Military Publishing, 1997.

Yerger, Mark C., *Waffen SS Commanders: Augsberger to Kreutz*, Atglen: Schiffer Military Publishing, 1997.

Yerger, Mark C., *Waffen SS Commanders: Krüger to Zimmermann*, Atglen: Schiffer Military Publishing, 1999.

Zaloga, Steven, *Bagration 1944: The Destruction of Army Group Centre*, Osprey Military: London, 1996.

Zawodny, J.K., *Nothing But Honor: The Story of the Warsaw Uprising, 1944*, Hoover Institution Press, 1978.

Ziemke, Earl F., *Stalingrad to Berlin: the German Defeat in the East*, Washington DC: Centre of Military History, United States Army, 1986.

Ziemke, Earl F., and Magna E. Bauer, *Moscow to Stalingrad: Decision in the East*, Washington DC: Centre of Military History, United States Army, 1987.

# NAME INDEX

**Operational Code Names -**

# FORMATION INDEX

## Eastern Volunteer Forces -

**Russian Units -**

**Finnish Units -**



**Latvian Units -**

## Axis Forces -

**Romanian Units -**



**Slovakian Units -**



**Hungarian Units -**



**Italian Units**



## Allied Forces –

**Red Army Units -**



**Soviet Partisan Units -**



**British Army -**